THE LOYAL ATLANTIC
Remaking the British Atlantic in the Revolutionary Era

Adding to a dynamic new wave of scholarship in Atlantic history, *The Loyal Atlantic* offers fresh interpretations of the key role played by Loyalism in shaping the early modern British Empire. This cohesive collection investigates how Loyalism and the empire were mutually constituted and reconstituted from the eighteenth century onward. Featuring contributions by authors from across Canada, the United States, and the United Kingdom, *The Loyal Atlantic* brings Loyalism into a genuinely international focus.

Through cutting-edge archival research, *The Loyal Atlantic* contextualizes Loyalism within the larger history of the British Empire. It also details how, far from being a passive allegiance, Loyalism changed in unexpected and fascinating ways – especially in times of crisis. Most important, *The Loyal Atlantic* demonstrates that neither the conquest of Canada nor the American Revolution can be properly understood without assessing the meanings of Loyalism in the wider Atlantic world.

JERRY BANNISTER is an associate professor and graduate coordinator in the Department of History at Dalhousie University.

LIAM RIORDAN is an associate professor in the Department of History at the University of Maine.

The Loyal Atlantic

Remaking the British Atlantic in the Revolutionary Era

EDITED BY
JERRY BANNISTER AND LIAM RIORDAN

UNIVERSITY OF TORONTO PRESS
Toronto   Buffalo   London

Reprinted 2013

ISBN 978-1-4426-4208-9 (cloth)
ISBN 978-1-4426-1109-2 (paper)

Printed on acid-free paper

Library and Archives Canada Cataloguing in Publication

The loyal Atlantic : remaking the British Atlantic in the revolutionary era /
edited by Jerry Bannister and Liam Riordan.

Includes bibliographical references and index.
ISBN 978-1-4426-4208-9 (bound). – ISBN 978-1-4426-1109-2 (pbk.)

1. United Empire loyalists.   2. American loyalists.   3. United States –
History – Revolution, 1775–1783.   4. Canada – History – Rebellion,
1837–1838.   5. Canada – History – 1841–1867.   6. Great Britain –
Colonies – America.   I. Bannister, Jerry, 1968–   II. Riordan, Liam, 1966–

FC423.L67 2012   971.02'4   C2011-906834-6

This book has been published with the help of a grant in aid of publication
from the Canadian-American Center at the University of Maine.

University of Toronto Press acknowledges the financial assistance to its
publishing program of the Canada Council for the Arts and the Ontario Arts
Council.

Canada Council   Conseil des Arts
for the Arts   du Canada

ONTARIO ARTS COUNCIL
CONSEIL DES ARTS DE L'ONTARIO

University of Toronto Press acknowledges the financial support of the
Government of Canada through the Canada Book Fund for its publishing
activities.

To Stephen J. Hornsby,
model Atlantic scholar, administrator, and colleague

Contents

Preface

The Loyal Atlantic explores the role of loyalism in sustaining and remaking the British Empire in the early modern era, especially in the period of change initiated by the American Revolution. The chapters represent parts of a much larger wave of international Loyalist studies that build on the new imperial history and Atlantic history. They examine the varied ways that loyalism functioned in the British Atlantic, which requires drawing upon different fields, such as aboriginal history, literary studies, and British, Irish, Canadian, Caribbean, and American history. In addition to this thematic range, our volume considers how loyalism developed over time. The depth and detail of the chapters reflect the different ways that loyalism was constituted and reconstituted from the eighteenth century through to the 1837 Rebellions in Upper and Lower Canada and their aftermath.

The volume's strength lies in its scope and diversity. The contributors work in a variety of fields and their original research breaks new ground in Atlantic scholarship. The chapters proceed chronologically from the late eighteenth to the mid-nineteenth century and geographically from the Northeast, to the South and Caribbean, and across the Atlantic Ocean. The paired chapters examine four major themes: aboriginal friendship and Loyalist identity formation; Loyalist print culture and literature; slavery and Loyalist migrations; and sectarian memory and Loyalist politics. Our basic premise is that loyalism fundamentally shaped the British Atlantic world. Loyalism was rooted deeply in a history that stretched back at least to the Restoration in 1660, and the full impact of colonization, the conquests of Canada, and the American Revolution cannot be understood properly without assessing the Loyal Atlantic. Loyalism should be understood not as a literal description of a particular group or party but rather as an amalgam of values, practices, laws, and politics that distinguished between who was loyal (and deserved the full rights and privileges of Britons) and who was disloyal (and subject to varied prohibitions and punishments). Loyalty was a highly contested and contingent process rather than a passive status. Loyalties could shift in unexpected ways, and the chapters in this volume trace their fascinating fluidities and contradictions in periods of crisis. Loyalism served as a broadly unifying and integrating set of values, yet it remained sufficiently elastic to permit accommodation to local circumstances that grew ever more varied as colonization expanded. Thus, we emphasize how early modern imperial formation was both durable and dynamic. While much recent Atlantic world scholarship focuses on inter-imperial negotiations, the focus here is on intra-imperial developments and the ways that differences were articulated and enforced.

The scope of this volume derives not only from wide-ranging reading and archival research, but also from sustained dialogue during an international and multidisciplinary conference on 'Loyalism and the Revolutionary Atlantic World,' hosted at the University of Maine in June 2009. All the chapters except the first are substantially revised versions of papers selected from conference presentations by scholars from US, Canadian, British, and Australian institutions. The thirty original panellists not only showed transnational range, they came from at least five different disciplinary traditions and included senior scholars, independent researchers, museum professionals, and doctoral candidates. We consider it noteworthy that the authors in this volume reflect varied locales across the English-speaking Atlantic: six from US institutions, three from Canada, and two from the United Kingdom. While the central planning and financial resources for the event came from the Canadian-American Center at the University of Maine, additional financial support from the Provost at the University of New Brunswick, the Maine Humanities Council, and the Castine Historical Society, located in a significant Loyalist town in Maine, added significantly to the success of the conference that initiated this volume.

The Loyal Atlantic contributes to American, Caribbean, Irish, and British history, as well as to Canadian history. One of the stubborn problems facing Canadian historians is that loyalism is too often assumed to refer only to the actual Loyalists who fled the American Revolution. Loyalism, however, was not the exclusive preserve of British Tories who used it to combat American Whigs: it encompassed a wide range of diverse peoples across the Atlantic world, including Quakers, German migrants, aboriginal peoples, African slaves, and most colonists in the British Caribbean. The vast majority of these people cannot be described as Tory in any meaningful sense; indeed, one finds significant Loyalist dissent from overbearing government authority everywhere that loyal refugees settled in substantial numbers, from the Six Nations' Grand River Reserve north of Lake Erie to New Brunswick and Nova Scotia, the Bahamas, and Sierra Leone. While Canadian historians have debated why Nova Scotia and Quebec did not join the American Patriots, we tend to forget that Bermuda, the Floridas, and the entire British West Indies did not join the rebels either. A borderland perspective certainly helps us to understand aspects of regional relationships in northeastern North America, but when this perspective fails to consider imperial and Atlantic contexts, it can too readily ossify into a stale US-Canadian dualism.

Just as loyalism encompassed more than just the refugees who arrived in Nova Scotia and Quebec in the 1770s and 1780s and settled in Upper Canada after 1791, it was also a much deeper and more contested force that had ramifications well into the 1830s. While the contributions here focus largely on the revolutionary era, in the first chapter we establish a longer chronological context for loyalism by assessing its place in the English Atlantic that took increasingly distinctive shape starting with the Restoration in 1660. This longitudinal approach is particularly meant to counter national-oriented assessments of loyalism that mostly limit their attention to the resistance movement that grew from 1765, the Revolutionary War, and the consequences of loyalism for post-war Canadian political culture. Just as historians of the American Revolution have taken pains to place the Patriots in a republican tradition that stretched back centuries, there is a similar imperative to situate the Loyalists in a much longer tradition of loyalism. This initial chapter draws together some of the vast recent scholarship about the early modern Atlantic world to consider its implications for reassessing loyalism and the place of Loyalists within a changing British Empire.

Subsequent chapters trace the complex ways British America took shape in the eighteenth and early nineteenth centuries by considering how ideas and movements flowed not only westward from the imperial centre, but also across the Canadian-US border, southward to the British West Indies, and eastward to the British Isles. Assessing the Loyal Atlantic requires an imperial framework to elucidate the repeated series of conquests that fuelled British colonization. For example, in the case of northeastern British America, this process encompassed the so-called conquest of Acadia in 1710, the expulsion of the Acadians, the conquest of Quebec, the voluntary and coerced migration of the Loyalists, the War of 1812, and eventually the Rebellions of 1837–38. English-Canadian scholars tend to see the Acadian deportations, the Planter migrations, and the Loyalist migrations as discrete events, yet they were parts of a larger struggle over loyalty to the British Crown and Empire, the limits to neutrality, and the meaning of sovereignty. In other words, they were each part of the many conquests of Canada.

These conquests were points on a historical continuum acted out across the British Atlantic from Ireland to the Maroon Wars in Jamaica, whereby migration (whether enslaved, coerced, or free) bolstered imperial policy. From Newfoundland to Georgia, which saw the first government-subsidized settlement project in British North America, and across the British West Indies, authorities sought to use Protestant settlers to serve imperial goals. The specific aim in Georgia was to create a buffer of Protestant settlers, many of them German speakers, to limit enslaved people's access to Spanish Florida. In every mainland British colony, at least, authorities increasingly understood that demography – the sheer force of incoming European migrants – was as important as armies or navies to achieve imperial goals. For conquest and colonization to succeed, migrants had to be loyal.

Thus, loyalty was both an idea and an act. British subjects chose actively or tacitly to resist, renounce, or support the Crown, and these decisions were negotiated and contested in a political world that could change quickly and unexpectedly. For example, if Britons in the West Indies largely remained loyal because the Empire provided critical support to maintain a stable slave society, it is all the more remarkable that so many enslaved people rallied to the imperial standard in North America when wartime turmoil suggested the possibility of successful escape from the status quo. Serious challenges remain, of course, to interpret what were often ambiguous commitments and meanings. Perhaps particularly during times of crisis, the political motivations and personal calculations that informed the decisions most people made remained elusive even to them, let alone to later scholars – but studying loyalism sheds light on the alliances and antagonisms that fed the organization of power in the British Atlantic world.

Co-editing this volume and collaborating on its ambitious first chapter has been a pleasure. We found ourselves in surprising agreement about most interpretive matters and without question benefited enormously from each other's specialized expertise. Historical scholarship will only benefit as we encourage and support multi-authored work – an aspect of our discipline that is woefully underdeveloped when compared with most other humanities, social sciences, and scientific approaches to research. As we turn to examine subjects on a larger geographic scale and remain committed to understanding ordinary people and local contingencies, it is increasingly imperative that historians embrace the opportunities of cooperative research, multi-authorship, and take careful stock of the potential benefits of new technologies to further our collective understanding of the past. We both trained as early modern Anglo-American historians, and, while one of us was born and raised in Canada and the other in the United States, in many ways we have had similar trajectories: one from the far east of Newfoundland to the centre of English Canada in Toronto for his graduate training, the other from the far west of California to the more traditional east coast metropolis of Philadelphia for his doctoral degree as an early Americanist. The Canadian began his graduate training concentrating on British history, while the *Californiano* did comparative work on colonial Spanish America. Thus, significant aspects of our careers have parallel lines, and we share a similar desire to understand our subjects and ourselves from comparative perspectives that overlap and inform one another.

Still, we have differences of opinion that suggest some of the conceptual challenges to rethinking the significance of loyalty in a period of upheaval. First, the most basic label with which to name the period we examine remains vexing. Given the deep divisions within British America and the fact that so many British colonies and territories never joined the rebellion that erupted in 1775, calling this period the 'revolutionary era' raises the danger of homogenizing complex phenomena and overstating the influence of the Patriots. In light of the remarkable resilience of a British Empire that emerged larger and more powerful in the nineteenth century than it ever had been prior to 1775, why not refer to rebellion and revolution in the 'loyalist era'? After debating this issue, we settled in this volume's subtitle for the more conventional term, most of all because a title needs to communicate principal parameters concisely and to correlate with a recognizable field of study. Does our use of revolutionary era imply that Patriots define or characterize the importance of the era by themselves? We hope not.

Second, our chief commitment throughout this project was to reassess this period and its changes without succumbing to the nation-state as the mandatory outcome and dominant perspective of people in that era. It is obvious to us that the nation did not – in fact, it could not – function in this way for most, if not all, of the eighteenth century. Yet, if the nation was weak and even non-existent in most of the places examined in this volume, its force today, even in the midst of rapid globalization, is inescapable, and imposes itself at many turns in our analysis. The profound way that loyalism has mattered to many Canadian political scientists and historians gives our subject a presence in Canadian scholarly and popular traditions that vastly exceeds its appeal (or even recognition) in either US or British national cultures. Not surprisingly, perhaps, this project benefited from support from a research centre dedicated to Canadian and Canadian-American studies, and a Canadian academic press is publishing it.

The real advantages of this Canadian commitment notwithstanding, the session at our initiating conference that sparked the greatest passion centred on the Australian scholar Cassandra Pybus's severe critique of historical frameworks limited to Atlantic and regional perspectives favouring Canada. Loyalism, to be sure, was a global phenomenon, but, as the chapters that follow demonstrate, it developed in regionally specific ways. By exploring the varieties of loyalism in the British Atlantic world, *The Loyal Atlantic* responds to the globalist critique of the supposedly parochial nature of Atlantic history. It demonstrates the need to balance synthetic global frameworks with new scholarship rooted firmly in specific geographical contexts, rigorous archival research, and powerful Atlantic connections that were forged with ever greater intensity over the course of the eighteenth century. Loyalism helps to explain imperial power and large structures of governance, but its importance also arises from its lasting resonance for self-understanding, public action, and collective memory tied to lived experience in particular places.

The paired chapters in Part I offer interpretive frameworks for understanding individual and group allegiance within an Atlantic context. Drawing on the theoretical literature about assessing identity, Keith Mason presents a fresh perspective on how Loyalist identities functioned and evolved during the revolutionary crisis. By matching his conceptual discussion with a sustained case study of a transatlantic Loyalist with significant ties to Virginia, Mason contextualizes the problem of identity and gives a compelling account of how allegiances could shift in unexpected ways. Mason draws not only on official sources such as the Loyalist Claims Commission, but also on popular songs, toasts, and rituals. John Reid's chapter on aboriginal concepts of friendship extends Mason's analysis by examining loyalty beyond the confines of British culture. Reid demonstrates how friendship operated in the long eighteenth century, and his analysis furthers our understanding of the relationships among loyalties, allegiances, and alliances. His chapter reveals salient continuities in aboriginal history that serve as powerful counterpoints to the fluidity of Loyalist politics during the revolutionary crisis. While Mason shows us how much changed in a short period of time, Reid emphasizes what endured after the Revolution.

In Part II the chapters about print culture by literary scholars also complement each other by their divergence. Where Philip Gould examines arguments over copyright law in eighteenth-century Britain to highlight issues of literary originality and the figure of the modern author in explaining Loyalists' pained response to *Common Sense*, Gwendolyn Davies reconstructs the migration that brought Loyalist printers to New Brunswick in the mid-1780s and the role they played for several decades in that province, northeastern British North America, and beyond. Gould's close focus on the textual interplay of New York and Philadelphia newspapers and imprints insightfully shows how what are usually framed as political disputes hinged on questions of authorship that were not just literary but had resounding legal and economic ramifications as well. Perhaps more than any other chapter in the volume, Gould's reminds us that historians generally, and scholars of loyalism in particular, can profitably approach their subjects with a broadened sense of the political. Issues of taste and cultural sensibility, such as the proper use of wit and satire to eviscerate an opponent, also make plain that British aesthetic values were crucial to Loyalists and Patriots alike, and lost no potency as a result of changes in formal politics in this period. Davies's painstaking investigation of the printing houses of John Ryan and Christopher Sower III (and their associates) combines the history of the book with business history, historical geography, and family history to demonstrate the pivotal role that printers played in shaping the post-war British Atlantic. While studies of the Loyalist diaspora once seemed to end with their subjects at isolated wilderness destinations, a slightly longer view shows these New Brunswick printers as important transregional and transnational actors.

While the Atlantic stage of Davies's printers and their contributions to the political and cultural development of eastern British North America is largely a success story of Loyalist refugees overcoming dislocation and loss, the challenges they faced pale when compared with the forced migration examined in Part III. An important literature about how enslaved people freed themselves with the assistance of British military forces in the course of the Revolutionary War, and especially the free black migration to Nova Scotia and the founding of Sierra Leone as a bulwark against slavery, directly challenges the complacent view of Patriots as liberators. Jennifer K. Snyder and Carole Watterson Troxler, however, consider the far more widespread situation of people of African descent who remained the legal property of others during and after the war. Snyder focuses on St Augustine, the capital of East Florida, which served as a refuge for thousands of Loyalists fleeing Patriot reprisals throughout the lower South. Despite wartime chaos, many of these Loyalists, especially those from plantation areas south of Savannah, brought slaves with them, and some even used the vagaries of war to seize more human property. Where Snyder principally considers the war years up to the final British evacuation of St Augustine in 1785, Troxler begins with the varied southern evacuations from Wilmington, North Carolina, through to Pensacola, West Florida, that sent Loyalists with their enslaved property throughout the Atlantic world, but above all to the British West Indies.

The Bahamian Islands offer an especially effective focal point because this colony was transformed by the Loyalist migration, including some new arrivals' attempts to remake the Bahamas as a slave society – an Atlantic crossroads of the most tragic and most representative sort. Yet the planter dream of a cotton-producing colony would not be sustained there. The Loyalist 'uses' of the Bahamas highlights some familiar political conflicts and contests over governance that beset much of post-war British North America, added to here by struggles over the 'amelioration' of slavery. Indeed, the ties of former Georgia and Carolina Loyalists to the Bahamas and the Maritime provinces – all places with new Loyalist majorities after the war – demonstrates that the Loyal British Atlantic may have been sundered by the American Revolution but certainly was not ended by it. Snyder and Troxler together insist that we attend to slavery's *expansion* in the British Atlantic as a result of the American Revolution.

The final paired chapters of *The Loyal Atlantic* examine Loyalist political culture in the nineteenth century. By extending the chronological framework for studying loyalism into a later period of reform and rebellion, Allison O'Mahen Malcom and Allan Blackstock show how the contested public memory of loyalism in general, and events such as the Glorious Revolution in particular, shaped politics across both the continental border and the Atlantic Ocean. By comparing how anti-Catholicism affected nativism in the United States and Orangeism in Canada, Malcom's transnational perspective shows the different ways that memory mutated in different political contexts. In doing so, she confronts the conventional view of the Orange Order and challenges readers to consider the full meanings of anti-Catholicism. Like Mason, Malcom examines the problem of identity and nationalism, but for her as they informed sectarianism. In the concluding chapter, Blackstock follows loyalism as it crossed back to the British Isles using an intensive examination of the Irish press to show how news of the Rebellion of 1837 was filtered through both British and Irish politics. Like Malcom, he demonstrates how the memory of loyalism functioned as a powerful sectarian tool. Blackstock's innovative framework challenges the traditional imperial assumption that ideas and movements only flowed westward from the British Isles to North America and the Caribbean.

Taken together, the contributions to *The Loyal Atlantic* offer new ways of thinking about loyalism and the Loyalists. It is no longer sufficient to merely decry the distortions that nationalism has imposed upon the interpretation of loyalism, whether it is a celebratory or denigrating bias. An Atlantic perspective now provides a useful transnational framework for analysis, but the dangers of too broad a global focus or too top-down an imperial one respectively threaten an overly general and an overly traditional perspective. The history of loyalism is diverse, but the skein of memory, identity, migration, and politics within a variegated yet integrated British Atlantic bind this history and this volume together.

Jerry Bannister and Liam Riordan

Acknowledgments

This project would not have been possible without the generous assistance of many individuals and institutions. We would like to thank the University of Maine, particularly Nathan Godfried, Chair of the History Department, and Jeff Hecker, Dean of the College of Liberal Arts and Sciences at the University of Maine. The endowment fund of the Canadian-American Center, University of Maine, provided a publication subvention, and we are extremely appreciative of its generous support. We would like to thank Robert Summerby-Murray, Dean of the Faculty of Arts and Social Sciences, for his help with securing funding from the Strategic Initiatives Fund at Dalhousie University. We also gratefully acknowledge the support of the Department of Foreign Affairs and International Trade Canada and the US Department of Education Title VI Program. Part of the research for the project was also funded through a standard research grant from the Social Sciences and Humanities Research Council of Canada.

Stephen Hornsby, to whom this volume is dedicated, has played numerous roles in bringing the book to print. As the Director of the Canadian-American Center at the University of Maine, he proposed the idea of a conference on loyalism and the Atlantic world in 2007 and helped provide financial and personal support for both the conference and the volume. Even more importantly, his scholarship and collegial engagement with both editors are keenly appreciated. We are also indebted to Elizabeth Mancke, John Reid, Scott See, and Shirley Tillotson for their helpful suggestions and encouragement.

Like any successful event, the 'Loyalism and the Revolutionary Atlantic World' conference that brought the contributors to this volume together in June 2009 required significant financial and personal contributions from a large number of people and several institutions. As the principal academic organizer of the conference, Liam Riordan is especially indebted to Betsy Arntzen's keen eye for organizational detail and tireless effort to make the event as stimulating and enjoyable as it was. Her level of commitment and engagement far exceeded the bounds of her title as Canadian Studies Outreach Coordinator at the Canadian-American Center at the University of Maine. Other important contributors to the conference, not mentioned elsewhere, included Lynn H. Parsons, emeritus professor of History at SUNY Brockport, who was an essential ally at the Castine Historical Society; Margaret Conrad, who facilitated ties to numerous scholars and helped secure financial support from the Provost at the University of New Brunswick as well as presenting a very fine paper on Edward Winslow; and a major grant from the Maine Humanities Council. Additional presenters and panel chairs who added greatly to our understanding of loyalism but were not able to contribute to this volume include: Todd W. Braisted, Ruma Chopra, Aaron (Nathan) Coleman, Timothy J. Compeau, Robert S. Davis, Susan Garfinkel, Edward M. Griffin, Gary Hughes, Bonnie Huskins, Maya Jasanoff, Brad A. Jones, Edward Larkin, James Leamon, Stephen Miller, Cassandra Pybus, Katherine Rieder, Stephen Sanfilippo (for Loyalist music!), Harvey Amani Whitfield, and Bradford J. Wood. Several University of Maine staff and History graduate students played essential supporting roles at the conference; among them were Suzanne Moulton, Robert Hodges, Peg Kearney, Edward (Ned) Martin, and Robert Woods.

We would like to thank the editorial staff at the University of Toronto Press for their exceptional work. We are particularly indebted to Len Husband for his tremendous support and encouragement, especially through the early stages of this project, and to Wayne Herrington for expertly shepherding us through the later stages. Barry Norris did an outstanding job of copy editing the entire manuscript. We are also grateful to Isaac Dorsch and Tanya Buckingham for their expert work in preparing the map, and to Natalie Neill for preparing the index. We are extremely lucky to have worked with such an impressive and diligent group of contributors. We are grateful for the time they generously took from their many personal and professional commitments to keep the project on schedule. This dedication was especially notable by Allison O'Mahen Malcom, and we would like to congratulate her on the birth of her son, James Victor Malcom, in January 2011.

Finally, we thank our families for their patience and support. In Maine, Liam Riordan would like to thank his wife, Susan Thibedeau, and his sons Cormac and Declan; in Nova Scotia, Jerry Bannister would like to thank his wife, Patti, and his sons Peter and Ryan. We owe them more than we can say.

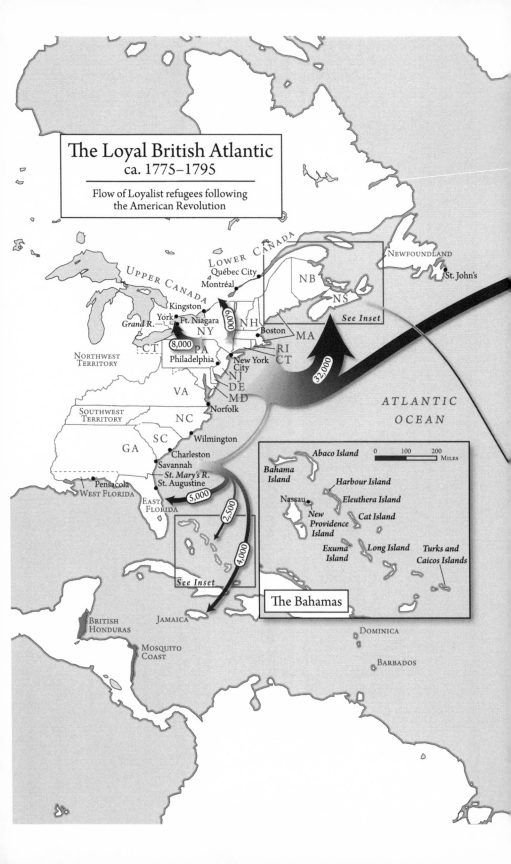

The Loyal British Atlantic
ca. 1775–1795

Flow of Loyalist refugees following
the American Revolution

NORTHWEST
TERRITORY

UPPER CANADA

LOWER CANADA

Québec City
Montréal

NB

NEWFOUNDLAND

St. John's

Kingston
York
Grand R.—
Ft. Niagara
NY

NH

Boston

MA

NS

See Inset

6,000

8,000
PA
Philadelphia

CT

RI
CT

New York
City

NJ
DE
MD

VA

Norfolk

32,000

ATLANTIC
OCEAN

SOUTHWEST
TERRITORY

NC

SC
GA

Wilmington

Charleston
Savannah
—St. Mary's R.
St. Augustine

5,000

2,500

Pensacola
WEST FLORIDA

EAST
FLORIDA

See Inset

4,000

Abaco Island

Bahama
Island

Harbour Island

0   100   200
MILES

Nassau

New
Providence
Island

Eleuthera Island

Cat Island

BRITISH
HONDURAS

JAMAICA

Exuma
Island

Long Island

Turks and
Caicos Islands

MOSQUITO
COAST

The Bahamas

DOMINICA

BARBADOS

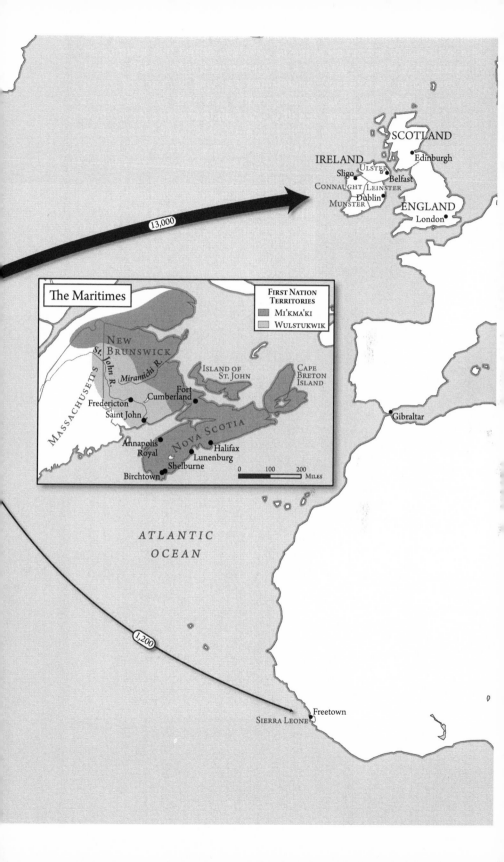

SCOTLAND

Edinburgh

IRELAND
ULSTER
Sligo
Belfast
CONNAUGHT LEINSTER
Dublin
MUNSTER
ENGLAND
London

13,000

The Maritimes

FIRST NATION
TERRITORIES
MI'KMA'KI
WULSTUKWIK

NEW
BRUNSWICK

St. John R.

Miramichi R.

ISLAND OF
ST. JOHN

CAPE
BRETON
ISLAND

MASSACHUSETS

Fredericton

Fort
Cumberland

Saint John

Annapolis
Royal

NOVA SCOTIA

Halifax

Lunenburg

Shelburne

Birchtown

0   100   200
MILES

Gibraltar

ATLANTIC
OCEAN

1,200

Freetown

SIERRA LEONE

THE LOYAL ATLANTIC
Remaking the British Atlantic in the Revolutionary Era

1

Loyalism and the British Atlantic, 1660–1840

JERRY BANNISTER AND LIAM RIORDAN[1]

This chapter explores the intertwined histories of Loyalists and loyalism in the British Atlantic world. The conceptualization of Loyalists has been unduly constricted by nationalistic perspectives and political priorities that have tended to focus on isolated individuals in ways that have prevented us from seeing how their specific expressions and experiences drew on a deep and dynamic tradition of loyalism that took particular shape in the early modern era around shifting relationships among English, British, colonial, American, and Atlantic formations. Loyalism has only very recently begun to be explored as an Atlantic subject, and the opportunity to reinvigorate our understanding of this essential force in its traditional, modern, and even postmodern expressions requires broad and multidisciplinary reflection.

The two great strengths of Atlantic scholarship are its diversity and its openness to debate. Since the moment that David Armitage coyly suggested that 'we are all Atlanticists now,' scholars have questioned the field's literal, littoral, and figurative boundaries.[2] While there is disagreement about the strengths and weaknesses of Atlantic versus global history, recent work has steadily expanded our horizons. Awareness of globalization has pushed early modern scholars to recognize, describe, and analyse varied transnational forces that, starting in the mid-fifteenth century, began to create an interconnected Atlantic. This new framework has shifted the geographic focus southward to the Caribbean, the French West Indies, the Spanish Atlantic, and the connections that bound west-central Africa and Brazil to one another. The value of this approach lies not only in its careful application to specific times and spaces, but also in its utility as a heuristic device. A remarkable wave of scholarship has produced an intellectual rainbow encompassing black, brown, red, white, and green Atlantics as well as Jesuit, Moravian, Quaker, Anglican, and Evangelical ones. Perhaps most forcefully, it has produced a renewed consciousness of early imperial Atlantics far different from the national orientation that almost all colonies would attain in the future. At its best, Atlantic history is an inclusive tool that enables scholars to transcend traditional boundaries (temporal, geographic, and disciplinary) and to place their work in a comparative framework. It offers new ways to conceptualize national historiographies and to assess anew varied critical themes such as agency, diaspora, borderlands, and entangled empires.[3] Like the so-called new imperial history, Atlantic studies tends to decentre early modern history and to challenge Eurocentric master narratives.[4]

Yet this torrent of Atlantic scholarship also has unwittingly reinscribed some of the verities of past scholarship that it aims to counter. This tendency is particularly strong for scholars working in US institutions (though hardly confined to them), for whom an often unspoken axiom plots imperial subjecthood as a backward social relation to be overcome by more modern forms of national citizenship. For Canadian historians, Atlantic scholarship has brought a renewed focus on political radicalism and revolution, but not on loyalism and counterrevolution. As a result, the study of loyalism in Canadian political culture remains mired in Whig-Tory binaries and relegated to outmoded notions of a 'Tory touch.'[5] Research on the revolutionary, or red, Atlantic spans a variety of perspectives – from the meta-narrative of *The Many-Headed Hydra* to detailed local studies of maritime communities – but it generally focuses on resistance to British authority.[6] From the failed war against the Maroons through the slave revolts that culminated in the Haitian Revolution, historians have given us a remarkably rich and complex picture of how Atlantic peoples created their own culture and communities outside the ambit of – though often in contested dialogue with – the imperial state.[7] In this Atlantic narrative, the American Revolution usefully appears within a broader transnational process of social agency, political struggle, and cultural negotiation. R.R. Palmer's landmark work, published a half century ago, has served as a classic point of departure, and, for many, the early modern Atlantic comes to its most appropriate close with the many challenges to imperial order in the revolutionary era.[8]

This approach obscures a crucial part of the story, however, for the Loyal Atlantic is central to understanding national, imperial, and Atlantic histories. Like any revolutionary ideology, loyalism in the British

Atlantic was a diffuse, complex, and potent phenomenon that traversed multiple borders. In fact, we can understand the revolution only in the context of counter-revolution, because both were so deeply interconnected in the making of the Atlantic world.[9] While historians have taken great pains to explore the complexity and multiplicity of revolutionary movements and ideologies, loyalism has received considerably less scholarly attention. Whereas Patriots are now understood to include a broad coalition of diverse interests that drew on varied precedents, Loyalists largely remain depicted as a one-dimensional, static group. Recent Canadian scholarship tells us much about liberalism, conservatism, and popular radicalism in the nineteenth century, but treats loyalism as essentially a synonym for British Toryism.[10] In one collection applying an Atlantic framework to Canadian history, Bryan Palmer sees international influences largely through the lens of revolutionary movements and ideas, and he depicts loyalism as a reactionary harbinger of patriarchy and paternalism.[11] Given the revolutionaries' widespread commitment to coercion to enforce conformity within their own ranks, this imbalanced scholarly assessment is strikingly ironic. Research on the red Atlantic favours the early anti-colonial trajectories of the United States and Haiti and tends to marginalize the more widespread accommodations with imperial power almost everywhere else. This volume begins to correct this overemphasis on the proponents of the revolutionary Atlantic by attending to the vital transatlantic commitments, experiences, and consequences of those who remained loyal to Britain. It focuses on the continuities as well as the changes in the British Atlantic world, and, we hope, will contribute to a dialogue among scholars in other national and linguistic traditions who assess additional Atlantic contexts of loyalism.

As the Iberian Atlantic historian Jeremy Adelman has brilliantly pointed out, we must avoid the nationalist teleology implicit in the 'age of revolutions' in order to understand the enduring 'legacies of empire and colonialism' that helped constitute the 'successor regimes' founded in the wake of the Atlantic revolutions. This framework demands a comparative assessment of what is best framed as the 'age of imperial revolutions,' which rejects the presumption of an inevitable decline of European empires. More interestingly, imperial transformations 'yielded new social practices in defining the internal life of sovereign politics,' and developments in Mexico, Brazil, Canada, and most of the Caribbean forcibly demonstrate 'the revitalization of the notion of empire itself,' and may provide crucial ground on which to assess 'the premodern roots of our transnational political vocabulary' as well as the 'pluralist foundations of our understandings of state authority.'[12] Future comparative work presumably will reveal striking contrasts as well as unexpected commonalities among loyalisms in different imperial traditions, but this fuller assessment of multiple dimensions of the Loyal Atlantic has only just begun. This chapter and those that follow reassert the place of the North Atlantic in the scholarly debate about the Atlantic world.[13] As recent studies by Stephen J. Hornsby, John G. Reid, and Elizabeth Mancke demonstrate, we need to reconsider the geographic and imperial dimensions of the break-up and reconstitution of the British Empire.[14] 'The Atlantic world was,' as Mancke notes, 'defined by states but colonized by empires.'[15]

The resistance to studying loyalism as a multifaceted international phenomenon arises in part from the ongoing force of national frameworks that shape how we study and explain the past. This nationalistic orientation has produced three basic views that treat Loyalists simplistically: in the US tradition, they are disparaged through condescension or lack of attention; in Britain after the Revolutionary War, they quickly became oddly embarrassing outcasts; and even their celebration as the best and brightest founders of English Canada offers a monocausal judgment of a more diverse, complex, and interesting phenomenon. As J.M. Bumsted pointed out twenty years ago, 'We must be prepared to consider and accept these people on their own terms for what they were – and were not – rather than for what subsequent generations have chosen to make them.'[16] The twenty-first-century incarnation of Loyalist popular memory, which links Canadian soldiers serving in Afghanistan with eighteenth-century British Loyalists, demonstrates the continued power and resiliency of Loyalist heritage.[17] While Canadian scholars have investigated the Loyalist myths that long permeated the writing of English-Canadian history, the challenge now is to move beyond debunking to place loyalism more fully in its international context.[18]

Loyalism (as a practice and as a body of thought, opinion, and self-understanding) needs to be recognized as a distinct, though interrelated, subject from the study of specific Loyalists (individuals who opposed Patriots during the American Revolution). It marks a process as much as a people, because allegiances shifted, often quickly and unexpectedly, in the Atlantic world. Though the theories of the late Clifford Geertz have fallen out of intellectual fashion, his insights remain useful for tracing such developments. Paraphrasing Geertz, Lauren

Benton makes an important observation in her analysis of legal regimes in world history: 'the global institutional order has its origins in the stories that people tell themselves about others.'[19] These stories change across time and place according to shifting currents of power, as allies become enemies, neutrals become rivals, and heroes become villains. Alan Taylor offers an especially evocative account of the varieties of loyalism in the fluid borderland from Montreal to Detroit. Retelling the stories of numerous figures that include First Nations people and Irish immigrants on both sides of the porous border, we learn about the fragile nature of the revolutionary settlement that remained highly contested until at least the outcome of a second Anglo-American war from 1812 to 1815.[20]

The subtle but at times decisive line separating loyalty and neutrality had enormous consequences for the peoples of the British Atlantic world well before the battles at Lexington and Concord.[21] As the Acadians discovered in 1755, refusal to swear an unconditional oath of allegiance could trigger punishment as dire as active resistance to the Crown; the difference between conditional and complete loyalty could form its own fault line of empire. The mass expulsion of the Acadian people from Nova Scotia was not an isolated event but part of the larger struggle that culminated in the Seven Years' War.[22] Yet, even as American colonists and Britons joined in rejoicing over the conquest of Quebec, they told themselves different stories and created different meanings of loyalty.[23] These evolving conceptions of loyalty, in turn, shaped the boundaries of the American Revolution. In Nova Scotia, for example, the shift from passive loyalty to the Crown in the early years of the Revolutionary War to a much more active loyalty, partially in response to coastal raids by rebel privateers, helped to keep the colony in British hands.[24]

The interaction between loyalism and Loyalists provides an important axis for work in the field. Loyalism was not the exclusive preserve of reactionary Tories who used it to combat Lockean liberalism; rather, it encompassed a wide range of peoples in colonial America, from ethnic and religious minorities to Mohawks and enslaved people of African descent to most of the white colonists in the British Caribbean.[25] This rich mixture of loyal people fuelled the modern development of a composite monarchy in which loyalty to Crown and Empire encompassed varied commitments and political traditions.[26] An Atlantic reassessment of revolutionary-era loyalism suggests that the once firm lines separating a 'first' and 'second' British Empire need to be reconsidered.[27] It would be a mistake to view *loyalist* as merely a literal description for a particular party, let alone an epithet for those supposedly on the losing side of history. Loyalism entailed far more than simply rejecting the Patriots and embracing the Crown. 'Loyalist,' as the *Oxford English Dictionary* reminds us, invokes a human condition premised on fidelity to promises, oaths, or words of honour; allegiance to sovereign or lawful governments; and a commitment to lawfulness and legality. Public professions of loyalty formed a central aspect of public life throughout the British Atlantic world, even if the penal laws were applied unevenly across Britain's possessions.[28] The requirement of public officials and military officers to swear the oaths of Protestant loyalty – specifically, the oaths of allegiance, supremacy, abjuration, and declaration – ensured that loyalism encompassed much more than tacit consent in its Lockean formulation. There is, of course, a vast grey area of ambiguous motives and meanings – the political attitudes of most people were rarely crystal clear even to themselves, let alone to those who study the past – but investigating loyalism sheds valuable light on the alliances and antagonisms that fed the organization of power in the Atlantic world.[29]

While the chapters in this volume mostly concern themselves with the crisis years after 1774 and especially the post-war force of loyalism in remaking the British Atlantic, it is important first to sketch some of the deeper traditions and cultural understandings that informed Loyalist action during and after the civil war that jettisoned thirteen colonies out of the Empire and onto an independent, yet often parallel, course with its former polity. These developments and personal commitments evolved in the context of violent English conquests that began in Ireland in the mid-seventeenth century and, in the imperial mind, culminated in the conquest of New France. If, as Ramsay Cook has argued, 'the central event in the history of Canada is the Conquest of 1760,' then we need to see that event as part of a much longer inter- and intra-imperial struggle over religious allegiance, royal sovereignty, and individual liberty.[30] While debates over the contested meanings of liberty have received significant attention recently, particularly in Michel Ducharme's prize-winning monograph, there remains a need to place this discourse in the broader context of the struggle over loyalty.[31] While the rejection of the rebels' republicanism became the focal point of loyalism after 1775, opposition to Roman Catholicism was its dominant feature for most of the eighteenth century. In addition to confronting France, Britain faced powerful aboriginal polities in the northeast for whom imperial loyalty was primarily an issue of diplomatic negotiation. Europeans did not begin to dominate most of the territory that became British North America until after the Loyalist migration to Canada in the late eighteenth century.[32] As John G. Reid demonstrates in his contribution to this volume, the notion of friendship remained a powerful force in negotiations between British and aboriginal peoples throughout the eighteenth century. Echoes of this history of friendship can still be heard in Canadian debates over the monarchy. The Royal Proclamation of 1763 forms an important basis for aboriginal land claims and, according to Michael Valpy, 'is rightly known as the aboriginal people's Magna Carta.' When Queen Elizabeth II visited Canada in 1997, Innu community leader Mary Pia Benuen told journalists in Labrador, 'The way I see it, she is everybody's queen. It's nice for her to know who the Innu are and why we're fighting for our land claim and self-government all the time.'[33]

Loyalism developed as the British Empire evolved and Britain's dominions themselves changed during the eighteenth century. The beliefs that Loyalists drew upon in their revolutionary self-fashioning, akin to the parallel process for Patriots, emerged from varied sources, yet a significant core of loyalism drew upon a contested sense of peoplehood that encompassed dynamic conceptions of social order, Englishness and Britishness (as overlapping and divergent identities), Protestant Christianity, monarchy, commerce, and empire.[34] The salience of each value changed over time in response to specific historical, local, and personal circumstances; what is most striking, however, is how such varied ways of making sense of self and society could be mutually reinforcing. As literary scholars have insightfully suggested, we need to conceptualize loyalism as an affective sensibility as well as a specific political program.[35] The emergence of a polite culture – rooted in Enlightenment fashion, fuelled by commercial expansion, and chronicled by a vibrant publishing industry – eventually would feed the popular belief in Britain that Patriots were *banditti* cut off from the civilizing influence of their king and country, little different from the thousands of convicts sent to colonial America prior to 1775. Seen in this light, loyalty was a matter of cultural as well as political allegiance.[36]

Scholars have long recognized the Patriot movement's embeddedness in deep traditions that drew on previous events and pre-existing ideologies that, in turn, influenced subsequent revolutionary movements. Similarly, loyalism was more than a discrete movement in an isolated handful of years. Just as Patriots drew on collective memories of radicalism that stretched back to the English Civil War, Loyalists drew on 'ancient' memories of loyalism. The Restoration of the Stuart crown in 1660 represented a watershed in the formation of the Loyal Atlantic.[37] Charles II's accession had a self-evident relevance for many late eighteenth-century observers about the dangers of rebellion leading to violence, regicide, and anarchic democracy that could be restrained and righted only by a return to monarchy. In addition to the political and historical ways that loyalism invoked the Restoration, the 1660s and 1670s also offered aesthetic forms that would resonate again in the Revolution. Samuel Butler's satirical polemic poem 'Hudibras' (1662–78), attacking the religious dissent of the Civil War, would remain popular into the eighteenth century and provided a direct model for the Loyalist poetry that flourished during the American Revolution and in post-war British Canada.[38] As Philip Gould and Gwendolyn Davies explore in their contributions to this collection, the legal, expressive, and business contexts of Loyalist print culture provide richly informative points of entry for understanding the Loyal Atlantic.

If republican ideology was a hybrid of classical ideas conceived in a Machiavellian moment, loyalism drew on principles deeply embedded in English politics, philosophy, and literature. These principles manifested themselves in an eclectic range of thinkers – from Hobbes and Locke to Burke and Durham – as Britons debated the covenants that bound subjects to their king. But they also found expression in the mercantilist system that bound the colonies to Britain. Based on the belief that the economic health of a nation depended on achieving a favourable balance of trade and a surplus of gold bullion, the British government sought to make its imperial system as self-sufficient as possible. The English Civil War had disrupted commercial networks, providing an opportunity for the Dutch to expand their North American trade. In response, the English Parliament passed a series of Navigation Acts from 1651 to 1696 that formed the statutory basis of mercantilism. The Navigation Act of 1673 sanctioned the creation of a system of duties and customs officers in the colonies to enforce imperial authority. From the perspective of London, the colonies represented mere extensions of the metropolis, parts of a single managed economy. The Navigation Acts acknowledged the right of colonial merchants to participate fully in imperial trade and to compete with English merchants in commodity markets. When mercantilism closed the British Empire to Dutch, French, and Spanish traders, it presented new opportunities for colonial merchants who were quick to take advantage of the system. Although the Navigation Acts placed significant restrictions on trade by favouring metropolitan interests, they also contributed to the growth of the Empire by giving colonial enterprises access to capital and markets. With notable exceptions, such as the smuggling of molasses and rum from foreign colonies in the West Indies, the mercantilist system functioned largely according to its design from the early eighteenth century to the outbreak of the American Revolution.[39] Although imperial rule across the Atlantic was uneven and complex, it followed discernible patterns.

The Empire's political and economic commitments did not function as isolated forces of domination and self-interest, and the intertwining imperial valences of control and succour for settlers are especially evident in the sweeping terrain of religion, nation, and empire. Imperial authorities endeavoured wherever possible to impose active obedience to the Crown and adherence to the Church of England. The Test Act of 1673 stipulated that office-holders not only had to swear allegiance to the monarch but also repudiate publicly the Roman Catholic doctrine of transubstantiation. Reception and enforcement of English law varied considerably, depending on when and how a particular colony was first established, but statutory law formed a loyalist continuity: the last of the Test Acts was not repealed until the Catholic Emancipation Act of 1829 and vestiges of the Navigation Acts remained in place until 1849. These statutes reflected a deep set of state-sanctioned beliefs about governance – a *mentalité* of rule, in other words – predicated on the axiom that officials acting in the name of the Crown had the inherent right to regulate both commerce and conscience. This right was continually negotiated and contested throughout the British Atlantic, its application stretching and shrinking according to changing balances of imperial, colonial, and aboriginal power, yet it remained part of the fabric of empire. It bequeathed questions that eventually tore the Empire apart: who should enjoy it (the king, Parliament, governors, colonial legislatures, local courts?); which royal house could wield it (the Stuarts or the Hanoverians?); and how should it be exercised (by statute, prerogative writ, custom, vote?).[40] The Act of Settlement of 1701 established the Hanoverian succession in English law, but enforcing loyalty to George I was a different matter. The anti-Catholicism that marked English (and, after 1707, British) loyalism was fuelled in large part by fear of the return of James II and his Stuart successors. Although the Jacobite Rebellion in

1715–16 failed, the domestic threat to the Hanoverians remained until 1746, when the Duke of Cumberland crushed the last serious Stuart insurrection at the Battle of Culloden. Fed by the rapidly expanding fiscal-military state, the British government by the mid-eighteenth century had unprecedented resources with which to enforce loyalty to the Crown.[41]

Prior to the American Revolution, few public commentators in the British Empire questioned monarchy itself: they took it for granted, like slavery, as a natural part of governance. The liberal impact of the Glorious Revolution on British political culture must be balanced against a loyalist legacy that emphasized the Battle of the Boyne as much as the Bill of Rights. As Allison O'Mahen Malcom argues in her chapter in this volume, the Glorious Revolution in Loyalist memory was above all a victory for Protestantism. By the nineteenth century, this memory had become synonymous with Toryism, but in the eighteenth century appeals to Protestant loyalism crossed party affiliations. English Whigs such as Joseph Addison drew on republican ideals of civic duty to argue that liberty and property depended on loyalty to a Protestant king: 'A Free-hold, tho' it be but in Ice and Snow, will make the Owner pleased in the Possession, and stout in the Defence of it; and *is a very proper Reward of our Allegiance to our present King*, who (by an unparallel'd Instance of Goodness in a Sovereign, and Infatuation in Subjects) contends for the Freedom of His People against Themselves; and will not suffer many of them to fall into a State of Slavery, which they are bent upon with so much Eagerness and Obstinacy.'[42]

Writing in the wake of the Jacobite uprising in 1715, Addison published *The Freeholder* with a clear political aim. He asserted, 'While many of my gallant Country-men are employed in pursuing Rebels half discomfited through the Consciousness of their Guilt, I shall labour to improve those Victories to the Good of my Fellow-Subjects; by carrying on our Successes over the Minds of Men, and by reconciling them to the Cause of their King, their Country, and their Religion.' His goal was 'to shew them the privileges of an *English* Free-holder which they enjoy in common with my self, and to make them sensible how these Blessings are secured to us by his Majesty's Title, his Administration, and his Personal Character.'[43] A recent scholarly collection on liberty in the British Empire reconsiders the importance of constitutional rights, but tends to gloss over Addison's argument that those rights were secured by the king. Jack Greene argues that the capacity for preserving liberty rested primarily on two institutions – juries and Parliament – that were recreated in the thirteen colonies and became functionally republican before they became anti-monarchical. Greene concludes, 'these conditions explain why, during the North American settler revolt that began in 1774–1776, the transition from monarchy to republican government was so easy in those polities that had the wherewithal to participate in the revolt.'[44] In this view, loyalty amounts to little more than a lack of wherewithal. By isolating liberty from monarchy, this perspective tends to overlook a political tradition that sees the Crown as a guarantor of liberty.[45]

The emphasis on the personal character of the king, which Addison had trumpeted in 1715, reached its apex in Lord Bolingbroke's *Idea of the Patriot King*. For Bolingbroke, the polity represented a family:

> The true image of a free people, governed by a PATRIOTIC KING, is that of a patriarchal family, where the head and all the members are united by one common interest, and animated by one common spirit: and where, if any are perverse enough to have another, they will soon be borne down by the superiority of those who have the same; and, far from making a *division*, they will but confirm the *union* of the little state. That to approach as near as possible to those ideas of perfect government, and social happiness under it, is desirable in every state, no man will be absurd enough to deny.[46]

The king enjoyed patriarchal status, but his power was not absolute. For Bolingbroke, the king's duty, '[t]o espouse no party, but to govern like the common father of people, is so essential to the character of a PATRIOTIC KING, that he who does otherwise forfeits the title.'[47]

To invoke Lord Bolingbroke, John Locke, Joseph Addison, or Alexander Pope in the eighteenth-century colonies was not so much a claim to share their politics as it was an assertion about cultural consistency and mastery of English 'classical' knowledge. As Philip Gould explores in his contribution to this volume, as well as elsewhere, taking the careful measure of Britishness was not solely a political discourse. Indeed the polemical exchanges of the mid-1770s could not be contained by mere partisan claims and immediately became 'literary disputes over matters of style and expression' that required the 'complex reconstruction of British American identities out of canonically English materials,' for in the shared Anglo-American eighteenth-century world, literary propriety and social and political stability were fully fused with one another.[48]

Lockean ideas circulated widely in the Atlantic world, but the principles of consent and contract must be placed in the larger context of early modern political culture. From the domestic regulation of women and children to the regulation of trade, public life was based on hierarchical ties that bound subjects to their king. British justice was deeply paternalistic and discretionary, and the law of master and servant supported the criminalization of breach of contract throughout the Empire.[49] And, as Brendan McConville argues, colonial America remained strongly monarchical and anti-Catholic right up to the eve of the American Revolution.[50] According to Gordon S. Wood, 'Royal authority never seemed more impressive and acceptable to the colonists than at mid-century, not simply because wars naturally favored a growth in the influence of the crown and the Anglican church was growing in strength, but also because the theoretical underpinnings of [the colonists'] social thought still remained largely monarchical.'[51] Moreover, confidence in the benefits of hierarchy was not simply voiced by elites and those paid to do their bidding in some vast exercise of social control. Popular culture, no less than abstract political and legal theory, was infused by a keen awareness of the ways in which popular interests benefitted from their special connection to the Crown. As the words of a Revolutionary War song to the tune of 'Drink, and let your Hearts at Rest' proclaimed in its chorus, 'Come soldiers come, nor fear to die, / For royal George and liberty.'[52] Given the strength of English and British attachments in all the late eighteenth-century colonies, T.H. Breen is surely correct when he cautions that, 'those who wish to posit a slow, simmering discontent among American colonists from 1765 forward run into a confounding fact: until the summer of 1774 – even later for some people – a majority of the white colonists expressed genuine pride in being members of the British Empire.'[53]

The imperial crisis that came to a head in 1775 and 1776 severed the shared, if multitudinous, sense of Britishness for many settlers in the thirteen rebellious colonies. Suddenly, a common orientation towards self-assessment within a British *habitus* became the terrain of violent polarization. For US historians, attention to this tipping point for Loyalists has been explained most influentially in Bernard Bailyn's landmark 1974 assessment of Thomas Hutchinson, yet three related issues make it an awkward foundation for future work on loyalism.[54] First, while Bailyn's biographical approach is masterfully realized and gives readers a movingly tragic understanding of an individual unable to comprehend rapid changes in Massachusetts society, the field needs more synthetic and analytical assessments. Biographical studies far outnumber all other approaches to Loyalists and, thus, despite the rich immediacy that effective biography permits, such assessments contribute to the scattered and particularistic state of the field. Second, despite *The Ordeal of Thomas Hutchinson*'s canonical status and myriad insights, its most fundamental interpretive commitment is to use Hutchinson's 'ordeal' from the mid-1760s to the mid-1770s as an exemplar of what made the *Patriot* movement so different from the Anglo-American status quo of the late eighteenth century: Hutchinson suffered because he could not fathom that rebel commitments were serious and genuine. The impulse to use Loyalists to explain Patriots thus remains a major conceptual barrier to our ability to understand loyalism. Finally, among Bailyn's most impressive achievements is to place Hutchinson as a skilled player in the patronage-based political culture of eighteenth-century Britain, shrewdly assessing the provincial-metropolitan relationship and inserting himself effectively into networks of Anglo-American politics powerfully described for the home country by Lewis Namier.[55] Yet the very strength of this transatlantic political context suggests a third way that Bailyn's brilliant assessment limits how the study of loyalism can be invigorated by Atlantic immersion.

A generation of scholarship about Georgian society has added such sweeping new dimensions to the Namierite interpretation of British politics that what once seemed to be a narrow world of complacent country gentleman has been almost completely overturned. T.H. Breen's synthetic assessment of this recent work and his suggestions about how it should reshape the ways in which we understand the American Revolution offer a rich base for reconsidering loyalism and Loyalists in their Atlantic context.[56] This revisionist scholarship argues that the strong commercial connections of eighteenth-century Britain created a more dynamic middle class than we have heretofore recognized, and thus British society in this era was more 'modern' than 'traditional,' especially given the effectiveness of the fiscal-military state and the rise of a self-confident British nationalism that made Englishness a contested identity for domestic and colonial provincial subjects trying to understand their place in the Empire and their relationship to metropolitan society. The ways in which nation and empire made both centripetal and centrifugal claims in the revolutionary period offer an especially promising point of entry for comparative work that situates colonial societies in relation to the three kingdoms of the British Isles as well as to non-British colonial societies and their empires.[57] Breen sets the British stage compellingly to explain Patriots in relation to these developments, especially their need to seize upon natural rights liberalism to free themselves from an assertive and aggressively English-centred sense of the Empire. Yet, what this vital new understanding of eighteenth-century British society means for loyalism and Loyalists remains largely unexplored.

These broad currents took specific shape in the crucible of resistance and loyalism starting in the mid-1760s that intensified from 1774 to 1776. While analysis of the American Revolution needs to be wary of casting New England as the synecdoche of the entire conflict – as the vanguard of the rebellion and the place where imperial force was applied most directly in the pre-war era – events there, and more particularly in Boston, demand close attention. Peter Oliver's remarkable 'Origin and Progress of the American Rebellion,' penned by 1781 and long available in a convenient scholarly edition, offers a profitable initial point of reference and still awaits definitive treatment. Oliver virulently decried both the materialism of the rebel elite's commitment to smuggling and its base manipulation of popular opinion to stir ordinary people to lawless violence that destroyed a just and balanced colonial society. Abetted by clergy who had 'quite unlearned the Gospel, & substituted Politicks in its Stead,' the passion of rebellion mindlessly corrupted the gullible in Massachusetts and beyond.[58] While his hostile denunciations of Patriots' self-interest, propaganda, and abuse of religion all offer telling leads about Loyalist self-understanding, Oliver's characterization of Loyalists especially calls for attention. He decried that '[t]he Foundations of Government were subverted; & every Loyalist was obliged to submit or be swept away by the Torrent' as early as 1771. In such tumult there were some who 'dared to say that their Souls were their own; but no one could call his Body his own; for that was at the Mercy of the Mob, who like the Inquisition Coach, would call a Man out of his Bed, & he must step in whether he liked the Conveyance or not.'[59] Related to Thomas Hutchinson by the marriage of their children and by close friendship, and bound together by business, legal, and governmental responsibilities, the Hutchinson-Oliver core provides an almost-too-easily-caricatured elite Loyalist profile at the dawn of the crisis. The Hutchinson-Oliver perspective was important to loyalism, yet the words and actions of these Loyalist paragons still have mostly been used to explain the rebels that they opposed rather than to provide a basis for analysing loyalism itself.[60]

The British army's withdrawal from Boston in March 1776 precipitated the first significant Loyalist diaspora, one of the major motifs of revolutionary-era loyalism that several contributors to this volume discuss. British military redeployment to New York City four months later shifted the central focus of the war and Loyalist activity to other regions, first the Mid-Atlantic, then, especially after 1778, to the southern colonies of Georgia, the Carolinas, and, at the very close, Virginia. The intersection of British military forces and loyalism is of crucial importance for several reasons, especially to include ordinary colonists, enslaved people of African descent, and Native Americans within our conceptualization of loyalism. Chapters here by Carole Watterson Troxler and Jennifer K. Snyder take up the complexities of African American relationships to loyalism and, especially, the persistence of enslavement, while John G. Reid considers aboriginal loyalism and allegiance. Since none of the contributors to this volume specifically examines colonists' service in Loyalist military units, a general discussion of this important subject seems necessary and reminds us that the public importance of loyalism becomes acute at times of war – an almost constant state in the long Anglo-American eighteenth century.

Military historian Paul H. Smith provides perhaps the most widely cited statistic about Loyalists: they constituted about 20 per cent of all white Americans in the thirteen rebellious colonies. He arrived at this conservative estimate by extrapolating from the nineteen thousand Loyalists he documented in the provincial corps of the British army. Based on an estimate that 15 per cent of all Loyalists served in these military units, a ratio derived from the large sample in Lorenzo Sabine's prosopographical work, Smith next used a family multiplier of four to arrive at a total estimate of five hundred thousand Loyalists.[61] While Smith's approach undercounts the full range of Loyalist sentiment, since active military service represented a deeply committed and high-risk form of loyalism, there can be little doubt that Loyalists were numerous, that their experiences merit more careful attention, and that a military history perspective can fruitfully reveal major dimensions of loyalism.

The war years assume particular importance from a Loyalist perspective for several reasons. The shift to the mid-Atlantic theatre starting in the summer of 1776 aimed to isolate rebellious New England and to draw on strong Loyalist and neutral commitments from prosperous New York, Pennsylvania, and adjoining colonies.[62] The expectation of strong civilian support among colonists was largely realized. The British performed impressively in the field, yet their efforts here ultimately failed. The significance of the British loss at Saratoga, New York, in October 1777 might not have been weighty in strictly martial terms, but its diplomatic and strategic ramifications, with open French financial and military support to the Patriots in its wake, made it a turning point. The entry of France and then Spain as open belligerents widened the war to include the West Indies, as well as defence of the home islands, the Mediterranean, and India. The dramatically expanded war encouraged new British diplomatic offers to the rebels. Yet, in April 1778, when the Continental Congress rejected the overtures of the Carlisle Commission, which sought a negotiated settlement open to a wide range of concessions short of complete independence, it became absolutely clear that the war would have no swift conclusion. The intensified phase of the war that followed, however, would be conducted with a reduced British military presence in North America: while 65 per cent of British land forces were deployed there at the start of 1778, by September 1780 that commitment had fallen to just 29 per cent.[63]

The final phase of the war in North America shifted to a southern strategy initiated with the invasion of Georgia in 1778. Loyalists' anticipated strength in the lower South shaped British leaders' strategic planning there, which historian Piers Mackesy judges a 'fresh start' that demonstrated 'a nice balance of military and political considerations' with a better chance of success than the effort in New England and the mid-Atlantic.[64] Not only would Loyalist provincial corps and militia contribute militarily, a return to civil government was anticipated where Loyalists would serve as influential leaders. Yet only in Georgia was civilian government restored, and the terror tactics employed on both sides in the southern theatre made it clear that quick reconciliation was impossible.[65]

While the weakness of Loyalist martial contributions is often seen as an important factor in the British failure to win the war, this criticism is often Janus faced. The brutality of Loyalists' combat in a 'vicious vendetta war' made meaningful stabilization impossible, yet Loyalists are also condemned for failing to have made sufficient personal sacrifices for British success. As Jim Piecuch points out in his detailed examination of the war in the Deep South, this caricature of white Loyalists as both too brutal and too passive mirrors a contemporary stereotype of aboriginal people. Loyalists surely played notable roles in the southern theatre, as well as in and around the major northern cities controlled by the British, but an overall assessment of the Loyalists' role in the war remains elusive in the face of tremendous local variation.[66] While the Loyalists' place in the war effort awaits additional careful archival research, the richest work on loyalism to date examines the Loyalist diaspora around the Atlantic world. This generally occurred in the form of chain migrations as individuals and families threatened by rebel assaults left their households to resettle near protection by British military forces. Thus, for example, many loyal residents of Falmouth (modern-day Portland, Maine) left the city after its bombardment by the British and plundering by rebel militia in October 1775.[67] A handful went to Britain, others to Halifax, and those who went to Boston, thinking it a safe haven, would depart once more by March 1776 – all well before the Declaration of Independence that supposedly initiated the Revolution. Similar local, regional, and Atlantic refugee trajectories occurred repeatedly throughout the rebellious colonies.

The significance of the Loyalist diaspora was highlighted a half-century ago by R.R. Palmer, who observed that the French Revolution displaced five subjects of that country for every thousand residents, a modest ratio against the staggering twenty-four per thousand displaced in America.[68] While this general statistic is often repeated and while there are many case studies of Loyalist settlement in post-war locales, the Loyalist out-migration in its global context has received systematic examination only with the recent publication of Maya Jasanoff's *Liberty's Exiles*. Her careful assessment of the imperial diaspora of Loyalists by 1785 has substantially reduced previous estimates of the out-migration from the thirteen colonies from a high of as much as one hundred thousand to sixty thousand. While this lower figure is overly conservative, especially since some Loyalist out-migration continued after 1785, her work re-emphasizes the diaspora's uneven geographic impact on the British Empire. Of the sixty-two thousand Loyalists Jasanoff documents, some thirty-eight thousand went to colonies in British North America, with the other principal destinations lagging considerably behind: thirteen thousand to Britain (among them five thousand free backs), five thousand to Florida (most of these to move again to the British West Indies after the evacuation of 1785), three thousand to Jamaica, and two thousand five hundred to the Bahamas.[69] Exceeding the importance even of this important numerical recovery, Jasanoff repositions Revolutionary War Loyalist refugees as a fascinating vanguard for central features of the nineteenth-century British Empire, especially the tension between its increasing liberalism and increasing hierarchy (alternately, its inclusive and exclusive impulses).[70]

Given the preponderant demographic weight of the Loyalist exodus to what would become Canada (see the map following the Acknowledgments) – by our judgment nearly two-thirds of the entire outmigration – half of the chapters that follow discuss British North America.[71] The Loyalist refugees were far from a homogeneous group, though; as David G. Bell and Neil Mackinnon have emphasized, once they arrived in Nova Scotia and New Brunswick, they were not particularly loyal participants in local politics.[72] Gwendolyn Davies's chapter in this volume adds to our understanding of Loyalist dissent in the post-war period by examining the roles played by interconnected networks of printers in the Maritimes. Though Loyalists came from varied backgrounds and expressed diverse political views that included a mixture of republican and monarchist doctrines, what they all shared was a deep opposition to rebellion. Most Loyalists opposed the idea of 'republican' America less vehemently than they rejected revolution as an acceptable means of enacting social change. The term 'republicanism' had so many connotations at the time, and still does in recent scholarship, that one hesitates to invoke it at all; but its quotidian, if contentious, presence seeped across polarized boundaries of partisanship in the revolutionary era. While republicanism would attain sharp and polemical meaning during the war and in post-war British North America, more generally it was a broad Enlightenment mode of thought, even a 'form of life,' whose values and ideals blended with monarchical colonial society, according to the historian Gordon S. Wood.[73] As a result, Loyalist refugees, especially those who had been long-term colonists, were not automatically anti-republican. Many had resented British policies in the 1760s and 1770s, but they refused to support military mobilization, outright independence, and a complete break with the Crown and Empire. Despite the wide diversity of peoples and motivations caught up in the Loyalist migrations, the close of the Revolutionary War brought a new formal line of demarcation that separated US citizens from British subjects that informed post-war meanings of loyalism in lasting ways.[74]

The area of Loyalist scholarship that has received the most prominent scholarly and public attention in recent years and that also includes a robust Atlantic approach examines the meaning of the American

Revolution for enslaved people. James W. St G. Walker's towering social history reconstructs the black Loyalists' experiences in Nova Scotia, and then follows some fifteen hundred black Nova Scotians to Africa in 1792, where they helped found Sierra Leone and where their descendants remained influential into the late nineteenth century.[75] Walker's pioneering scholarship recently has been extended in especially influential studies. Chief among them is Cassandra Pybus's micro-biographical recovery of black Loyalists from slavery, through wartime mobilization, and then on to London, Sierra Leone, and even a handful to the founding of Botany Bay, Australia. In her well-crafted prose, careful archival scholarship, and, above all, her move far beyond the Atlantic, Pybus charts numerous courses for future work.[76]

Yet for all the importance of some twenty thousand slaves who seized advantage of war's turmoil to flee bondage, the eight to ten thousand formerly enslaved people who used British support to depart the rebellious colonies permanently are overshadowed demographically, though not historiographically, by the nearly eighteen thousand displaced people of African descent who were forced to relocate after the war as the property of Loyalists. Maya Jasanoff reminds us that we must attend to the critical line of inclusion *and* exclusion that loyalism entailed, not just for people of African descent but also for different First Nation groups and for white Loyalists as well. The chapters in this volume by Carole Watterson Troxler and Jennifer K. Snyder follow Loyalists and their enslaved property to the Bahamas and East Florida, respectively, to examine the persistence and expansion of slavery in the post-war British colonies and to offer an important corrective to recent overly celebratory work about the British as slave liberators in the American Revolution.[77]

An important area where loyalist and imperial studies have informed one another, especially for Canadian scholars, has been in the assessment of changes to formal British political structures and political culture as a consequence of the Revolutionary War. For British North America, the period after 1783 was characterized by counter-revolution and the struggle for reform. The metropolitan government created two new colonies – New Brunswick in 1784 and Upper Canada in 1791 – designed to be bulwarks of Protestant loyalism. This 'second' British Empire strove to achieve greater control than its predecessor, as the home government adopted counter-revolutionary policies to exert a tighter hold on its colonial possessions, and the system of representative government established in most Atlantic colonies was intended to keep popular impulses in check.[78] The Colonial Office, founded in 1801, circumscribed the powers of elected assemblies, and governors were expected to rely upon their executive and legislative councils, both of which were filled with unelected officials.[79] But the system never worked according to design: colonial assemblies repeatedly contested the authority of the appointed councils; persistent public criticism of the governors' regimes created a divisive political climate; and efforts to curb political opposition damaged the legitimacy of local government.[80] In borderlands such as the Eastern Townships of Quebec, the War of 1812 tested the allegiance to British authority and hardened political differences.[81] The conflicts of the 1820s and 1830s in British North America echoed the pre-war crises of the 1760s and 1770s in the thirteen colonies and culminated in the rebellions of 1837–38 in Upper and Lower Canada, which were firmly suppressed.

The imperial response to the rebellions forms a revealing episode in the history of the Loyal Atlantic. London commissioned Lord Durham to investigate the governance of British North America and to suggest ways to stabilize its colonies. Durham's report of 1839 claimed that the colonists' core grievance centred on their lack of the full rights and privileges of free-born Englishmen that their peers enjoyed on the other side of the Atlantic. Added to this was a second enduring problem: in what way did French Catholics in the colonies, whom Durham viewed as inherently backward, belong to the British Empire? His solution harkened back to the union of Britain and Ireland in 1801. He proposed the Union of the Canadas as a way to control French Catholics by subsuming them in a polity with a Protestant majority. Like generations of British officials before him, Durham viewed governance as a means to combat threatening, foreign people within a loyal social order.[82] This volume's two closing chapters expand the bounds of loyalist studies geographically and chronologically. Allison O'Mahen Malcom traces the Loyal Atlantic up the St Lawrence River in order to compare patterns of sectarian politics and memory in nineteenth-century Canada and the United States, while Allan Blackstock tracks loyalism back to Ireland and Britain in order to explore the transatlantic dimensions of the 1837 Rebellions in Upper and Lower Canada.

Studying loyalism contributes directly to the ongoing debate between Atlantic and global historians. Loyalism in the revolutionary period was primarily an Atlantic, rather than a global, phenomenon.

It was fashioned from over a century of intensive metropolitan-colonial exchange, and the post-war diaspora sent only a handful of Loyalists to Asia and Australia, even though loyalism increasingly informed British political culture beyond the Atlantic after 1783. To see loyalism primarily through the wide lens of globalism risks losing the crucial hybrid quality of Loyalists as Americans *and* Britons, and in rushing to engage contemporary globalization skips over critical developments before and during the American Revolution.[83] As Keith Mason explores in the next chapter of this volume, over time the Loyalists developed a sharp sense of identity as their relational point of reference shifted from American rebels to British imperial authorities. Loyalism took shape in specific experiential contexts best understood through case studies and local analyses that reveal their larger importance when framed within circumatlantic analysis.[84]

Careful attention to pressing local imperatives demonstrates the importance of contingency, unexpected consequences, and variation. Our view of the British Atlantic depends as much on the period we study as the places we examine. Loyalism shows how much could change in a remarkably short period of time; how victors could turn into refugees; and how loss could turn into triumphal mythology. Because nationalist verities have dominated historical perception from the founding of the discipline as an academic profession – and nationalism still shapes our understanding despite the vaunted influence of globalization – it remains to be seen how a revisionist scholarship that places Loyalists in their Atlantic context can contribute to a more complete assessment of the Age of Imperial Revolutions. The Atlantic world was created from mass, mostly involuntary migration involving millions of people over hundreds of years. Seen in that context, Loyalists offer a quintessentially Atlantic story.

Forty years ago, in a collection of Loyalist documents, G.A. Rawlyk argued that a comparative approach was the best way to understand the varied causes and effects of the American Revolution. The chapters that follow demonstrate how far we have come since 1968, when Rawlyk could safely summarize loyalism as *revolution rejected*.[85] For the hundreds of thousands of people who did not embrace the American Revolution, loyalism was just as powerfully an affirmation of fidelity as rejection of rebellion. Loyalists were not on the losing side of history, fleeing the supposedly inevitable ascendancy of republicanism; rather, they contributed to the contingent development of what would become the world's largest empire in the nineteenth century, while many others remained within the United States and participated in its later national development. These Loyalists had diverse backgrounds and commitments as well as different memories and notions about what loyalty meant that included unpredictably mixed assessments of multivalent English and British cultural, legal, commercial, and political ways of understanding themselves and their world. Like the boundary between Canada and the United States, the relationship between republicanism and monarchism in the Atlantic world was marked by violent conflict, ambivalent desire, and protracted negotiation among the peoples who claimed or rejected a bond with the British Empire and Crown. While their stories are rooted in an Atlantic history that stretches back many generations, their legacy is still felt, contested, and debated.

NOTES

1 For their incisive comments on earlier versions of this chapter, we thank Phillip Buckner, Jack Crowley, and Stephen Hornsby.
2 David Armitage, 'Three Concepts of Atlantic History,' in *The British Atlantic World, 1500–1800*, 2nd ed., ed. David Armitage and Michael J. Braddick (London: Palgrave Macmillan, 2009, orig. 2002), 11. The literature assessing the field is now quite enormous, but for two useful starting points, see Alison Games, 'Atlantic History: Definitions, Challenges, and Opportunities,' *American Historical Review* 111 (2006): 741–57; and Jack P. Greene and Philip D. Morgan, eds., *Atlantic History: A Critical Appraisal* (New York: Oxford University Press, 2009).
3 For a sense of the theoretical debate, see the forum, 'Entangled Empires in the Atlantic Word,' *American Historical Review* 112 (2007): 710–99; and Eliga Gould, 'Entangled Atlantic Histories: A Response from the Anglo-American Periphery,' *American Historical Review* 112 (2007): 1415–22.
4 Kathleen Wilson, 'Histories, Empires, Modernities,' in *A New Imperial History: Culture, Identity and Modernity in Britain and the Empire, 1660–1840*, ed. Kathleen Wilson (Cambridge: Cambridge University Press, 2004). For applications of new imperial approaches to North American history, see Phillip Buckner, ed., *Canada and the British Empire* (Oxford: Oxford University Press, 2008); Phillip Buckner and R. Douglas Francis, eds., *Canada and the British World: Culture, Migration, and Identity* (Vancouver: University of British Columbia Press, 2006); and John McLaren, A.R. Buck, and Nancy E. Wright,

eds., *Despotic Dominion: Property Rights in British Settler Societies* (Vancouver: University of British Columbia Press, 2005).

5 See Louis Hartz, *The Liberal Tradition in America* (New York: Harcourt Brace, 1955); Louis Hartz, ed., *The Founding of New Societies* (New York: Harcourt Brace, 1964); S.F. Wise, 'Liberal Consensus or Ideological Battleground: Some Reflections on the Hartz Thesis,' *Canadian Historical Association, Historical Papers* (1974): 1–14; H.D. Forbes, 'Hartz-Horowitz at Twenty: Nationalism, Toryism, and Socialism in Canada and the United States,' *Canadian Journal of Political Science* 2 (1987): 287–315; Peter Smith, 'Civic Humanism vs. Liberalism: Fitting the Loyalists In,' *Journal of Canadian Studies* 26 (1991): 25–43; Janet Ajzenstat and Peter J. Smith, 'The "Tory Touch" Thesis: Bad History, Poor Political Science,' in *Crosscurrents: Contemporary Political Issues,* 3rd ed., ed. Mark Charlton and Paul Barker (Toronto: Nelson, 1988), 84–90; Gad Horowitz, 'Conservatism, Liberalism, and Socialism in Canada: An Interpretation (1966),' in *The Development of Political Thought in Canada: An Anthology,* ed. Katherine Fierlbeck (Toronto: Broadview Press, 2005); and Katherine Fierlbeck, *Political Thought in Canada: An Intellectual History* (Toronto: Broadview Press, 2006). Horowitz's article, the most reprinted study in Canadian political science, originally appeared in 1966 in the *Canadian Journal of Political Science.*

6 Jesse Lemisch, *Jack Tar vs. John Bull: The Role of New York's Seamen in Participating the American Revolution* (New York: Garland, 1997); Peter Linebaugh and Marcus Rediker, *The Many-Headed Hydra: Sailors, Slaves, Commoners and the Hidden History of the Revolutionary Atlantic* (Boston: Beacon Press, 2000); David S. Cecelski, *The Waterman's Song: Slavery and Freedom in Maritime North Carolina* (Chapel Hill: University of North Carolina Press, 2001); Paul Gilje, *Liberty on the Waterfront: American Maritime Culture in the Age of Revolution* (Philadelphia: University of Pennsylvania Press, 2004); and Christopher P. Magra, *The Fishermen's Cause: Atlantic Commerce and Maritime Dimensions of the American Revolution* (Cambridge: Cambridge University Press, 2009).

7 Ira Berlin, 'From Creole to African: Atlantic Creoles and the Origins of African-American Society in Mainland North America,' *William and Mary Quarterly,* 3rd series, 53 (1996): 251–88; David Geggus, ed., *The Impact of the Haitian Revolution in the Atlantic World* (Charleston: University of South Carolina Press, 2002); Nathalie Dessens and Jean-Pierre Le Glaunec, eds., *Haïti, regards croisés* (Paris: Éditions Le Manuscrit, 2007); Laurent Dubois, *A Colony of Citizens: Revolution and Slave Emancipation in the French Caribbean, 1787–1804* (Chapel Hill: University of North Carolina Press, 2004); and Emma Christopher, *Slave Ship Sailors and Their Captive Cargoes, 1730–1807* (Cambridge: Cambridge University Press, 2006).

8 R.R. Palmer, *The Age of the Democratic Revolution*, 2 vols. (Princeton, NJ: Princeton University Press, 1959–64).

9 On this point, see Eliga Gould, 'Revolution and Counter-Revolution,' in *British Atlantic World* (see note 2); Alan Taylor, 'The Late Loyalists: Northern Reflections of the Early American Republic,' *Journal of the Early Republic* 27 (2007): 1–34; and a parallel call for the need to integrate British Whig and Tory historiographic traditions to understand Britain in its interactive imperial context by David Armitage, *The Ideological Origins of the British Empire* (Cambridge: Cambridge University Press, 2000), 9–17.

10 For a sense of this scholarship, see Allan Greer and Ian Radforth, eds., *Colonial Leviathan: State Formation in Mid-Nineteenth-Century Canada* (Toronto: University of Toronto Press, 1992); Allan Greer, '1837–38: Rebellion Reconsidered,' *Canadian Historical Review* 76 (1995): 1–19; Allan Greer, *The Patriots and the People: The Rebellion of 1837 in Rural Lower Canada* (Toronto: University of Toronto Press, 1993), 145–6; Cecelia Morgan, *Public Men and Virtuous Women: The Gendered Languages of Religion and Politics in Upper Canada, 1791–1850* (Toronto: University of Toronto Press, 1996); Jeffrey L. McNairn, *The Capacity to Judge: Public Opinion and Deliberative Democracy in Upper Canada, 1791–1854* (Toronto: University of Toronto Press, 2000); and Carol Wilton, *Popular Politics and Political Culture in Upper Canada, 1800–1850* (Montreal; Kingston, ON: McGill-Queen's University Press, 2000).

11 Bryan Palmer, 'Popular Radicalism and the Theatrics of Rebellion: The Hybrid Discourse of Dissent in Upper Canada in the 1830s,' in *Transatlantic Subjects: Ideas, Institutions, and Social Experience in Post-Revolutionary British North America*, ed. Nancy Christie (Montreal; Kingston, ON: McGill-Queen's University Press, 2008), 403–29.

12 Jeremy Adelman, 'An Age of Imperial Revolutions,' *American Historical Review* 113 (2008), 320, 323, 339. The ongoing importance of imperialism within the new United States is emphasized in Carroll Smith-Rosenberg, *This Violent Empire: The Birth of an American National Identity* (Chapel Hill: University of North Carolina Press, 2010). See also Jeremy Adelman, *Sovereignty and Revolution in the Iberian Atlantic* (Princeton, NJ: Princeton University Press, 2006).

13 On the need to reconsider the North Atlantic, see John J. McCusker and Russell R. Menard, *The Economy of British America, 1607–1789*, 2nd ed. (Chapel Hill: University of North Carolina Press, 1991), 112–13; Peter Pope, 'Comparisons: Atlantic Canada,' in *A Companion to Colonial America*, ed. Daniel Vickers (New York: Blackwell, 2003); and Luca Codignola and John G. Reid, 'Forum: How Wide Is the Atlantic Ocean?' *Acadiensis* 34 (2005): 74–87.

14 Stephen J. Hornsby, *Surveyors of Empire: Samuel Holland, J.W.F. Des Barres, and the Making of The Atlantic Neptune* (Montreal; Kingston, ON: McGill-Queen's University Press, 2011); idem, *British Atlantic, American Frontier: Spaces of Power in Early Modern British America* (Lebanon, NH: University Press of New England, 2005); John G. Reid and Elizabeth Mancke, 'From Global Processes to Continental Strategies: The Emergence of British North America to 1783,' in *Canada and the British Empire* (see note 4), 22–41; Elizabeth Mancke, *The Fault Lines of Empire: Political Differentiation in Massachusetts and Nova Scotia, ca. 1760–1830* (New York: Routledge, 2004); and John G. Reid, with contributions from Emerson W. Baker, *Essays on Northeastern North America: Seventeenth and Eighteenth Centuries* (Toronto: University of Toronto Press, 2008).

15 Elizabeth Mancke, 'Empire and State,' in *British Atlantic World* (see note 2), 193.

16 J.M. Bumsted, *Understanding the Loyalists* (Sackville, NB: Mount Allison University, Centre for Canadian Studies, 1986), 39–40.

17 On this current Loyalist memory, see the *Loyalist Gazette* 47 (Spring 2009), which has a front-page story on the war in Afghanistan and, as the editor notes, 'a special message to share: linking Loyalist courage both past and present.' On the distinctions between heritage and history, see David Lowenthal, *The Heritage Crusade and the Spoils of History* (Cambridge: Cambridge University Press, 1998).

18 On this point, see J.M. Bumsted, 'British North America in Its Imperial and International Context,' in *Canadian History, A Reader's Guide, Volume 1: Beginnings to Confederation*, ed. M. Brook Taylor (Toronto: University of Toronto Press, 1994).

19 Lauren Benton, *Law and Colonial Cultures: Legal Regimes in World History, 1400–1900* (Cambridge: Cambridge University Press, 2002), 263.

20 Alan Taylor, *The Civil War of 1812: American Citizens, British Subjects, Irish Rebels, and Indian Allies* (New York: Knopf, 2010); and idem, *The Divided Ground: Indians, Settlers, and the Northern Borderland of the American Revolution* (New York: Knopf, 2006) on the same cross-border region in the late eighteenth century.

21 Robert M. Calhoon, 'Loyalism and Neutrality,' in *The Blackwell Encyclopedia of the American Revolution*, ed. Jack P. Greene and J.R. Pole (Oxford: Blackwell, 1991), 247–59.

22 Geoffrey Plank, *An Unsettled Conquest: The British Campaign against the Peoples of Acadia* (Philadelphia: University of Pennsylvania Press, 2001); John Mack Faragher, *A Great and Noble Scheme: The Tragic Story of the Expulsion of the French Acadians from Their American Homeland* (New York: Norton,

2005); and N.E.S. Griffiths, *From Migrant to Acadian: A North American Border People, 1604–1755* (Montreal; Kingston, ON: McGill-Queen's University Press, 2005).

23 Fred Anderson, *Crucible of War: The Seven Years' War and the Fate of Empire in British North America, 1754–1766* (New York: Vintage, 2000), chaps. 46, 72.

24 On this point, see Roger Marsters, *Bold Privateers: Terror, Plunder and Profit on Canada's Atlantic Coast* (Halifax: Formac, 2004), chap. 8. On the threat of rebellion in Nova Scotia and Loyalist responses, see Ernest Clarke, *The Siege of Fort Cumberland: An Episode of the American Revolution* (Montreal; Kingston, ON: McGill-Queen's University Press, 1995); and Barry Cahill, 'The Treason of the Merchants: Dissent and Repression in Halifax in the Era of the American Revolution,' *Acadiensis* 26 (1996): 52–70.

25 William H. Nelson, *The American Tory* (London: Oxford University Press, 1961); and Andrew Jackson O'Shaughnessy, *An Empire Divided: The American Revolution and the British Caribbean* (Philadelphia: University of Pennsylvania Press, 2000).

26 G. Koenigsberger, 'Composite States, Representative Institutions and the American Revolution,' *Historical Research* 62 (1989): 135–53; J.H. Elliott, 'A Europe of Composite Monarchies,' *Past and Present* 137 (1992): 48–71; and P.J. Marshall, 'Empire and Authority in the Later Eighteenth Century,' *Journal of Imperial and Commonwealth History* 15 (1987): 105–22.

27 Work re-evaluating the periodization of British imperial history includes P.J. Marshall, *The Making and Unmaking of Empires: Britain, India, and America c. 1750–1783* (New York: Oxford University Press, 2005); and Stephen Conway, *The British Isles and the War of American Independence* (New York: Oxford University Press, 2000).

28 On this point, Rhys Isaac's pioneering studies of the cultural theatre of oaths and other contested expressions of authority remain highly useful. See, particularly, Rhys Isaac, 'Dramatizing the Ideology of Revolution: Popular Mobilization in Virginia, 1774 to 1776,' *William and Mary Quarterly*, 3rd series, 33 (1976): 357–85.

29 Several points raised here also appear in Jerry Bannister, 'Canada as Counter-Revolution: The Loyalist Order Framework in Canadian History, 1750–1840,' in *Liberalism and Hegemony: Debating the Canadian Liberal Revolution*, ed. Jean-François Constant and Michel Ducharme (Toronto: University of Toronto Press, 2009), 126.

30 Ramsay Cook, *Watching Quebec: Selected Essays* (Montreal; Kingston, ON: McGill-Queen's University Press, 2005), 190. On the relationships among loyalism, republicanism, and identity in French Canada, see Jacques Monet, *The Last Cannon Shot: A Study of French-Canadian Nationalism,*

1837–1850 (Toronto: University of Toronto Press, 1969); Louis-Georges Harvey, *Le printemps de l'Amérique française: américanité, anticolonialisme et républicanisme dans le discours politique québécois, 1805–1837* (Montreal: Boréal, 2005); Serge Courville, 'Part of the British Empire, Too: French Canada and Colonization Propaganda,' in *Canada and the British World* (see note 4), 129–41.

31 Michel Ducharme, 'Canada in the Age of Revolutions: Rethinking Canadian Intellectual History in an Atlantic Perspective,' in *Contesting Clio's Craft: New Directions and Debates in Canadian History*, ed. Michael Dawson and Christopher Dummit (London: Institute for the Study of the Americas Press and the Brookings Institution, 2009), 162–86; Michel Ducharme, *Le concept de liberté au Canada à l'époque des Révolutions atlantiques (1776–1838)* (Montreal; Kingston, ON: McGill-Queen's University Press, 2010); and Philip Girard, 'Liberty, Order, and Pluralism: The Canadian Experience,' in *Exclusionary Empire: English Liberty Overseas, 1600–1900*, ed. Jack P. Greene (Cambridge: Cambridge University Press, 2010), 160–90.

32 John G. Reid, 'Pax Britannica *or* Pax Indigena? Planter Nova Scotia (1760–1782) and Competing Strategies of Pacification,' *Canadian Historical Review* 85 (2004); John G. Reid et al., *The 'Conquest' of Acadia, 1710: Imperial, Colonial, and Aboriginal Constructions* (Toronto: University of Toronto Press, 2004); and Emerson W. Baker and John G. Reid, 'Amerindian Power in the Early Modern Northeast: A Reappraisal,' *William and Mary Quarterly*, 3rd series, 51 (2004): 77–106.

33 Michael Valpy, 'The monarchy: offshore, but built-in,' *Globe and Mail*, 13 November 2009.

34 T.H. Breen provides a useful introduction to this large literature in 'Ideology and Nationalism on the Eve of the American Revolution: Revisions *Once More* in Need of Revising,' *Journal of American History* 84 (1997): 13–39. Among the most important work that Breen discusses are influential studies by Linda Colley, John Brewer, and Kathleen Wilson (see citations below). The interior and psychological dimensions of loyalism, especially its familial and fraternal connotations, merit detailed attention, given the persistence of Patriots' pathological descriptions of Loyalists' character and motives, but this demands more attention than we can give it here.

35 Edward Larkin provides a brief and compelling assessment of how sensibility reveals important Anglo-American continuities in the revolutionary period that are obfuscated by the dominance of political analysis. See his 'What Is a Loyalist?' *Common-Place* 8 (October 2008), http://www.commonplace.org; and Jay Fliegelman, *Prodigals and Pilgrims: The American*

Revolution Against Patriarchal Authority (Cambridge: Cambridge University Press, 1982). Sarah Knott insightfully examines sensibility and the American Revolution, but, unfortunately, explains its ramifications only for Patriots and their new nation in *Sensibility and the American Revolution* (Chapel Hill: University of North Carolina Press, 2009).

36 Eliga Gould, *The Persistence of Empire: British Political Culture in the Age of the American Revolution* (Chapel Hill: University of North Carolina Press, 2000); Paul Langford, *A Polite and Commercial People: England, 1727–1783* (Oxford: Oxford University Press, 1989); Linda Colley, *Britons: Forging the Nation, 1707–1837* (New Haven, CT: Yale University Press, 1992); Kathleen Wilson, *The Sense of the People: Politics, Culture and Imperialism in England, 1715–1785* (Cambridge: Cambridge University Press, 1995); John Brewer, *The Pleasures of the Imagination: English Culture in the Eighteenth Century* (London: Harper Collins, 1997); and Gwenda Morgan and Peter Rushton, *Eighteenth-Century Criminal Transportation: The Formation of the Criminal Atlantic* (New York: Palgrave Macmillan, 2004).

37 On the complexities of the 1660s and the debate over whether there was a 'Restoration,' see Neil Keeble, *The Restoration: England in the 1660s* (Oxford: Blackwell, 2002). On the need to correct the long-standing overemphasis on the Civil War with more scholarly attention to the Restoration, see Ronald Hutton's landmark study, *The Restoration: A Political and Religious History of England and Wales, 1658–1667* (Oxford: Clarendon, 1985).

38 On Loyalist poetry and its predecessors, see Winthrop Sargent, ed., *The Loyalist Poetry of the Revolution* (Philadelphia: n.p., 1857); Thomas B. Vincent, ed., *Narrative Verse Satire in Maritime Canada, 1779–1814* (Ottawa: Tecumseh Press, 1978); and Bruce Ingham Granger, *Political Satire in the American Revolution* (Ithaca, NY: Cornell University Press, 1960).

39 Jerry Bannister, 'Mercantilism,' in *Oxford Companion to Canadian History*, ed. Gerald Hallowell (Toronto: Oxford University Press, 2004); and Steven Sarson, *British America, 1500–1800: Creating Colonies, Imagining Empire* (London: Hodder Arnold, 2005), chap. 2.

40 This point draws on Jerry Bannister, 'The Oriental Atlantic: Governance and Regulatory Frameworks in the British Atlantic World,' in *Britain's Oceanic Empire: Atlantic and Indian Ocean Worlds, 1500–1850*, ed. H.V. Bowen, Elizabeth Mancke, and John G. Reid (Cambridge: Cambridge University Press, forthcoming).

41 John Brewer, *The Sinews of Power: War, Money, and the English State, 1688–1783* (London: Unwin Hyman, 1989); Geoffrey Plank, *Rebellion and Savagery: The Jacobite Rising of 1745 and the British Empire* (Philadelphia: University of Pennsylvania Press, 2006); John Brewer, 'The Eighteenth-century British

State: Contexts and Issues,' in *An Imperial State at War: Britain from 1689 to 1815*, ed. Lawrence Stone (New York: Routledge, 1994); and John Brewer and Eckhart Hellmuth, 'Introduction: Rethinking Leviathan,' in *Rethinking Leviathan: The Eighteenth-Century State in Britain and Germany*, ed. John Brewer and Eckhart Hellmuth (Oxford: Oxford University Press, 1999).

42 Joseph Addison, *The Freeholder* 1, 23 (December 1715), in *Literature and the Social Order in Eighteenth Century England*, ed. Stephen Copley (London: Croom Helm, 1984), 35; emphasis added.

43 Ibid.

44 Jack P. Greene, 'Introduction: Empire and Liberty,' in *Exclusionary Empire* (see note 31), 13.

45 On 'rights' as a grant from the king (and thus reversible) from the Glorious Revolution to the revolutionary period, see Jack N. Rakove, *Declaring Rights: A Brief History with Documents* (New York: Bedford/St Martin's Press, 1998).

46 Henry St John, 1st Viscount Bolingbroke, *The Idea of the Patriot King* (1752), in *The Eighteenth Century Constitution: Documents and Commentary*, ed. E.N. Williams (Cambridge: Cambridge University Press, 1965), 86.

47 Ibid., 85.

48 Philip Gould, 'Wit and Politics in Revolutionary British America: The Case of Samuel Seabury and Alexander Hamilton,' *Eighteenth-Century Studies* 41 (2008): 385.

49 Douglas Hay, 'Property, Authority and the Criminal Law,' in *Albion's Fatal Tree: Crime and Society in Eighteenth-Century England*, ed. Douglas Hay et al. (New York: Pantheon, 1975); and Douglas Hay and Paul Craven, eds., *Masters, Servants, and Magistrates in Britain and the Empire, 1562–1955* (Chapel Hill: University of North Carolina Press, 2004). On the influence of Hay's work, see David Garland, *Punishment and Modern Society: A Study in Social Theory* (Oxford: Oxford University Press, 1990).

50 Brendan McConville, *The King's Three Faces: The Rise and Fall of Royal America, 1688–1776* (Chapel Hill: University of North Carolina Press, 2007).

51 Gordon S. Wood, *The Radicalism of the American Revolution* (New York: Random House, 1991), 18.

52 *Loyal and Humorous Songs* (New York: Hugh Gaine, 1779), 25. The sole known copy of this chapbook of popular songs, itself incomplete, is held at the American Antiquarian Society in Worcester, Massachusetts.

53 T.H. Breen, *American Insurgents, American Patriots: The Revolution of the People* (New York: Farrar, Straus and Giroux, 2010), 36.

54 Bernard Bailyn, *The Ordeal of Thomas Hutchinson* (Cambridge, MA: Harvard University Press, 1974).

55 Lewis Namier, *The Structure of Politics at the Accession of George III*, 2nd ed. (New York: St Martin's Press, 1957).

56 Breen, 'Ideology and Nationalism.'

57 Two forums in the *American Historical Review* can usefully be read side-by-side for a sense of the interpretive promises and challenges of such comparative work: 'The New British History in Atlantic Perspective,' *American Historical Review* 104 (1999): 426–500; and 'Revolutions in the Americas,' *American Historical Review* 105 (2000): 92–152. While scholars of the British Atlantic now struggle with the volume and variety of work in the field, placing it in dialogue with the non-British Revolutionary Atlantic remains to be done.

58 Peter Oliver, *Peter Oliver's 'Origin and Progress of the American Rebellion': A Tory View*, ed. Douglas Adair and John A. Schultz (Stanford, CA: Stanford University Press, 1961), 105.

59 Ibid., 97.

60 This is largely true even of the stimulating argument in Edward Larkin, 'Seeing through Language: Narrative, Portraiture, and Character in Peter Oliver's "The Origin & Progress of the American Rebellion,"' *Early American Literature* 36 (2001): 427–54.

61 Paul H. Smith, 'The American Loyalists: Notes on Their Organizational and Numerical Strength,' *William and Mary Quarterly*, 3rd series, 25 (1968): 259–77; and Lorenzo Sabine, *Biographical Sketches of Loyalists of the American Revolution*, 2nd rev. ed. (Boston, 1864).

62 Ruma Chopra's *Unnatural Rebellion: Loyalists in New York City* (Charlottesville: University Press of Virginia, 2011) was published too recently to be assessed properly here, but it promises to make a significant contribution to the field. See also Judith L. Van Buskirk, *Generous Enemies: Patriots and Loyalists in Revolutionary New York* (Philadelphia: University of Pennsylvania Press, 2002). Unfortunately, other wartime Loyalist urban centres have not been as carefully studied.

63 Statistic quoted in Stephen Conway, 'Britain and the Revolutionary Crisis, 1763–1791,' in *Oxford History of the British Empire*, vol. 2, *The Eighteenth Century*, ed. P.J. Marshall (Oxford: Oxford University Press, 1998), 341.

64 Piers Mackesy, *The War for America, 1775–1783* (Lincoln: University of Nebraska Press, reprint 1984; orig. 1964), 256.

65 On the severity of the southern war, see Ronald Hoffman, Thad W. Tate, and Peter J. Albert, eds., *An Uncivil War: The Southern Backcountry during the American Revolution* (Charlottesville: University Press of Virginia, 1985).

66 Jim Piecuch's monograph is now the starting point on Loyalists in the lower South; see *Three Peoples, One King: Loyalists, Indians, and Slaves in the*

Revolutionary South, 1775–1782 (Columbia: University of South Carolina Press, 2008), 4–8. See also Charles Royster, *A Revolutionary People at War: The Continental Army and American Character, 1775–1783* (New York: Norton, 1979), 277. On the severity of the war around New York City, see David J. Fowler, '"Loyalty Is Now Bleeding in New Jersey": Motivations and Mentalities of the Disaffected,' in *The Other Loyalists: Ordinary People, Royalism, and the Revolution in the Middle Colonies, 1763–1787*, ed. Joseph S. Tiedemann, Eugene R. Fingerhut, and Robert W. Venables (Albany: State University of New York Press, 2009), 45–77; John Shy, 'Loyalism in the Lower Hudson Valley,' in John Shy, *A People Numerous and Armed: Reflections in the Military Struggle for American Independence*, rev. ed. (Ann Arbor: University of Michigan Press, 1990, orig., 1976).

67 James S. Leamon, *Revolution Downeast: The War for American Independence in Maine* (Amherst: University of Massachusetts Press, 1993), 60–73.

68 Palmer, *Age of the Democratic Revolution*, vol. 1, 188. Several important studies have taken up strands of this forced migration, especially into British North America. Important work on Loyalists in Canada not cited elsewhere in this chapter includes Ann Gorman Condon, *The Envy of the American States: The Loyalist Dream for New Brunswick* (Fredericton, NB: New Ireland Press, 1984); Jane Errington, *The Lion, the Eagle, and Upper Canada: A Developing Colonial Ideology* (Montreal; Kingston, ON: McGill-Queen's University Press, 1987); Janice Potter-MacKinnon, *While the Women Only Wept: Loyalist Refugee Women in Eastern Ontario* (Montreal; Kingston, ON: McGill-Queens University Press, 1993); and Esther Clark Wright, *The Loyalists of New Brunswick* (Fredericton, NB: private press, 1955).

69 These figures, their sources, and Jasanoff's interpretive decisions are insightfully discussed in an appendix to *Liberty's Exiles: American Loyalists in the Revolutionary World* (New York: Alfred A. Knopf, 2011), 351–8. Although superseded in some ways by her book, an earlier essay remains a superb introduction to a range of important themes; see Maya Jasanoff, 'The Other Side of Revolution: Loyalists in the British Empire,' *William and Mary Quarterly*, 3rd series, 65 (2008): 205–32.

70 Jasanoff, *Liberty's Exiles*, 13, 91, 346–9. On Loyalists in Britain, Mary Beth Norton, *The British Americans: The Loyalist Exiles in England, 1774–1789* (New York: Little Brown, 1972), remains indispensable.

71 The refugee figures in Map 1 build on Jasanoff's higher range of estimates and as modified by figures in R. Cole Harris, ed., *Historical Atlas of Canada*, vol. 1, *From the Beginning to 1800* (Toronto: University of Toronto Press, 1987), plates 32, 44; R. Louis Gentilcore, ed., *Historical Atlas of Canada*, vol. 2, *The Land Transformed, 1800–1891* (Toronto: University of Toronto Press,

1987), plate 7; Carole Watterson Troxler, 'Loyalist Refugees and the British Evacuation of East Florida, 1783–1785,' *Florida Historical Quarterly* 60 (1981): 1–28; and Taylor, 'Late Loyalists.'

72 David G. Bell, *Early Loyalist Saint John: The Origin of New Brunswick Politics, 1783–1786* (Fredericton, NB: New Ireland Press, 1983); and Neil MacKinnon, *This Unfriendly Soil: The Loyalist Experience in Nova Scotia, 1783–1791* (Montreal; Kingston, ON: McGill-Queen's University Press, 1986).

73 Wood, *Radicalism*, 95–6. This quotation and his discussion of the 'traditional *patrician* bias' of republicanism (106, emphasis added) appear in a chapter entitled 'The Republicanization of Monarchy.' For an essential introduction to the overburdened scholarship about this key term, see Daniel T. Rogers, 'Republicanism: The Career of a Concept,' *Journal of American History* 79 (1992): 11–38.

74 On the contested borderland between New England and the Maritime provinces, see Joshua M. Smith, *Borderland Smuggling: Patriots, Loyalists, and Illicit Trade in the Northeast, 1783–1820* (Gainesville: University Press of Florida, 2006). For the New York-Upper Canada borderland, see Taylor, *Civil War*; and idem, *Divided Ground*.

75 James W. St G. Walker, *The Black Loyalists: The Search for a Promised Land in Nova Scotia and Sierra Leone 1783–1870* (New York: Africana Publishing, 1976); see also Ellen Gibson Wilson, *The Loyal Blacks* (New York: Capricorn, 1976). On the debate over black loyalism, see the exchange between Barry Cahill, 'The Black Loyalist Myth in Atlantic Canada,' and James Walker, 'Myth, History and Revisionism: The Black Loyalists Revisited,' *Acadiensis* 29 (1999): 76–105. On the period after the War of 1812, see Harvey Whitfield, *Blacks on the Border: The Black Refugees in British North America, 1815–1860* (Lebanon: University of Vermont Press, 2006).

76 Cassandra Pybus, *Epic Journeys of Freedom: Runaway Slaves of the American Revolution and Their Global Quest for Liberty* (Boston: Beacon Press, 2006). See also the groundbreaking study by Alexander X. Byrd, *Captives and Voyagers: Black Migrants across the Eighteenth-Century British Atlantic World* (Baton Rouge: Louisiana State University Press, 2008); and the essays collected in *Moving On: Black Loyalists in the Afro-Atlantic World*, ed. John W. Pulis (New York: Garland Publishing, 1999).

77 Jasanoff, *Liberty's Exiles*, 351–2, 358. For the overstatement of black liberation by the British, see, most influentially, Simon Schama, *Rough Crossings: Britain, the Slaves, and the American Revolution* (New York: Ecco/Harper Collins, 2006; orig. London, 2005). The best study of the black experience in the revolutionary South remains Sylvia R. Frey, *Water from the Rock: Black Resistance in a Revolutionary Age* (Princeton, NJ: Princeton University Press,

1991). While most Loyalist slave masters took their human property to the British West Indies, slavery persisted in British North America as well; see Carole Watterson Troxler, 'Re-enslavement of Black Loyalists: Mary Postell in South Carolina, East Florida and Nova Scotia,' *Acadiensis* 37 (2008): 70–85; and D.G. Bell, 'Slavery and the Loyalist Judges of New Brunswick,' *University of New Brunswick Law Journal* 9 (1982): 9–42.

78 We agree with Elizabeth Mancke that hierarchical imperial governance was not only a response to the loss of the thirteen colonies; see her important revisionist insights in 'Early Modern Imperial Governance and the Origins of Canadian Political Culture,' *Canadian Journal of Political Science* 32 (1999): 3–20. Powerful arguments about the authoritarian shift in the British Empire include C.A. Bayly, *Imperial Meridian: The British Empire and the World, 1780–1830* (London: Longman, 1989); and Colley, *Britons*. See also J.C.D. Clark, *English Society 1660–1832: Religion, Identity, and Politics during the Ancien Régime*, 2nd ed. (Cambridge: Cambridge University Press, 2000), 300–1, which places the Canada Act of 1791 as part of the 'rebirth of Anglican hegemony.'

79 After Burke's Act of 1782 abolished the Board of Trade, responsibility for administering the colonies passed to the Home Office and then to the Secretary of War. In 1801 a War and Colonial Office was created under a new Secretary of State for War and the Colonies. On the development of the Colonial Office, see Phillip Buckner, 'The Colonial Office in British North America, 1801–50,' in *Dictionary of Canadian Biography*, vol. 8, ed. George W. Brown et al. (Toronto: University of Toronto Press, 1966–).

80 Phillip Buckner, *The Transition to Responsible Government: British Policy in British North America, 1815–1850* (Westport, CT: Greenwood Press, 1985); Ian Radforth, 'Sydenham and Utilitarian Reform,' in *Colonial Leviathan* (see note 10); Bayly, *Imperial Meridian*, 195–209; and Allan Greer, 'Historical Roots of Canadian Democracy,' *Journal of Canadian Studies* 34 (1999): 7–26.

81 J.L. Little, *Loyalties in Conflict: A Canadian Borderland in War and Rebellion, 1812–1840* (Toronto: University of Toronto Press, 2008). On the creation of nationalist mythologies based on the War of 1812, see Colin M. Coates and Cecilia Morgan, *Heroines and History: Representations of Madeleine de Verchères and Laura Secord* (Toronto: University of Toronto Press, 2002); and Taylor, *Civil War*.

82 *Lord Durham's Report on the Affairs of British North America*, vol. 2, ed. C.P. Lucas (Oxford: Clarendon Press, 1912 [1839]); Janet Ajzenstat, *The Political Thought of Lord Durham* (Montreal; Kingston, ON: McGill-Queen's University Press, 1988); and Stéphane Dion, 'Durham et Tocqueville sur la colonisation libérale,' *Journal of Canadian Studies* 25 (1990): 60–77.

83 P.J. Marshall insightfully assesses the global reach of the British Empire in the late eighteenth century in *The Making and Unmaking of Empires*, yet this invigorating framework for reassessing empire is misleading as an approach to loyalism that was more fully Atlantic than imperial. For an accomplished assessment of the late nineteenth-century formation of globalization, see Michael Lang, 'Globalization and Its History,' *Journal of Modern History* 78 (2006): 899–931.

84 A persuasive call for the need to stress internal-external connections as we move to larger geographic frameworks of analysis appears in Lynn Hunt, 'The French Revolution in Global Context,' in *The Age of Revolutions in Global Context, c. 1760–1840*, ed. David Armitage and Sanjay Subrahmanyam (New York: Palgrave Macmillan, 2010), 22, 30, 34–35.

85 G.A. Rawlyk, ed., *Revolution Rejected, 1775–1776* (Scarborough, ON: Prentice-Hall, 1968).

PART I

Interpretive Frameworks of Allegiance and Imperial Transition

2

The American Loyalist Problem of Identity in the Revolutionary Atlantic World

KEITH MASON

The twin issues of allegiance and identity loomed large in the turbulent era of the American Revolution. While they agonized over how to position themselves in this complex, traumatic, and fluid contest, both fledgling Americans and Britons struggled to get to grips with the wider implications of a struggle that many commentators elected to perceive as a transatlantic civil war. In Britain itself pamphleteers, writing from a variety of different vantage points, competed with each other in declaiming the potential horrors of this kind of deeply regrettable and destructive conflict. 'It is not our natural enemy, it is not French or Spaniards, nor rebel Scots, that we are contending with,' exclaimed a vexed American sympathizer, 'it is our friends, our brethren with whom we have this unhappy and unnatural contest.' 'The present War,' declared a remorseless British critic of the rebels, 'is of all Wars the most unnatural' because it is an 'unwarrantable civil War.'[1] The colonists themselves expressed similar sentiments. Fearing considerable 'carnage and desolation,' several raised the spectre of a vicious contest that would 'dissolve that union which has so long subsisted between the mother country and her colonies.'[2] For them, however, the alternative of submission and perpetual 'slavery' was far worse.

Viewing the conflict through the lens of civil war almost invariably forced contemporaries on both sides of the Atlantic to reflect – often with considerable unease – on their understandings of identity. Their concerns were felt at several different levels. For some the conflict raised issues of personal integrity and consistency: one observer noted, for example, that the 'evils of civil war' prevent us from being 'true to ourselves.' Others highlighted the threat posed to the vital bonds of family, kin, and fraternity, declaring that the struggle 'confound[s] all the social ties of blood.' A further issue was the shadow these events cast on the durability of social hierarchies previously considered fixed and enduring. The Revolution was particularly pernicious, according to another writer, because it scrambled 'those distinctions among men which God and nature have established.'[3]

As the cultural historian Dror Wahrman perceptively highlighted several years ago, however, the crisis went deeper still. For Wahrman the fundamental dilemma was that both *sameness* and *difference* characterized the relationship between Britons and Americans – the latter itself, of course, a rather problematic designation during this era. The resulting tension between the two, he maintains, 'irrepressibly surfaced and resurfaced, self-contradictory and unresolvable, to destabilize each supposedly well-demarcated superimposition of identity categories on the alignments of the American crisis.'[4] As a result, even when considered as a civil war the conflict lacked a definitive and transparent character. It was certainly not reducible to a simple 'us' versus 'them' dichotomy founded on consistent criteria of difference, but nor could the two main protagonists be seen simply in the guise of brethren who had been unnaturally torn asunder. Instead, as Wahrman insists, it was that rather unusual creature, namely 'a war without a stable "other."'[5] The resulting confusion, he argues, played itself out differently on each side of the Atlantic. If the victorious colonists moved gradually and falteringly towards an encompassing, new sense of (national) identity, the British were compelled to consider what identity actually entailed amid the contagion of revolution, military defeat, and imperial reconfiguration.[6]

Wahrman was primarily concerned with how metropolitans and, to a lesser extent, rebel colonists experienced and meditated upon the revolutionary crisis. This chapter seeks to broaden the debate by exploring how the third major player in this struggle engaged with these issues in the midst of schism within the British Atlantic community. In other words, I want to examine the American Loyalist 'problem of identity.' Though there were some loose parallels with the challenges confronting both the British and the revolutionaries, as Wahrman describes, their dilemma was nevertheless rather distinctive. Partly for this reason and partly because the Loyalists are clearly central to the whole controversy, it merits more careful scrutiny than it has so far received. Most tellingly, their pivotal role in the crisis actually helped to define the American Revolution as a civil war. Put simply, they were at the cutting edge of the conflict that ravaged many local communities.

The Loyalist presence, along with the issues it generated, added to the crisis's transatlantic cross-currents. It simultaneously complicated the British response to the struggle and helped to shape the all-important debates over citizenship and nationhood in the new republic.[7]

Beyond that, the major fault line of the revolutionary era actually ran through the heart of Loyalist populations. Many in their ranks bore the burden of being the ultimate Anglo-Americans. As Maya Jasanoff has argued, they had an intensely felt dual allegiance as both 'British' and 'American,' and this tension obviously shaped the question of their own identity in intriguing ways.[8] On the one hand, Loyalists – black as well as white – defined themselves, in the last resort, as British subjects or (in the case of Native Americans) as allies. Because of its perceived protective role, this was manifested principally through a steadfast, although sometimes strategic, commitment to the monarchy. For a variety of political, ideological, and cultural reasons, they became the 'King's friends.'[9] Yet Loyalists were also often seen in the guise of 'His Majesty's *Americans*.'[10] This designation is entirely apt because, although most rejected the republican connotations that became irrevocably associated with that identity, they nevertheless did remain 'American' in terms of their culture and inheritance. Those who became refugees then carried the values associated with this background into the wider British Empire in a way guaranteed to provoke misunderstandings or outright clashes with fellow Britons, rival settlers, and most explicitly with the imperial authorities.[11]

A final crucial dimension was the Loyalists' own complicated history. Their distinctive trajectory of harassment, persecution, and, for many, exile was central to how they saw themselves and others. In particular, their subsequent experiences in the remaining areas of the British Atlantic – the Maritimes, Upper and Lower Canada, the greater Caribbean, Sierra Leone, and the metropolis itself – as well as still further afield in the Pacific, had potentially disruptive effects on their notions of identity, whether personal or collective.[12] For them, as for many other transient groups, migration constituted a series of social deaths and rebirths, a repeating circuit of dislocation and dismemberment, marked nevertheless by an unceasing desire to reconstitute the self through family, friends, and community.[13] By turning the spotlight on the intriguing question of Loyalist identity, therefore, one can further illuminate the terrain Wahrman is attempting to navigate. When viewed through the prism of this fresh perspective, however, his central argument about the unsettling impact of Atlantic civil war on its principal participants and observers looks slightly less compelling and possibly needs qualifying, if not challenging outright. This is principally because, in the case of the Loyalists, the conflict itself actually hardened their sense of identity. It was the subsequent experience of exile that destabilized it.

Before turning to these questions, however, I must address two initial issues – one socio-cultural, the other definitional. The first relates to the sheer diversity of those inclined to support the imperial cause. Perhaps because loyalism proved particularly attractive to minorities of different kinds, the 'King's friends' were characterized by a degree of heterogeneity that is hard to exaggerate. Like the revolutionaries they opposed, Loyalists came from a variety of different socio-economic, cultural, religious, ethnic, and racial backgrounds. Among whites, they were recruited from all classes – the very rich, the very poor, and the middling orders. In their ranks were ex-governors and placemen, and labourers and artisans from the major Atlantic cities. Loyalists also had different motives and ambitions, ranging from the protection of privilege to the seizing of fresh opportunities. There were those who supported Britain because their position, livelihood, or aspirations depended upon it, and those who backed the imperial power out of a simple concern for loyalty and the rule of law. Their lived experiences of revolution and war also varied markedly. Some spent the conflict in the relative shelter of garrison towns like New York, while others served in the hazardous campaigns of the provincial regiments. There were those who departed early from the rebellious colonies, and those who left only when they had to. Still others, of course, chose to remain in the newly independent United States or to return there after the tensions generated by the conflict had died down. Some successfully carved out a career on the basis of their previous misfortunes. Others turned their back on the past and tried to create a new life for themselves while confronting fresh challenges as exiles.[14]

In addition, there were, of course, black Loyalists desperate to take advantage of wartime disruption in order to gain an often-tenuous grasp on freedom. As Gary Nash has pointed out, the Revolution constituted the largest slave rebellion in North American history.[15] However, this uprising was carried on individually rather than collectively, with the principal instrument being flight. Lured by imperial proclamations and promises, slaves simply fled to British lines. Although heavily outnumbered by those who left the colonies as the slaves of white exiles, eight to ten thousand black Loyalists subsequently joined the out-migration from the fledgling United States; hundreds even received small plots of land in Nova Scotia and later Sierra Leone.[16] Given their previous status in the American colonies and their earlier fraught relationship with their now-republican white masters, they became identified as 'black Britons.' Like their white Loyalist counterparts, they felt that this status, along with the sacrifices they had made, gave them the moral leverage to make demands on the imperial authorities. Also, like their fellow migrants, they brought with them values that were at least partly 'American.' As Graham Hodges points out, the ex-slaves' settler mentality centred ironically around 'black republicanism,' the notion of propertied independence underpinned by landholding.[17] Another leading characteristic was the commitment of many to forms of evangelical religion. Black Loyalist preachers – including the Baptists David George, George Liele, and Moses Baker, and the Methodists Moses Wilkinson, John Ball, and John Marrant – established thriving congregations among refugees in such far-flung locales as Nova Scotia, Sierra Leone, Jamaica, and the Bahamas.[18]

Finally, there were Native Americans among the ranks of the Crown's supporters. Although their allegiance was essentially diplomatic and strategic and they were inclined to reject the demands of harder forms of loyalty, they were keen to maintain long-standing relations with the imperial power based on what they saw as reciprocal patterns of 'friendship' and gift exchange. Their hope was that imperial authorities then would act as a counterweight to the growing power of white settler populations, whether American or indeed Loyalist.[19] That proved forlorn in the cases of the Cherokees and the Creeks, who were abandoned to the pressing encroachments of the United States by the peace treaty of 1783. Partly as a result of Joseph Brant's astute bargaining, however, the Haudenosaunee did receive a modicum of land and protection following their migration to Upper Canada. Yet despite this assistance, they were still at pains to emphasize their independence. One British general reported their insistence that they 'were a free People subject to no Power upon Earth, that they were faithful allies of the King of England, but not his Subjects.'[20]

The degree of heterogeneity among Loyalist populations raises several important questions. What sense of (collective) identity, if any, did Loyalists possess? How might it have changed over time during the late eighteenth century? And at what level did it function or have meaning? These queries lead naturally to the second, rather more theoretical, issue, which concerns the definition of identity itself.

A rather problematic and contentious matter, this has long been the subject of considerable debate among scholars from a variety of different disciplines. While aware of these wider controversies, I want to draw specifically on one suggestive critical commentary with a view to considering its typology as a possible framework for studying the American Loyalists in the midst of transatlantic civil war. In their article 'Beyond "Identity,"' the historian Frederick Cooper and the sociologist Rogers Brubaker try to disaggregate the term's several meanings and to analyse them separately.[21] In the process, they usefully pinpoint at least three different notions that feed into the idea of identity as generally understood: 'identification,' 'self-understanding,' and 'commonality'/'connectedness.' The first, 'identification,' essentially denotes the processes by which one defines oneself and, in turn, is defined by 'others.' In the case of the Loyalists, this principally meant the American revolutionaries and the British authorities. 'Self-understanding,' by contrast, designates one's inherent sense of who one is and one's social situation, independent of 'identification' as far as is possible. At a practical level, it revolved around the traits ascribed by the Revolution's opponents to themselves. Finally, 'commonality'/'connectedness' constitutes an attempt to engage with the vexed question of collective identity or, as Brubaker and Cooper prefer to call it, 'groupness.' While 'commonality' refers to the sharing of some common characteristics, 'connectedness' speaks to the relational ties that link people together. Brubaker and Cooper argue that, while neither of these traits in itself automatically engenders 'groupness,' in conjunction they provide the conditions that indeed can do so. Their aim in using these terms is to distinguish more readily between instances of strongly binding, intensely felt 'groupness' and looser forms of affinity, affiliation, and allegiance – arguably an important distinction in the case of the rather heterogeneous Loyalist population.

Drawing on Brubaker and Cooper's typology, this chapter explores the American Loyalist problem of identity in the revolutionary Atlantic world. The discussion falls into three parts. The first section focuses primarily on the leadership's understanding of the crisis and its attempts to create a hegemonic sense of Loyalist identity in the midst of imperial rupture and civil war. This analysis rests upon a fresh reading of the claims of the Loyalist Claims Commission at the National Archives in London, buttressed by references to other kinds of evidence – principally pamphlets, addresses, toasts, songs, and rituals. The second part traces the trajectory of an individual Loyalist – James

Parker of Virginia – and considers the applicability of Brubaker and Cooper's terminology at this microcosmic level. Parker, as a Scot, typifies a particular strand of loyalism that can be characterized as 'middling' in social orientation, British in terms of cultural background, and provincial yet imperial in terms of political perspective. In addition, by drawing on his extensive correspondence, one can track the fluidity of an individual Loyalist mentality as it evolved from the start of the revolutionary crisis to the experience of exile. Finally, the third section explores the degree to which a distinct Loyalist identity was sustained under the potentially disruptive conditions of the postwar diaspora. The emphasis here is on the experiences of rank-and-file refugees as they tried to re-establish themselves in regions of the British Atlantic beyond the metropolis. By adopting this multilayered approach, I intend to present a rounded portrait of the Loyalist movement that highlights the complexity of their problem of identity over time and across space.

– I –

Let me start, then, with the leadership's sense of identity as revealed in the records of the Loyalist Claims Commission, which provide a surprisingly valuable entrée into the topic. Used in the past primarily to establish rather dubious estimates of wealth and social standing, the records actually contain more revealing material on essentially elite Loyalist language and sensibility, as well as on that elite's social networks and individual narratives.[22] Although occasionally formulaic and conventional in their phrasing, the Claims nevertheless shed valuable light on the Revolution's opponents' assumptions about their own identity, or at least of those who are represented in this documentation. Their sheer repetition and very banality speak to how some well-connected Loyalists saw themselves and their world. How did they describe the American Revolution itself? A sampling of the terms used reveals that they, like other parties, had some difficulty both in characterizing the conflict they were embroiled in and in pinpointing its origins. To them it seemingly arose out of nowhere. Like the British observers on whom Wahrman mainly focuses, they certainly perceived the crisis as a 'civil war.' That particular phrase recurs repeatedly in the Claims. Besides that designation, the description most favoured was simply the 'troubles.' Other terms used were the rather bland and almost wistful 'unhappy disturbances,' 'dissensions,' and 'unhappy dissensions.' All euphemistically convey a sense of upheaval, division, and regret without clearly identifying or even indicating the conflict's root causes and the underlying issues involved.

This uncertainty, however, did not prevent the Loyalist claimants from being forthright in defining themselves against the principal 'others' they confronted – their revolutionary adversaries. In this regard they did not share the equivocation characteristic of Wahrman's British commentators. On the contrary, Brubaker and Cooper's process of 'identification' is fully at play in this documentation. The Patriots were routinely described in purely negative terms, as 'rebels,' 'revolters,' 'ring leaders of sedition,' 'malecontents,' 'enemies of the British government,' 'leaders of faction,' 'disloyal inhabitants,' and 'lawless rabble.' The qualities associated with the revolutionaries were also predictably unflattering. They included 'malice and resentment,' 'usurped authority,' 'interest,' 'ill treatment,' 'violation,' and 'vengeance.' Perhaps even more significant was the way that deceit and disguise loomed large as defining characteristics of the American rebels – they were not as they appeared or claimed to be. Leading Loyalists frequently pictured Patriots as cynical demagogues stirring up the populace, dishonourable men whose much-vaunted 'love of country' simply masked their own ambition.

These concerns were echoed in contemporary polemical Loyalist literature. Nestor's 1778 address to the Pennsylvania militia, for example, opens with a conventional bromide concerning the affinities between both sides in the revolutionary struggle: 'For my Countrymen you are, and, if you are not my Friends, I am yours.' For Nestor, the problem is that the populace had been tricked into 'all the horrors of civil war' by 'interested Men' or a 'few pretended Patriots' employing 'artful Addresses and Management.' Nestor then probes further into the question of who was to blame for the crisis: 'Your Resentments are awakened by the unavoidable Calamities which must attend on all civil Wars; but, in the present Case, against whom ought your Indignation to be roused?' His answer is clear: 'Against those who have called you from your peaceful Occupations into the Horrors of Bloodshed and Desolation, all which might have been prevented, had not the Ambition and Avarice of Leaders stood in the way of all Accommodation!'[23]

The duplicity of the revolutionary leadership is described with even greater penetration in Peter Oliver's *Origin and Progress of the American Rebellion* (1781).[24] Exploring the 'Hydra of Rebellion,' he concentrates on Massachusetts Bay, 'the *Volcano* from whence issued all the Smoak, Flame & Lava which hath since enveloped the whole British American Continent.' Oliver's main thesis in this standard counter-narrative is that revolutionary discourse, rather than expressing high-minded idealism, served the self-interested motives of an ambitious group of Boston politicians and merchants who manipulated and distorted language to secure political and financial gains for their families and associates. As Edward Larkin argues, however, the text has an even deeper, more profound dimension. Its most striking feature is the degree to which it displays suspicion towards the very medium of storytelling it employs. With language itself so thoroughly debased in the revolutionaries' representations, Oliver turns to other devices – namely, the eighteenth-century poetic convention of 'characters' and even contemporary portrait theory, to underpin his account. What ultimately emerges as a result is a hybrid text – part history, part visual sketch. By this means, he successfully trumps the revolutionaries' more performative notions of identity with a reassertion of the traditional notion of character as fixed and transparent.[25]

Associated with disguise and deceit in many prominent Loyalists' thinking were the Americans' social pretensions and insubordination. Like Britons, in their writings, songs, and poetry Loyalist commentators relentlessly lampooned the perceived humble origins of many of the Revolution's civilian and military leaders,[26] frequently mocking them as lowly artisans: cobblers, barbers, and pedlars, a set of 'worthless Fellows' who were 'mostly bankrupts, and mean People.'[27] These kinds of observations on the dangers of levelling and social mobility were, of course, a familiar feature of the emerging revolutionary debate on natural equality. But they were also, in effect, a code for discussing the danger that shaped how most elite Loyalists experienced the conflict from the outset: the threat posed by the unsettling of identity categories that previously had been reassuringly fixed, reliable, and consistent. The critique of the Revolution's social implications was inseparable from the now-familiar unease about the broader undermining of the stability of identity itself.

Turning to how leading Loyalists described themselves in relation to their 'self-identification,' the principal motifs were consistency and integrity. The most common terms deployed in the Claims were 'loyal and faithful subjects' and 'friends of government,' who were zealously 'attached to the King and Constitution of Great Britain.' Among the characteristics underpinning their stance were 'loyalty,' 'allegiance,' and 'duty.' Highlighting the price they paid for their 'noble' stance, terms like 'victim,' 'sufferer,' and 'exile' recur. While all these characteristics were universally acclaimed, loyalty to the king was by far the most prominent. At one level this sentiment, as Brendan McConville argues, was in many respects a natural outgrowth of a colonial political culture that, up to almost the very moment of independence, had been decidedly monarchical and imperial, Protestant and virulently anti-Catholic. Shaped by what they saw, heard, and read, many provincials had earlier identified themselves as Britons and referenced versions of British and English history as their own. They had willingly proclaimed their love of the nation's Protestant monarchs and loathing for the king's enemies. Across eighteenth-century British North America, loyalism therefore had been essentially normative.[28]

The revolutionary crisis of 1774–76 was transformative, however, in more ways than one. First, as Jerry Bannister and Liam Riordan maintain, it 'decisively severed the shared, if multitudinous, sense of Britishness for settlers in the thirteen rebellious colonies' and paved the way for the gradual emergence of a rival 'American' identity.[29] Second, because it pivoted firmly around the issue of kingship in a fashion that we are only just beginning to understand fully, the crisis resulted in the transmogrification of the earlier, broadly diffused colonial loyalism into the exclusive preserve of a particular group or faction. As American Patriots metamorphosed into revolutionaries, they engaged in the ritualistic and metaphorical king-killing that Winthrop Jordan described so ably several years ago.[30] Royal symbols were attacked and desecrated in a wave of iconoclastic violence that culminated in the legendary toppling from its pedestal of George III's equestrian statue in New York during July 1776. In an action that strongly referenced earlier English history, the crowd decapitated it in emulation of Charles I's regicide. What is even more interesting, however, is the fate of the king's head. Stripped of its laurel leaf crown, it was carried off by members of the crowd to a Manhattan tavern. Their intention was that George's head eventually be displayed at Fort Washington atop a spike, like that of a common executed criminal, but Loyalists managed to recapture the piece and eventually sent it to London, where it was seen by the exiled Thomas Hutchinson, among others. The statue's head therefore was a potent political football in this era of civil war.[31]

Leading Loyalists' commitment to the monarch hardened in reaction to this kind of iconoclastic violence and, in the process, became their principal defining characteristic. In the context of revolution in the British world, this was a perfectly understandable position to adopt. After all, as J.G.A. Pocock insists, 'in English memory the alternative to monarchy was not the republic but the dissolution of government, civil war, regicide.'[32] In 1776 the Anglican minister William Smith could draw on this still vivid recollection to fight a rearguard action against the lure of Thomas Paine's *Common Sense*. He did so by instancing the black time when 'republicanism triumphed over the Constitution.' The same precedent obsessed Camillus. Writing from New York in October 1776, he argued that prompt military action would relieve the former colonists 'from the most degrading Species of Tyranny, Republican Tyranny.' According to him, this had an obvious pedigree in earlier British history: 'The experiment has already been made during the Usurpation of OLIVER CROMWELL, and Experience has shewed it by the Restoration of KING CHARLES the Second, to be totally incompatible with the Magnitude and Majesty of a great Empire.'[33]

So, in 1774–76, the diffuse, broadly based colonial loyalism of the mid-eighteenth century became fractured and reconfigured. It became defined against Protestant revolutionary 'others' and in opposition to the twin causes of republicanism and independence. And in most of the areas lying outside British military control, it was often a minority position, although one that retained a potentially wide social and ethno-religious constituency that encompassed poorer whites, free blacks, slaves, and Native Americans as well as members of the former colonial elites.

How did leading Loyalists display their allegiance in this contested political environment? And to what extent did they attempt to reach out to tap and possibly control this wider support? Aside from assisting and actually fighting with the British, the most striking action they took was to develop distinct forms of political organization that mimicked and rivalled those of the revolutionaries. This happened from the outset of the crisis that was to culminate in war. As early as January 1775, for example, some Loyalists in Petersham, Massachusetts, formed an association on the basis that they 'will not acknowledge or submit to the pretended authority of any Congress, Committees of Correspondence, or any other unconstitutional Assemblies of men, but will at the risk of our lives, if need be, oppose the forcible exercise of all such authority.' They also agreed to stand by each other and repel force with force in the event that their persons or property be threatened by 'any committees, mobs or lawful assemblies.' The revolutionaries, in turn, charged the

Loyalists with contemptuously comparing 'the strength and wisdom of the grand council of America, to an insignificant mob, and an unlawful assembly,' and insinuated that they were intent on manifesting 'principles inimical to the liberties of America.' They decided to break off all commercial connections with those who had been 'agreeable neighbours' now turned 'traitorous paricides to the cause of freedom,' until they 'have repented of their evil principles and became friends to the common rights of mankind.'[34]

As well as organizing themselves politically, white male Loyalists also confirmed their sense of collective identity through cultural manifestations such as toasts, songs, and rituals. Indeed, they often defined themselves through whom they toasted, when, and how. Offered daily in taverns, toasts were often centrepieces of festive dinners.[35] They had a complex impact on those present, generating a renewed sense of unity and resolve, a collective bonhomie, and an awareness of a shared past and a common set of goals in the present. Toasts, however, had an impact beyond the specific occasion itself because they were sometimes published in newspapers, pamphlets, and anthologies,[36] thus making the transition from the private to the public sphere. In the process, they became a convenient means of simultaneously broadcasting a strongly held political identity and of encouraging further support among the wider populace.

Loyalist toasts could be either a celebration or an abnegation, an invocation of praise or blame. Often they took the form of a curse aimed at the 'other,' as is evident in this widely distributed example from the war years: 'The Continental Congress, with all their subordinates, may their commissions prove death warrants, and their sword belts be exchanged for halters.' The toast continued in a similar vein: 'Let the root of faction be consumed, and the branches of rebellion perish for ever. A speedy downfal[l] to the allies of treason.' On the other hand, toasts could entail a positive expression of Loyalist identity by highlighting and reinforcing shared core values: 'Veneration to the parent state that amply provided for, and nobly fought in defence of her children. Rewards to the honest sons of America, who withstood the torrents of disobedience . . . The noble fabrick of the British constitution: May it never moulder or decay, but unblemished withstand despotic rage, and republican subtilty. Health and long-life to all the friends of British monarchy.'[37] Whether they took the form of critique or affirmation, toasts therefore remained powerful public acts of affiliation and allegiance.

Songs were another effective vehicle for expressing Loyalist sentiments. Often they were sung in the same contexts and venues as toasts – most notably, taverns. As was the case with toasts, their content varied significantly. In every case, however, they were a valuable means of affirming Loyalist identity. Some simply referred back to the same motifs that had been a familiar feature of the colonial era – the celebration of royal birthdays and other key dates in the commemorative calendar remained a prominent feature. This was exemplified in a refrain reputedly sung on the queen's birthday on Long Island in 1779. It was characterized by a pronounced idyllic, pastoral tone: 'Arise sweet messenger of morn, With thy mild beams the isles adorn, For long as shepherds sport and play, 'Tis this shall be a holiday . . . Come all ye loyal British souls, Let love and honour crown your bowls, Rejoice, rejoice, and sport and play, This source of many holiday.'[38]

Other songs, however, served as political commentaries and often had a hard, satirical edge to them. This was evident, for example, in 'The Procession, with the standard of faction, a cantata,' which opened, "Twas on the morn when Virtue wept to see Discord stalk forth in robes of Liberty, The Sons of Faction met, (a ghastly hand!) To fix their Standard in our bleeding land. Pleas'd with the play thing roar'd the youthful train, Wond'ring their parents had grown young again.'[39] During the war, a more martial tone became evident: 'Rise Britannia's sons arise and see, Rebellions strife intrude on thee, Brave intrepid sons of war, Quick yourselves, for arms prepare, Scourge the traitors that rebel, And the horrid monster quell; And all your liberties maintain, Under great George's milder reign.' The song concluded with the rousing verse: 'Crush the foes of Britain's crown, And rebellion trample down; And all your liberties maintain, Under great George's milder reign.'[40] Many of the era's other songs also stood as paeans to martial values: 'Stand around my brave boys with heart and with voice, And all in full chorus agree, We'll fight for our king, and as loyal we'll sing, And let the world know we'll be free, And let the world know we'll be free.' It continued: 'The rebels will fly, as with shouts we draw nigh, And echo shall victory bring, Then safe from all harms, we'll rest on our arms, And chorus it, Long live the king.'[41] The final refrain was actually repeated no less than five times for effect.

Loyalism was also expressed in the form of direct action and ritual attack. Often this involved targeting totems of revolutionary thought and authority with a view to fatally undermining their power and influence. In some instances it was rebel literature that incurred Loyalist wrath. One target was *The Crisis*, a series of essays that first appeared in London in January 1775 but was then widely circulated across the colonies. Its author, who remains unknown, called for Americans to defend their rights if necessary by force of arms. Naturally this publication, along with the inflammatory arguments it contained, incensed Loyalists. In one incident it was publicly burnt at a coffee house door in 1775 by 'Mr. Murray, late of the Kingdom of Ireland, who has distinguished himself on many occasions, as a staunch Friend to the Constitution.' As he engaged in his pyromaniacal gesture, which probably deliberately imitated an earlier parliamentary-sanctioned event in New Palace Yard, Westminster, Murray insisted that 'any Man who opposed him in so meritorious an Act, ought and he made no doubt would be deemed equally culpable with the Author of so base and infamous a Publication.'[42]

People, rather than printed literature, were more frequently the focus of Loyalist action. In areas where their authority was rather tenuous, local revolutionary officials were often attacked and abused. Sometimes these assaults were an expression of a popular loyalism that operated largely beyond elite control. In 1782 a group of refugees based on the Delmarva Peninsula ransacked the home of Robert Appleton, an unpopular Delaware revolutionary official, and carried him away as a captive to their retreat. When he refused to preach a Methodist sermon, the refugees ordered a black fugitive to whip him with a rope. Appleton was then forced to destroy official papers and to promise that he would never serve warrants on Loyalists again. How should we understand this incident? It seems that, drawing on conversion procedures common in evangelical meetings, his captors first exhorted Appleton to repent his 'sins' and acknowledge his guilt. But when this failed with the official's adamant refusal to deliver a sermon, they proceeded to engage in a ritual debasement and inversion that aimed symbolically at turning political and social relations upside down. To puncture his haughtiness and pomposity, Appleton was punished by one of the lowliest members of society – a black male. By these actions this particular gang of Loyalist sympathizers clearly was expressing its group identity in an inclusive fashion. But at the same time these Loyalists were demonstrating the depth of the cultural and ideological threat they posed to revolutionary authority through their rather jaundiced view of conventional social relations, their possible acceptance of a rough equality even between races, and their willingness to challenge lingering notions of order, hierarchy, and deference. In this way, they highlighted once again the civil war dimension central to the American Revolution and flagged the potential of variants of loyalism that lay largely beyond elite influence.[43]

– II –

In this second part of the chapter, I want to supplement the preceding analysis with a microhistory of the Virginia Loyalist, James Parker. Focusing on a particular individual allows for a more dynamic, developmental approach to the issue of Loyalist identity, because one can track Parker's changing reactions to the challenges of revolution, war, and exile.

A Scottish migrant who achieved economic success as a merchant in pre-revolutionary Norfolk, Parker eventually became a stalwart supporter of the British cause. Having fought with Governor Dunmore to stem the revolutionary tide in the Chesapeake, he saw service in various military theatres before settling in London. What is particularly striking, however, is that Parker did not simply define his loyalism against the American rebels; during the long years of war and exile, his identity was also forged by his disillusionment with and struggles against the British authorities. For Parker, loyalism represented a distinctive position and approach to the conflict. To be a Loyalist certainly did not mean blindly accepting the dictates of British officialdom. This is clearly evident in the extensive commentary on American affairs contained in his letters to his close friend and fellow Scot, Charles Steuart – correspondence that is particularly valuable because it provides a rare glimpse into the evolving identity of an individual British sympathizer.[44]

Parker was one of many Lowland Scots who migrated to the Chesapeake during the eighteenth century. After serving as a tobacco factor for a prominent Glasgow firm, he entered into partnership at Norfolk with a fellow Scot, William Aitchison, in the late 1750s.[45] Their business so flourished that the eve of the imperial crisis found him a prosperous, independent merchant actively involved in Atlantic commerce and with connections spanning colonial boundaries. In Virginia Parker was certainly aware of the processes of 'identification.'[46] As a Lowland Scot, he was a member of a cultural minority that felt threatened by an emergent, latently intolerant Anglo-American majority. As William H. Nelson famously put it, 'Almost all the Loyalists were, in one way or another, more afraid of America than they were of Britain.'[47] That was particularly true of the Chesapeake's Scottish community. Despite some affinity for another non-metropolitan culture, they carried their traditional ambivalence towards the English across the Atlantic. 'No other immigrant group, at least until the Irish influx of the nineteenth century,' Ned Landsman claims, 'arrived in America with such pronounced preconceptions, and such wariness, of their fellow settlers.' 'Probably no other group initially,' he concludes, 'was quite so protective of its social distinctiveness.'[48] Nor were the colonists themselves particularly welcoming – they wanted little to do with the Scottish immigrant community. Clearly there was a fundamental culture clash between the two groups that their shared provincialism could not disguise and perhaps even magnified. The Scots were seen as outsiders who were becoming too successful, too aggressive, and increasingly too close to government. They were also vulnerable in the 1760s to the Wilkite charge that their commitment to 'liberty' was, at the very least, suspect. As the imperial crisis unfolded, the Scots increasingly were seen as sympathetic to 'tyranny,' and they became scapegoats, targets for colonial discontent.[49]

In the Virginian context, then, the way Parker and his associates were being identified may help account for his ultimate commitment to the British cause. That said, it is important to emphasize that he was not a stereotypical Chesapeake Scottish trader. Unlike his fellows, Parker ventured outside the immigrant community's narrow orbit and displayed an unusual degree of commitment to the colony. In a rare move for a 'sojourner,' for example, he married into a native Virginia family. Moreover, Parker built up a considerable economic stake in the Chesapeake during the 1760s and 1770s as his commercial ventures flourished. Finally, he even became involved in local politics. Beginning in the late 1750s his career therefore followed a different course from that normally pursued by Scottish migrants and indeed others with a primarily imperial rather than colonial perspective. Far from viewing his stay merely as a stepping-stone *en route* to a prosperous future back in Britain, Parker seemed settled in Norfolk – a civic-minded, wealthy merchant with a growing young family and local kin ties. Rather than planning a return to Scotland, he was beginning to adopt the mantle of a Virginian gentleman.[50] His attachment to the colony and his 'self-understanding' set him apart from his fellows in the Chesapeake.[51] It was more characteristic of the Middle Colony Scottish administrators, merchants, and educators who were later inclined to support the revolutionary cause.[52]

Parker's eventual Loyalist stance, therefore, was not preordained. Before finally siding with the British authorities, he had to undertake a personal odyssey. Its difficulty is evident in his initial sympathy for the colonists' constitutional case. Unlike some future Loyalists, he did not see the settlers as perpetual clients, had no illusions about the British government's intentions, and even felt that the colonists actually had legitimate grounds for protest. Believing they had a right to control their local affairs, he resented the heightened level of parliamentary interference during the 1760s and refused to accept the concept of virtual representation that the imperial authorities employed as a defence. '[I]t was no part of the Original plan of Settlement,' Parker insisted, 'that a Briton should lose part of his liberty by moving to any part of the Empire.'[53] By overstepping the bounds of its legitimate authority, the British government had jeopardized the harmony, security, and prosperity of the king's overseas subjects. Colonial opposition therefore was perfectly legitimate if conducted legally and peaceably. Indeed, his underlying sympathy for the colonists' constitutional position led Parker to oppose the Sugar Act in 1764. The following year he even supported the Virginians in their defiance of the Stamp Act and sat on the committee that drafted Norfolk's resolves.[54]

When and why, then, did Parker embark upon the political journey that eventually was to take him back to Britain an embittered man? Arguably there were two principal watersheds. The first was the anti-inoculation riots that broke out during 1768 and 1769. In summer 1768 Parker and other members of the Scottish community decided to immunize their families against smallpox. This was an extremely controversial, even provocative, step because most Norfolk residents strongly opposed the practice. The Scots immediately became the focus of considerable antagonism whipped up by prominent native Virginians who would later support the Revolution. Already a dispute over a medical procedure was assuming the overtones of a political and ethnic struggle. The controversy also rapidly became violent: the inoculationists' Norfolk townhouses were attacked and their families assaulted. After a lull, new riots broke out the following May, when a ship owned by one of the inoculators, Cornelius Calvert, arrived ravaged with smallpox. Calvert, the native-born mayor of the borough, employed a Scot, Dr John Dalgleish, to inoculate some slaves who had been exposed to the disease. Given the community's sensitivity towards the issue, news of this incident spread like wildfire. A crowd attacked Calvert's house before moving on. Parker's residence was their next target, but, armed with a gun, he managed to drive off the rioters.[55]

Being a victim of crowd action had a profound effect on Parker. In particular, it clarified the issue of how he was being identified. For Parker, inoculation was not the real issue in the disturbances but merely 'the shadow of a pretence' for the expression of hostility towards him as a Scot.[56] Having lived in Norfolk for more than twenty years, the realization dawned that his 'weak prejudiced' neighbours still viewed him as an alien not entitled to equal protection under the law.[57] With the long-latent rivalry between the two factions now blossoming, Parker's social position suddenly assumed a new precariousness. In October 1769, he informed Steuart that 'the mob are setting up a Rope Work' to compete against the business established earlier by himself and some Scottish associates.[58] Shortly afterwards, the two sides put up rival slates in local elections, with supporters of the Scottish faction wearing orange badges and the English 'true blue.'[59] With the growth of ethnic and imperial tension, Parker's socio-political aspirations were in jeopardy.

If the inoculation riots heightened Parker's sense of embattled identity, they also shifted his attention away from the origins of the imperial crisis to its ramifications for social order in North America. Like many other Loyalists, he began to link the colonial cause inextricably with debtors and mob violence. Parker clearly felt that the crowd had singled him out as much for his vigorous pursuit of Virginian defaulters as for his Scottish origins. He increasingly saw American unrest as motivated at least partly by the desire to evade financial obligations to British merchants.[60] Also, having himself been a victim, Parker abhorred crowd action. He spoke contemptuously of the 'mobility' and the threat they posed to good order.[61] As well as the danger to person and property, Parker was also concerned about the subversion of government processes and the threat of anarchy. He and his friends were under attack because they had 'in a constitutional manner commenced against persons who have already treated us with insufferable Violence.' Nor, to Parker's dismay, were the local authorities any help; some officeholders, after all, had participated in the disturbances themselves. Their abdication of responsibility left innocent people like Parker subject to intimidation at the hands of unelected mobs. If anarchy was the eventual outcome, he asserted prophetically, 'there will be no living in America for us.'[62]

The second watershed was the introduction of the Continental Association. Confronted by colony-wide decisions that portended further serious damage to his interests, Parker hardened his commitment to the Crown and Empire. Prior to 1774 he had hoped that the British government would reconsider its policy and repeal some of the offending legislation. But the colonists' decision to introduce the Continental Association seemed to raise the stakes with its renewed stress on economic retaliation, even extending to non-exportation. In addition, the associators clearly were intent on compelling others to join the movement or else suffer the consequences. Rather than narrowing the growing gulf between the colonies and the metropolis, the Continental Congress had widened it and thereby intensified the imperial crisis. Like other prospective Loyalists, Parker felt angry, embittered, and vulnerable. Congress's irresponsibility proved to him that the colonists were no longer capable of managing their own affairs. To prevent outright rebellion, he fully supported the parliamentary intervention he had previously deplored. He was now delighted that the 'administration are firmly resolved to support authority.'[63]

Any doubts Parker harboured about British legislation, any lingering sympathy he had for the colonists' constitutional case, evaporated. From now on, as he responded to the mounting imperial crisis, his thoughts and actions followed a predictable course. When the Norfolk Committee formally asked him to sign the Association in December 1774, Parker refused point blank because he 'had taken the Oath of Allegiance to his Majesty.'[64] This decision reflected his belief that the British inevitably would prevail. After all, eighteenth-century monarchies had numerous informal weapons at their disposal and, if they failed, ultimately could use fear and force to ensure obedience. Like other Loyalists, Parker was contemptuous of the Patriots' courage in the face of such an awesome threat: '[N]otwithstanding all the noise of arming & mustering,' he believed, 'the Colonists never will attempt fighting.'[65] As late as April 1775, he claimed that, despite Patriot 'boastings,' 'the moment any force appears to oppose them it will be all over.'[66] Even news of the opening skirmishes at Lexington and Concord did not fundamentally dent his confidence.

It was British authority, however, that collapsed in Virginia during early 1775. Parker's business partner, William Aitchison, was more astute when he warned that 'there is no contending against such numbers.'[67] In the face of popular mobilization, Governor Dunmore found he could not retain his influence from Williamsburg, and eventually abandoned the capital to try to retain control of the situation from a warship stationed off Norfolk.[68] But, by the late summer, the governor's position there – along with the plight of the town's merchants – had become intolerable. As Parker declared, 'what few friends Government have in this province are either obliged to go off or Subjected to insult & danger.' His earlier hopes of a speedy reassertion of imperial authority dashed, he contemplated leaving himself. '[A] very little force at first would have secured this Country,' Parker lamented, 'it will now however take more time & more force.'[69] Yet, in a refrain he was to repeat many times subsequently, he did not ascribe this transformation to Patriot success but to British failure: Lord North's administration had 'Starv'd the Cause.'[70] The disenchantment that was to characterize the peripatetic war years and his exile in London had begun.

Having initially defined his Loyalist identity against the American revolutionaries, Parker now began to turn against the British authorities in whom he had put his faith.[71] As he moved with the army from New York to Philadelphia and then back to New York again, his attitude towards wartime developments in America was characterized by the confusion, uncertainty, and apprehension typical of other Loyalists.[72] He found the revolutionaries' success inexplicable, frustrating, and galling. After all, the Continental Army did not seem a formidable opponent: its generals were inept, its ranks often unfilled, and its common soldiers undisciplined. 'As to their strength here,' Parker asserted, 'I never shall be able to find any reason why they have not been Crushed long ago.'[73] Moreover, the American civilian and military leadership seemed riven with crippling rivalries and divisions. As late as June 1779, for example, Parker suggested, 'There is no doubt but that the rebels are split[t]ing to pieces in all quarters.'[74] He also took heart from what appeared to be mounting popular disenchantment with the revolutionary cause as the war dragged on. Like many others, he felt there was a great deal of closet loyalism in certain regions that the imperial forces could exploit to their advantage. In particular, the Eastern Shore of Maryland and Virginia and the southern backcountry figured prominently in his calculations. While acknowledging that, 'Tis true, there have been many misrepresentations respecting the loyalty of people in certain districts,' he pointed to the efforts that residents of the Delmarva Peninsula had made 'to free themselves' as 'proof positive, that a little proper Management would soon set all things right in that quarter.'[75]

Given these favourable conditions, what accounted for the British lack of success? For Parker, it basically came down to incompetent leadership and a failure of will. As with many other Loyalists, a particular target of his wrath were the Howes, whose lack of aggression, he believed, played a major part in Britain's downfall. '[T]he fatal brothers,' as he contemptuously dubbed them, had 'brought many of the best friends to the British Government on this Continent to destruction & death.'[76] Parker even accused them of treachery, of refusing to act as long as Lords North and Germain remained in office. According to him, 'no malefactor ever finished his course at Tyburn more deserving a halter than the fatal brothers.'[77] The reasons for Britain's failure to put down the rebellion went beyond personalities, however. A failure of will in the highest reaches of government combined fatally with a damaging lack of consistency in policy. Pivotal in Parker's mind was the sending of the Carlisle Commission to negotiate with the Americans in 1778. He saw this as a disaster that sent completely the wrong signals. As far as Parker was concerned, 'every soft Silken plan of peace offered to the Rebels, will have no other effect than furnishing them with opportunitys of adding to repeated insults.'[78] Moreover, the terms suggested by the Commission represented a betrayal of the Loyalists' interests. 'Such weight and power will be thrown into the rebel scale,' Parker claimed, 'as will enable them to deprive all who have opposed them, of either p[e]ace or Security.'[79] The only hope was that Congress would hold out for complete independence, and this is indeed what eventually transpired. The Commission returned to England empty handed and in virtual disgrace.

Why had this vain attempt at reaching an accommodation with the revolutionaries even been attempted? Parker detected the hand of metropolitan political intrigue. He felt that the colonists 'would have long ere now been humbled to the dust' without the 'Aid of the factious party at home.'[80] Parker felt that the machinations of the pro-American element in British parliamentary politics were continually undermining the pursuit of the war effort. A report that Lord Chatham himself had entered the ministry in early 1778, for example, had 'greatly disconcerted' British followers at Philadelphia. And Parker saw the efforts of the Commission as an attempt to 'shut the mouths of the Minority.'[81]

If Parker dismissed the possibility of reaching some sort of accord with the rebellious colonists, which policy did he favour himself? Unsurprisingly, he adamantly retained faith in a vigorous military solution to the problem. '[I]f our troops had been permitted to do their duty,' Parker asserted in early 1779, 'the rebels could never have come into the scale of importance.' He concluded that, 'When duty & inclination go

together all difficultys are removed or surmounted.'[82] Parker therefore
was buoyed by Sir Henry Clinton's appointment as commander-in-
chief because, '[b]y all accounts he is well disposed to Crush the rebel[l]
ion.'[83] But, with the evacuation of Philadelphia in June 1778, disillusionment quickly set in. It seemed that vacillation remained the order of the
day. 'Ignorant of the Situation of Affairs at home,' Parker declared, 'I
cannot unfathom the reason why such an Army as we have here, with
such a General Should without trying Washington's strength, march to
New York & embark for Britain.'[84] Nor could he understand the army's
subsequent passivity and lack of campaigning. 'Not but they have still
the power to finish it right,' Parker asserted, 'but such long periods of
inactivity would ruin Romans.' He concluded, 'If the regular Generals
cannot do anything, benefit by the example of Brant & Buttler, why not
try a little irregularity.' If, for example, the British sent General Sir John
Vaughan after Washington and Lord Dunmore back into Virginia with
a thousand men, it 'wd. soon finish this business.'[85]

Parker also advocated a firm line with civilians suspected of collud-
ing with the Patriots. Here he was certainly not alone. As Robert M. Calhoon points out, many Loyalists, especially those residing in garrison
towns, increasingly saw the conflict as an instrument of vengeance and
retribution.[86] Particularly after the triple blow of Burgoyne's defeat, the
news of the French alliance, and the Continental Congress's rejection of
the ill-fated Carlisle Commission, they felt strongly that the Americans
should be punished for their sins of disobedience and ingratitude. After
some Long Island residents had been found guilty of concealing and
aiding the revolutionaries in early 1779, for instance, Parker warmly
welcomed their banishment to the American lines and the turning
over of their estates to distressed Loyalists. According to him, this was
'going to work properly.'[87] Similarly, he approved the policy of confiscation practised in South Carolina following the Charleston expedition.
Parker had only praise for the efforts of his friend, John Cruden, in putting overseers on rebel plantations. '[I]t is said he reforms more Rebels
than the troops,' he claimed, 'Indeed this method has always appeared
highly proper in my eyes, & the radical cure.'[88] Parker essentially was
advocating a war of occupation and pacification. If this course was pursued, there was every prospect of success. For him there was nothing
inevitable about the outcome of the conflict; instead it was largely a result of a fateful combination of rebel cunning and British incompetence.
Summing up his perspective on the war in July 1778, he declared, 'By

Cruelty[,] Cowardice[,] falsehood & Unanimity have a Set of the Worst men on Earth become important.' Meanwhile, 'one of the most power-full Nations on it, her councils thwarted by her factious Nobles & her force misapplied either by ignorance or design hath these three years contended to little Purpose.'[89]

The principal victims of this unfortunate coincidence were, of course, the Loyalists. What was to happen to them after the war was over? Parker hoped that he, his relations, and friends would receive just compensation for their suffering and losses. Only in this way could the Empire be true to its own best standards of liberality, humanitarianism, and civility. But, because he was keen to minimize the burden on the British Treasury, it was important that the rebellion should first be crushed '& let proper enquiry then be made, & every man Stand according to his Merit.'[90] That would ensure that any available compensation would go to those who truly deserved it. In the case of the Virginia Loyalists, according to him, this meant only those who had actively supported Lord Dunmore from the outset of the conflict. Hence, when he heard that his fellow Norfolk merchant Neil Jamieson (who had earlier served on the town's committee of correspondence) had put in a claim, Parker thought that this was 'stealing a March.' On the other hand, Parker thought that his own case was solid. 'If Government after the Rebellion is quelled make good the loss of any,' he declared, 'I am Conscious I have never sin[n]ed against the Constitution either in thought or deed & hope then for redress.'[91] This was a refrain that Parker repeated in his last American letter to Charles Steuart in January 1781. He asserted, 'There are not many from the province that with justice has a better right to look up to Government for a little aid than myself.' But his confidence was somewhat dented by his concern that 'friends or int[e]rest' might ultimately count for more than 'sufferings or Merit itself.'[92]

– III –

Although his trajectory as a British-born exile returning to the metropolis was not typical of the diaspora as a whole, Parker's final observations provide a useful entrée into the question of post-war Loyalist identity in the wider Atlantic world. As is readily evident in his remarks, this was characterized by an underlying tension between solidarity and fragmentation arising out of the revolutionary crisis and war years. On the one hand, some factors still acted to bind the Loyalist exiles loosely together. First, and most fundamentally, there was their displacement during the Revolution. Although it did not act as the equivalent of the later Confederate 'lost cause,' the memory of the conflict retained the emotional power to act as an adhesive for Loyalists in its immediate aftermath. Loyalist identity, as a result, essentially was based on a narrative of war, exile, and the struggle for redemption. Second, following their flight from the United States, the Loyalists assumed a shared status as migrants and settlers. Finding themselves living in 'new worlds,' they confronted similar problems of re-establishing themselves and adapting their inherited social values and structures to unfamiliar environments, whether in the Maritimes, Upper Canada, Jamaica, the Bahamas, or Sierra Leone. Third, enduring kinship, social, and economic ties among diaspora members may have opened and then consolidated channels of communication between otherwise far-flung Loyalist communities. Finally, there was the Loyalists' actual experience of exile and their resulting liminal status: like others in the Atlantic basin caught between worlds, they found themselves suspended between the past and the present.[93]

Perhaps more important to the shaping of Loyalist identity, however, was the refugees' relationship with Britain. As Parker's story demonstrates, this had two main dimensions. First, as they had chosen to remain 'British' in a contested political environment, they shared a determination to assert their rights as British subjects or allies. Under these circumstances, they also felt that the imperial authorities had a quasi-contractual obligation to meet their demands.[94] Second, because the British government had begun to conceive of them as wards of state, Loyalists started to think of themselves as an interest group with a special status within the Empire that reflected their distinctive history of service and sacrifice. Loyalism, as Christopher Sparshott has suggested, almost became a commodity as the exiles traded on their past politics to secure the best possible compensation deal from the imperial bureaucracy.[95] And whenever the authorities fell short, many Loyalists drew upon what Maya Jasanoff has termed a 'discourse of grievance' founded upon the perception that they had suffered from persecution and discrimination.[96] This was well expressed in the assertion of the bitter Anglican minister William Clark, who declared in 1790 from Nova Scotia, 'The People of New England never treated me with that barbarity the Government of Old England has, all things considered.'[97] These kinds of sentiments shaped black as well as white settler attitudes towards the land grant, and the compensation and pension arrangements they were offered. Having begun by defining themselves against the embryonic forces of American nationalism, many Loyalists increasingly identified themselves in terms of their rather fraught relationship with the imperial authorities.

As they vied with each other for resources from the government, Loyalists began to develop a competitive political culture to some degree akin to the one they had left behind in the United States. As different groups and factions jockeyed for position in contests over compensation, land, and provisions, it became clear that Loyalist cohesion would become somewhat attenuated. Instead, as Neil MacKinnon eloquently puts it, a 'scramble over the spoils of defeat' developed as everyone attempted to secure their own corner within the Empire.[98] Under these circumstances, economic and ethno-cultural divisions among Loyalists came to the fore. This was hardly surprising, since Loyalist exile settlements across the Atlantic world often constituted, to use John McLeod's phrase, 'composite communities.'[99] This was reflected, for example, in the Anglican clergyman Jacob Bailey's rather alarmed characterization of his neighbours in the Annapolis Valley, Nova Scotia. He described them as 'a collection of all nations, kindreds, complexions and tongues assembled from every quarter of the Globe, and till lately equally strangers to me and each other.'[100] In Upper Canada the outcome of this diversity was rather marked. A mosaic of quasi-corporate communities developed throughout that region at the behest of the settlers themselves. There, divisions among the Loyalists were so profound that, along the St Lawrence valley, exiles formed distinct townships centred around ethnicity and religion. Catholic Highlanders, Scottish Presbyterians, German Calvinists, German Lutherans, and English Anglicans all tended to live apart from each other.[101]

The most important fissure, however, ran, perhaps predictably, along racial lines. At one level the same dynamic operated in the case of black Loyalists as white. Both tended to define themselves against 'others,' first the American revolutionaries and then the British. Once in exile they also tried to use their wartime 'sacrifices' as a weapon to demand concessions from the imperial authorities. Finally, having gained their freedom, they were looking for many of the same things as white Loyalist settlers – land, independence, and practical assistance to help them establish themselves in a new and challenging environment. In their principal destinations such as Nova Scotia, however, they faced both neglect and hostility. Though Lord Sydney considered the black veterans 'entitled to some protection and favour,' their plight was a low priority in Whitehall and in Halifax. Hence they were slow to receive land grants and provisions and, despite earlier promises, these were never on the same scale and quality as those proffered their white counterparts. Many had to accept positions as indentured servants or sharecroppers because there was no other means of earning a living. Meanwhile, black Loyalists confronted the prejudice of white settlers and were discriminated against in all spheres ranging from the law courts to job markets. Occasionally, as in the case of the Shelburne riot in 1784, they were the victims of overt white violence. These harsh conditions inclined the black Loyalists towards cultural and social separatism centring, in particular, around evangelical religion. Eventually, many, under the leadership of figures such as Thomas Peters, elected to abandon Nova Scotia in favour of Sierra Leone, only to find that white domination was as pronounced there as in the Maritimes and that they had to confront many of the same challenges.[102]

To conclude, Loyalist populations clearly did not experience the late eighteenth-century Atlantic civil war and its aftermath in the same ways as either the American revolutionaries or the British. Both their central dilemma and trajectory were different. While the former colonists were set (albeit hesitantly) upon revolution and nation building and the imperial power was wallowing in the disillusionment attendant upon military defeat, the Loyalists were getting to grips directly with the consequences of persecution, displacement, and, in many cases, exile.[103] These sharp differences had profound consequences for each party's understanding of both the conflict itself and their sense of identity. While the revolutionaries absorbed themselves in debates over the construction of a new sense of national destiny and the British were left to ponder what the concept actually meant, there was no such underlying uncertainty about the Loyalist position, at least initially. They developed a rather sharper, more immediate sense of collective identity coming out of the Atlantic civil war than the other major participants in the struggle. Because of their position at its cutting edge, they thought more unequivocally in terms of 'us' versus 'them' than either the rebels or the imperial power. That said, there was an undoubted dynamism to Loyalist identity as the 'other' shifted over time for them. Having begun by defining themselves exclusively against the embryonic forces of American nationalism, they identified themselves in the post-war world against the British imperial authorities for as long as their active mutual engagement continued into the 1790s.

At the same time, any strong sense of collective identity began to dissipate under conditions of migration and exile. Two factors were primarily responsible. First, the types of communities Loyalists established across the Atlantic world inevitably differed as a result of the interaction of variables such as the size of the population flow to a particular area, the migrants' composition in terms of regional origins, socioeconomic background, ethnicity, race, and gender, and the density and mentality of the receiving population. In some areas, such as New Brunswick, Upper Canada, and the Bahamas, Loyalists arguably became the dominant element. In others, notably Nova Scotia, Grenada, Jamaica, and Sierra Leone, they constituted enclaves amid an established settler or indigenous population. Meanwhile, in provincial Britain, Loyalists dispersed and eventually were absorbed into the wider society. The resulting variety in local experience naturally had profound implications for how the refugees perceived themselves and acted. In regions where they were clearly in the majority, for example, they were perhaps more prone to division and rivalry than where they remained an embattled, defensive minority.

Second, internal cohesion was eroded by the sheer heterogeneity of these exile populations. Under these circumstances the processes of migration and resettlement involved the refugees in a series of disputes about what their loyalism should bring them. All agreed that the British government ought to reward their resolve, but their rival expectations invariably generated sharp disagreements and conflicts as individual Loyalists contemplated their relationship to the larger imperial community. From this perspective, post-war loyalism appears less as a cohesive movement possessing a clear sense of collective identity and more as a fluid political culture in which every Loyalist held a personal vision of his or her place in the Empire. In a sense there was a loose parallel here with their revolutionary opponents. While Americans struggled to work out what it meant to be a citizen of the United States in the 1780s and 1790s, Loyalists were simultaneously engaged in the equally complex task of defining what it was to be a British subject. This level of contestation meant that, even in a Loyalist bastion such as New Brunswick, the elite's 'dream' of establishing an orderly, hierarchical society that would provide a rival to the new republic was vigorously challenged by rank-and-file settlers. When, for example, fifty-five leading exiles petitioned for five-thousand-acre estates (ten times the average grant), popular protest succeeded in blocking the request. Similarly, the election of 1785 sparked street riots in Saint John as different factions expressed opposition to the elite based in Fredericton. Partly for these reasons, some other Loyalist colonies, like Cape Breton, simply failed altogether.[104]

With their trajectory differing markedly from those pursued by either the revolutionaries or the British, the American Loyalists' 'problem of identity' was clearly distinctive. In the process, it demonstrates that the dynamics of the late eighteenth-century struggle in the British Atlantic were even more complex than Wahrman suggests. As loyalism was shaped by both internal contestation and external relationships with 'others,' it was also fluid and subject to change over time. From being a 'normative,' expansive, and almost unthinking stance among at least the majority of the white settler population earlier in the eighteenth century, it became the self-conscious preserve of embattled, vulnerable minorities during the revolutionary era. Being more prone than the other parties to the conflict to think in terms of 'us' versus 'them' dichotomies, Loyalists arguably emerged from the Atlantic civil war with a sharper sense of collective self than either the British or the revolutionaries. The problem was that this could not be sustained under the challenging conditions of migration and exile. Defining themselves against the British authorities rather than their revolutionary enemies in the post-war era simply could not provide the cohesion needed to overcome mounting internal divisions. Instead, these tensions were exacerbated, and any strong sense of collective identity dissipated, especially as the exiles' close engagement with the imperial government began to fade in the 1790s. As a result, no single, monolithic Loyalist tradition could be passed on to subsequent generations, even in the main area of resettlement, Canada. During the nineteenth century, this provided ample scope for an ongoing redefinition of loyalism and the emergence of multiple visions that were essentially inventions, the fulfilment of quests for 'usable pasts' that spoke to contemporary anxieties and interests. In this way, at least, the fluidity and diversity characteristic of the late eighteenth century continued unabated.[105]

NOTES

1 Quoted in Dror Wahrman, 'The English Problem of Identity in the American Revolution,' *American Historical Review* 106 (2001): 7. On eighteenth-century

notions of identity, see also idem, *The Making of the Modern Self: Identity and Culture in Eighteenth-Century England* (New Haven: Yale University Press, 2004); and Ronald Hoffman, Mechal Sobel, and Fredrika Teute, eds., *Through a Glass Darkly: Reflections on Personal Identity in Early America* (Chapel Hill: University of North Carolina Press, 1997). For an insightful discussion of allegiance and the related concept of 'friendship,' see John G. Reid, in this volume.

2 'Meeting of the Freeholders and other Inhabitants of the County of Dunmore, Virginia, June 1774' and 'Form of the Covenant sent to every town in Massachusetts, June 1774,' both in Peter Force, ed., *American Archives: Documents of the American Revolution, 1774–76,* http://dig.lib.niu/amarch/ (accessed 22 November 2010).

3 Wahrman, 'The English Problem of Identity,' 8.

4 Ibid., 10.

5 Ibid., 38.

6 Two thoughtful recent analyses of the development of American national identity in the revolutionary era are Liam Riordan, *Many Identities, One Nation: The Revolution and its Legacy in the Mid-Atlantic* (Philadelphia: University of Pennsylvania Press, 2007); and Carroll Smith-Rosenberg, *This Violent Empire: The Birth of American National Identity* (Chapel Hill: University of North Carolina Press, 2010). On Britain, see Wahrman, *Making of the Modern Self.*

7 For a good introduction to the role of the Loyalists in community conflict, see the contributions in *Loyalists and Community in North America,* ed. Robert M. Calhoon, Timothy M. Barnes, and George A. Rawlyk (Westport, CT: Greenwood Press, 1994). Central to understanding citizenship in the early republic is James H. Kettner's notion of 'volitional allegiance'; see his *The Development of American Citizenship, 1608–1870* (Chapel Hill: University of North Carolina Press, 1978), chap. 7. On relations between the British and their Loyalist allies, at least in the vital region of the lower South, see Jim Piecuch, *Three Peoples, One King: Loyalists, Indians, and Slaves in the Revolutionary South, 1775–1782* (Columbia: University of South Carolina Press, 2008).

8 Maya Jasanoff, 'The Other Side of Revolution: Loyalists in the British Empire,' *William and Mary Quarterly* 65 (2008): esp. 222–7.

9 The phrase is used by Wallace Brown, among others, in the title of his book *The King's Friends: The Composition and Motives of the American Loyalist Claimants* (Providence, RI: Brown University Press, 1965). For a comparison with the role of the monarch in the French Atlantic, see Gene E. Ogle, 'The Trans-Atlantic King and Imperial Public Spheres: Everyday Politics in Pre-Revolutionary St. Domingue,' in *The World of the Haitian Revolution,* ed. David P. Geggus and Norman Fiering (Bloomington: Indiana University Press, 2009).

10 For the resonances associated with this term, see J.M. Bumsted, *Understanding the Loyalists* (Sackville, NB: Mount Allison University, Centre for Canadian Studies, 1986), 35.

11 For the kinds of conflicts that could arise in areas as widely dispersed and different as the Bahamas, New Brunswick, and Sierra Leone, see Jasanoff, 'The Other Side of Revolution,' esp. 224–7.

12 On Loyalist exile and diaspora, see Jasanoff, 'The Other Side of Revolution'; and Keith Mason, 'The American Loyalist Diaspora and the Reconfiguration of the British Atlantic World,' in *Empire and Nation: The American Revolution in the Atlantic World*, ed. Eliga H. Gould and Peter S. Onuf (Baltimore: Johns Hopkins University Press, 2005), 239–59. For an introduction to the Pacific dimension, see Cassandra Pybus, *Epic Journeys of Freedom: Runaway Slaves of the American Revolution and their Global Quest for Liberty* (Boston: Beacon Press, 2006).

13 A recent illuminating analysis of the problem of identity in the Atlantic world (admittedly in a rather different context) is James Sweet, 'Mistaken Identities: Olaudah Equiano, Domingos Alvares, and the Methodological Challenges of Studying the African Diaspora,' *American Historical Review* 114 (2009): 279–306.

14 For an introduction to the diversity of Loyalist populations along with some suggestive individual case studies, see Mason, 'The American Loyalist Diaspora.'

15 Gary Nash, *Race and Revolution* (Madison, WI: Madison House, 1990), 57.

16 James W. St G. Walker, *The Black Loyalists: The Search for a Promised Land in Nova Scotia and Sierra Leone, 1783–1870* (New York: Africana Publishing, 1976); John W. Pulis, ed., *Moving On: Black Loyalists in the Afro-Atlantic World* (New York: Garland Publishing, 1999); Simon Schama, *Rough Crossings: Britain, the Slaves, and the American Revolution* (London: BBC Books, 2005); and Pybus, *Epic Journeys of Freedom*. For those African Americans who left the United States as the slaves of white Loyalists, see the chapters by Carole W. Troxler and Jennifer K. Snyder, in this volume.

17 Graham R. Hodges, ed., *The Black Loyalist Directory: African Americans in Exile after the American Revolution* (New York: Garland, 1996), xv.

18 See, for example, John W. Pulis, 'Bridging Troubled Waters: Moses Baker, George Liele, and the African America Diaspora to Jamaica,' in *Moving On* (see note 16).

19 For a thoughtful discussion of the motivation of Native Americans, at least in the lower South, see Piecuch, *Three Peoples*, esp. 'Introduction.' On 'friendship,' see Reid, in this volume. For one important group of Native

American Loyalists, the Haudenosaunee, see Alan Taylor, *The Divided Ground: Indians, Settlers, and Slaves* (New York: Knopf, 2006).

20 Quoted in Alan Taylor, *The Civil War of 1812: American Citizens, British Subjects, Irish Rebels, & Indian Allies* (New York: Knopf, 2010), 27.

21 Rogers Brubaker and Frederick Cooper, 'Beyond "Identity,"' *Theory and Society* 29 (2000): 1–47.

22 See, in particular, American Loyalist Claims Series 1 (AO12), American Loyalist Claims Series 2 (AO13), and American Loyalist Claims Commission (T79), National Archives of the United Kingdom. The sample underpinning my analysis of language rests on a reading of every fifth claim from Massachusetts, Pennsylvania, and the Chesapeake region (Maryland, Virginia, North Carolina). On the notion of sensibility in the late eighteenth century, see Sarah Knott, *Sensibility and the American Revolution* (Chapel Hill: University of North Carolina Press, 2009). Especially note her plea on 177 that much work needs to be done on Loyalist discourses.

23 'To the militia of Pennsylvania,' (1778), Evans Collection 15919.

24 Douglass Adair and John A. Schutz, eds., *Peter Oliver's Origin & Progress of the American Rebellion: A Tory View* (San Marino, CA: The Huntington Library, 1961). The following quotations are from 9, 51.

25 Edward Larkin, 'Seeing through Language: Narrative, Portraiture, and Character in Peter Oliver's The Origin and Progress of the American Rebellion,' *Early American Literature* 36 (2001): 427–54.

26 For some examples, see 'Loyal and Humerous Songs on Recent Occasions . . .,' (1779), Evans Collection 16326.

27 Quoted in Mary Beth Norton, *The British-Americans: The Loyalist Exiles in England 1774–1789* (London: Constable, 1974), 140.

28 Brendan McConville, *The King's Three Faces: The Rise and Fall of Royal America, 1688–1776* (Chapel Hill: University of North Carolina Press, 2006). I would like to thank Elizabeth Mancke for suggesting the use of the term 'normative' in this context.

29 Jerry Bannister and Liam Riordan, in this volume.

30 Winthrop Jordan, 'Familial Politics: Thomas Paine and the Killing of the King, 1776,' *Journal of American History* 60 (1973): 294–308.

31 McConville, *The King's Three Faces*, esp. 309–11; Arthur S. Marks, 'The Statue of King George III in New York and the Iconology of Regicide,' *American Art Journal* 13 (1981): 61–82.

32 J.G.A. Pocock, 'Monarchy in the Name of Britain: The Case of George III,' in *Monarchisms in the Age of Enlightenment*, ed. Hans Blom, John Christian Laursen, and Luisa Simonutti (Toronto: University of Toronto Press, 2007), 300.

33 'To the Public. Considerations on the Present Revolted State of America, addressed to its Inhabitants at Large,' New York, 18 October 1776, Evans Collection 43108.

34 'Proceedings of the Town of Petersham,' 2 January 1775, Evans Collection 49293.

35 On the tavern setting, see David Conroy, *In Public Houses: Drink and the Revolution of Authority in Colonial Massachusetts* (Chapel Hill: University of North Carolina Press, 1995); and Peter Thompson, *Rum, Punch, and Revolution: Taverngoing and Public Life in Eighteenth-century Philadelphia* (Philadelphia: University of Pennsylvania Press, 1998). For the role of toasts in the party politics of the post-revolutionary United States, see Simon P. Newman, *Parades and the Politics of the Street: Festive Culture in the Early American Republic* (Philadelphia: University of Pennsylvania Press, 1997).

36 See, for example, those collected in 'Loyal and Humerous Songs on Recent Occasions . . .,' (1779), Evans Collection 16326.

37 Ibid., 53, 54, 55.

38 Ibid., 61.

39 Ibid., 73.

40 Ibid., 68–9.

41 Ibid., 69.

42 'To the Public. The Crisis being deemed by the Parliament of England a Libel, and consequently ordered to be burnt . . .,' (1775), Evans Collection 14512. On the circulation, impact, and earlier neglect of *The Crisis* in the historiography, see T.H. Breen, *American Insurgents, American Patriots: The Revolution of the People* (New York: Hill and Wang, 2010), 261–74.

43 Details of this incident can be found in 'Localism, Evangelicalism, and Loyalism: The Sources of Discontent in the Revolutionary Chesapeake,' *Journal of Southern History* 56 (1990): 42–3; and Robert M. Calhoon, 'The Reintegration of the Loyalists and Disaffected,' in *The American Revolution: Its Character and Limits*, ed. Jack P. Greene (New York: New York University Press, 1987), 60.

44 Parker's correspondence can be found in the Parker Papers at the Liverpool Record Office (henceforth LRO). His career and revolutionary experience can also be tracked in the companion Steuart Papers at the National Library of Scotland (henceforth NLS). I drew on these sources heavily in an earlier article; see Keith Mason, 'A Loyalist's Journey: James Parker's Response to the Revolutionary Crisis,' *Virginia Magazine of History and Biography* 101 (1994): 139–66.

45 On the role of Glasgow merchants, see T.M. Devine, *The Tobacco Lords: A Study of the Tobacco Merchants of Glasgow and Their Trading Activities c. 1740–90* (Edinburgh: John Donald, 1975). For the activities of Scottish migrants,

see Alan L. Karras, *Sojourners in the Sun: Scots in Jamaica and the Chesapeake, 1740–1800* (Ithaca, NY: Cornell University Press, 1993). On Norfolk's commercial activity and the rise of its merchant oligarchy, see Thomas M. Costa, 'Economic Development and Political Authority: Norfolk, Virginia, Merchant-Magistrates, 1736–1800' (PhD diss., College of William and Mary, 1991), chaps. 2 and 3.

46 On 'identification,' see Brubaker and Cooper, 'Beyond Identity,' 14–17.

47 William H. Nelson, *The American Tory* (Oxford: Oxford University Press, 1961), 85–115; quotation on 91.

48 Ned C. Landsman, *Scotland and Its First American Colony, 1683–1765* (Princeton, NJ: Princeton University Press, 1985), 261–2.

49 See John E. Selby, *The Revolution in Virginia, 1775–1783* (Williamsburg: University of Virginia Press, 1988), 15.

50 'Notes on the Parker Family – Memoir by Mrs Charles Parker written in 1835,' 920 PAR I 60, LRO. Information on Parker's property holdings comes from 'Estimates of losses sustained by James Parker, in Virginia and North Carolina, in consequence of his taking up arms, agreeably to the calls of government, in 1775,' London, 9 March 1784, 920 PAR I, 19/5, LRO; Brent Tarter, ed., *The Order Book and Related Papers of the Common Hall of the Borough of Norfolk, Virginia, 1736–1798* (Richmond: Virginia State Library, 1979), 136, 138, 146, 148, 149, 152–3, 161, 172.

51 Brubaker and Cooper, 'Beyond Identity,' 17–19.

52 I would like to thank Ned Landsman for this suggestion.

53 James Parker to Charles Steuart, Norfolk, 7 June 1774, Steuart Papers, MSS 5028, f. 206, NLS.

54 Adele Hast, *Loyalism in Revolutionary Virginia: The Norfolk Area and the Eastern Shore* (Ann Arbor. MI: UMI Research Press, 1982).

55 Descriptions of this incident can be found in James Parker to Charles Steuart, Norfolk, May [ ], 1769, Steuart Papers, MSS 5025, ff. 123–4 and James Parker to Charles Steuart, Norfolk, 20 Oct. 20, 1769, MSS 5025, ff.215–21, NLS. For an illuminating study that describes the wider context for these events in rich detail, see Elizabeth Fenn, *Pox Americana: The Great Smallpox Epidemic of 1775–1782* (New York: Hill & Wang, 2002).

56 James Parker to Charles Steuart, Norfolk, May [ ], 1769, Steuart Papers, MSS 5025, ff. 123–4, NLS.

57 James Parker to Charles Steuart, Norfolk, 6 May 1769, Steuart Papers, MSS 5025, ff. 128–9, NLS; James Parker to Charles Steuart, Norfolk, 27 January 1775, Steuart Papers, MSS 5029, f. 14, NLS.

58 James Parker to Charles Steuart, Norfolk, 20 October 1769, Steuart Papers, MSS 5025, f. 218, NLS. For details of the Scots' rope works, see 'Declaration

of William Calderhead re James Campbell & Co.,' Glasgow, 22 May 1809, 920 PAR I 37, LRO. On economic competition in Norfolk, see Costa, 'Economic Development and Political Authority,' 167–9.

59 Thomas J. Wertenbaker, *Norfolk, Historic Southern Port* (Durham, NC: Duke University Press, 1962), 13.

60 See the entries in the City of Norfolk Order Books: (1) 1761–1769 and (2) 1770–1782, Virginia State Library, Richmond, VA; James Parker to Charles Steuart, Norfolk, 7 June 1774, Steuart Papers, MSS 5028, f. 206, NLS.

61 See, for example, James Parker to Charles Steuart, Norfolk, 6 May 1769, Steuart Papers, MSS 5028, f. 206, NLS.

62 James Parker and Dr. Campbell to the Governor of Virginia, Norfolk, 28 May 1769, Steuart Papers, MSS 5025, f. 125; James Parker to Charles Steuart, Norfolk, 20 July 1774, Steuart Papers, MSS 5028, f. 231, NLS.

63 James Parker to Charles Steuart, Norfolk, 26 October 1774, Steuart Papers, MSS 5028, f. 273, NLS.

64 James Parker to Charles Steuart, Norfolk, 6 December 1774, Steuart Papers, MSS 5028, f. 292, NLS.

65 James Parker to Charles Steuart, Norfolk, 28 December 1774, Steuart Papers, MSS 5028, f. 301, NLS.

66 James Parker to Charles Steuart, Norfolk, 6 April 1775, Steuart Papers, MSS 5029, f. 39, NLS.

67 William Aitchison to James Parker, 14 November 1774, 920 PAR I 2, LRO.

68 James Parker to Charles Steuart, Norfolk, 12 June 1775, Steuart Papers, MSS 5029, ff. 62, 66, 73, 77, NLS.

69 James Parker to Charles Steuart, Norfolk, 25 September 1775, Steuart Papers, MSS 5029, f. 104, NLS.

70 Quoted in William Dabney, 'Letters from Norfolk: Scottish Merchants View the Revolutionary Crisis,' in *The Old Dominion: Essays for Thomas Perkins Abernethy*, ed. Darrett B. Rutman (Charlottesville: University of Virginia Press, 1964), 119.

71 For an intelligent analysis of similar tensions between British officialdom and Loyalists in occupied New York, see Ruma Chopra, 'Loyalist Persuasions: The Case of New York City' (unpublished paper given to the conference on Loyalism and the Revolutionary Atlantic World, University of Maine, Orono, 4–7 June 2009).

72 Robert M. Calhoon, *The Loyalist Perception and Other Essays* (Columbia: University of South Carolina Press, 1989), 170.

73 James Parker to Charles Steuart, Philadelphia, 15 April 1778, 920 PAR I 13/1, LRO.

74 James Parker to Charles Steuart, New York, June 1779, 920 PAR I 13/1, LRO.

75 James Parker to Charles Steuart, Philadelphia, 22 May 1778, 920 PAR 1, 13/1, LRO.

76 James Parker to Charles Steuart, New York, 8 November 1778, 920 PAR 1, 13/1, LRO.

77 James Parker to Charles Steuart, New York, 29 August 1779, 920 PAR 1 13/1, LRO; James Parker to Charles Steuart, New York, 11 October till 9 November 1779, 920 PAR 1 13/1, LRO.

78 James Parker to Charles Steuart, [Long Island], 6 July 1778, 920 PAR 1 13/1, LRO.

79 James Parker to Charles Steuart, Philadelphia, 9 June 1778, 920 PAR 1 13/1, LRO.

80 James Parker to Charles Steuart, Philadelphia, 3 May 1778, 920 PAR 1 13/1, LRO.

81 James Parker to Charles Steuart, Philadelphia, 9 April 1778, 920 PAR 1 13/1, LRO.

82 James Parker to Charles Steuart, [New York], 3 February 1779, 920 PAR 1 13/1, LRO.

83 James Parker to Charles Steuart, Philadelphia, 19 May 1778, 920 PAR 1 13/1, LRO.

84 James Parker to Charles Steuart, Philadelphia, 1 June 1778, 920 PAR 1 13/1, LRO.

85 James Parker to Charles Steuart, New York, 29 August 1779, 920 PAR 1 13/1, LRO.

86 Calhoon, *The Loyalist Perception*, 157, 160. On the garrison town mentality, see Robert M. Calhoon, Timothy M. Barnes, and George A. Rawlyk, eds., *Loyalists and Community in North America* (Westport, CT: Greenwood Press, 1994), especially 6–9.

87 James Parker to Charles Steuart, [New York], 3 February 1779, 920 PAR 1 13/1, LRO.

88 James Parker to Charles Steuart, Charleston, 14 January 1781, 920 PAR 1 13/1, LRO.

89 James Parker to Charles Steuart, [ ], 12 July 1778, 920 PAR 1 13/1, LRO.

90 James Parker to Charles Steuart, New York, 16 July 1777, 920 PAR 1 13/1, LRO.

91 James Parker to Charles Steuart, Philadelphia, 22 December 1777, 920 PAR 1 13/1, LRO.

92 James Parker to Charles Steuart, Charlestown, 16 January 1781, 920 PAR 1 13/1, LRO.

93 Mason, 'The American Loyalist Diaspora,' 239–59.
94 For an insightful analysis of how Loyalists perceived this contractual relationship, see Carole W. Troxler, 'Refuge, Resistance, and Reward: The Southern Loyalists' Claim on East Florida,' *Journal of Southern History* 55 (1989): 563–96.
95 Christopher Sparshott, 'Personal Visions of the British Empire: Re-examining the Loyalist Experience at the end of the American Revolution' (unpublished paper delivered to the Newberry Seminar on Early American History and Culture, Chicago, 17 November 2005), 4.
96 The phrase comes from Maya Jasanoff, 'An Imperial Disaster? The Loyalist Diaspora after the American Revolution' (unpublished lecture given at the University of British Columbia, Vancouver, 20 October 2010).
97 Quoted in Neil MacKinnon, *This Unfriendly Soil: The Loyalist Experience in Nova Scotia, 1783–1791* (Montreal; Kingston, ON: McGill-Queen's University Press, 1986), 183.
98 Sparshott, 'Personal Visions of the British Empire,' 35; and MacKinnon, *This Unfriendly Soil*, 183.
99 John McLeod, *Beginning Postcolonialism* (Manchester: Manchester University Press, 1998), 207.
100 Quoted in J.M. Bumsted, 'The Cultural Landscape of Early Canada,' in *Strangers within the Realm: Cultural Margins of the First British Empire*, ed. Bernard Bailyn and Philip D. Morgan (Chapel Hill: University of North Carolina Press, 1991), 383.
101 Norman Knowles, *Inventing the Loyalists: The Ontario Loyalist Tradition & the Creation of Usable Pasts* (Toronto: University of Toronto Press, 1997), 18.
102 Walker, *The Black Loyalists*.
103 On the complexity of identity formation in the early American republic, see Riordan, *Many Identities, One Nation*; and Smith-Rosenberg, *This Violent Empire*. For the subsequent collision of identities on the North American continent, see Taylor, *Civil War*.
104 For New Brunswick, see Ann Gorman Condon, *The Envy of the American States: The Loyalist Dream for New Brunswick* (Fredericton, NB: New Ireland Press, 1984), 107–12; and David G. Bell, *Early Loyalist Saint John: The Origins of New Brunswick Politics, 1783–1786* (Fredericton, NB: New Ireland Press, 1983), 104–15. I would like to thank Jerry Bannister for drawing my attention to these incidents.
105 On nineteenth-century developments in Canada, see Knowles, *Inventing the Loyalists*; David Mills, *The Idea of Loyalty in Upper Canada, 1784–1850* (Montreal, Kingston, ON: McGill-Queen's University Press, 1988); and Bumsted, *Understanding the Loyalists*, 13–14.

3

Imperial-Aboriginal Friendship in Eighteenth-century Mi'kma'ki/Wulstukwik

JOHN G. REID

It is hardly surprising that historical studies of the American Revolution and its era traditionally have emphasized polarization and the rending of the British Atlantic world. The Declaration of Independence can provide a convenient point of differentiation, as salient for historians as it was for those who grappled at the time with a series of disputes that were often obscure and disordered. To be able to distinguish clearly between Loyalists and Patriots, despite the affinities they might have in social background and even political philosophy, was a luxury that brought with it a degree of clarity that has formed the basis for countless studies of the Revolution and its consequences. In a limited sense, these categories are justifiable enough. The Revolution, after all, did succeed in its goal of independence, while the Loyalist refugees found out through their forced migration that adherence to the cause of the Crown had created for them a costly demarcation. They, in turn, brought significant changes to the areas in which they settled.

Yet, there is a wider context in which continuity, rather than discontinuity, attended the revolutionary and post-revolutionary eras. The Empire itself continued, in North America and elsewhere. More significantly, it continued – as did the British Atlantic world – to embody a complex web of negotiated relationships that varied widely not only in their linkages with the composite Crown at the head of the imperial structure but also in the texture they derived from the nuances and the imperatives of locality and region. The Revolution was not, of course, unimportant to imperial evolution – as P.J. Marshall argues, it stimulated a movement away from the notion of an empire based primarily on a common Britishness to one in which non-British peoples took a variety of prominent, if not necessarily powerful, roles.[1] Yet the complexity of empire both predated the Revolution and survived it.

Nowhere was this complexity more evident than in the experience of native North Americans in their relationships with the Crown. The historiography of native North America in the era of the Revolutionary War and its aftermath has tended to emphasize the involvement of aboriginal nations in the conflict and the new pressures exerted after 1783 both in the new republic and in an attenuated British North America. It is many years now since William H. Nelson argued that loyalism in the thirteen colonies and on their frontiers was conspicuous among cultural and religious minorities, and that many aboriginal participants calculated that 'the British government was the only force they could rely on to check the rapid advance of agricultural settlement.'[2] As Nelson also pointed out, even for those native leaders who might have opted for neutrality, involvement in the revolutionary conflict was difficult to avoid in the actively contested areas. Thus, as Colin G. Calloway observes in an extended treatment of native experiences during the Revolution, 'Indians could not keep the war out of Indian country.'[3] For Timothy J. Shannon, who identifies the especially damaging impact on the Houdenasaunee (Iroquois), 'the . . . Revolution was a period of prolonged trial for Native Americans in general.'[4] Alan Taylor also uses the Houdenasaunee as a key example of the destructive force that could issue from the sundering of traditional lands in the immediate post-war era: 'In competition with one another, the republic and the empire defined a border that controlled the Indians. That division cost the Iroquois their place as the keepers of a borderland between. Formerly a middle ground, Iroquoia became a divided ground.'[5]

Yet, as Taylor also observes in distinguishing his work from the portrayal of peoples further west and earlier in time than Richard White's *The Middle Ground*, there were many variations in aboriginal experience, among which, for Taylor, 'the common ground is the struggle by native peoples to adapt creatively to the transforming power of intruding empires.'[6] In the more northeasterly portions of British North America – which could be seen more realistically as British after the Revolution than before – the transforming power of empire became evident much later than in the settled portions of the rebelling colonies. Older negotiated relationships such as those that joined the Mi'kmaq and Wulstukwiuk with the Crown persisted well beyond the immediate post-war era.[7] In their complexities, which could include the construal of neutrality as a form of cooperation with the Crown, these relationships bore witness not only to a distinctive aboriginal experience of the later part of the 'long' eighteenth century, but also to an empire and a British Atlantic world in which fluid and long-standing linkages could emerge changed but still alive from the revolutionary era. Loyalist settlement, to be sure, combined with Celtic migrations to threaten such intricate balances. Yet, just as the loyal Atlantic can be seen as a continuing and normative phenomenon, so the aboriginal-imperial friendship that had been essayed in Mi'kma'ki and Wulstukwik since the earlier years of the century would retain its currency in important respects and thus create an element of continuity to which the Revolution, in itself, was incidental.[8]

'Friendship' was a frequently used descriptor, on the imperial side, for the imperial-aboriginal relationship in Nova Scotia during the early-to-middle decades of the eighteenth century. The term was embodied in the most formal of imperial documents regarding the colony, and was also used less formally to define imperial goals in making and preserving the treaty relationship that joined the British with the Mi'kmaw and Wulstukwiuk nations. During the American and French Revolutions and their aftermaths, 'friendship' faded from explicit imperial terminology. The word still made occasional appearances, but the reports of governors and other senior officials to London on aboriginal matters now referred more frequently to 'fidelity,' 'allegiance,' and 'loyalty.' That this should be characteristic of the era of loyalism is not surprising. Yet the influence of the earlier ascendancy of 'friendship' did not disappear, but persisted in two important and complementary forms. First, it continued to inform the demands of aboriginal leaders for reciprocity, and during the recurrent warfare that spanned the later years of the 'long' eighteenth century these demands necessarily carried weight. Accordingly, and the second element of the persistence of 'friendship,' imperial officials proved repeatedly to be willing in practice to compromise on the more rigid doctrines they professed to uphold, so that even loyalty and allegiance could come with strings attached. Aboriginal understandings of the nature of friendship remained largely stable during the period, while imperial terminologies proved mutable. This instability partly reflected broader changes taking place within the Empire, as the loss of the rebelling colonies was accompanied by the increasing presence of non-British peoples in Asia and elsewhere who were not easily accommodated within traditional concepts of loyalty. Nevertheless, in Mi'kma'ki and Wulstukwik, an extended history of imperial-aboriginal relations exercised a formative influence even after 'friendship' had waned as a formal imperial value in this part of North America.

'Friendship,' as an expression of good relations between aboriginal populations and the newcomers who arrived in increasing numbers during the seventeenth and eighteenth centuries, was a term applied so frequently in North America that it would be impossible to account comprehensively for its use and evolution. Most famously embedded in the language of British-Houdenasaunee relations as 'the covenant chain of friendship' or 'the chain of friendship,' the word resonates in the English/British documentation surrounding relationships formed or attempted in every part of North America where a significant colonial population existed, even where relations might generally be characterized as anything but friendly.[9] Friendship was not, of course, a term peculiar to the British Empire. As early as in 1603, royal instructions to Pierre Dugua de Mons as lieutenant-general in the French colony of Acadie had enjoined him to reach a relationship of 'paix, alliance, conféderation, et bonne amitié, correspondance et Communication' with aboriginal inhabitants, and the extended use of such terminologies was reflected, for example, in the discussions leading to the crucial French-Houdenasaunee peace agreement of 1701.[10] However, the great variety of contexts in which friendship was sought, proclaimed, or appealed to left little scope for a general definition of what it meant beyond the obvious usage to represent harmonious or peaceful relations. Often a conveniently ambiguous term – bridging the perceptual gap between imperial and aboriginal participants who understood their associations quite differently – in itself it said little about the way in which friendship might relate to other facets of any given relationship.

Even in its broader eighteenth-century sense in the English language, friendship could apply to a wide, though not unlimited, spectrum of affinities, ranging from active support reinforced by fellowship to the simple absence of enmity.[11] As Naomi Tadmor has shown, however, eighteenth-century friendship was particularly characterized by the notion of mutual serviceability in a context where friends were stakeholders in one another's well-being. Although it was common for friends to be united also by bonds of affection – and family members were frequently counted as friends – a social associate of many years' standing might not qualify as a friend in this sense. Friendship could flourish in a relationship of equality or near-equality, but it could also be unequal.[12] In a political sense, the notion of 'the King's friends,' often applied among others to Loyalists in the American Revolution, was one of the most obvious examples of an unequal friendship. Thus, friendship – in an imperial-aboriginal context or in a broader range of individual and collective relationships – implied harmony and mutuality, although as a descriptor it did not necessarily offer a detailed delineation of the dynamics of a given relationship.[13]

More closely defined was the imperial understanding of friendship with the aboriginal populations of eighteenth-century Nova Scotia. In addition to prescribing incentives for intermarriage between colonists and aboriginal inhabitants, the royal instructions issued to Governor Richard Philipps in 1719 defined the governor's responsibilities in the area of aboriginal relations in language that had no precedent in the instructions issued to governors of other colonies, and would remain unique until partially adopted for Georgia in 1754:

> And whereas We have judg'd it highly necessary for His Majesty's Service that you shou'd cultivate and maintain a strict Friendship and good Correspondence with the Indian Nations inhabiting within the precincts of Your Government, that they may be reduc'd by Degrees not only to be good Neighbours to His Majesty's Subjects, but likewise themselves become good subjects to His Majesty; We do therefore direct you upon your Arrival in Nova Scotia to send for the several Heads of the said Indian Nations or Clans, and promise them Friendship and protection on his Majesty's Part. You will likewise bestow on them, as your Discretion shall direct, such presents as you shall carry from hence, in His Majesty's Name, for their use.[14]

Over the terms in office of successive governors, the instruction underwent periodic revisions – most notably the introduction in 1749 of a phrase requiring governors to 'enter into a treaty with them' – though retaining its most essential import and wording.[15] Regarding Nova Scotia, it reached into the Loyalist era in instructions issued to Governor John Parr in 1784 that extended also to Cape Breton and the Island of St John (later known as Prince Edward Island).[16] In the interim, the wording had been used not only for Georgia but also, immediately following the 1763 Treaty of Paris, for Quebec and for East and West Florida.[17] It was later applied to New Brunswick, as included in successive instructions issued to Governor Thomas Carleton in 1784 and (as lieutenant-governor) in 1786.[18] In Nova Scotia – along with Cape Breton and the

Island of St John – its persistence past 1786, when the resident governorship of the province was reduced to a lieutenant-governorship and
new instructions were sent to Guy Carleton, Lord Dorchester, as 'Captain General and Governor in Chief in and over our Province of Nova
Scotia,' is likely despite incomplete documentation.[19] At least until
that time and probably beyond, the instruction applied to governing
officials of all four of the colonies that embodied the British claim to
Mi'kma'ki and Wulstukwik.

An offer of friendship, in the theoretical framework held by some
western European jurists to justify imperial expansion, was capable
of having a coercive purpose, in that an indigenous people refusing
'trade and friendship' could be treated legitimately as an enemy.[20] In
this case, however, the reason for the offer was more pragmatic. The
genesis of the distinctive instruction issued to Philipps in 1719 lay in an
extended re-evaluation of aboriginal relations by the Board of Trade.
Its localized origins were owed, in turn, to the Nova Scotia council-
lor William Shirreff and the colony's lieutenant-governor at the time,
Thomas Caulfeild. Shirreff, with Caulfeild's support, advocated British
emulation of what he took to be French practices of systematic gift-
giving along with encouragement to intermarriage. For Caulfeild, it
was necessary for Nova Scotia's survival that aboriginal inhabitants
should be won over 'by kindly using of them, on which foundation
their friendshipp is wholy founded.'[21] Philipps's instructions of 1719
reflected these arguments and the more general assertion of the Board
of Trade itself that, 'We are convinced from all the Accounts that We
have received from America, that nothing so much contributed to
Strengthen the hands of the French in those parts, as the Friendship
they maintain, and the Intermarriage they make with the Indians.'[22]
Two years later, the Board of Trade issued a lengthy report on the trade
and government of all the British colonies in North America. As well as
improving colonial governance, the report urged that it was essential
to British interests in America to curb French expansion and to cultivate 'a good understanding with the Native Indians.' Accordingly, the
Nova Scotia instruction regarding intermarriage 'should be extended
to all the other British Colonies.' Presents should be regularly distributed, and trade promoted on terms attractive to aboriginal partners.
Moreover, 'the Several Governors of Your Majesty's Plantations should
endeavor to make Treaties and Alliances of Friendship with as many
Indian Nations as they can.'[23] Although this ambitious program was
never carried into full effect, the relevant instruction to Nova Scotia

governors for the ensuing 65 years was founded on the notion that British-aboriginal relations represented a work in progress and must be based on friendship. The interdependence on which mutual service-ability was based would be created through diplomatic activity facilitated by gifts.

The instruction was not without its own complexities. That the incremental process was intended to end in the aboriginal nations' becoming 'good subjects to us' might be taken in isolation to imply that they were already subjects in some sense, just not good ones. However, the preceding opposition of the aboriginal nations to 'our subjects,' to whom they were to become good neighbours, indicates that they were seen differently than as subjects. Similarly, the entering into a treaty could be read, in eighteenth-century usage, as meaning either entering into a formal agreement or simply entering into negotiation. The Board of Trade's phrasing of 1721, 'to make Treaties,' clearly indicated the former, as did the reference to 'a treaty' introduced to the Nova Scotia instructions in 1749, although by the time the equivalent phrase was used in Governor Parr's initial instructions in 1782 (following many years of intermittent treaty-making) it told the governor 'to have interviews from time to time with the several heads of the Indian Nations or Clans, and to endeavour to enter into Treaty with them,' suggesting a negotiated relationship rather than necessarily a further formal agreement. The emphasis on friendship, however, remained unchanged.[24] Ambiguities also existed in the English texts of the major treaties that were concluded. The treaty of 1725, reached in Boston and subsequently ratified by both Mi'kmaq and Wulstukwiuk, distinguished between 'Indians' and 'His Majesties Subjects,' as in the phrase, 'that the Indians shall not molest any of His Majesties Subjects or their Dependants in their Settlements already made or Lawfully to be made.'[25] The British-Mi'kmaw treaty of 1752 gave an opposite indication in providing for dispute resolution between 'the Indians now at peace and others His Majesty's Subjects,' while the Maliseet and Passamaquoddy treaty of 1760 similarly referred to 'the said Tribes . . . and his Majesty's other subjects.'[26] The Mi'kmaw treaties of 1760–61, however, reverted to a variant form of the 1752 phrasing that distinguished between 'my Tribe' and 'any of His Majesty's Subjects or their Dependants in their Settlements already made or to be hereafter made.'[27]

The confusion of terminology, to be sure, had limited significance in that these formulae, like the submission clauses that were embedded in all of the treaties, represented elements of political philosophy that in cross-cultural negotiations were inherently open to a variety of interpretations. The mutability, however, highlighted the consistency with which friendship was held to define the desired relationship, whether in the consistent designation of the treaties as enshrining 'peace and friendship' or in the revealing comment of Governor Charles Lawrence in 1760 that the trade provisions of the treaties had the principal advantage of ensuring 'the friendship of these Indians.'[28]

Friendship carried obligations that could be understood despite cultural barriers, in contrast to a concept such as subjection. In the context of other Algonkian-speaking groups, Sir William Johnson, Superintendent of Northern Indians, commented in 1764 to his fellow-officer Henry Bouquet, 'I fear for the Consequences of the Words, *Subjection* And *Dominion* said to be acknowledged by the Ottawa and the Chipeweighs, they have no words to Express any thing like either.' Trying to impose such a template, for Johnson, could only lead to 'Jealousy and Resentment,' whereas 'for my part I should rather covet to bring them to terms, which I had Reason to Expect they would keep.'[29] Friendship, in its eighteenth-century English sense – varied as were the relationships it might be taken to embrace – depended at its core on the will and the ability to render support and service on a mutual basis. In the absence of more tangible ways to be of service, gratitude might suffice for the time being, but reciprocal support lay at the heart of friendship.[30] Reciprocity and the nurturing of an ongoing relationship were also crucial to aboriginal interpretations of linkages with the British Crown and Empire, and were frequently rendered in English translations as embracing 'friendship.' Definition of the relationship in this way emerged early in the English-Wabanaki interactions that came to be closely linked, through the negotiation of the treaty of 1725 by Penobscot negotiators in Boston, with Mi'kmaw and Wulstukwiuk treaty processes. 'In times of Peace,' commented an early Wabanaki delegation to the Massachusetts council in 1701, 'friends use to discourse with one another.'[31] As Katherine Hermes has shown, reciprocity was also from the beginning a key point of contact between English law and the legal principles of Algonkian-speaking peoples, not only in negotiations that flowed from specific incidents of conflict resolution but also in the more general aboriginal insistence that colonizers must at least recognize and make some atonement for the disruptions that resulted from their presence.[32]

Crucial on the aboriginal side to the expression of friendship, and to fulfilment of the reciprocal obligations it imposed, was gift-giving.

Both a symbolic embodiment of friendship and an economic redress for the costs associated with tolerating a non-native presence, gifts could come in the literal form of presents offered either routinely or at key moments of negotiation, or in the form of trade on favourable terms. The New England merchant Thomas Bannister commented in 1715 that the British in northern New England and Nova Scotia 'must verry clearly perswade' aboriginal inhabitants 'that they shall find them another Sort of People than those in New England' and 'must undersell the French and take especial care the Indians are not cheated in the Prices of their Furrs. These [approaches] in Time, I believe, would beget Trust and Confidence and at last an intire Friendship.'[33] For William Shirreff, meanwhile, gift-giving and trade through a royal magazine to be established at Annapolis Royal would 'by Degrees gain them to the British Interest.'[34]

Although the arguments of merchants such as Bannister and Shirreff were pragmatic, the measures they recommended during the years leading up to the issuance of Philipps's instructions were exactly those that, if carried into effect, were well suited to meeting aboriginal demands and contributing to the peace and friendship that was central to successive treaties from 1725 to the later years of the eighteenth century. Reciprocity would have to prevail if the treaties were to provide for a relationship capable of being nurtured on a continuing basis, and it would entail arrangements that were asymmetrical, to allow for the gift of toleration that proceeded tacitly from the aboriginal side. As the trade official Alexander Grant noted of commerce with the Wulstukwiuk in the era immediately following the treaty of 1760, the agreed tariff was 'much to their advantage, in order to Indian Intercourse, and gain their affections to the British Nation, of whom they had bad impressions, and with whom they were little acquainted.'[35]

That friendship and its obligation of reciprocity should be both formally and informally embraced on the imperial side over an extended portion of the eighteenth century was a product in part of what was for eastern North America an unusual configuration of aboriginal and imperial interests. Nova Scotia – which represented the entirety of the British claim in Mi'kma'ki and Wulstukwik until the separation of the Island of St John in 1769, and which still covered most of the territory until the further separation of New Brunswick and Cape Breton in 1784 – had a continuous British imperial presence from 1710 onwards. British colonization, however, was largely absent. Outside the British presence at Annapolis Royal and intermittently at Canso, existing colonial settlements, primarily around the Bay of Fundy, were Acadian. Even the establishment of Halifax in 1749 and Lunenburg in 1752 brought only a few thousand settlers. The *Grand dérangement* of 1755–62 destroyed the Acadian communities, though not eradicating a diminished Acadian presence elsewhere, while the subsequent repopulation during the 1760s by New England Planters and other British-sponsored groups largely replicated Acadian patterns of settlement and did not fully replace the Acadian numbers. Colonial settlement remained largely peripheral to the far more extensive inland areas that remained aboriginal territory. Thus, imperial-aboriginal relations were pursued not only on the basis of limited imperial influence over territory but also in the absence of colonial settlement that was spatially significant. This was neither a 'middle ground' nor a 'divided ground,' but the site of an imperial claim that had the real (if fragile) substantiation of a long-standing regime, first at Annapolis Royal and then at Halifax, yet where the influence of that regime was exerted only in subregions within the whole. As successive governors acknowledged during the era immediately following the treaties of 1760–61, alienation of aboriginal friendship in these circumstances was not a realistic option.[36]

The Revolutionary War provided further evidence that Mi'kmaw and Wulstukwiuk leaderships continued actively to pursue reciprocity through gift-giving. At times imperial officials competed with one another in their eagerness to comply, even though the languages of friendship and allegiance (in an era when loyalty in the form of allegiance had become central to the coordination of opposition to revolutionary forces) were frequently conflated in the accompanying rhetoric.[37] The onset of hostilities prompted a heated debate between Governor Francis Legge and his critics as to how best to go about securing a solid relationship with the aboriginal population. It was conducted in terms that were ambiguous regarding both the formal status of the aboriginal people and whether they were likely to participate in hostilities, but that betrayed no doubt as to the importance of conciliation. For Legge, reporting to London in late 1775, it was urgently necessary 'to endeavour to engage the Indians of this Province on the part of the Crown.' Sending messengers to the strategically significant St John valley, Legge admitted that expense would be involved, but believed that a hostile aboriginal population 'woud be more formidable to the settlers here than an Army of Americans.'[38] Six months later, however, the soon-to-be provincial superintendent of Indian affairs, Michael Francklin, lamented Legge's failure to ensure that the aboriginal population was 'cherished and taken care of.' His apprehensions that 'they may be seduced to act against us' – based on observations in the vicinity of Fort Cumberland, on the Isthmus of Chignecto – received apparent confirmation when a small number of Mi'kmaq and Wulstukwiuk participated in an unsuccessful rebel attack on the fort in 1776.[39] A further critique of the province's efforts came in the following year from the Miramichi fish merchant John Cort that 'the cultivating the Savages friendship' had been neglected when 'with a few trifling presents and fair words . . . they might be made very serviceable subjects.'[40] Cort's advocacy notwithstanding, in spring 1779 his property was plundered by a group of Mi'kmaq apparently encouraged by revolutionaries. The resulting incident and ensuing negotiations led representatives of all Mi'kmaw communities on what was later to become the Gulf shore of New Brunswick to enter into a treaty with Francklin confirming previous treaties and promising that 'we will behave Quietly and Peaceably towards all his Majesty King George's good subjects treating these upon every occasion in an honest friendly and Brotherly manner.'[41]

Although imperial-aboriginal friendship prevailed, this final Mi'k-maw treaty of the eighteenth-century series also represented the culmination of an intensive series of diplomatic exchanges that had seen some Mi'kmaq and Wulstukwiuk reach agreement with revolutionary emissaries in 1776 and launched at least three years of internal debates among aboriginal leaders as to the direction to be pursued.[42] One Mi'kmaw chief informed the Continental agent John Preble in early 1777 that 'their Tribe is determin'd to Rest easely and remain Neutral during the Contest between the Old England people and Boston men,' while Preble was also convinced that there were Wulstukwiuk leaders who were 'harty in our Cause.'[43] Yet, on the imperial side, a series of diplomatic missions reported with a melding of the languages of friendship and subjection. For Colonel Arthur Goold, following a meeting in the spring of 1777 with the Wulstukwiuk chief Pierre Tomah – 'frere Pierre' to Goold as he recalled Tomah's 'ancienne amitie' with the Crown – the outcome had been to confirm 'the firmest friendship' and to prompt eight chiefs to take oaths of allegiance. To be sure, it was not enough to stop Tomah from steering a pragmatic course for the remainder of the war years, cultivating either side in turn.[44] Richard Bulkeley, Nova Scotia's provincial secretary, confirmed during the summer of 1777 that clothing and ammunition would be sent to Mi'kmaq in the Tatamagouche area who had requested them. 'The Lieutenant Governor,' Bulkeley wrote, 'is always ready to give relief to all the King's good and faithfull Subjects,' although at the same time he was apologetic for responding so slowly to a Mi'kmaw message that had taken seventeen days to reach Halifax.[45] Francklin himself, a year prior to the treaty of 1779, won praise from Lieutenant-Governor Richard Hughes for his convening of 'a Grand Meeting of the Chiefs' at the mouth of the St John River, which had resulted in 'a Treaty of firm Peace and Amity' as well as the taking of oaths of allegiance.[46]

While the languages of friendship and subjection coexisted in communications to London, a consistent theme was the obligation of offering gifts. From the Island of St John, the acting governor, Phillips Callbeck, cited in 1777 'the Indians avowed Dispositions to Rebellion in these parts . . . [and] the Treaties that I have had made with Seven tribes of them to whom, and others that are daily visitting me I am obliged to give provisions and presents.'[47] The gifts that went with Francklin's treaties were measured in sums to which London eventually objected, but from the beginning Francklin had made it clear that they were indispensable. Aboriginal forces, he warned in 1778, could inflict a 'Deadly Wound' on Nova Scotia, destroying the interior settlements and putting pressure on Halifax, and 'Belts of Wampum accompanied with the most liberal Promises of presents' were reaching both Mi'kmaq and Wulstukwiuk from the revolutionaries.[48] Hughes followed up by informing the Secretary of State, Lord George Germain, in early 1779 that the expense of Francklin's treaty on the St John had been £577 2s 9d, a sum that handsomely exceeded the Nova Scotia council's budget of £100 for the purpose. Germain was understanding, agreeing to provide an extra £500, but worse was to come in the wake of Franklin's treaty of 1779 and other distributions of supplies elsewhere in Mi'kma'ki and Wulstukwik.

By October 1779 Francklin was forwarding to Germain accounts totalling £1,543 2s 101/2d. Germain, who earlier in the year had been expressing confidence in the possibility of persuading aboriginal forces in the region to fight for the Crown, now baulked at the cost.[49] Francklin had already expressed scepticism as to whether any military support could be expected, even if gift-giving was intensified, and cited the traditional Mi'kmaw-French affinity as giving reason to believe that a more realistic goal was to keep aboriginal force from being deployed on the other side now that France had joined the war.[50] Hughes, meanwhile, stood firm on the need to sustain the necessary expenditures for presents, commenting that 'the expediency of preserving the Indians in their present Sentiments of Allegiance and Tranquility (which can only be done by these Supplies) remains still in its full Force.'[51] This eloquent statement that allegiance here was a thoroughly contingent value, and dependent on the maintenance of friendship in its time-honoured form, encapsulated well the experience of the war years.

Beginning during the late years of the Revolutionary War and continuing after the Peace of Paris, however, the Loyalist migration changed the spatial dynamics abruptly and irrevocably. Both the Loyalists themselves and the Scottish migrants whose inflow proceeded in parallel – though the Scots were centred primarily on eastern Nova Scotia, Cape Breton, and the Island of St John, rather than distributed throughout as were the Loyalists – presented a lethal threat to the aboriginal economy and the environmental balances on which it depended. Land encroachment, the severing of transportation routes that were essential to the maintenance of the necessarily mobile resource harvest, and the depletion of the resources themselves all proceeded at a brisk pace. There were local nuances, associated with the persistence of more extensive 'back countries' in Cape Breton and New Brunswick, by comparison with the more complete encroachments that quickly emerged in peninsular Nova Scotia and the Island of St John. Nevertheless, the Mi'kmaw elder Peter Paul, born in 1779 and thus experiencing the Loyalist era as a child and a young man, was undoubtedly expressing a sweeping reality when eventually he looked back with dismay on the changes he had seen during his then-eighty-six years of life and declared that '[the] Indian . . . have no country now.'[52]

The sudden introduction of colonial settlement as a major factor influencing the imperial-aboriginal relationship could be expected to alter the tenor of the exchanges taking place, not least because imperial claims to territory were now increasingly underpinned by the encroachment and environmental degradation that came as part and parcel of settlement. Yet those Mi'kmaq and Wulstukwiuk with whom imperial representatives came in contact retained the ability to manage their accessibility and to set the agenda for meetings during which the Crown's duty of reciprocity would be discussed. Late in the Revolutionary War, Michael Francklin made the important point to London that unless he had gifts to offer, even he, as an experienced imperial-aboriginal diplomat, would find it impossible to get a hearing from aboriginal leaders. 'It has ever been the Custom,' Francklin reported, 'even in times of the most Profound Peace, to Assist the

Indians Occasionally with Provisions from the Kings Stores, but now it is indispensably necessary, for it is totally impossible to see, or be seen by the Indians, or can a Messenger be sent to, or from them, without an Expence of Provisions, exclusive of such, who by age, Sickness or Accident are in such distress as to require assistance.'[53] The emerging pattern was that those aboriginal individuals who were most acutely damaged by dispossession were visible, while communities and leaderships that retained coherence also retained the ability to be accessible or inaccessible – and thus to tailor meetings with imperial officials to fit the expression of demands for discharge of the reciprocal obligations of the Crown that alone could provide even the most minimal redress for the results of colonization.

Such demands frequently characterized the recorded aboriginal-imperial meetings of the post-revolutionary era. Francklin's successor, George Henry Monk, grew accustomed to fielding insistent claims for gifts, and was confronted on other occasions with pointed directives. On 23 January 1794, Monk wrote apologetically to Governor John Wentworth of Nova Scotia regarding 'the incessant and pressing Applications made by the Indians for more general Supplies.' Monk continued:

> They have repeatedly urged me to write for them to your Excellency, but their remarks and representations were such that I wished rather to discourage than to communicate them. They persisted in their request, and observed that every one refused to write for them, because it was the duty of the Superintendent to inform the Governor of whatever the Indians had to say, and added that if I would not write for them, they would go in a Body to Halifax, and speak for themselves to your Excellency.[54]

Monk conceded, and wrote up a petition that complained of the encroaching settlements and made specific reference to the treaties: 'That when they made peace with the English, there was Country enough in Nova Scotia for all the English, French, and Indians then in the Province,' but since then the promise of British brotherhood had been betrayed and gifts had been inadequate. Now, 'the Mickmacks have little or no hunting Ground; no regular Supplies; no Brothers, except among themselves; and know not where to go or what to do.'[55] Although Monk recorded a series of testy exchanges with Mi'kmaq with whom he came in contact that winter, the former provincial chief justice, Isaac

Deschamps, was convinced that for the Mi'kmaq there was no lack of 'Inclination to remain on Friendly terms with the inhabitants and peaceable' if supplies were provided them.[56] It was a friendship, however, that continued to depend on reciprocity. In February 1794, Monk met the Mi'kmaw Francis Emable, who had been hunting all winter between Canso and Antigonish, with poor results and who asked Monk bluntly, 'what was to be done about the Indians?' Asked what he meant, Emable questioned further, 'what are they to do to live? What has the Governor ordered for them?'[57] In the following month another Mi'kmaw, Louis Anthony, informed Monk that 'the Indians ought to get more and that the Governor would give them more and that all the Indians would see the Governor about it soon.'[58] Cape Breton Mi'kmaq, two years later, took a more direct approach. The colony's acting governor, David Mathews, reported to London that during the winter of 1796 'many families' had simply moved into his house for periods of weeks at a time, 'when they considered themselves intitled to remain and be supported by the King's representative.'[59] The following winter, for Mathews, was no better: 'these Savages . . . continue to be a very heavy and solid burthen on my Private Property as they consider my House a rightful home whenever they choose to come to Sydney, and, seldom a day passes without one or more families of them, taking up their Quarters with me.'[60]

Some years later, Governor Wentworth of Nova Scotia – who was a firm advocate of the need to distribute gifts and willing on occasion to do battle with London for the budgetary capacity to do so – attributed to Mi'kmaq whom he suspected of French sympathies an explicit demand for reciprocity, referring to 'Support from His Majesty, which they considered as an obligation of Loyalty.'[61] A petition to Governor Sir John Sherbrooke later in the era of the Napoleonic Wars from a group of Mi'kmaw families living in the Halifax area struck a different tone in noting that they were in 'a very suffering Condition at this season as the Game has become so scarce that they cannot live in the Woods, and their Business of making Baskets, Ax-handles &c. is so over done that they cannot find Sale for what they make,' but still placed reliance on the governor as 'the representative of King George Who has always been their Friend.'[62] For the land surveyor Titus Smith, travelling through northern Nova Scotia in 1802, it was noticeable that, 'Notwithstanding the low condition to which the Indians are reduced they still retain a considerable portion of national pride.'[63] However, for Smith, it was not easy to make contact with Mi'kmaq whose geographical knowledge he wished to draw upon: 'saw very frequently,' he recorded near Falmouth one day, 'very old blazed Paths of the Indians, heard some Guns near and saw the Tracks of Indians, but did not find their Camp.'[64] The same elusiveness consistently frustrated the efforts of imperial officials and others to estimate the aboriginal population. Although some tried to do so, the New Brunswick Loyalist and former military officer John Coffin had to admit in 1806 that, 'as to the number of Indians in this and the neighbouring province [Nova Scotia], you might as well attempt to number the Spruce trees.'[65]

Despite the mounting disruptions brought about by colonization, therefore, calls for reciprocity continued to characterize Mi'kmaw and Wulstukwiuk representations during the meetings they orchestrated. Indeed, given the displacement and resource depletion of the era, such calls intensified. Although the language of friendship was dwindling on the imperial side, demands for gifts continued to be compelling, for reasons inseparable from the threat of aboriginal force that was apprehended on the imperial side, even if not explicitly communicated on the aboriginal. An increasingly dispossessed and greatly outnumbered aboriginal population inevitably had less ability to present an armed threat on the scale that governors and others had necessarily feared prior to the major migrations. In time of war, however, they might yet prove – as the Loyalist settler and half-pay officer Daniel Lyman argued for New Brunswick – 'sufficiently numerous to be very troublesome, particularly if they are encouraged by our enemies.'[66] Settlement had caused enormous disruption for the aboriginal population, but it had also created a host of isolated settlements that would be difficult to defend. The renewal of warfare with France in 1792 – along with frequent tensions and, ultimately, warfare in 1812 with the United States – increased the possibility that those settlements might indeed need defending.

Accordingly, Governor Thomas Carleton of New Brunswick, who earlier in his governorship had attributed Wulstukwiuk obstruction of settlement in the upper St John valley to 'the insolence of the Savages,' had become convinced by 1794 of 'the Importance of cultivating a friendly disposition in the Savages, and securing their future attachment.'[67] For Governor Wentworth of Nova Scotia in 1796, the advantage of distributing gifts to needy Mi'kmaq was that 'these People would probably otherwise have been disaffected and required Coercion.'[68] That the outlay involved had inflated George Henry Monk's accounts far beyond budget prompted Wentworth, like Francklin and Hughes before him, to defend the need vigorously on military grounds: 'the Supply could not be withheld, but they should be driven by irresistible necessity to plunder the dispersed Settlers, which would soon have brought on murders and devastation in the interior Settlements and occasioned a necessity to employ at least one good Regiment to protect the Scattered Inhabitants and destroy the Indians.' As matters stood, however, Wentworth had 'instructed them in their Loyalty and received engagements of their fidelity.'[69]

Such imperatives persisted throughout Wentworth's long governorship. By late 1807, as war with France continued and war with the United States became a pressing possibility, the governor was assuring London that he had instructed Monk to 'collect and secure the obedience of these People [Mi'kmaq], and their aid in case of necessity. Otherwise, they might prove very mischievous upon the scattering unprotected settlements and make it necessary to employ some strength for their defence – As it is the fixed Habit of these Savages to engage with those who will subsist, clothe, and please them with trifling Presents.'[70] Even so, Monk believed that, in the event of an invasion of Nova Scotia, 'it appears generally to be their intention . . . to remain neuter until they can form an Opinion of the Strength of the Enemy and then in their own words "to join the strongest Party."' Diplomatic exchanges with 'the Indians of Canada' had reinforced this intention for some, although Monk believed that the solution lay in 'management and relief' and was careful to note that 'in some other Districts the Indians are better disposed, and, in Cumberland they have declared that it is their wish to remain neuter but if they are compelled to fight, it shall be for their King George.'[71]

In raising the question of aboriginal neutrality, Monk touched an issue that had been unresolved in Nova Scotia for a number of years. Wentworth had been a consistent advocate of recruiting aboriginal forces for military service in the British cause. Proposing to London in 1793 the raising of a Mi'kmaw corps of sixty to one hundred men had brought Wentworth only discouragement from the secretary of state, Henry Dundas.[72] However, the governor persisted in regarding the Mi'kmaq as at least a potential defence force, and attempted to make gift-giving conditional on their agreement to serve as such. Claiming partial success in this effort, he reported in late 1793 that he had 'secured usefulness from some, and subjection from all of them, greatly to comfort of the dispersed Cottagers.'[73] Wentworth's most uncompromising statement on the matter came three years later, when he instructed military officers in the Guysborough area on the distribution of gifts:

> It will also be useful to inform the [Mi'kmaw] men, that I expect them to be faithfull to the King, and to take arms with us, in case of an invasion – all those that are in this District [Halifax] have so engaged. The women and children are all to encamp on an Island in the Bason, and receive Rations, while the men assist us in defending the Country, according to their own manner, and not attached to any Regiment. Major Monk will command them. If any man refuses this just testimony of Loyalty and love of his Country Whether Indian, Acadian, British or Black man, let him depart to Old France, whither I will certainly send him, when his recusance his [sic] established.[74]

Although Wentworth continued as late as 1807 to speculate on the value of an aboriginal defence force, the interim years saw strong suggestions, peaking in the spring and summer of 1804, that the arrival of a rumoured French force would have prompted Mi'kmaq in significant numbers to join the invaders. 'The Indians,' Wentworth assured the acting governor of New Brunswick, 'are intirely unequal to giving us any serious trouble,' but the notion of enlisting aboriginal defenders was, for the time being, conspicuously absent.[75]

The outbreak of the War of 1812 prompted new discussions about enlisting aboriginal military support, and the secretary of state, the Earl of Bathurst, advanced to the Nova Scotia governor, Sir John Coape Sherbrooke, a convoluted argument that, if the aboriginal forces of the region were likely to be drawn into hostilities on one side or the other, it might as well be the British side, provided their 'Excesses' could be kept under control. Lieutenant-Colonel Joseph Gubbins reported the following year, however, that, as least as far as New Brunswick was concerned, any such plans had been abandoned. This was a good thing in Gubbins's view, because they would have invited retaliation.[76] In the meantime, New Brunswick's acting governor, Major-General George Stracey Smyth, had reported with evident relief that a series of agreements had been concluded with aboriginal groups in Charlotte County, the St John valley, the Miramichi, and elsewhere, 'for the purpose of securing their Neutrality.'[77] From an imperial perspective, this benevolent neutrality, it seemed, was the ideal outcome of negotiations with aboriginal inhabitants who were not to be encouraged to behave as subjects but could still be approached as friends.

Neither during the Revolutionary War, therefore, nor in the decades that followed did the Mi'kmaq or Wulstukwiuk fit any pattern of aboriginal loyalism that involved fighting for or as allies of the Crown. Here, no Thayendanegea (Joseph Brant) emerged as an iconic figure urging and practising armed struggle on the Loyalist side; nor did a constellation of nations, as in the southern colonies, find it necessary, though ultimately futile, as Jim Piecuch has pointed out, 'to fight alongside the British to insure that they retained their land.'[78] Rather, although there were variations and dissidence at some points, the notion of reciprocity based on aboriginal tolerance of the non-native presence, and the offering of gifts and support in return, was a thread in imperial-aboriginal exchanges that continued throughout an era that was remarkable for the infrequency of aboriginal participation in actual armed conflict of any kind, despite the fears regularly expressed by imperial administrators. Beyond 1815, aboriginal statements such as those reported in 1847 by Abraham Gesner, Commissioner for Indian Affairs for Nova Scotia, showed a marked consistency:

> Naturally jealous, they look to the fulfilment of the Treaty, the terms of which are stamped on the minds of each succeeding generation. The small presents made to them from the grants of the Legislature, they consider as testimonies of respect, and they pride themselves upon such bounties rather than consider them in any way humiliating. For the lands, forests, and fisheries, long since taken from them, they are of the opinion that the Government should make a far greater compensation than they have ever received, or the permanent protection contemplated by the Chief at the time when they laid down their arms and 'smoked the pipe of peace.'[79]

On the imperial side, however, consistency was just as markedly absent, at least in the terminologies that governed understandings of the status of aboriginal inhabitants vis-à-vis Crown and Empire. While royal dominion over territory was a constant assumption, the instruction of 1719 – and its succeeding appearances – enshrined friendship as the starting point of a hoped-for journey to subjecthood that was explicitly dependent on diplomatic initiatives and aboriginal assent.[80] The ambiguities in imperial terminology that appeared in the wording of the treaties were minor compared to those that emerged during the revolutionary and post-revolutionary eras, when allegiance and the obligation of military service became conflated at times with the demands of friendship.

In part, the change reflected wider imperial tendencies. This was an era when every North American colony divided over a multiplicity of issues to which the concept of allegiance alone, following the Declaration of Independence, was capable of bringing any semblance of manageability. It was also an era when the Empire as a whole was adjusting to the addition of diverse non-British peoples through a confusing array of legalities that clothed an increasing authoritarianism at the imperial centre and led to the eclipse of the competing notion of an empire representing a community of British communities.[81] Finally, this was a time of persistent imperial tension and warfare, when governors and other administrators prior to 1815 had to cope with the daily pressure of balancing potential assets and threats – a process that, as Timothy D. Willig has demonstrated, could lead to significant variations, and thus to 'multiple chains of friendship,' even within the limited geographical compass of Upper Canada.[82] That inconsistency reigned in the approaches of imperial officials to Mi'kmaq and Wulstukwiuk, therefore, was not surprising in itself.

What was, on the face of it, more surprising was that aboriginal leaders persisted in seeking reciprocity despite abrupt and wholesale encroachment by colonial settlement from the early 1780s onwards. The adverse results of that settlement – measured in displacement, hunger, and disease – made the demand for the Crown's support ever more urgent, while the dilemmas of imperial officials meant that those demands could never be ignored, even if the response fell short of the need. Consequently, no matter how gift-giving might be rendered in the guise of humanitarian relief and moral responsibility, it continued at a deeper level to be a necessary response to aboriginal insistence. The Mi'kmaq and Wulstukwiuk were not loyalist in the accepted mould of aboriginal Loyalists elsewhere, who made the difficult and complex decision to fight, only to pay the price in abrupt and devastating land loss.[83] Although land loss was a cumulative and destructive element of the Mi'kmaw and Wulstukwiuk experience as well during the later years of the 'long' eighteenth century, their prevailing link to the Crown was that of friendship, in the particular sense that belonged to the long-standing relationship whose origins were in both an extended aboriginal diplomacy and an imperial approach that belonged to the earlier years of the old colony of Nova Scotia.

Friendship in this sense, as imperial officials were continually forced to recognize, was just as crucial to the maintenance of empire as more active aboriginal loyalism might be elsewhere. As Jerry Bannister and Liam Riordan point out in this volume, the essence of loyalism was 'an affirmation of fidelity,' and, as Keith Mason shows, also in this volume, the stresses of displacement became integral to the experience of the Loyalist refugees. In Mi'kma'ki and Wulstukwik, fidelity was not founded on fealty to the Crown, but a value given to a relationship based on friendship – reciprocal at best, contingent and contested in its everyday reality. Displacement at the hands of migrants who included prominently the Loyalist refugees did not erase the fidelity, even though it had consequences that stretched friendship and reciprocity to the limit.

Just one strand among the many that gave the loyal Atlantic its distinctive – if at times mutable – texture, this affinity persisted throughout the revolutionary and post-revolutionary eras. Even the violent dispossession that ultimately accompanied colonial settlement could not forever obscure its significance, which was necessarily rediscovered as Canada's 1982 Constitution prompted the treaty-based legal cases that were successively adjudicated by the Supreme Court of Canada during the late twentieth century and beyond. That eighteenth-century treaties of peace and friendship retained their currency even after more than two centuries of turbulent change underscores the centrality of imperial-aboriginal friendship in the loyalist era itself. To define loyalism only in terms of allegiance to the Crown in the face of a revolutionary threat is to underestimate the tenacity of negotiated relationships with the Crown and its representatives that long predated the revolutionary crisis. Friendship and reciprocity were continuing values even in an evolving and globalizing empire.

NOTES

1 See P.J. Marshall, *The Making and Unmaking of Empires: Britain, India, and America, c. 1750–1783* (Oxford: Oxford University Press, 2005), 373–6.
2 William H. Nelson, *The American Tory* (Oxford: Clarendon Press, 1961), 87, 102–3; quotation from 87.
3 Colin G. Calloway, *The American Revolution in Indian Country: Crisis and Diversity in Native American Communities* (Cambridge: Cambridge University Press, 1995), 30.

4 Timothy J. Shannon, *Iroquois Diplomacy on the Early American Frontier* (New York: Penguin Books, 2009), 172.

5 Alan Taylor, *The Divided Ground: Indians, Settlers, and the Northern Borderland of the American Revolution* (New York: Knopf, 2006), 405–6.

6 Ibid., 11. See also Richard White, *The Middle Ground: Indians, Empires, and Republics in the Great Lakes Region, 1650–1815* (Cambridge: Cambridge University Press, 1991).

7 This essay follows the convention by which 'Mi'kmaq' is used as a plural noun, while 'Mi'kmaw' is both the singular noun and the corresponding adjective. Also, I have used the terms Mi'kma'ki and Wulstukwik to refer respectively to the territories of the Mi'kmaq and Wulstukwiuk (Maliseet). Mi'kma'ki extended throughout the present-day Maritime provinces (as well as to the Gaspé and Gulf islands) with the exception of the Wulstukw (St John) Valley and territories surrounding it and to the west, while Wulstukwik is defined as including the entire Wulstukw Valley. For the suggestion that neither Wulstukwiuk nor Mi'kmaq had exclusive use of the lower Wulstukw region but that both were present there in this era, see Greg Marquis, 'The Story of a Map: W.F. Ganong and Tribal Boundaries in New Brunswick,' in *Papers of the Thirty-Ninth Algonquian Conference*, ed. Karl S. Hele and Regna Darnell (London: University of Western Ontario, 2008), 479–517. This essay deals primarily with an area corresponding to the colonies that came out of 'old' Nova Scotia: Cape Breton, Island of St John/ Prince Edward Island, New Brunswick, and Nova Scotia.

8 For an outline of more general considerations pertaining to the argument sketched here, see John G. Reid and Elizabeth Mancke, 'From Global Processes to Continental Strategies: The Emergence of British North America to 1783,' in *Canada and the British Empire*, ed. Phillip Buckner (Oxford: Oxford University Press, 2008), 22–42.

9 The frequency with which the term 'friendship' was used can be confirmed by even the most cursory survey of Alden T. Vaughan, general ed., *Early American Indian Documents: Treaties and Laws, 1607–1789*, 20 vols. (Washington, DC: University Publications of America, 1979–2004). On friendship as envisaged by the Hudson's Bay Company, see J.R. Miller, *Compact, Contract, Covenant: Aboriginal Treaty-Making in Canada* (Toronto: University of Toronto Press, 2009). On the Covenant Chain and its evolution and contexts, see, for example, Francis Jennings et al., eds., *The History and Culture of Iroquois Diplomacy: An Interdisciplinary Guide to the Treaties of the Six Nations and Their League* (Syracuse, NY: Syracuse University Press, 1985); Daniel K. Richter, *The Ordeal of the Longhouse: The Peoples of the Iroquois League in the Era of European Colonization* (Chapel Hill, NC: University of North Carolina Press,

1992); Daniel K. Richter and James H. Merrell, eds., *Beyond the Covenant Chain: The Iroquois and Their Neighbors in Indian North America, 1600–1800* (Syracuse, NY: Syracuse University Press, 1987); and Timothy J. Shannon, *Indians and Colonists at the Crossroads of the Empire: The Albany Congress of 1754* (Ithaca, NY: Cornell University Press, 2000). Among studies that pursue these issues into the late eighteenth and early nineteenth centuries, see Colin G. Calloway, *Crown and Calumet: British-Indian Relations, 1783–1815* (Norman: University of Oklahoma Press, 1987); and Timothy D. Willig, *Restoring the Chain of Friendship: British Policy and the Indians of the Great Lakes, 1783–1815* (Lincoln: University of Nebraska Press, 2008).

10 Royal Letter to de Mons, 8 September 1603, France, Archives des Colonies, C11D, I, ff. 17–21. On the peace of 1701, see Gilles Havard, *The Great Peace of Montreal of 1701: French-Native Diplomacy in the Seventeenth Century* (Montreal; Kingston, ON: McGill-Queen's University Press, 2001). For friendship in a Delaware-Swedish context, see Robert A. Williams, Jr, *Linking Arms Together: American Indian Treaty Visions of Law and Peace, 1600–1800* (New York: Routledge, 1999), 109.

11 See 'Friend,' 'Friendship,' *Oxford English Dictionary Online*, http:// dictionary.oed.com (accessed 5 August 2010).

12 Naomi Tadmor, *Family and Friends in Eighteenth-Century England: Household, Kinship, and Patronage* (Cambridge: Cambridge University Press, 2001), 168, 171–9, 211–15, 218, 236, 243–4. On a view of friendship emerging in the late eighteenth century that was more social and sentimental than that portrayed by Tadmor, see Sarah Knott, *Sensibility and the American Revolution* (Chapel Hill: University of North Carolina Press, 2009), 113–22. Within a 'sentimental coterie,' argues Knott, friendship 'shucked off its early modern tinge of patronage relations, hierarchy, and economic self-interest' (113).

13 Wallace Brown, *The King's Friends: The Composition and Motives of the American Loyalist Claimants* (Providence, RI: Brown University Press, 1965). For a revealing discussion of the choice of the Labrador merchant George Cartwright in the same era to treat Inuit visitors as friends, 'a label he otherwise reserved for British gentlemen,' see Stephen Hay, 'A Popular Culture of Paternalism: Alcohol in the Fisheries and Fur Trade of Cartwright's Labrador, 1770–1786' (paper presented to the Canadian Historical Association 2009 Annual Meeting, Ottawa, 26 May 2009), 32–3.

14 Instructions to Richard Philipps, 14 July 1719, National Archives of the United Kingdom (hereafter cited as UKNA), CO5/189, 427–8.

15 Revisions to the wording of the instruction can be traced in Leonard W. Labaree, *Royal Instructions to British Colonial Governors, 1670–1776*, vol. 2 (New York: American Historical Association, 1935), 469–70; for Georgia, see 474.

16 Instructions to John Parr, [1784], UKNA, CO218/9, ff. 122–3. The instruction was new in 1784 to the Island of St John, since it had not been included in the only preceding instructions – those issued to Governor Walter Patterson: Instructions to Walter Patterson, 27 July 1769, UKNA, CO227/1, ff.15–38.

17 The instruction was also adapted at the same time for Grenada, with the substitution of 'Caribbeans or wild Negroes in the several islands' for 'Indians'; Labaree, *Royal Instructions*, vol. 2, 478–9.

18 Instructions to Thomas Carleton, 18 August 1784, Provincial Archives of New Brunswick, RS330, B1b, Instruction 63; Instructions to Thomas Carleton, 23 August 1786, ibid., RS330, B4b, Instruction 64.

19 Dorchester's instructions appear in the relevant Nova Scotia documentary series only in a truncated form. For reasons unknown, the document ends in mid-sentence, partway through Instruction 18: Instructions to Guy Carleton, Lord Dorchester, 23 August 1786, UKNA, CO218/10, ff. 1–16. An extended draft, including the key aboriginal instruction, exists in another series – UKNA, CO189/2, 334–491 – although it is in rough form, with some blank pages and others where the text at some point has been lightly crossed through in pencil. The aboriginal instruction appears on 457–8, with the pencil crossing appearing on 458 but not on 457. Surviving sealed original copies of governors' instructions are rare because they were transmitted to the governors personally; in this case, the situation is complicated by the fact that Dorchester's widow had most of his papers burned soon after his death. See Labaree, *Royal Instructions*, 'Introduction,' vol. 1, xi–xii; Library and Archives Canada, 'Sir Guy Carleton, 1st Baron Dorchester fonds,' http://collectionscanada.gc.ca (accessed 5 August 2010). However, the existence of instructions of the same date to Dorchester in his New Brunswick capacity (Instructions to Guy Carleton, Lord Dorchester, 23 August 1786, UKNA, CO189/1, 145–253) – which include the aboriginal instruction on 227–8 – and the rough draft of the instructions covering Nova Scotia, Cape Breton, and the Island of St John suggest strongly that the aboriginal instruction would have remained in force in these areas also.

20 See Ken MacMillan, 'Imperial Constitutions: Sovereignty and Law in the British Atlantic,' in *Britain's Oceanic Empire: Atlantic and Indian Ocean Worlds, 1500–1850*, ed. H.V. Bowen, Elizabeth Mancke, and John G. Reid (Cambridge: Cambridge University Press, forthcoming).

21 [Shirreff] to Board of Trade, 18 March 1715, UKNA, CO217/1, No. 96; Shirreff to Board of Trade, 24 May 1715, Ibid., No. 120; Caulfeild to Board of Trade, 1 November 1715, UKNA, CO217/2, No. 8.

22 Board of Trade to Lords Justices, 19 June 1719, UKNA, CO218/1, f. 207.

23 Board of Trade to George I, 8 September 1721, UKNA, CO324/10, 412–18.

24 Ibid.; Instructions to John Parr, 23 August 1782, UKNA, CO218/9, f. 33.

25 Articles of Peace for Nova Scotia, 15 December 1725, UKNA, CO217/4, ff.348–9.

26 Treaty of Peace and Friendship, 22 November 1752, UKNA, CO217/40, f. 229; Treaty of Peace and Friendship, 23 February 1760, UKNA, CO217/18, f. 27.

27 See, for example, Treaty of Peace and Friendship, 25 June 1761, Nova Scotia Archives and Records Management (hereafter cited as NSARM), RG1, Vol. 165.

28 Lawrence to Board of Trade, 11 May 1760, UKNA, CO217/17, ff. 59–60; for 'peace and friendship,' see the treaties cited in notes 26 and 27 above.

29 Sir William Johnson to Henry Bouquet, 6 December 1764, in James Sullivan et al., eds., *The Papers of Sir William Johnson*, vol. 4 (Albany: University of the State of New York, 1921–62), 610–11; see also Johnson to Cadwallader Colden, 11 December 1764, 616.

30 Tadmor, *Family and Friends in Eighteenth-Century England*, 179.

31 Massachusetts Council Minutes, 27 December 1701, UKNA, CO5/862, No. 101(ii).

32 Katherine Hermes, ' "Justice Will Be Done Us": Algonquian Demands for Reciprocity in the Courts of the European Settlers,' in *The Many Legalities of Early America*, ed. Christopher L. Tomlins and Bruce H. Mann (Chapel Hill: University of North Carolina Press, 2001), 128 and *passim*.

33 Thomas Bannister to Board of Trade, 15 July 1715, UKNA, CO5/866, No. 53. On gift-giving, see also Miller, *Compact, Contract, Covenant*, 22–5.

34 William Shirreff to Board of Trade, 24 May 1715, UKNA, CO217/1, No. 120.

35 Alexander Grant to Board of Trade, 18 November 1763, UKNA, CO217/20, f. 296.

36 Allusion is made here, as above, to two justly celebrated studies: White, *Middle Ground*; and Taylor, *Divided Ground*. For supporting analysis regarding Nova Scotia, see John G. Reid et al., *The 'Conquest' of Acadia, 1710: Imperial, Colonial, and Aboriginal Constructions* (Toronto: University of Toronto Press, 2004), 206–9 and *passim*; and John G. Reid, '*Pax Britannica* or *Pax Indigena*? Planter Nova Scotia (1760–1782) and Competing Strategies of Pacification,' *Canadian Historical Review* 85 (2004): 669–92.

37 On the role of allegiance, see Maya Jasanoff, 'The Other Side of the Revolution: Loyalists in the British Empire,' *William and Mary Quarterly*, 3rd series, 65 (2008): 223–4.

38 Letter of Francis Legge, 4 November 1775, UKNA, CO217/52, f. 8.

39 Francklin to John Pownall, 4 May 1776, UKNA, CO217/52, f. 144. On Francklin, see Lewis R. Fischer, 'Michael Francklin,' in George W. Brown et al., *Dictionary of Canadian Biography*, vol. 4 (Toronto: University of Toronto Press, 1966–), 272–6; on the siege of Fort Cumberland, see Ernest Clarke, *The Siege of Fort Cumberland, 1776: An Episode in the American Revolution* (Montreal; Kingston, ON: McGill-Queen's University Press, 1999).

40 Memorial of John Cort, [8 April 1777], UKNA, CO217/27, f. 299.

41 Treaty, 22 September 1779, UKNA, CO217/54, ff. 221–2.

42 Minutes of Watertown Conference, 10–17 July 1776, in *Early American Indian Documents* (see note 9), vol. 20, 828–41; Memorial of Joseph Bennett, 7 January 1777, UKNA, CO217/28, ff. 11–3; Reid, '*Pax Britannica* or *Pax Indigena*?,' 688.

43 John Preble to Massachusetts Council, 27 January 1777, Massachusetts State Archives, Massachusetts Archives, vol. 196, 171a.

44 Goold to Tomah, 11 May 1777, UKNA, CO217/53, f. 112; Goold to Mariot Arbuthnot, 28 May 1777, UKNA, CO217/53, ff. 120–1; Richard I. Hunt, 'Pierre Tomah,' in *Dictionary of Canadian Biography*, vol. 4 (see note 39), 735–6.

45 Bulkeley to [Chief Anthony Urry], 2 July 1777, Inland Letter-Book, 1760–84, NSARM, RG1, vol. 136, 252.

46 Hughes to Lord George Germain, 12 October 1778, UKNA, CO217/54, f. 13.

47 Callbeck to Germain, 2 September 1777, UKNA, CO226/6, f. 188.

48 Francklin to Germain, 6 June 1778, UKNA, CO217/54, ff. 70–1.

49 Hughes to Germain, 16 January 1779, UKNA, CO217/54, ff. 151–2; Germain to Francklin, 3 May 1779, ff. 178–9; Francklin to Germain, 24 October 1779, ff. 223–6; Germain to Hughes, 4 December 1779, ff. 235–6; Germain to Francklin, 4 December 1779, ff. 237–8.

50 Francklin to Germain, 3 August 1779, UKNA, CO217/54, ff. 202–4.

51 Hughes to Germain, March 1780, UKNA, CO217/55, ff. 33–4.

52 'Biography of Peter Paul – Written February 16th, 1865, from his own Statement by an Amanuensis' (unattributed newspaper clipping), NSARM, MG9, vol. 5, 'Scrapbook of Dr. George Patterson on Indians.' For more detailed discussion of Mi'kmaw and Wulstukwiuk dispossession, see John G. Reid, 'Empire, the Maritime Colonies, and the Supplanting of Mi'kma'ki/Wulstukwik, 1780–1820,' *Acadiensis* 38 (2009): 78–97.

53 Francklin to Lord George Germain, 4 May 1780, UKNA, CO217/55, f. 37.

54 Monk to Wentworth, 23 January 1794, UKNA, CO217/65, f. 150.

55 Petition of Mickmack Indians, [23 January 1794], UKNA, CO217/65, f. 148.

56 Deschamps to Monk, 4 November 1793, Library and Archives Canada (microfilm at NSARM), Monk Papers, MG23, Letterbook, Indian Affairs, 1783–1797, 1040.

57 Report of George Henry Monk, 26 February 1794, Monk Papers, Letter-book, Indian Affairs, 1783–1797, 1067–8.

58 Ibid., 6 March 1794, 1072.

59 Mathews to Duke of Portland, 7 July 1796, UKNA, CO217/112, f. 93.

60 Mathews to Portland, 2 August 1797, UKNA, CO217/113, f. 211.

61 Wentworth to Lord Hobart, 3 May 1804, UKNA, CO217/79, f. 16; for Wentworth's representations to London on expenditures for gifts, see Wentworth to Portland, 21 April 1797, UKNA, CO217/68, ff. 106–8.

62 Petition of Samuel Paul et al., n.d. [c. 1814], NSARM, RG1, vol. 430, no. 149⅓.

63 Titus Smith, 'Survey of the Eastern and Northern Parts of the Province in the Years 1801 and 1802 With General Observations Thereon,' NSARM, RG1, vol. 380, 115.

64 Titus Smith, 'Field Book of Western Nova Scotia,' 1801, NSARM, RG1, vol. 380A, 27 August 1801.

65 John Coffin to Edward Winslow, 14 July 1806, in W.O. Raymond, ed., *Winslow Papers, A.D. 1776–1826* (Saint John: New Brunswick Historical Society, 1901), 555.

66 Memorial of Daniel Lyman, c. 1790, UKNA, CO188/4, f. 391; on Lyman's background, see List of MLAs, CO188/6, f.141.

67 Thomas Carleton to Henry Dundas, 20 November 1792, Carleton Letter-Book, 1791–5, Provincial Archives of New Brunswick, RS330, A3b; Carleton to Portland, 19 December 1794, ibid. On later negotiations specifically concerning the Wulstukwiuk centre of Meductic and the associated treaty of 1807, see D.G. Bell, 'A Commercial Harvesting Prosecution in Context: The Peter Paul Case, 1946,' Carleton County Historical Society, http://www.cchs-nb.ca/html/Peter_PaulL.html (accessed 24 July 2009).

68 Wentworth to Portland, 8 October 1796, Wentworth Letter-Book, 1783–1808, NSARM, RG1, vol. 49.

69 Wentworth to Portland, 21 April 1797, UKNA, CO217/68, f. 106–7.

70 Wentworth to Castlereagh, 26 October 1807, UKNA, CO217/81, ff. 244–5.

71 Report of George Henry Monk, 23 April 1808, UKNA, CO217/82, ff. 202–5.

72 Wentworth to Dundas, 3 May 1793, UKNA, CO217/64, f. 172; Dundas to Wentworth, 6 July 1793, f. 216.

73 Wentworth to Dundas, 23 July, 9 November 1793, PRO, CO217/64, 236–7, 288.

74 Wentworth to John Stuart, Thomas Cuttler, and William Nixon, 30 December 1796, Wentworth Letter-Book, 1796–1800, NSARM, RG1, vol. 52.

75 Wentworth to Gabriel George Ludlow, 17 April 1804, Wentworth Letter-Book, 1800–5, NSARM, RG1, vol. 53; see also Wentworth to Sir Robert S.

Milner, 18 April 1804, 489–90; and Wentworth to John Despard, 30 May 1804, 507–9. For Wentworth's hopes expressed in 1807, see Wentworth to Castlereagh, 26 October 1807, UKNA, CO217/81, f. 245.

76 Bathurst to Sherbrooke, 26 August 1812, UKNA, CO217/89, ff. 214–15; Howard Temperley, ed., *Gubbins' New Brunswick Journals, 1811 & 1813* (Fredericton: New Brunswick Heritage Publications, 1980), 77.

77 Smyth to Bathurst, 31 August 1812, UKNA, CO188/18, ff. 70, 73; see also specific agreements, 10 and 11 July 1812, Smyth Correspondence, 1812–1819, PANB, RS336, A2a, 1812/1, 1812/2.

78 Among many treatments of Thayendenegea and his sister Koñwatsiat-siaéñni (Molly Brant), see Barbara Graymont, 'Thayendenegea,' *Dictionary of Canadian Biography*, http://www.biographi.ca (accessed 5 August 2010); Graymont, 'Koñwatsiatsiaéñni,' ibid.; and Taylor, *Divided Ground*, 86–96 and *passim*. See also Jim Piecuch, *Three Peoples, One King: Loyalists, Indians, and Slaves in the Revolutionary South, 1775–1782* (Columbia: University of South Carolina Press, 2008), 35; and, on the coherence of 'nativist' loyalism, Gregory Evans Dowd, *A Spirited Resistance: The North American Indian Struggle for Unity, 1745–1815* (Baltimore: Johns Hopkins University Press, 1992), 47–61.

79 Abraham Gesner, 'Report on Indian Affairs,' 29 September 1847, *Journal and Proceedings of the House of Assembly (Nova Scotia)*, 1847, appendix 24, 117.

80 On *dominium*, see Ken Macmillan, *Sovereignty and Possession in the English New World: The Legal Foundations of Empire, 1576–1640* (Cambridge: Cambridge University Press, 2006), 6–7; see also, on the significance of the Royal Proclamation of 1763 for royal dominion vis-à-vis aboriginal territories, Stuart Banner, *How the Indians Lost Their Land: Law and Power on the Frontier* (Cambridge, MA: Belknap Press of Harvard University Press, 2005), 84–95.

81 See Marshall, *Making and Unmaking of Empires*, 373–9 and *passim*.

82 Willig, *Restoring the Chain of Friendship*, 1–9 and *passim*; quotation is at 6.

83 See Piecuch, *Three Peoples*, 332–4; and Shannon, *Iroquois Diplomacy*, 192–3.

PART II

Transnational Print Culture and Loyalist Expression

4

Loyalists Respond to *Common Sense*: The Politics of Authorship in Revolutionary America

PHILIP GOULD

Since its publication in 1776, Thomas Paine's *Common Sense* has eclipsed the many, angry Loyalist responses to this mercurial pamphlet, which made the bold (and false) argument that American independence was already a *fait accompli*. Perhaps because of the very success of the revolutionary movement, culminating in political independence later that year, scholars tend to dismiss the Loyalist rebuttals as either rhetorically inept or simply doomed to the inexorable forces of national history. In the late nineteenth century, for example, the first major literary historian of the Revolution, Moses Coit Tyler, argued that the quality of Loyalist writing declined precipitously in 1776, due partly to the realization of 'the uselessness of further discussion' since the revolutionary movement 'could not be checked by mere word.'[1]

As this volume attests, serious historical scholarship on the Loyalists has grown in recent years, yet it still tends to be dismissive of those who responded to Paine's influential pamphlet.[2] This essay recuperates some of this important Loyalist writing, not to gauge its aesthetic value per se but rather to reconsider the episode in a transatlantic context – specifically, the convergence between revolutionary politics and eighteenth-century arguments about authorship that extended well beyond revolutionary Philadelphia.[3] By seriously accounting for these rebuttals to *Common Sense*, we can begin to see how political writing in revolutionary America effectively mobilized discourses that were not themselves strictly 'political.' In this case, the exchanges between American Loyalists and Paine and his patriotic allies made use of the rhetorical figure of the 'author': authorship became one of the most important devices with which each side aimed to establish literary – and thereby political – credibility.

The political crisis over American independence was concurrent with important legal proceedings and public debates in Britain during the 1770s over the meanings of authorship and literary property. Paine, himself a Briton, went to America in 1774, the year of a landmark House of Lords ruling on copyright law. (Other key figures, such as the Loyalists James Chalmers and William Smith and the Patriot John Witherspoon, were also English or Scottish emigrants to British America.) The first part of this chapter thus aims to clarify the transatlantic context for the publication and reception of *Common Sense* by analysing the legal controversy in Britain surrounding copyright law, which involved questions about the nature of literary property and literary originality, questions that were resonant as well in the political literature of British America at this time. As historians of authorship have argued, these issues turned on the figure of the proprietary author – the individual who produced his own original work and therefore owned it – and concerned how one could measure the 'value' of this special kind of commodity called 'literature.' With this transatlantic context in mind, the analysis then turns to Loyalist responses to *Common Sense*. The literature of politics in 1776 is rife with references to literary originality: pamphlets and newspaper writing demonstrate the transatlantic circulation of ideas about authorship at this moment of political unrest in British America – ideas, moreover, that also allow us to reconsider the meanings of 'freedom of the press.'[4]

Authorship and Literary Value

Loyalists were so appalled by *Common Sense* that they could not help but attack its author, who ostensibly remained anonymous. Across the Atlantic, metropolitan Britons were contesting the nature of authors and their literary works – indeed, for much of the eighteenth century, the subject revolved around the legal controversy over copyrights. In the aftermath of the lapse of the Licensing Act in 1695, Parliament had passed the Statute of Anne in 1709, which tried to bring some control over the publishing industry by establishing limited terms of copyright: twenty-one years for existing works and fourteen years for new ones, renewable for another fourteen years. (The first copyright law passed by the US Congress, in 1790, was modelled largely on the British statute.) The Statute of Anne represented something of a compromise position on copyright law in that it protected copyright holders but only for a limited period of time. When the terms of copyright began to expire in the 1730s and 1740s, many booksellers began to challenge in the British courts the term limits Parliament had placed on their property. These legal battles culminated with the landmark decision by the House of Lords in the case of *Donaldson v. Becket* (1774), upholding the statutory limitation on the duration of copyrights.

The legal issues in *Donaldson* devolved upon the relation between literary property and the common law. The fundamental question facing British jurists was whether or not literary property fell under the domain of the common law; if it did, copyright holders would maintain *perpetual* ownership of their literary works. As the famous Scottish bookseller Alexander Donaldson summarized the issue, 'Whether at common law an author and his assignees have a perpetual and exclusive right of selling and vending his own works?'[5] The important point here is that, in practice, the powerful London booksellers owned most copyrights and monopolized the British publishing industry by controlling who could attend the private auctions – at venues such as the Chapter Coffee House – where rights to copy were bought, sold, traded, and sometimes divided up. Because the common practice was for authors to sell their copyrights to these 'topping' booksellers, the latter had a great financial stake in the proceedings of the 1760s and 1770s on the legal principle that authors exercised the common law right to their 'property.' (This common law right to property, of course, transferred to the bookseller-publisher upon the sale of copyright.) As one historian of the book has put it, the London booksellers 'virtually invented the modern proprietary author, constructing him as a weapon in their struggle with the book sellers of the provinces.'[6] Provincial booksellers and publishers such as Donaldson, on the other hand, were set upon breaking the hold of this metropolitan monopoly, maintaining that, similar to patents on mechanical inventions, rights to copy under the Statute of Anne were subject to regulation under statutory law.

None of these legal arguments would have been imaginable without the important changes taking place during this era in the very meaning of print. The gradual transformation of printing from a political to an economic activity, as Grantland Rice has argued, had ramifications for the development of modern authorship: 'It was the separation of the economic from the political domain and the concomitant rewriting of the political legislation of censorship into the economic laws of copyright and literary property which allowed the birth of the professional writer.'[7] Indeed, the figure of the modern author, the person who individually produces original literary works for money, was central to the common law argument about literary property (and, as we shall see, to the British American reception of *Common Sense*, which came only two years after the *Donaldson* case). This is the figure in whom the famous theorist Michel Foucault long ago ascribed the 'author function' as a crucial development that marked 'the privileged notion of *individualization* in the history of ideas.'[8] Foucault's famous question – 'What is an author?' – has helped to frame the argument for the rise of the modern professional author in eighteenth-century Britain. Mark Rose summarizes these changes in this way:

> All of these cultural developments – the emergence of the mass market for books, the valorization of original genius, and the development of the Lockean discourse of possessive individualism – occurred in the same period as the long legal and commercial struggle over copyright. Indeed it was in the course of that struggle under the particular pressures of the requirements of legal argumentation that the blending of the Lockean discourse and the aesthetic discourse of originality occurred and the modern representation of the author as proprietor was formed.[9]

While Rose acknowledges that the legal judgment in *Donaldson* did not favour the London booksellers, he also persuasively argues for the widespread circulation of the figure of the modern author in the British press's coverage of the trial. The London monopoly might have lost the *Donaldson* case, but its efforts helped to popularize the figure of the modern author.[10]

British debates over copyright focused as well on matters of literary originality and value that are central to modern authorship. The first actually was not that controversial – even those critics who advocated statutory limitations on copyright agreed that famous writers such as Shakespeare, Milton, and Pope had produced works of original genius. While writing against the London booksellers, Lord Kames, for example, admitted that '[t]he composer of a valuable book has great merit with respect to the public: his proper reward is approbation and praise, and he seldom fails of that reward.'[11] This kind of language, however, notably removed literary value from the process of invention and individual labour; rather, it made the value of literature a function of public opinion, substituting fame for financial compensation as the 'reward' for one's labours. On the other hand, those critics who advocated proprietary rights under the common law went much further in promoting an ideology of literary genius, or what Foucault calls the 'author function.' This usually contrasted the originality of authors with the meanness and greed of the provincial printers. Lord Mansfield, for example, wryly debunks Donaldson's motives for reprinting Pope's edition of Homer: 'Patriot Donaldson, Sir, has still greater attributes than his counsel have given him . . . He is the rival of the famed [twelfth-century Greek scholar and archbishop] Eustathius, he is, Sir, an editor and a commentator; he has refined upon the edition of Pope's Homer, published by the poet himself, by expunging 23,851 lines from the notes; these lines, commentator Donaldson thought unnecessary.'[12]

The question of literary originality was directly related to the matter of labour – the work that went into writing a book. One of the best cases defending proprietary authorship in the name of literary labour came from William Warburton, Bishop of Gloucester, literary executor to Alexander Pope, and one of the era's most renowned men of letters. In his *Letter from an Author, to a Member of Parliament, Concerning Literary Property*, Warburton emphasizes that the work involved in producing a piece of literature was like no other form of labour. Working deductively at first, he distinguishes between 'moveable' property and 'immoveable' property (such as landed estates), then divides the former into 'natural' and 'artificial' forms, the latter marked by human improvement. In addressing human labour, he makes the crucial distinction between labour of the hand and labour of the mind: 'as an *Utensil* made; a *Book* composed.'[13] The key idea here is that such a composition is not just a physical artefact – paper, binding, printed text – but the ideas inhering intangibly within it. As Warburton puts it, 'the complete Idea of a Book being such a Composition as is here spoken of, together with a *Doctrine contained*. But under this Idea it assumes another Nature, and becomes a *Work of the Mind*.'[14] Hence, artistic labour is something at once both extraordinary and typical, outside the ambit of most normal persons' capacities ('by a long and painful Exercise of that very Faculty which denominateth us MEN'), yet protected as much by law as the labour required to make a spoon or a rifle.

Even this formulation, however, raised important questions about the value of the printed book. While common law advocates emphasized the labour that went into making a literary work – the pains it took a writer to produce a book – those advocating statutory limits on copyright emphasized literature's public utility, an ideal demanding the free circulation of printed matter. A related issue concerned the nature of literary property vis-à-vis the common law. Warburton, for example, argued that literature was a form of property insofar as it was useful and capable of being 'ascertained.' Those who opposed proprietary rights (and the monopoly of the London booksellers) countered that literary property was not property at all in the conventional sense: it lacked substance and was 'incorporeal.' According to Warburton, even great literature was 'detached from any physical existence'; another opponent criticized the London booksellers for contriving a 'modern invention' of property that had 'nothing real in it'; yet another talked about the *'metaphorical property'* in books.[15] Lord Kames similarly argued that the literary virtues of style and form simply lacked a *'corpus'* that could be 'possessed [and] transferred from hand to hand.'[16]

These disputes over literary originality helped to shape the debates on the other side of the Atlantic about *Common Sense*. Both Loyalist and Patriot writers in British America wielded the ideology of literary originality and modern authorship in their attempts to gain political legitimacy in the public sphere of political debate. By focusing on the figure of the author and on the quality of original writing he was able to produce, each side operated from the premise that literary form and political ideology were inextricably connected. The transatlantic dissemination of these important ideas about authorship was complicated by the impending political crisis that culminated in political independence for the newly declared United States. Yet the Loyalist response to *Common Sense* testified to the continued presence – indeed, to the imposing cultural authority – of metropolitan Britain. Loyalist writers looked to British literary figures rhetorically to legitimize their own authorial stature; they wrote as 'Englishmen' and accessed those metropolitan authorities to lay claim to the virtues of literary originality. As we shall see, this strategy often characterized the Patriot side as well. The question of the 'author' – who could write well, who could claim knowledge of British literary culture – consumed both sides of the political debate in revolutionary British America.

'To Write or Not to Write'

Loyalist responses to *Common Sense* appeared as pamphlets and in newspapers, and were reprinted widely in British America, though mostly in Philadelphia and New York. The flamboyant Philadelphia printer and bookseller Robert Bell (the self-proclaimed 'Provedore to the Sentimentalists'), who was printing works on both sides of the political crisis, published the first major pamphlet responding to *Common Sense*, James Chalmers's *Plain Truth; Addressed to the Inhabitants of America, Containing, Remarks on a Late Pamphlet, Entitled Common Sense* (1776). During the spring of 1776 there also appeared in Philadelphia newspapers an important series of letters under the pseudonym 'Cato,' written by William Smith, the provost of the College of Philadelphia, who, despite his opposition to British imperial regulations, opposed the independence movement. Feeling personally slighted by 'Cato,' Paine responded with a series of letters in the Philadelphia press under the name of 'The Forester.' The newspaper exchanges between 'Cato' and 'The Forester' were accompanied by numerous anonymous squibs, poems, parodies, rebuttals, and counter-charges, as Loyalist and Patriot writers assailed and defended Paine's pamphlet. Perhaps the most effective Loyalist response to *Common Sense*, however, was printed in New York, but not published there, probably out of fear of patriotic reprisals.[17] Written by the Anglican minister Charles Inglis, *The Deceiver Unmasked* appeared two months later in Philadelphia under the new (and attenuated) title, *The True Interest of America Impartially Stated in Certain Strictures on a Pamphlet Intitled Common Sense*.

Notwithstanding their outrage over a work that brazenly advocated American independence, Loyalists responding to *Common Sense* were on the defensive from the outset. Because they were aware of the pamphlet's immediate popularity, they were forced to engage its particular arguments and ended up getting lost in the details of political debate. But one strategy Loyalists employed was more effective in challenging the very idea of political independence that Paine heralded. That was their focus on its style – a direct indication, they claimed, of the character of the pamphlet's author. Whether or not these Loyalists knew it was Paine (some, like William Smith, surely did, as we will see), they seized upon the convention of anonymity in political writing and inverted it to recast *Common Sense* as the work of a writer deliberately intent upon deluding British Americans. Coupled with wariness about this anonymous conspirator was suspicion about his admittedly powerful writing style. Loyalists desperately tried to turn their adversary's literary talents into moral vices. This meant returning 'art' to its original meaning of artifice. One Loyalist, writing as 'Rationalis' in the Philadelphia newspapers, put it this way: 'But to my great grief I have too often seen instances of persons in every class of life, whose publications, at the same time they have reflected honor on the parts and genius of the authors, have been so shamefully wanting in candor as to attempt, by the cadence of words, and force of stile, a total perversion of the understanding.'[18] Similarly, the preface to *The True Interest of America Impartially Stated* declares, 'The following pages contain an answer to one of the most artful, insidious and pernicious pamphlets I have ever met with.' This attack links artifice to author. He is guilty of 'Catechresis' – 'that is, in plain English, an abuse of words . . . Thus have I seen a book written by a popish bigot, entitled *Mercy and Truth; or Charity Maintained*; in which the author very devoutly and charitably damns all heretics.'[19]

Unfortunately for the Loyalist cause, the first major pamphlet responding to *Common Sense*, James Chalmers's *Plain Truth* (1776), was so ineptly written that patriotic writers (including Paine) were easily able to put the opposition on the defensive. The letters William Smith (writing as 'Cato') penned for the Philadelphia newspapers were far better prose, but when Paine came around to rebut them he immediately seized upon his adversary's supposedly inferior literary ability.[20] 'The Forester' makes snide remarks about 'Cato''s style – his 'manner of writing has as much order in it as the motion of a squirrel' – and critiques the absence of literary originality. This is significant for what it begins to show us about British American understandings of originality vis-à-vis metropolitan literature and culture. Paine concludes the first 'Forester' piece by mocking 'Cato''s use of the cliché, 'The eyes of all Europe are upon us':

> This stale and hackneyed phrase hath had a regular descent, from many of the King's speeches down to several of the speeches of Parliament; from thence it took a turn among the little wits and bucks of St. James's; till after suffering all the torture of senseless repetition, and being reduced to a state of vagrancy, it was charitably picked up to embellish the second letter of Cato. It is truly of the bug-bear kind, contains no meaning, and the very using it discovers a barrenness of invention. It signifies nothing to tell us 'that the eyes of all Europe are upon us,' unless he had likewise told us what they are looking for.[21]

The passage is most significant in this respect: it challenges the traditional notion of Paine as an 'American' writer, a cultural nationalist spurning all things English, while the Loyalists remain the only true (and hence doomed) anglophiles. We might recall that in *Common Sense* Paine had called for cutting all ties between Britain and America – indeed, he had proclaimed they were already severed and that America represented a de facto nation waiting for its legal and political institutionalization as a state. But 'The Forester' here offers a more complex model of transatlantic culture, which puts a particular kind of burden on the British American writer: 'Cato' is guilty of 'senseless imitation' of an already overused and debased version of Englishness. To be an 'original' American thus requires transatlantic cultural reach. Co-opting metropolitan cultural literacy for the Patriot cause, 'The Forester' alienates loyalism as something, uncannily, un-English.

In the exchanges over *Common Sense*, the subject of literary originality began to take on a life of its own. It culminated in the fourth 'Cato' letter, in which Smith writes a parody of Hamlet's famous soliloquy as a way of displaying the predicament facing the Loyalist writer at that time of crisis. Because of what it suggests about the Loyalist cultural position, and the scathing critiques it elicited from Patriots, it is worth quoting in its entirety:

ALAS POOR CATO!

What a buzz hast thou raised about thine ears? How canst thou proceed in thy lucubrations? If the following soliloquy can yield thee any consolation, thou art welcome to place it either in front or in rear of thy next letter. Thou wilt perceive thyself more indebted for it to William Shakespeare than to Thy Friend and Reader, HAMLET.

> To write or not to write; that is the question –
> Whether 'tis nobler in the mind to bear
> Th' unlicens'd wrongs of furious party zeal,
> Or dip the pen into a nest of hornets.
> And still, by teasing, wake them? To write, to answer –
> No more? And by a single answer end
> The thousand scorns and heart-aches which an author
> Is born to suffer – 'Tis a consummation
> Devoutly to be wished! To write, to answer,
> Reply, perchance rejoin – aye, there's the rub!
> For in replies, and answers, and rejoinders,
> Who knows what deadly broils and feuds may come,
> When we have shuffled off this mortal zest
> Of mutual forbearance. There's the curse
> That makes calamity of *wordy war*.
> For who would bear the scoffing of the times,

The Tory's hated name, the *Tool of Power*,
The contumely of the *pension'd Slave*,
When he himself might his *quietus* make
With a *dry quill*? Who would endure the Pain*
This foul discharge of wrath from Adam's sons
Marshall'd in dread array, both old and Young,
Their pop-guns here, and there their heavy Cannon,
Our labor'd pages not deemed worth a Rush
But that the dread of something worse to come,
Some undiscover'd mischief puzzles thought,
And makes one rather court the ancient path
Than fly to others that we know not of!
And thus the native hue of resolution
Is sicklied o'er with the pale cast of fear,
And enterprises of great pith and moment
With this regard, their currents turn awry.

Some writers, in imitation of our ancestors, yet spell this word Payne

This moment in political debate registers an important feature of Loyalist authorship in its transatlantic context. Posing as 'Cato,' Smith not only appropriates canonical English literature but he does so to sentimentalize his position as a martyred author. The solitary feature of the modern author becomes part of the political persona meant to oppose the patriotic movement. What is most interesting, then, about Smith's burlesque is the almost complete lack of irony vis-à-vis the Shakespearean model. Instead of satirizing his own position, by ironically elevating his newspaper writing to the level of Shakespearean tragedy, Smith instead takes it as a serious model to announce the high stakes of Loyalist authorship. 'Cato' identifies with Hamlet; in a sense he becomes Hamlet – besieged, anxious, ambivalent (insofar as he dislikes British imperial policy but wants to remain loyal to the Empire), and ultimately unable to do anything. The very subject of authorship enables this identification; suffering seems to be its necessary precondition. 'Cato' writes against the rising tide of patriotic dissent, which has now made American independence a viable option and is increasingly bent on silencing Loyalist opposition. This makes 'Cato''s preference for sentimental identification over urbane wit comprehensible, since his writing and Shakespeare's are now aligned to accomplish the same thing: dramatize a tragic situation.

Patriots were quick to point out 'Cato''s lack of originality in parodying this passage from Shakespeare: Hamlet's famous soliloquy was already a shopworn model for writing burlesque by the 1770s.[22] Paine seized upon 'Cato''s faux-burlesque as further proof of his lack of originality. The Hamlet passage had alluded to a number of prominent Patriots such as Benjamin Rush, Thomas Young, James Cannon, and Paine himself via the pun on 'Pain.'[23] So, in the next 'Forester' letter, Paine became even more vindictive, inverting the very premise of 'Cato''s isolation. 'His fourth letter is introduced with a punning Soliloquy – "Cato"'s title to soliloquies is indisputable; because no man cares for his company.'[24] Paine extends the critique of what he calls 'punning nonsense' as a meagre form of wit that condemns the writer to imitation, a problem that 'Cato' apparently cannot escape. As he says elsewhere, 'In this part of the debate ['Cato'] shelters himself chiefly in quotations from other authors, without reasoning much on the matter himself; in answer to which, I present him with a string of maxims and reflections, drawn from the nature of things, without borrowing from any one. Cato may observe, that I scarcely ever quote: the reason is, I always think.'[25]

The larger contours of political debate are apparent here. The dispute over charters and rights, American liberties and parliamentary authority, could easily slide into literary critique, as though literary quality demonstrated political credibility. More to the point: the inability to write well – and to show mastery of the canons of taste themselves – invalidated the opposition's political position. In this case 'Cato' appeals to an increasingly hostile public through the medium of wit (the parody of Hamlet), which, in light of the worsening political situation for Loyalists in 1776, unsurprisingly slides into sentimental appeal. To discredit the position of the Loyalist martyr who faces the dangers of censorship and intimidation, Paine recasts it as merely an imitative gesture that lacks any sort of original invention. Questions of whether to feel sorry for the Loyalist objector or to take Loyalist complaints seriously become lost in questions of taste. To claim that the Loyalist writer lacks originality, in other words, is not merely a sideshow to political debate; rather, it is integral to the rhetorical strategies involved in discrediting the opposition. While Smith employs Hamlet to express his own tormented captivity, Paine scorns such a model as a form of cultural imitation that is the corollary to political enslavement.[26] The trope of the original writer – the author – provides the position from which to leverage political debate.

The importance of literary originality in political debate also helps to explain 'The Forester''s snub about 'Cato''s Scottish ancestry. As the repartee between the two continued, they became aware of each other's real identities. ('Cato,' as we have seen, punned on Paine and 'Pain.') 'The Forester' responded in kind. Aware of Smith's Scottish origins, he offers the offhanded barb that 'the poetical merit of the performance' proves that 'though the writer of it may be an Allen, he'll never be a Ramsay.'[27] If an 'Allen' is shorthand for a Scotsman, 'Ramsay' refers here to the famous Scottish poet and antiquarian Allan Ramsay, whose anthologies of popular ballads were popular in eighteenth-century British America. Using a canonical Scottish writer to measure 'Cato''s failings is significant, for Ramsay advocated a version of the literary imagination that recalled earlier debates at the turn of the eighteenth century between the Augustan wits (like Pope and Swift) and their Whig adversaries (like Richard Blackmore), who championed the powers of the individual's creative imagination. Ramsay espoused a Whiggish understanding of the primacy of inspiration over literary decorum. The epigraph, for example, to the 1751 edition of his collected poems comes from Mathew Prior's translation of Anacreon, which rejects the rules of criticism in favour of pleasing 'the fair, the gay, and the young.' The preface distances the poems from the classical tradition, while Ramsay praises all poets, ancient and modern, whose 'souls are warmed with true poetic flame.'[28] He urges any poet to be 'an Original': 'Throughout the whole, I have only copied from nature; and with all the precaution have studied, as far as it came within the ken of my observation and memory, not to repeat what has been already said by others, tho' it be impossible sometimes to stand clear of them.'[29]

Loyalists, too, made this charge against the author of *Common Sense*. Coming to 'Cato''s defence in the Philadelphia press, they took the similar approach of shaping political debate through the figure of the credible author. For example, in the 3 April 1776 *Pennsylvania Gazette*, an entry entitled 'The Forester and the Lion' points out the distortions in patriotic newspaper pieces. Here, the Loyalist 'Aesop Junior' (and it may have been Smith himself) retells the fable of the man and the lion where the two dispute which is the superior species; the lion comments that you cannot trust the 'marble monument' of a man vanquishing a lion because it was sculpted by men themselves. In other words, the bias of authors distorts their works. The essay goes on to criticize 'The Forester' for not allowing 'Cato' to finish writing all of his letters to the press before responding to any of them. 'The Forester,' he claims, is 'a person who could not argue the matter in dispute fairly with his opponent, but relied upon the work and ingenuity of others of his own side to prove the matter in controversy.' He goes on to complain that 'The Forester,' faced with 'Cato''s rational arguments, resorts to citing 'the book called *Common Sense*, and takes it for granted that thy point is already proved.' One should note the ironies infusing authorship and originality this moment presents. At a time when anonymous authorship was still quite the norm for political writing, both sides nevertheless claimed the political high ground by upholding the figure of the original author. Apparently unaware, however, that 'The Forester' was also the author of *Common Sense*, the Loyalist critique of the Forester's imitative literary sensibility ends up, in effect, unwittingly critiquing Paine for citing *himself* as the ultimate authority. This moment registers the logic of literary originality carried to its extreme: the point where one becomes the source of one's own literary inspiration.

The Liberty of Readers

The publication and reception of *Common Sense* dramatically heightened the politicization of print culture in Philadelphia. Numerous exchanges took place debating the merits or defects of the pamphlet, and they became increasingly hostile and partisan as the independence movement gained momentum. The writer 'Cassandra,' for example, scoffed at the idea of dealing with imperial negotiators and scorned those Loyalists who would receive them with open arms; 'Cato' attacked Cassandra and *Common Sense* alike, and 'The Forester' responded in kind. 'Queries to Cato' appeared in Benjamin Towne's *Pennsylvania Evening Post* ('But are you not a most furious, violent, and implacable enemy to the liberties of this country? – Or, in other words, are you not a RANK TORY?'); and another Loyalist writing under the moniker 'R' came to 'Cato''s defence to rescue him from patriotic abuse.[30] 'Cato' wrote a nasty squib to the Patriot writer 'Tiberius' that impugned his style and corrected his diction. A number of Patriot essays by 'Sincerus' and other writers appeared in Philadelphia newspapers defending *Common Sense* and the Patriot movement, and Robert Bell soon published them under the misleading yet marketable title, *Additions to Common Sense*, as a way of getting back at Paine and the Bradfords, who were publishing a new, expanded edition of *Common Sense*. Bell also brought out subsequent editions of *Common Sense* and

Plain Truth, as well as an *Additions to Plain Truth,* to tap the rising market for political writings.

All of this writing led some to consider the effect of the political crisis on the overall quality of the public press. As we have seen, Loyalists had been complaining about the need for a free and open press that adequately expressed competing political views. Indeed the principle of the freedom of the press was a cornerstone to the concept of 'English liberties' that British Americans were debating at the time. Prominent printers, moreover, such as Robert Bell and James Rivington, who wished to print writing on both sides of the political controversy, voiced much the same complaints against the patriotic movement's attempt to suppress the expression of political dissent. Scholars have long noted the harassment and intimidation that British American printers sympathetic to the Loyalist cause experienced, and in the current volume Gwendolyn Davies shows how many of them recreated transatlantic circuits of cultural dissemination in the Canadian communities to which they fled as exiles.[31]

Yet the proliferation of political writing opened up the issue of a 'free press' to considerations of quality as well. Some commentators began to consider just what the increased production – and rancour – of political discourse was doing to the quality of print culture in general. What was happening to literary standards in the midst of the rapid politicization of print? This issue invariably focused on readers of newspapers and pamphlet literature. Similarly, across the Atlantic, the literary property debates focused on British readers as the counterpart to the author – that is, these debates readily considered the role of consumers as well as producers in capitalist print economies. As we have seen, these debates were highly self-conscious about the ramifications that copyright law held for British readers, particularly the effect statutory regulation of copyrights would have on the overall circulation and quality of British print culture. By limiting the terms of copyright, the *Donaldson* case was seen (by the provincial booksellers anyway) as a victory for British readers. As Trevor Ross has argued, 'If authors and [London] booksellers were the apparent losers in the decision of 1774, the clear winners were English readers, who could now look forward to multiple editions of canonical works.'[32]

The most considered statement about the dilemma of American readers in this tumultuous period came from John Witherspoon, the prominent Presbyterian minister and president of the College of New Jersey, who was also an important critic of rhetoric and oratory. Writing as

'Aristides,' Witherspoon's assessment of 'the Independent controversy in the newspapers' appeared on 13 May 1776 in *Dunlap's Pennsylvania Packet*.[33] He was undoubtedly aware of the bitter complaints that Loyalist writers – and those printers like Bell who wished to continue issuing work on both sides of the political controversy – were making about the patriotic movement's increasingly violent activities to stifle political dissent. Indeed, Witherspoon begins by recasting this issue entirely. Wryly noting that Loyalists like 'Cato' tended to complain about the problem of censorship, Witherspoon counters with the provocative claim that the real problem in 1776 was not the repression but the proliferation of political writing. 'Much has been said about the liberty of the press,' he complains, 'suffer me to say a few words for the liberty of readers.'[34]

Witherspoon's patriotic politics evidently intensified his critiques of Loyalist writers such as Chalmers and Smith.[35] Yet his insights about the production and consumption of newspaper writing at this time had more far-reaching ramifications. Read in light of the British debates about copyright law taking place in the 1770s, Witherspoon initially sounds like the advocates for limited copyright during the British debates: he places faith in the free circulation and consumption of literary works to secure the quality of the literary public sphere. By considering the respective roles of authors, printers, and readers in the publication process, 'Aristides' aims to sort out just what is driving the notable decline in the literary value of contemporary newspapers and pamphlets. Literary value, he argues, can exist only with real freedom of choice for readers. Pointing out, for example, that *Plain Truth* and *Common Sense* are expensive pamphlets, he argues, 'I apprehend it is the undoubted right of every author to set what price he pleases upon the productions of his genius, and of every printer upon the productions of his press, leaving it always to the free will of the Public to determine whether they will purchase these productions at that price or any other.'[36]

What corrupts this ideal image of an open market for printed matter, however, is corrupt printers such as the 'illustrious and exalted R.B. [Robert Bell], provedore (as he calls himself) to the sentimentalists.'[37] Witherspoon's criticism of the flamboyant and profiteering Bell is not exactly political – unlike the Sons of Liberty, he does not object to Bell's willingness to profit from Loyalist pamphlets. Rather, Witherspoon complains that the printer intentionally and artificially inflated the value of *Plain Truth* by advertising the pamphlet – duplicitously – as the

'first edition.'[38] Do you refer to your wife, he mocks Bell, as your first
wife? By marketing the pamphlet this way, and hedging on the number
of copies of *Plain Truth* initially printed, Bell presumably manipulated
the demand for a poorly written pamphlet. Bell, in turn, defended himself by publishing an addendum to Josiah Tucker's *The True Interest of
Britain Set Forth in Regard to the Colonies* (1776), which includes 'A Short
Answer to Some Criticisms,' taking Aristides to task for failing to recognize that the sales of *Plain Truth* necessitated a second edition.

Yet Witherspoon's critique is unique in focusing on the practices of
newspaper publishing. Since British American newspapers commonly
reprinted other writings, the political crisis created problems of dupli-
cation and demand. The increased amount of political writing was not
merely bad, he argues, but it was being reproduced at alarming rates
and at the expense of readers' literary sensibilities. Many readers like
Aristides subscribed to numerous papers simultaneously, so that they
were repeatedly subjected to the same poorly written essays: '[I] am to
pay three times for the most part of Cato's letters, and if they were to be
published in a pamphlet I would not give a rush for them all together.'
He goes on:

> Pray, Sir, how much copy money would you have given for a pamphlet in
> which you had found that ridiculous pun upon Mount Seir[39] which is to
> be seen in one of Cato's letters, and the wretched parody upon Hamlet's
> soliloquy? Parody in general is one of the lowest kinds of writing that has
> yet found a name, and that poor speech has been repeated, imitated, and
> mangled so often that it must excite disgust in every person who has any
> acquaintance with newspapers and pamphlets to see it again.[40]

The passage is significant not as an attack on 'Cato''s literary deficien-
cies but for its dramatization of the degree to which commentators
such as Witherspoon understood the value of print in both aesthetic
and financial terms. The subjects of good and bad writing and the relative cost of newspapers and pamphlets are closely interwoven and
inseparable.

This kind of critique begins to reveal that the fundamental problem
for readers is not the politicization of print but the commercialization
of politics. This becomes even more striking in the other major issue
Witherspoon addresses: the payment of newspaper writers. The professionalization of newspaper writing was hardly the norm at this
time in British America – indeed, the 'Aristides' piece may be the first

important articulation of this principle. Yet Witherspoon is concerned not really with newspaper writers per se but with the overall quality of print culture during the political crisis. His real fear is that the medium is becoming quickly debased because unscrupulous editors like Bell are actually auctioning off newspaper space to the highest bidders. 'Sir,' he addresses Bell, 'if you have paid for or even solicited from the authors the papers you have published, you are wholly acquitted of blame further than sometimes a mistaken choice. But, on the contrary, which I strongly suspect, if you and others are paid for inserting political pieces, I affirm you take your money and deceive your readers.'[41]

Such a position re-imagines the role of the printer in the economy of newspaper publishing. Rather than sell space in the newspaper to those willing to pay for it, the printer becomes the buyer of writing that presumably is worth printing – writing that has intellectual and formal value. The production of that value lies originally with the writer himself (or herself), though it is ultimately a collaborative process involving artistic originality and editorial judgment. Put another way, Witherspoon moves printers from the supply to the demand side of the print economy, at once empowering them and making them responsible for judging literary merit and ultimately preserving the quality of a 'free' press. One might say that the newspaper medium functions properly so long as printers and writers know their proper roles. Even as he makes such a claim, however, Witherspoon hedges almost imperceptibly in the face of the very market forces he is supporting. Recognizing that he is advocating for professionally paid newspaper writers, he recoils from the prospect of writing as a commodity. 'In this view an able writer is a treasure to a publisher of any periodical paper, and ought certainly to be paid liberally, either in money, or thanks, or both.'[42] In fact, writers generally received very little of either. But Witherspoon makes it 'both,' which suggests an important tension between literary and financial registers of value, one that he maintains by policing the boundaries of even this inchoate version of literary professionalism. The literary marketplace functions properly when it is overseen (in a potently vague phrase) 'under proper direction.'

Loyalists and the Canon

The controversy over *Common Sense* in 1776 reveals the degree to which the literary and political histories of the American Revolution were intimately bound up in one another. Rather than simply see Loyalists as the 'losers' in the debate over the pamphlet, we might begin to reconsider the very nature of the debates themselves. Political writing functioned as a discursive arena where many kinds of issues were contested simultaneously. The transatlantic contexts of copyright and authorship help to unfold the multiple levels on which political discourse operated, opening up current literary and cultural questions about what it meant to be an author, what constituted original writing, and how one could ascertain literary value. It is easy to overstate the case: these audible stirrings of modern conceptions of literature and authorship were concurrent with traditional understandings of corporate authorship and originality informing, for example, Jefferson's avowal that the Declaration of Independence was meant to embody the 'common sense' of the people in 1776. This enquiry into the reception of *Common Sense* not only takes Loyalist responses seriously but also unsettles the monumental and hyper-canonical status of Paine's work – the very status that has marginalized Loyalist rebuttals. If we are willing to award Paine the prize of 'literary genius,' we should recognize the historical emergence of a concept that, while taking inchoate and uneven forms in 1776, circulated in a print culture distributed on both sides of the political divide. The debates over genius, over originality and proprietary authorship, moreover, present us with a far different view of the overall effect of *Common Sense*. Rather than simply creating the tidal wave of patriotic sentiment that inexorably overwhelmed Loyalist dissent, the pamphlet also elicited a series of critical commentaries – one might say a form of literary and cultural criticism – that make it look far less the unifying document that it supposedly was in 1776. Pamphlets, newspaper essays, letters, satires, squibs, literary burlesque, critiques of burlesque, and so forth: these expressed very real debates over form, style, and what it meant to be an original author – a real writer – in revolutionary British America.

NOTES

1 See Moses Coit Tyler, *The Literary History of the American Revolution, 1763–1783*, vol. 1 (New York: Frederick Ungar, 1957), 479–80. Tyler's history was initially published in 1897. For British and European responses to Paine, see Richard Gimbel, *A Bibliographical Check List of Common Sense. With an Account of Its Publication* (New Haven, CT: Yale University Press, 1956).

2 With the exception of Samuel Seabury, there is no Loyalist writer acknowledged as a major literary figure in early American literary and cultural studies. Loyalists generally fare badly in this regard. See, for example, Bruce Granger, *Political Satire in the American Revolution, 1763–1783* (Ithaca, NY: Cornell University Press, 1960); Kenneth Silverman, *A Cultural History of the American Revolution* (New York: Columbia University Press, 1987); Everett Emerson, ed., *American Literature, 1764–1789: The Revolutionary Years* (Madison: University of Wisconsin Press, 1977), esp. 59–72; and Robert A. Ferguson, *The American Enlightenment, 1750–1820* (Cambridge, MA: Harvard University Press, 1997), esp. 80–123.

3 This approach is even in keeping with Paine scholarship itself, particularly the recent emphasis on Paine the author, whose writing (as one study puts it) 'can best be understood through an analysis of his participation in the various debates in which his texts are produced.' These 'are often just as much about authorship and the dissemination of ideas as they are about the nature of government.' See Edward Larkin, *Thomas Paine and the Literature of Revolution* (Cambridge: Cambridge University Press, 2005), 12; see also Robert A. Ferguson, 'The Commonalities of *Common Sense*,' *William and Mary Quarterly*, 3rd series, 57 (2000): 465–504.

4 For the important relations between literary originality and political polemics at this time, see my 'Wit and Politics in Revolutionary British America: The Case of Samuel Seabury and Alexander Hamilton,' *Eighteenth-Century Studies* 71 (2008): 383–404.

5 Reprinted in *The Literary Property Debate: Six Tracts, 1764–1774* (New York: Garland: 1975), 21.

6 Mark Rose, 'The Author as Proprietor: *Donaldson v. Becket* and the Genealogy of Modern Authorship,' *Representations* 23 (1988), 54. See also his *Authors and Owners: The Invention of Copyright* (Cambridge, MA: Harvard University Press, 1993).

7 Grantland Rice, *The Transformation of Authorship in America* (Chicago: University of Chicago Press, 1997), 79–80.

8 Foucault's famous essay from the late 1960s, 'What Is an Author?' defines the 'author function' as a cultural construction that is comprehensible in the context of historical and epistemological changes in the nature and privatization of knowledge. The essay is not a 'sociohistorical analysis of the author's persona' but rather a preliminary consideration of the advent and effect of 'studies of authenticity and attribution' of authorship. It is included in *The Foucault Reader*, ed. Paul Rabinow (New York: Pantheon, 1984), 101–20.

9 Rose, 56.

10 Some critics have contested Rose's argument for overstating the hold capitalist ideologies of literary property exerted on early American culture. Meredith McGill argues that the important case of *Wheaton v. Peters* (1834) shows the degree to which both Lockean and utilitarian understandings of literature were operative in the Court's written proceedings; see 'The Matter of the Text: Commerce, Print Culture, and the Authority of the State in American Copyright Law,' *American Literary History* 9 (1997): 21–59, and idem, *American Literature and the Culture of Reprinting, 1834–1853* (Philadelphia: University of Pennsylvania Press, 2002). David Saunders also has challenged the Rose/Foucault argument about the relation between copyright law and commercial capitalism, emphasizing that the value of print was affected in highly contextual ways by legal rights and liabilities, aesthetics, and developing ideas about an author's inward personality; see *Authorship and Copyright* (London: Routledge, 1992).

11 Reprinted in *Literary Property Debate* (see note 5), 18.

12 See *The Parliamentary History of England, from the Earliest Period to the Year 1803*, vol. 17 (London: T.C. Hansard, 1813), 1098.

13 *A Letter from an Author, to a Member of Parliament, Concerning Literary Property* (London: John and Paul Knapton, 1787), 7.

14 Ibid., 7–9.

15 Ibid., 5–6.

16 Reprinted in *Literary Property Debate* (see note 5), 18.

17 In the copy at the John Carter Brown Library, there is the following inscription that explains its publication history:

> This pamphlet was first presented at New York, in March 1776; when advertised for Sale, the whole Impression was seized and burned by the *Sons of Liberty*. The Author, with much Trouble and no less Hazard, conveyed a copy to Philadelphia, after expunging some Passages that gave greatest offence, softening others, inserting a few adapted to the Spirit of the Times, and altering the Title Page. Two Editions of it were sold at Philadelphia in the course of a few Months. The Author's chief View was to prevent, if possible, the Declaration of Independency until the Commissioners, who were then soon expected from England, should arrive – They, he thought, would probably terminate the unhappy Contest. On this Principle, many Expressions are used which may seem to favour the Congress; but without these the Pamphlet could not be published – they were intended to soothe the Disaffected, gain their Confidence, and thereby obtain the Object principally aimed at.

18 'Rationalis' was the author of the Loyalist piece appended to the pamphlet *Plain Truth*, 76.

19 See *The True Interest of America Impartially Stated, in Certain Strictures on a Pamphlet Intitled Common Sense. By an American*. (Philadelphia: James Humphreys, 1776), v–vi.

20 Paine's 'Forester' letters appeared in Philadelphia newspapers, among them the *Pennsylvania Journal* and the *Weekly Advertiser*, on the following dates: To Cato (written 28 March 1776; published 3 April 1776); To Cato (written 8 April 1776; published 10 April 1776); To Cato (published 24 April 1776); To Cato (published 8 May 1776).

21 *The Writings of Thomas Paine*, vol. 1, ed. Moncure Daniel Conway (New York: Burt Franklin, 1969), 133.

22 See 'The Pausing American Loyalist,' quoted in Tyler, *Literary History*, vol. 2, 54–5. On the other side of the Atlantic, Adam Smith pointed out in his lectures on belletristic writing that *Hamlet* was terribly overused as the subject of parody. 'But so far is it from being a sign of any passages being a mean one that a parrodie [sic] has been made upon it, that 'tis rather a sign of the contrary, as the more sublime and Pompous a passage is the greater the contrast will be when the phraseology is applied to trivial subjects. Thus we see the soliloquy of Hamlet, the last speech of Cato, have undergone more parodies than any others I know, and indeed make very good ones.' Reprinted in *Lectures on Rhetoric and Belles Lettres*, ed. J.C. Bryce (Indianapolis: Liberty Fund, 1985), 46.

23 For these figures in Philadelphia revolutionary politics, see Eric Foner, *Tom Paine and Revolutionary America* (New York: Oxford University Press, 1976), esp. 115–30.

24 *Writings of Thomas Paine*, vol. 1, 144.

25 Ibid., 148–9.

26 Smith was not alone. Responding favourably to 'Cato' in James Humphreys's Loyalist newspaper, *The Pennsylvania Ledger*, on 11 May 1776, 'A Planter' followed with another version of Hamlet's speech that again lacked irony while condemning republican conspiracies: 'It must be so Cato – thou reasonest well! . . . 'Tis Heaven itself that teaches us/To avoid the ruinating schemes/Of bad, designing, mercenary men.'

27 *Writings of Thomas Paine*, vol. 1, 145.

28 See *Poems by Allan Ramsay*, vol. 1 (London: A. Millar and W. Johnston, 1751), iii.

29 Ibid., iv–v.

30 *Pennsylvania Evening Post*, 14 March, 21 March 1776.

31 See Gwendolyn Davies, in this volume. For analysis of the position of colonial printers during the revolutionary crisis, see Richard Buell, 'Freedom
of the Press in Revolutionary America,' in *The Press and the American Revolution*, ed. Bernard Bailyn and John B. Hench (Worcester, MA: American
Antiquarian Society, 1980), 59–85; and Stephen Botein, ' "Mere Mechanics"
and an Open Press: The Business and Political Strategies of Colonial American Printers,' *Perspectives in American History* 9 (1975): 127–225.

32 Trevor Ross, 'Copyright and the Invention of Tradition,' *Eighteenth-Century
Studies* 26 (1992): 14.

33 It is reprinted in *The Miscellaneous Works of the Reverend John Witherspoon,
DD, LLD, Late President of the College of New Jersey* (Philadelphia: William
Woodward, 1803), 313–21.

34 Ibid., 316.

35 Witherspoon castigated 'Candidus' for poor form. *Plain Truth* was so 'ri-
diculously ornamented with vapid, senseless phrases, and feeble epithets,
that his meaning could hardly be comprehended. He often put me in the
mind of the painted windows of some old Gothic buildings which keep
out the light. If Common Sense is some places wanted polish, Plain Truth
was covered over from head to foot with a detestable and stinking var-
nish'; see *Pennsylvania Packet*, 13 May 1776.

36 *Miscellaneous Works*, 314.

37 Ibid., 315.

38 One should note that Witherspoon certainly did not invent such an argument. Earlier in the eighteenth century, Warburton had argued that the
'vulgar Prejudice' against professional writers actually resulted from the
self-serving practices of printers. While writers, he admitted, sometimes
did pressure printers to issue second editions, more often it was printers who were guilty of rushing 'new' editions into print, which devalued
those first editions that readers had just purchased. Like Warburton, Witherspoon takes seriously the role of artistic genius while still acknowledging
the limitations of the author's role in the material process whereby literary value is determined. For Witherspoon, it seems, only printers like Bell
could make such trash as *Plain Truth* valuable.

39 Witherspoon refers here to 'Cato''s response to the Forester in the
3 April 1776 issue of the *Pennsylvania Gazette* that ends with Smith's trying
again to put his wit on display. Challenging what *Common Sense* says
about the Bible and monarchy, 'Cato' writes:

>   I cannot find any modern kings rejected by Heaven, but MOUNSIER
>   the KING OF FRANCE. It is in the 25th chapter of Ezekiel; and I am

sure our author is so deeply versed in scripture, could not have over-
looked it, if it had not been for the treaty he proposes with this King.
The reader will readily allow that the application is much more natural than that which the author has made of the 8th chapter of the 1st
book of Samuel.

Son of Man, set thy face against MOUNTSEIR (Heb. Mounseir, or
Monseur) and prophecy against it (Heb. Him) and say unto him, thus
saith the Lord God: Behold O Mountseir or Mounsier, I am against
thee – because thou hast had a perpetual hatred, and has shed the
blood of the children of Israel [that is, the French Protestants] by the
force of the sword – Therefore, as I live, saith the Lord God, I will prepare thee unto blood, and blood shall pursue thee. – Thus will I make
Mountseir, or Monsieur, most desolate – because thou hast said these
two nations, and these two countries [here Britain and America are
clearly pointed out] shall be mine, and we will possess it – whereas
the Lord was there – as much to say, [you shall not have these two
countries Monsieur! The Lord intends them for his own use – they
shall be free Protestant countries].

The reader may peruse the remainder of the chapter, which he may
do as well as the author of Common Sense; and, some may say, perhaps as well as CATO.

40 *Miscellaneous Works*, 317–18.
41 Ibid., 317.
42 Ibid.

5

New Brunswick Loyalist Printers in the Post-war Atlantic World: Cultural Transfer and Cultural Challenges

GWENDOLYN DAVIES

On 13 February 1766, *Halifax Gazette* journeyman printer Isaiah Thomas articulated his opposition to the Stamp Act by printing a revenue stamp upside down on a page of the newspaper and inserting above it a woodcut depicting the devil jabbing at the halfpenny revenue stamp with a pitchfork. Overprinted on the text of the paper were the words, 'Scorn and Contempt of America pitching down to Destruction. D—ils clear the way for B———s and STAMPS.'[1] Because of this flagrant challenge to British authority, Thomas was dismissed from the *Halifax Gazette* and returned to New England, where he was eventually to continue his anti-British attacks in the *Massachusetts Spy*, first published in Boston in 1770.[2] By mid-April 1775, with political tensions in the Boston area escalating, Thomas spirited his printing press and type forty miles inland and, on 3 May, resumed newspaper publishing in Worcester, Massachusetts.[3] There he remained for the rest of his career, building a network as an influential printer, authoring an enduring two-volume *History of Printing in America* (Worcester, 1810), and founding the American Antiquarian Society to preserve the print heritage of the United States.

Thomas's brief association with Nova Scotia now seems a footnote in time, but it nonetheless illustrates the contiguousness in Canadian and American printing culture in the years leading up to the American Revolution.[4] The Tory targets of Thomas's virulent attacks in the *Massachusetts Spy* were among the sixty to seventy thousand Loyalist refugees who left the United States at the cessation of hostilities, approximately thirty thousand of whom entered the Maritime provinces of British North America, where they escalated the introduction of printing shops, newspapers, reading societies, educational institutions, theatrical performances, and book production in the region at a rate atypical of an early stage of colonial development.[5]

Although geographical distance and the immediate challenge of building a social and physical infrastructure militated against the emergence of a Loyalist school of writing in the Maritimes at the end of the eighteenth century, the example of Loyalist poets such as Jonathan Odell in Fredericton and Jacob Bailey in Annapolis Royal nonetheless laid the foundation for a regional literary and cultural consciousness that found expression in the next two generations of Maritime writers. Joseph Howe, Oliver Goldsmith, Jr, Griselda Tonge, Thomas Chandler Haliburton, Bliss Carman, Sir Charles G.D. Roberts, H.A. Cody, Sophia Almon Hensley, and Alice Jones were all among the children and grandchildren of regional Loyalists who saw in the imagined community of the Loyalists' poetry, essays, sermons, diaries, letters, and dramatic prologues the emergence of a distinctive sense of cultural identity. 'Many have been the chances and changes of my pilgrimage,' noted poet Deborah How Cottnam in 1794 as she reflected on her transition from upper-middle-class life in Salem, Massachusetts, to teaching school in Saint John. But for her students – as for her Nova Scotian great granddaughter, the poet Griselda Tonge (1803–25) – Cottnam's life, values, and literary talent stood as an inspiration for successive generations of young women ('Oh, that on me the power had been bestowed!').[6]

Central to this process of cultural transition as the Loyalists moved into what would become Maritime Canada were the Loyalist printers, who, having been forced to take sides in the polarized political environment of America in the years leading up to the Revolution, now found themselves among the refugee exiles. Disseminators of public debate, prisms of insight into societal patterns, and representatives of Loyalist views, they now emerged as seminal agents of cultural transfer and creation in the newly settled communities where they published broadsheets, monographs, almanacs, sermons, government documents, and newspapers. The polarization accompanying the war had revealed that printers were not, as Stephen Botein has noted, 'mere mechanics,' but men of 'independent intellect and principle.'[7] They played an enabling, if sometimes contested, role in arguments about authorship at a time of political crisis (see Philip Gould in this volume), *and* they began to inform part of an emerging middle class in both the United States and British North America.[8] Thus, they had considerable impact on the fledgling Loyalist communities to which they migrated in terms of both what they published and where they disseminated it.

John Ryan of Rhode Island and Christopher Sower (Sauer) III of Pennsylvania effectively illustrate the transitional roles in which Loyalist printers found themselves in moving to British North America. Migrating separately to the newly established city of Saint John in 1783 and 1785, respectively, they brought different social and political approaches to their professional work. A pacifist German Baptist (Dunker) and the product of a Pennsylvania German printing dynasty, Sower articulated a conservative vision as printer, publisher, and eventual political aspirant in the new colony of New Brunswick. Sacrifices for the Crown had created a sense of defensiveness, perhaps even desperation, in Sower, and he took full advantage of well-placed London connections to negotiate his appointment as king's printer and deputy postmaster general of New Brunswick in 1785. In his bid for political office in 1795, Sower appears to have had aspirations for gentrification, a thesis reinforced by his building a large, isolated rural retreat on the Hammond River twelve miles outside Saint John, where locals began referring to him as 'Colonel Sower.'[9] Such moves – not inconsistent with the post-war upward mobility of prominent American printers and publishers such as Timothy Green III and Isaiah Thomas, who added the designation 'Esquire' to their names – nonetheless isolated Sower from many of his fellow Loyalists in the colony.[10] And although he demonstrated masterly technical skills as a printer in his production of the *Royal Gazette and New Brunswick Advertiser*, his publishing venture as king's printer reflected sublimation to official expectation more than a forward-looking engagement with his new society.

Equally talented as a master printer in the design and execution of his newspapers, the six foot two, quietly astute John Ryan always seemed more attuned to constituency opinion and public debate than Sower. Ryan, his wife, and partner William Lewis had all acted in amateur theatricals in New York City, where Lewis and Ryan had published the *New York Mercury; or General Advertiser* at the end of the Revolution.[11] They subsequently demonstrated the same kind of community involvement that developed local trust in Saint John. Immersing themselves in the spirit of municipal politics, they were declared freemen of the city after its incorporation and became actively involved in a newly formed branch of the Freemasons.[12] After 1785 Ryan assumed full responsibility for their printing and publishing establishment, eventually becoming king's printer when Sower left the colony in 1799. Even during the period when they were publishing competitively in New Brunswick, however, it was clear that Ryan, unlike Sower, had begun to develop a network of apprentices, journeymen, and printers, including his own sons, who would build the foundations of future printing and publishing ventures throughout the Maritime provinces and in the wider British Atlantic. Thus, as case studies of how two Loyalist printers positioned themselves in rebuilding careers fractured by war, Sower and Ryan speak eloquently to the varying degrees of success that Loyalist printers experienced in the region. Moreover, cast under the critical lens of a 'history of the book' approach, they are of interest not only for the practical process they represent in establishing a print culture framework on the east coast of British North America, but also for their role in enabling the emergence of divergent political and cultural voices through their publications.

The pre-war careers of many Loyalist printers were remarkably homogeneous. As Carol Sue Humphrey notes, many pre-revolutionary printers had learned their trade from the Green family printing dynasty, which had flourished in New England for almost two hundred years, or through 'the networks that resulted from the apprenticeship system.'[13] Intermarriage within printing families strengthened those bonds, so that when printer Margaret (Green) Draper joined other Loyalists in the evacuation of Boston to Halifax in March 1776, she already had a familial connection to the city through her uncle, who had established its first press in 1751.[14] Loyalist printer John Howe of Halifax trained his brother-in-law, William Minns, before the latter began his own print shop and newspaper in that city, and John Ryan of Saint John was succeeded as king's printer by his Loyalist refugee brother-in-law, Jacob Mott, in 1808. Among the Loyalist printers in British North America, as in pre-war America, apprenticeship in one print shop began to provide employees for another. For example, in 1820 David Howe left the printing business established by his father, John Howe, in Halifax, to become co-editor of the *St Andrews Herald* in St Andrews, New Brunswick, while in 1815 Gabriel F. Mott left his family print shop in Saint John for his uncle's establishment in Newfoundland.[15]

While pre-war printers in the middle colonies often had been identified in relationship to Benjamin Franklin's entrepreneurial network, a sense of a *cognoscente* of printers nonetheless had prevailed in the old British America.[16] Moreover, the Stamp Act had briefly unified printers throughout the colonies, not only because of the financial and civil challenges that it represented, but also because it threatened 'the precious economic lifeline between the printing business and the paper trade.'[17] Supply networks, notes John Bidwell, had 'provided the printing craft not just with materials and equipment but also order and continuity.' Important, then, as family or religious ties might have been in unifying pre-war printers, 'credit strategies,' 'political alignments,' and 'lines of supplies' were fundamental to how printers and publishers did business.[18] When 'the revolutionary crisis' came, adds David D. Hall in *The Colonial Book in the Atlantic World*, 'a stance of neutrality, which a long line of printers used to shield themselves from factionalism, ceased to be an option.' 'Anyone who affiliated with the Loyalists,' he adds, 'risked being put out of business by a mob.'[19]

The situation in Boston in 1775 at the outbreak of war revealed just such divisions. After the battles of Lexington and Concord in April, the British had fortified themselves within Boston. Four Loyalist printers remained in the city and published two newspapers, while Patriots such as Benjamin Edes and Isaiah Thomas fled inland to Watertown and Worcester, respectively, to carry on their publishing. But, by mid-March 1776, the British had evacuated Boston, forcing Loyalist printers such as Margaret Draper, John Howe, John Hicks, and Nathaniel Mills to sail to Halifax with the retreating military forces.[20] While Margaret Draper proceeded to Britain to press claims for her losses, Howe, Mills, and Hicks made their way back to America, where, by November 1776, they had opened a printing office in British-held New York City (Mills and Hicks eventually joining forces with the Loyalist printers Alexander and James Robertson).[21] After the British took Newport, Rhode Island, on 8 December 1776, Howe became the official printer for the Provincial Forces in Rhode Island, publishing his first issue of the *Newport Gazette* on 16 January 1777.

Howe's *Newport Gazette* was initially a small publication because of a scarcity of large paper, and it relied on equipment originally buried by the editor of the Patriot newspaper, the *Newport Mercury*.[22] Also employing what George Edward Cullen has described as 'curious boldface roman' Scottish type originally belonging to the Boston print shop of Mein and Fleeming, the *Newport Gazette* was an unabashedly pro-British newspaper strong on examples of congressional malaise.[23] Married during this period into what was to be the Loyalist Minns family of printers, Howe took as an apprentice Newport native John Ryan, who would later join William Lewis in publishing the *New York Mer-*

cury; or General Advertiser.[24] In 1780, after British troops had left Rhode Island, John Howe returned to Halifax, where, in December, he began to publish the *Halifax Journal*, which survived for the next one hundred years, and where he trained his sons John, David, and Joseph to be printers and publishers in Nova Scotia and New Brunswick. Joseph also became an iconic Canadian poet, essayist, champion of Responsible Government, and opponent of Confederation. Meanwhile, Howe's former apprentice John Ryan, now married into the Mott family of printers, joined other refugees immigrating to Saint John.[25]

The Loyalist printers faced especially daunting challenges in 1783 in coming to an undeveloped Maritime region where most communities had yet to be surveyed. They settled in ports with access to the latest news arriving on ships, incoming letters that individuals might share with the public, fresh supplies of books and stationery (both staples of the print shop), and to business advertising essential for printers' revenue.[26] Pre-war printing economies had relied on what John Bidwell describes as family, credit, political, religious, and supply-line ties.[27] All of these connections were in disarray, but family proved the most durable. The initial cost of setting up a print shop was daunting at any time and presented special challenges in the inflationary post-war period. Carol Humphrey estimates that at the time of the Revolution it cost a printer in New England about one-fifth to one-third of an expected yearly income of approximately £247 to establish a printing business.[28] In most cases, a family-run print shop had just one press and one or two apprentices, but the most successful ventures, such as those operated by Benjamin Franklin and David Hall in Philadelphia in the 1750s, or Isaiah Thomas and Ebenezer T. Andrews in Boston and Worcester in the 1790s, were two- or three-press shops.[29]

For any Loyalist printer trying to re-establish a professional life in Nova Scotia, New Brunswick, or Prince Edward Island after the war, major capital expenses included at least one printing press, type, composing sticks, type cases, galleys, chases, ball stocks, and an imposing stone. Prior to the American Revolution, nearly all presses and type in America had been imported.[30] As a result, an active business existed in used presses, all of which were difficult to transport. John Bidwell has noted that 'even with sufficient capital in hand' master printers in America often had difficulty shopping for essential equipment, sometimes even booking passage overseas to deal with suppliers directly, sometimes ordering from overseas 'sight unseen,' and more frequently buying used equipment at home.[31] By far the most expensive investment in equipment was for type, usually imported from large printing centres such as Paris, Amsterdam, and London. Although attempts to produce local type were made by a number of American foundries before the end of the eighteenth century (and Franklin and Thomas 'sold new or used fonts on the side'),[32] many North American printers continued to rely on British foundries such as Caslon in London, Baine in Edinburgh, or Wilson in Glasgow for their supplies. Shipping, insurance, wharfage, and agents' fees for transferring type were high, and printers often experienced delays in receiving their purchases. With type weighing up to a thousand pounds and costing up to £80, some North American printers experimented with octavo gatherings of four leaves instead of eight in their publications or with mixing type as a way of saving on wear and replacement costs.[33] Loyalist printer John Howe working in Rhode Island in 1779 serves as a case in point. Clearly lacking a capital 'R' in his typesetting of Sir George Collier and Major General William Tryon's 'Address to the Inhabitants of Connecticut' in the *Newport Gazette* in 1779, Howe imaginatively improvised to make relevant words intelligible while missing a critical letter.[34]

Howe's wartime challenges probably helped prepare him for setting up shop in Halifax in 1780, where, according to tradition, he began publishing with a fifty-year-old Benjamin Franklin press.[35] Other Loyalist printers, such as the Robertsons of Shelburne, were equally effective in integrating used equipment into their new locations, although Benjamin Franklin actively blocked the removal of a Philadelphia press from the Robertsons' New York shop in May 1783 by insisting that the provisional treaty, which prohibited British forces from carrying away any property of the inhabitants, entitled him to recover the press.[36] By far the best-prepared Loyalist printer entering the region was Christopher Sower III, who, provided with a printing press and other equipment by his influential friend Brook Watson, former commissary general of British forces in New York and now a member of Parliament for the City of London,[37] arrived in Saint John in 1785 announcing that he possessed 'a set of the very best Types, entirely new, and cast by the most celebrated Letter-Founders.'[38]

Representing the third generation of a printing dynasty in Germantown, Pennsylvania, Sower had seen his father's type foundry, ink-making, and printing business, valued at £7,000, confiscated by the Patriots in 1777. Having sacrificed his own business during the war to serve the British as a sometime printer, German translator, and undercover agent, he had operated a book and stationery business in London after 1783 while pressing his claims for reparation. His 22 March 1784 memorial to the Loyalist Claims Commission provides insight into the pre-war prosperity of a well-established thirty-year-old family printer. He valued his seized 'large dwelling House, Printing office and sundry other Buildings with three and a half acres of Land' in Germantown at £600; 'three printing presses, with English and German types and all other necessary Materials for carrying on the Printing Business' at £660; stocks of books (three thousand primers, three hundred *Death of Abel*s in German) at £37 20s; and a five-year loss of income from both his printing office and his book, stationery, and drug shop at £900.[39] By contrast, when Sower died in 1799 after fourteen years in New Brunswick, his total estate, including debts owed, was evaluated at £348 6s 10d, with £70 of the total for 'printing press and materials.'[40]

When Sower arrived in Saint John from London in 1785, he discovered that a two-press print shop was already firmly established in the city. With the dissolution of the *New York Mercury; or General Advertiser* in 1783, Kentish-born printer William Lewis led a Loyalist company of ninety-one men, women, and children to New Brunswick carrying everything needed to set up a print shop.[41] After the arrival of his former partner John Ryan, the two began publishing the first New Brunswick newspaper, the *Royal St John's Gazette and Nova Scotia Intelligencer*, in December 1783, just eight months after the first Loyalist refugees had landed in the still-unformed province. By mid-1784, the Ryan-Lewis office was augmented by a second press and set of type after Ryan successfully petitioned Lieutenant-Governor Thomas Carleton on 27 February 1784 to import 'a printing Press and Types' that he had left in New York 'not knowing what Encouragement he might meet with in a new Country.'[42]

Now well equipped to operate a two-press shop, Lewis and Ryan nonetheless faced other challenges, especially finding a source of paper to meet the demands of government printing jobs that had begun to come their way. During the war years, as Arthur Schlesinger has pointed out, 'the scarcity of newsprint owing to the cutting off of imports, the spiraling of costs of the domestic variety, and the shortage of journeymen due to wartime demands and distractions' had resulted in American printers issuing smaller editions, ceasing to publish for weeks at a time, and raising prices for subscriptions.[43] Cognizant of the importance of information distribution during the war, George Washington had exempted papermakers from military service and given at least 'one publisher a supply of tent cloth for making paper so that his soldiers could have access to a newspaper.'[44]

Inevitably, then, Loyalist refugee printers establishing themselves in the Maritimes in the post-war period relied on importing expensive paper from Britain or making their own. The process, notes Carol Humphrey, 'required skilled workmen, who were difficult to find, and large numbers of rags, which were always scarce,'[45] forcing printers throughout North America to actively solicit rags, linen, old sails, and 'junk.'[46] An account entry by Captain Daniel Lovett of Saint John in April 1798 shows that he received 11s 8d from John Ryan for 'old Sails,' suggesting that Ryan took advantage of port city resources for papermaking.[47] Ryan may well have been driven to this extremity by the continuing uncertainty of his import sources, for he implored his readers on 31 March 1789 to 'excuse his intruding again on their good nature, by being obliged to alter the form of this *Gazette,* which is wholly occasioned by disappointments in a supply of Printing paper.'[48] His publishing rival, Christopher Sower, also apologized profusely to his readers of 11, 18, and 25 April 1797 because he had to print the *Royal Gazette* on wrapping paper. Although he had 'laid in a stock of printing paper, in his opinion sufficient to last him until he could receive a fresh supply from England,' he had 'exhausted his store' and was 'now under the disagreeable necessity of making use of brown paper until the arrival of some vessel from London.'[49] And, in 1800, Jacob Mott, who had purchased the *Saint John Gazette and the General Advertiser* in April 1799, offered cash or books from his printing shop in exchange for clean linen and cotton rags.[50] A 15 August 1800 newspaper response to Mott's plea satirically argued that his offer of a penny a pound for rags was not going to entice Moll, Betty, or Sue to stoop and soil her hands in picking up 'shreds' or 'dish cloths' for the welfare of the printer and the production of news. Adopting a tone of mock irony that anticipated Thomas McCulloch and Thomas Chandler Haliburton's later Nova Scotian newspaper satires on the region's decline in moral values, the writer ended his diatribe on the follies of those wedded to 'gewgaws and superfluous commodities' by pontificating: 'to prevent being ragged, save your rags!'[51]

By far the most immediate initial challenge for Lewis and Ryan, however, was a purely physical one. Saint John, as Loyalist diarist Sarah Frost noted from the deck of the *Two Sisters,* was 'the roughest land I ever saw,'[52] or, as Clarence Ward put it, little more than an uphill path through the woods.[53] The boundary lines of Prince William Street had just been run by the surveyor Paul Bedell, and the building lots and cross streets were still identified only by roughly cut fir posts or by blazes upon trees. In the middle of lot 59, on the east side of Prince William Street (between Duke and Princess), Lewis and Ryan built a two-room log cabin that served as dwelling place, printing shop, and newspaper office.[54] They began publishing their eight-by-thirteen inch three-column weekly on 18 December 1783, and from the start were inextricably drawn into what David Bell has argued was a 'political climate . . . that many likened . . . to the mood of the old colonies on the eve of the Revolution.'[55]

Even before the Loyalist evacuees had left New York, notes Bell, six hundred heads of refugee households had signed a memorial against the proposal that fifty-five elite Loyalists receive individual fiefdoms of five thousand acres of the best land at the expense of the disbanded military and refugee families awaiting passage to what was then Nova Scotia. Although assured by Sir Guy Carleton that he would forward 'their remonstrance to Governor Parr,' the incoming Loyalists brought their sense of grievance and alarm with them to Saint John.[56] A highly charged environment marked by class violence, executive manipulation of regulations and election results, and subsequent trials for libel and sedition unfolded in the city from 1783, building to the election of 1785. Lewis and Ryan's publication of an anonymous vernacular sixty-line poem by 'A Spectator' on 29 January 1784 suggested that Loyalist disillusionment with the 'fifty-five' was at public boil, especially in its venomous denunciation of Reverend John Sayre, Secretary of the New York Agency:

> May he, the author of our woes,
> Far fiercer than our rebel foes,
> Have his due portion near a lake,
> Which is ordain'd to such by fate;
> May living worms his corps devour,
> Him and his comrades fifty-four:
> A scandal to both church and state,
> The rebel's friend, the public's hate.[57]

This was followed by a dialogue by 'A Plain Dealer' on 26 February 1784 critical of both the land distribution process and the agents. And on 4 March 1784 Lewis and Ryan published a letter by 'A Soldier' that again attacked, among others, government land agents. All of this challenged an inchoate civil authority, and on 10 March 1784 Lewis and Ryan were charged before a Sunbury County grand jury with printing, publishing, and spreading 'among the subjects of our said lord the King a certain seditious and scandalous libel.'[58] By putting the weight of sedition on Lewis and Ryan as printers rather than on the contributors to the newspaper, the magistrates made the printers a searing public symbol of administrative displeasure with those who dared challenge executive authority in the colony. Even though Lewis and Ryan had publicly demurred on 4 March 1784 that 'pieces tending to scurrility or faction' would 'not be attended to' in their newspaper, they had published the letter from 'A Soldier' on the very day their editorial policy had appeared.[59] The charges of sedition and libel that ensued were designed to be a visible condemnation of their perceived role as an incubus for dissent in the public sphere.

Despite these charges Lewis and Ryan continued to publish according to their convictions. On 9 September 1784 they printed a proposal by David Melville for the subscription publication of a three-hundred-page 'Accurate History of the Settlement of his Majesty's Exiled Loyalists.' Melville's prospectus indicated that he would explore the 'disputes between the inhabitants and their Agents, so called' and that he would show the suffering among the refugees because of delayed land allocations, withheld donations, and taxation levied upon them. Although copies do not survive, instalments were supposedly printed in the *St John's Gazette*.[60] Moreover, by signing the Huggeford Petition of Grievance with 342 other Saint John Loyalists on 24 December 1784 that protested the agents' handling of land issues, Lewis and Ryan clearly demonstrated that they had not been intimidated by the libel and sedition charges in March.

They were to be less fortunate following the election of 1785. By that time Christopher Sower III had arrived in Saint John from England as king's printer and deputy postmaster general.[61] Publishing every Thursday, Lewis and Ryan had carved out a strong commercial niche with the solid advertising base essential for the survival of a non-subsidized newspaper, and had enjoyed a monopoly on printing official items such as the charter for the new city of Saint John and various government bills. They therefore had reason to resent Sower's appointment, not only because it threatened to cost them all government printing business but also because they had to remove the word 'Royal' from their newspaper masthead in deference to Sower's official *Royal Gazette and New Brunswick Advertiser*.

On one level Lewis and Ryan may have had little to fear. They had already built up a viable subscription, contributor, and reader constituency as the first newspaper in the city. And they had already demonstrated their ability to attract the kind of readership that, as Jeffery L. McNairn has discussed in his analysis of reader engagement in nineteenth-century Upper Canada, had made 'a conscious decision to participate in the public sphere and to support a particular vehicle for that participation.'[62] Moreover, Sower's *Royal Gazette* inevitably was shaped by his mandate as king's printer and deputy postmaster general (the latter role gave him free copies of the latest newspapers from other places as source material but compelled him to publish long lists of uncollected letters in his newspaper). His well-executed, three-column Tuesday paper, which was regularly distributed as far away as Fredericton (two to three days by sleigh in winter), was a compendium of British and American extracts, government reports, shipping activities, advertisements, and local events (of particular interest were partisan letters sent to the paper during the intense Saint John election of 1785). Marie Tremaine has pointed out that official items and advertisements could so dominate the *Royal Gazette*'s layout as to make it 'a formal and monotonous journal.'[63] A cross-section of Sower's print-shop production reinforces a sense of his professional commitments: almanacs, legal blanks, a handbill preventing Assembly members from wearing ice creepers in the Assembly room,[64] a 1786 New Year's Masonic sermon, confessions by condemned criminals, and, in the *Gazette*, even the details of a drunken murderer wandering the streets of Saint John in 1797 with a bouquet of flowers in one hand and a severed hand in the other.[65] As had been clear in his pre-war and wartime career, Sower used print to reinforce governing authority in the public sphere.

Thus, it was as the representative of good order that Sower clashed most visibly with Lewis and Ryan. He began publication of his newspaper by stressing that 'neither disrespect to Government, nor abuse or ridicule of fellow subjects will be permitted in this paper.'[66] His report of the Mallard House riot in Saint John, where troops quelled violence between the Lower Covers (including disbanded Loyalist soldiers) and the Upper Covers (better-off Loyalists) during the November 1785 election for the Provincial Assembly, self-righteously played upon public emotions by employing words such as 'fear,' 'mob,' 'violent,' and 'outrageous.'[67] The five months of bitter dissent between entrenched privilege and its opposition in Saint John that culminated in

the riot 'became one of the most dramatic and, it may be, formative episodes in New Brunswick political history,' argues Bell.[68] Sower clearly
saw his fellow printers as having crossed to the dark side, identifying
Lewis to the Speaker of the House of Assembly as being in McPher-
son's Coffee Room on 24 January 1786 when seditious words allegedly were uttered.[69] There was already a 'history' between Lewis and
Sower dating back to New York in 1783, when Sower's attempts to
collect money from a publishing venture in the city had led indirectly
to Lewis' incarceration for debt.[70] When, on 22 February 1786, Lewis
and Ryan published a letter signed 'Americanus' in which the anonymous author urged readers to 'Submit not to petit Tyrants,' they were
arrested and charged with 'printing and publishing a scandalous and
seditious libel.'[71] Their arrest, notes Bell, was the government's attempt
to neutralize them 'through intimidation or financial ruin.'[72] The tactic
worked. Dissolving their partnership on 1 April 1786, Lewis and Ryan
stood trial and were found guilty of sedition by the Supreme Court in
Saint John on 2 May 1786. They were each fined £20 and costs and 'ordered to provide surety of £100 for good behaviour for six months.'[73]
Lewis disappeared from public view at this juncture, but Ryan continued to publish his newspaper, the *St John's Gazette and the Weekly Advertiser* (by 1787 called the *Saint John Gazette and the Weekly Advertiser*),
as an unofficial 'municipal printer' until he sold it to his brother-in-law,
Jacob Mott, in 1799.[74]

Clearly, the authorities' perception of Ryan as subversive did not
long endure. As early as 1787 he was invited to compete against Sower
for the contract to print the journals of the House of Assembly of New
Brunswick, a tender usually awarded automatically to the king's printer.
Sower was bitter at losing business to Ryan, but surviving correspondence suggests that Sower's excellence as a master printer was offset
by his inability to work well with people.[75] Disappointed in his political aspirations and claiming ill health, Sower resigned as king's printer
in 1799 and travelled to the United States with his printer-apprentice
son, Brook Watson Sower (named after his father's influential London
friend), to negotiate a partnership in his brother Samuel's type foundry
business. His death from apoplexy while visiting Baltimore ended the
peregrinations that had taken him across the Atlantic four times, relocated him from London to colonial New Brunswick, and brought him
back to the United States to a family dynasty of German-English printers that had been disrupted but not destroyed by the Revolution (see
Map 5.1).

Map 5.1

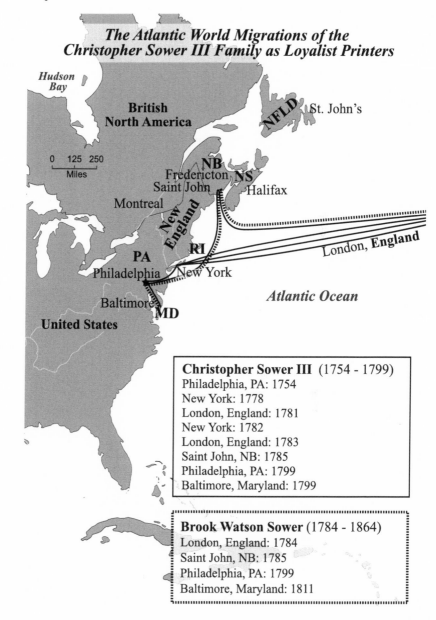

The Atlantic World Migrations of the
Christopher Sower III Family as Loyalist Printers

Christopher Sower III (1754 - 1799)
Philadelphia, PA: 1754
New York: 1778
London, England: 1781
New York: 1782
London, England: 1783
Saint John, NB: 1785
Philadelphia, PA: 1799
Baltimore, Maryland: 1799

Brook Watson Sower (1784 - 1864)
London, England: 1784
Saint John, NB: 1785
Philadelphia, PA: 1799
Baltimore, Maryland: 1811

While Sower's life reflects the complexity of one Loyalist printer's career in the British Atlantic during and after the war, it also reveals an impact on the next generation. His son had been born in London in 1784, raised in New Brunswick, initially trained in Saint John, and apprenticed in Pennsylvania to printer Zachariah Poulson after Sower's death. Brook Watson Sower's early printing career was inextricably tied to the fortunes of his father. With one Sower uncle in Baltimore as a printer and type founder, another Sower uncle in Pennsylvania as a newspaper publisher, and a maternal uncle with a print shop in Philadelphia, Brook Watson decided to remain in the United States after completing his apprenticeship in Philadelphia. Founding the publishing firm B.W. Sower & Company in Baltimore, he printed the first diamond edition of the Bible in America in 1812.[76]

The outmigration from New Brunswick experienced by Christopher Sower's son was replicated by the children of John Ryan. Appointed king's printer after Sower resigned the position in 1799, Ryan enjoyed a new level of personal security at the beginning of the nineteenth century. He brought changes to the *Royal Gazette,* adding to its news content, enlarging its pages, increasing its type size, and giving it a new sense of style.[77] In 1806, however, faced with a growing family requiring career options, he made a reconnaissance trip to Newfoundland, whose population of approximately twenty-five thousand had no newspaper. Confirming that two hundred merchants and middle-class endorsers in St John's would support a newspaper, Ryan paid £200 as bond to the Newfoundland Court of Sessions for a licence as a printer and publisher in the city.[78] Leaving his wife, Amelia (Mott) Ryan, in Saint John to manage his New Brunswick affairs – and his Loyalist brother-in-law, Jacob Mott, to become king's printer – John Ryan, with his eldest son, Michael, began publishing the *Royal Gazette and Newfoundland Advertiser* on 27 August 1807. Eventually setting up a thirty-by-twenty foot printing office and stationer's shop on Duckworth Street in St John's adjoining their rented dwelling place,[79] Ryan's family-run operation not only intermittently trained or employed five sons and a Saint John nephew, Gabriel F. Mott,[80] it also integrated his wife and daughters into the business. A visitor to St John's provides a detailed account of 'the daily routine of a newspaper family at the time':

the various departments of exertion left no individual, young or old, male or female, unoccupied. The father took the literary lead, and wrote the leading article; the son-in-law (a half-pay purser in the Navy) sometimes sported a quiet quill on a little quackery in political economy; the mother, not having much pretensions to letters, except in type (for she could assist a compositor in a pinch), collected and arranged little recipes for preserves, pickling, and pretty progeny; whilst the daughters who were spinsters, professing total ignorance of the latter composition, confined their talents to aiding in the composition of type and correcting the press, which usually went on during the hour of tea, when every avowed contributor considered himself a privileged guest.[81]

This glimpse into the operations of what Maudie Whelan identifies as the Ryan family press confirms that Loyalist daughters and wives such as Amelia (Mott) Ryan in Saint John and St John's – and her sister-in-law Ann (Hinton) Mott in Saint John – played as significant a role in the household printing operations in post-war British North America as women had sometimes done in pre-revolutionary America.[82]

But Ryan found, as did many first-generation middle-class Loyalists, that opportunities for his children were limited in the British colonies. Chafing at the lack of support to sustain Michael's editorship of the *New Brunswick Chronicle* in Saint John in 1804 or the *Fredericton Telegraph* in 1806–07, he took Michael with him to Newfoundland. When Michael's attempts in 1810 to establish a mercantile newspaper in St John's were thwarted by officialdom's decision to permit only one paper, Ryan noted bitterly to Governor Keats that Michael had been forced to move to the West Indies because of local resistance to expanding publishing.[83] In Barbados, Michael succeeded in publishing the *Globe*, a paper that was as vigilant in representing the voice of the common man against class privilege as had been his father's *St John's Gazette and New Brunswick Advertiser* in the mid-1780s. Tried and exonerated by the Court of Grand Sessions on 10 June 1819 on charges of printing sedition and libel, Michael Ryan was carried triumphantly through the streets of the capital, Bridgetown, by his supporters.[84] He eventually became Printer to the Barbados House of Assembly in much the same way as his father had overcome similar charges to later enjoy government favour in New Brunswick and then Newfoundland.

Michael Ryan's Barbados career – the outcome of three generations of British American printers from Margaret (Green) Draper to John Howe to John Ryan – shows that, by the nineteenth century, the British Atlantic had truly become a 'zone of exchange and interchange, circulation and transmission.'[85] The younger Ryan brought to Barbados the spirit of the press learned in his father's printing establishments in Saint John and St John's, and his brothers, the Newfoundland publisher, Lewis Kelly, and twenty-one-year-old Ingraham would set off independently to Bridgetown to ostensibly join Michael in the family trade. Both died young, however, one en route to Barbados and the other from illness on the island. To these family losses in the 1820s was added that of Michael Ryan himself in 1829, lost at sea when his ten-gun brig disappeared on the return voyage from Newfoundland, where he had visited his parents.[86] His widow, continuing the tradition of female involvement in the printing business, became 'editress of the *Globe'* after his death, and four years later married the editor of the Port of Spain *Gazette* in nuptials reported in the *New Brunswick Royal Gazette* of Fredericton. Thus, the map of Ryan family migration shows figures traversing the western Atlantic, especially the densely travelled routes connecting New Brunswick, Newfoundland, and Barbados. To these can be added unexpected trajectories, for Ryan's nephew, Gabriel F. Mott, left the familiar Saint John–St John's axis to head for the Alabama Territory in 1819, where he edited the Blakely *Sun* before moving to New York in 1822 to copublish the *Weekly Museum.* Thus, the Ryan map (see Map 5.2), like the Sower one, not only suggests the complexity and scope of British Atlantic print culture in the post-war era but also effectively illustrates how Loyalist printers were crucial agents in creating the north-south and transatlantic corridors that followed in the wake of forced Loyalist migrations.

In 1832, with four of his five sons dead (the youngest had been killed in a winter sliding accident in St John's), John Ryan took his employee, John Collier Withers, into partnership in running Newfoundland's *Royal Gazette* and withdrew from active publishing. The agreement he had signed with Governor Sir Erasmus Gower in 1806 had required 'that previously to the printing of each number of the said Paper, he shall submit the perusal of the proposed contents thereof, to the Magistrates in the said Court of Sessions' and not include any matter 'which in their opinion or the opinion of the Governor . . . may tend to disturb the peace of his Majesty's Subjects.'[87] Subsequent conditions forbade Ryan from allowing anything negative about Britain to appear in the newspaper, including 'any comments on the policy of any nation.'[88] Nonetheless, 'the appearance of a local press,' notes Jerry Bannister, 'marked a formative stage in the monitoring of state power. For the first time, the court calendar and the outcomes of trials were published, providing a basis of accountability that far outstripped the traditional forms of communication.'[89] Thus, the press provided a *'public* space' in which official abuse could be checked and in which 'the bourgeoisie could fix its place in the social environment, identify its local interests, and promote its own particular causes.'[90]

By 1828–29, pressure for representative government had coalesced, and Ryan's signature on a petition for an assembly suggests that, despite his public role as editor of the *Royal Gazette,* he had not lost the convictions of the man who had signed the Huggeford Grievance against elite privilege in New Brunswick more than forty years earlier.[91] Yet a September 1830 editorial in the *Royal Gazette* argued that Newfoundland could ill afford a local legislature, although Patrick O'Flaherty notes that it might well have been written by Withers, rather than Ryan, who seems to have dropped out of the public gaze after leaving the running of the paper to his employee. In any event, the editorial failed to deter reformers from petitioning for a local legislature and sending a delegation to Britain to present it. When Ryan died in 1847 after years of suffering the 'infirmities of advanced age,' he was described as 'the father of the Press in British North America,' having worked as printer, publisher, and mentor in the Atlantic world for more than sixty years.[92]

Ryan's importance as 'the father of the Press' also lies in his role as an agent of transfer, transition, and change in the liminal years after the Loyalists arrived in east coast British North America. Establishing himself with Lewis as both publisher and printer, he developed the name recognition that ensured his centrality to New Brunswick's discourse and led to his eventual appointment as king's printer. Both Rosalind Remer and Stephen Botein argue that newspaper publishing enabled American printers to 'take pride in the intellectual dimensions of their craft,'[93] and Lewis and Ryan surely possessed a sense of social and intellectual engagement with their profession. Moreover, as early as 26 February 1784, only nine months after the Spring Fleet landed in Saint John, Lewis and Ryan began to negotiate the transitional space between American and refugee identity by enabling readers to self-define through the wide-ranging material in their newspaper. In addition to the politically sensitive content that catapulted Lewis and Ryan into libel court, on 26 February 1784 they also published a local poem by 'Celia,' a voice for Harmony, who, 'Weeping Incessantly these seven long years' waiting for peace, had been reunited with her 'reverend sire' only to find herself now 'banished from the Muse in this

Map 5.2

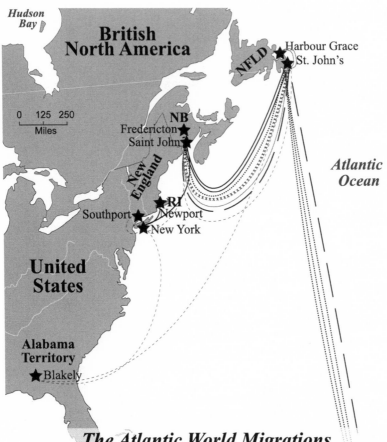

The Atlantic World Migrations of the John Ryan Family as Loyalist Printers

The Atlantic World Migrations of the John Ryan Family as Loyalist Printers

John Ryan (1761 - 1847)

Newport, RI: 1761
New York, NY: 1780
Saint John, NB: 1783
St. Johns, NFLD: 1807
Saint John, NB: 1814
St Johns, NFLD: 1815

Michael Ryan (1784 - 1829)

Saint John, NB: 1784
Fredericton, NB: 1806
St. John's, NFLD: 1807
Bridgetown, Barbados: 1813
St. John's, NFLD: 1828
Barbados (enroute): 1829

Lewis Kelly Ryan (? - 1821)

Saint John, NB: ?
St. John's, NFLD: 1813
Barbados (enroute): 1821

Robert B. Ryan (1802 - 1819)

Saint John, NB: 1802
St. John's, NFLD: 1813

John Ryan Jr. (? - 1860)

Saint John, NB: ?
St. John's, NFLD: 1813
Harbour Grace, NFLD: 1823
St. John's, NFLD: 1823

Ingraham B. Ryan (1805 - 1824)

Saint John, NB: 1805
St. John's NFLD: 1813
Bridgetown, Barbados: 1824

Gabriel F. Mott (1797-1875)

New York: 1797
Saint John, NB: 1798
St. John's, NFLD: 1815
Blakely, Alabama Territory: 1819
New York City: 1819 *
Southport, Connecticut: 1870 *

* approximate dates

new world' – a social plea that the newspaper could circulate but little redress given the political climate that dominated much of the publication throughout 1784–85.[94]

Nonetheless, the newspaper did initiate a book infrastructure in the city. It announced, for example, plans to publish a thousand copies of David Melville's polemical 1784 book on the Loyalists, as well as a book on freemasonry and almanacs designed for the region.[95] It also advertised bookbinder Neville Williams, who was eager to repair old volumes or bind the laws of the newly minted colony, and the availability of songbooks, Bibles, children's picture books, and seamen's journals at a local merchant. The paper also noted that dry-goods dealer William Campbell had imported Johnson's *Dictionary* and Smollett's *Roderick Random*, and carried the announcement by Frederictonians Ludlow, Fraser, and Robertson of the sale, in August 1798, of the indigenously written *The New Gentle Shepherd*, by Lieutenant Adam Allen.[96]

The *St John Gazette* reveals how Lewis and Ryan – and, after 1785, Ryan alone – published local sermons, almanacs, political doggerel, legal documents, personal letters, and literary productions for a refugee population still coming to terms with its identity. At the same time, through reprints of international articles and notices of shipping and commercial activity, the newspaper situated itself within an interconnected Atlantic world. David Hancock notes that recent scholarship has seen the eighteenth-century Atlantic as a 'bridge more than a barrier,' adding that 'newspaper publishing and advertising and a network of permanent retail shops linked the outer reaches of the kingdom to the 'goods-rich' metropolis.'[97] Ryan's notices concerning the comings and goings of ships from London – or merchants' advertisements mentioning a London account – reinforced Saint John's place in a wider economic, mercantile, and intellectual world.[98] While most of the cash-starved Loyalists could ill afford the various consumer goods imported through London- or Glasgow-based mercantile networks, the list of disposable luxuries available – from walnuts and mangoes to cinnamon, nutmeg, cloves, and India soy – indicates a growing international consumer trade in Saint John within several years of settlement.[99] Moreover, advertisements for novels such as *Clarissa Harlow* or practical guides such as *Ferguson's Astronomy* or *Moore's Navigation* speak to the way newspapers provided a conduit for participation in the wider Atlantic world.[100]

While Sower's *Royal Gazette* lacked the personal character informing Lewis and Ryan's publication (J. Russell Harper celebrates the 'utter abandon' of a classic Ryan advertisement), it nonetheless reflected Sower's interest in keeping readers abreast of what other printers and newspapers in the region were publishing.[101] For example, the 9 March 1790 issue advertised a new collection of Robert Burns' poetry to be published by James Robertson in Charlottetown, Sower's own edition of *The Last Words, Dying Speech and Confessions* of two recently executed Saint John burglars, and the prospectus of the *Nova-Scotia Magazine*, a literary periodical published by John Howe in Halifax and edited by classical scholar and teacher the Reverend William Cochrane. The *Nova-Scotia Magazine* was of particular importance. At the height of its popularity, it had a circulation of over three hundred regional subscribers, mainly Loyalists, and in March 1790 (when Sower ran his advertisement) was just concluding its reprint of the unedited script of William Dunlap's enormously popular 1789 American play, *The Father; or, American Shandyism* ('our readers not being likely to meet it in any other shape').[102] The conciliatory note in the play, where the ward of an American colonel marries a British officer from Halifax, was palpable ('We are no longer enemies, your Honour'). And the Cochrane-Howe initiative in publishing the play – not merely as representative of what was fashionable elsewhere, but perhaps also as a 'next step' in local cultural development – reflects the seminal role Loyalist printers such as Howe, Ryan, and Sower played.

Scholars are familiar with the surge in post-war dramatic productions in the United States, but it is less well known that the Loyalists brought an equally strong taste for plays into the Maritime region in the 1780s.[103] They relished not only the productions themselves but also locally written prologues that articulated regional points of view. Tellingly, then, interspersed with other advertisements throughout Ryan and Sower's years of publishing were announcements of dramatic productions such as *The Busy Body, The Gamester, The Citizen,* and *Douglass: The Noble Scotch Shepherd,* most of them performed in the Long Room of Mallard's Tavern in Saint John or the Theatre in Fredericton.[104] Significantly, locally written prologues – such as *On Opening A Little Theatre In This City,* performed in Saint John in 1795, and *Speed the Plough,* performed in Fredericton on 21 May 1803 – were not retrospective in tone but stressed commercial initiative as both the foundation and the future of the new province:

> What rais'd this City on a dreary coast,
> Alternately presenting rocks and frost,

Where torpid shell-fish hardly found a bed,
Where scarce a pine durst shew a stunted head?

Twas commerce – commerce smooth'd the rugged strand,
Her streets and buildings overspread the land;
Her piers the mighty Fundy's tides control,
And navies ride secure within her mole.[105]

Before the Seven Years' War, notes David Shields, the poetry of the
British Empire in America had 'promulgated' both 'a commercial mythology' and various elements of imperial discourse, none of which
survived the Revolution. 'Autarky disappeared completely from the
poetic discourse of the republic,' he adds. 'The notion of metropolitan
privilege, the metaphor of the empire as a political family in which patriarchal authority is exercised over offspring territories, the image of
the virtuous monarch, all vanished in the United States.' It nonetheless
persevered after the war, he argues, 'in the work of Loyalist poets in
Halifax,' citing *America* by Jacob Bailey of Annapolis Royal as an illustra-
tion.[106] Bailey's sentiments – or those of Roger Viets of Digby in his long
poem, *Annapolis Royal* (1788) – shared a great deal with New Brunswick
Loyalist dramatic prologues and newspaper verse that also developed
tropes of community growth and cultural coherence within the context
of the wider British Atlantic. The New Year news carrier's poem published in the *Royal Gazette* on 2 January 1798 was typical of a range of
popular writing in the post-war period that, like dramatic prologues,
reveal the role of the press in shaping a sense of identity. Celebrating
Britain as a political power asserting its role on the international military stage, it nonetheless focused readers on New Brunswick's future
within that construct, where, protected from 'democratical pollution,'
'smiling commerce here with glee/Resume her wonted energy!!!!!'[107]
    Despite the rhetoric of 'commerce' informing the poems and pre-
ludes of New Brunswick's Loyalist *literati*, the small cities on the
Maritime and Newfoundland seaboard could not support the kind of
post-war literary entrepreneurialism, particularly an explosion of book
production, described by Rosalind Remer in her analysis of the publishing economy of Philadelphia in the early republic.[108] Impeded by
small populations (St John's had six thousand, Philadelphia forty-four
thousand), the demands of early settlement, and a local populace often
hard-pressed to pay its newspaper subscriptions, even an innovative
printer and publisher like Ryan had little opportunity to rise financially

in the world. After the destructive St John's fire of 1817, which wiped out Ryan's printing business and home – and after the great fires of 1837 and 1877 in Saint John, which destroyed major portions of that city – there are practical problems in locating records of the printer-supplier networks that integrated Ryan and Sower into the commercial infrastructure of the British Atlantic world. Although he was described as John Ryan, 'Esquire,' at the time of his death in 1847, Ryan's estate was valued under £700.[109] By comparison, the sale price of Isaiah Thomas's US printing and publishing business in 1794 was approximately £7,580.[110] But Thomas, like Benjamin Franklin, had established a network of printing shop investments and had become a supplier to other printers – something that Ryan never seems to have achieved despite Saint John newspaper co-ownership with his former apprentice, William Durant, between 1807 and 1815, the period when he was establishing himself in Newfoundland. Ryan's return to Saint John in 1814 to sell off his partnership and divest himself of property there completed his permanent move to St John's.[111]

Yet, if Ryan left only a modest estate, his professional legacy remains significant. He initiated printing policies in eastern British North America that drew upon and contributed to communication networks essential to the coherence of the British Atlantic in the post-war period. As the publisher of the first newspaper in Newfoundland, notes Patrick O'Flaherty, Ryan 'brought to the attention of a remote and backward colony developments in the great world beyond its headlands.'[112] More enduringly, in New Brunswick, Ryan, along with William Lewis, began a tradition of editorial independence from government that would come to be seen as a crucial function of the press and the public sphere in modern political life. The newspaper and printing offices of John Ryan and his brother-in-law, Jacob Mott, trained, among others, William Durant, Henry Chubb, and George Lugrin, representatives of a whole new generation of New Brunswick printers and publishers of Loyalist background.[113] They continued Ryan's model of editorial independence, and in 1883 Saint John honoured both Ryan and Sower as founding provincial printers during a special arbour day ceremony at Queen's Square marking the one hundredth anniversary of the contribution of the Loyalists to New Brunswick.[114]

By far the most influential figure to emerge from the interconnected group of New Brunswick printers and publishers who prospered from Ryan's substantial legacy was Henry Chubb, sometime partner of Durant, brother-in-law of Lugrin (who became king's printer in 1814), and staunch defender of reform during his long tenure with the *New Brunswick Courier* from 1811 to 1855. Chubb's office trained a generation of journalists, including the New York publisher Robert Sears and the literarily inclined New Brunswick editors Robert Shives and James Hogg.[115] Thus, although Ryan's family network of Ryan-Mott printers never materialized because of the early deaths of his sons, he nonetheless helped to create independent-minded printer-publishers who took New Brunswick from its early Loyalist decades into the Victorian era. Just as Lewis, Ryan, and even Sower had tested the liminality of the social and cultural space occupied by the Loyalists upon first arrival and had employed their newspapers to refigure the refugees' place within an emerging public sphere, so their printer-publisher successors in nineteenth-century New Brunswick began to secure that space by fashioning a regional sense of place within the Atlantic world.

NOTES

1 Francis G. Walett, *Patriots, Loyalists & Printers* (Worcester, MA: American Antiquarian Society, 1976), 19–20; and Hugh Amory, 'The New England Book Trade, 1713–1790,' in *A History of the Book in America*, vol. 1, *The Colonial Book in the Atlantic World*, ed. Hugh Amory and David D. Hall (Cambridge: Cambridge University Press, 2000), 334–5. See also Patricia Lockhart Fleming, 'Mapping Innovation: First Printers and the Spread of the Press,' in *History of the Book in Canada*, vol. 1, *Beginnings to 1840*, ed. Patricia Lockhart Fleming, Gilles Gallichan, and Yvan Lamonde (Toronto: University of Toronto Press, 2004), 63.
2 John Bidwell, 'Part Two: Printers' Supplies and Capitalization,' in *A History of the Book in America*, vol. 1, 1, 179.
3 Isaiah Thomas, *The History of Printing in America* (New York: Weathervane Books, 1970; orig. 1810), 273–4.
4 George Edward Cullen, 'Talking to a Whirlwind: The Loyalist Printers in America: 1763–1783' (PhD diss., West Virginia University, 1979), 29–30. Cullen indicates that Richard Draper feigned horror in the *Massachusetts Gazette* on 27 February 1766 at receiving the *Halifax Gazette* with a 'bloody-red Stamp on each, as terrible as Death to Printers.' Draper also pronounced the quality of the stamped paper to be so thin and so poor that the print was scarcely legible. That Draper received the Halifax paper in Boston underscores the relationship of American and Canadian print culture.

5 The overall figure of 'at least sixty thousand loyalists with fifteen thousand slaves in tow' is given in Maya Jasanoff, 'The Other Side of Revolution: Loyalists in the British Empire,' *William and Mary Quarterly*, 3rd series, 65 (2008): 208, http://www.historycooperative.org/journals/wm/65.2/jasanoff.html. Wallace Brown and Hereward Senior estimate seventy thousand Loyalists left the United States, thirty-five thousand of whom came to the Maritime provinces; see *Victorious in Defeat: The Loyalists in Canada* (Toronto: Methuen, 1984), 32, 38. See also Maya Jasanoff, *Liberty's Exiles: American Loyalists in the Revolutionary World* (New York: Alfred A. Knopf, 2011), 160.

6 [G.E.C. Tonge], 'To My Dear Grandmother On Her 80th Birth Day,' *Acadian Recorder*, 5 March 1825. See Gwendolyn Davies, 'Researching Eighteenth-Century Maritime Women Writers: Deborah How Cottnam – A Case Study,' in *Working in Women's Archives: Researching Women's Private Literature and Archival Documents*, ed. Helen M. Buss and Marlene Kadar (Waterloo, ON: Wilfrid Laurier University Press, 2001), 35–50; and idem, 'Literary Culture in the Maritime Provinces,' in *History of the Book in Canada*, vol. 1 (see note 1), 368–83.

7 Stephen Botein, 'Printers and the American Revolution,' in *The Press & the American Revolution*, ed. Bernard Bailyn and John B. Hench (Boston: Northeastern University Press, 1981), 45.

8 For the economic and class difference between a printer and a publisher, see James N. Green, 'Part One: English Books and Printing in the Age of Franklin,' in *History of the Book in America*, vol. 1 (see note 1), 265.

9 J. Russell Harper, 'Christopher Sower, King's Printer and Loyalist,' *Collections of the New Brunswick Historical Society* 14 (1955): 95–103.

10 Carol Sue Humphrey, *'This Popular Engine': New England Newspapers during the American Revolution, 1775–1789* (Newark: University of Delaware Press, 1992), 59.

11 Maudie Whelan, 'Journalism in Newfoundland: A Beginning History' (unpublished MA thesis in Journalism, Carleton University, 1993), 35, note 58.

12 William Franklin Bunting, *History of St John's Lodge, F. & A.M. of Saint John, New Brunswick, Together With Sketches of All Masonic Bodies in New Brunswick, From A.D. 1784 to A.D. 1894* (Saint John, NB: J. & A. McMillan, 1895), 8, 15.

13 Humphrey, *'This Popular Engine,'* 47–51.

14 Leona M. Hudak, *Early American Women Printers and Publishers: 1639–1820* (Metuchen, NJ: Scarecrow Press, 1978), 397.

15 Printer David Howe, born in Halifax in 1790, was in partnership with his brother, John Howe, Jr, in the Halifax family print shop before he moved to St Andrews, New Brunswick, in 1820 to co-edit the *St Andrews Gazette*.

David Howe returned to Halifax in 1825 and was drowned in St Margaret's Bay, Nova Scotia, in 1826. See Terence M. Punch and Allan E. Marble, 'The Family of John Howe Halifax Loyalist and King's Printer,' *Nova Scotia Historical Quarterly* 6 (1976): 320. For information on Gabriel F. Mott, see endnote 80.

16 Green, 'Age of Franklin,' 271. Also see Ralph Fresca, *Benjamin Franklin's Printing Network: Disseminating Virtue in Early America* (Columbia: University of Missouri Press, 2006), 196–206.

17 Bidwell, 'Printers' Supplies and Capitalization,' 178–9.

18 Ibid., 182, 183.

19 David D. Hall, 'Part One: The Atlantic Economy,' in *History of the Book in America*, vol. 1 (see note 1), 160.

20 Humphrey, '*This Popular Engine*,' 37. John Howe and Margaret Draper published the *Massachusetts Gazette and Boston News-Letter* until the evacuation of Boston in March 1776. See John N. Grant, 'John Howe, Senior,' in *Eleven Exiles: Accounts of Loyalists of the American Revolution*, ed. Phyllis R. Blakeley and John N. Grant (Toronto; Charlottetown: Dundurn Press, 1982), 26–7; and Arthur M. Schlesinger, *Prelude to Independence: The Newspaper War on Britain, 1764–1776* (New York: Alfred A. Knopf, 1958), 237, 258, 295. See also Botein, 'Printers and the American Revolution,' 39–40.

21 Cullen, 'Talking to a Whirlwind,' 289. Cullen says that Mills, Hicks, and Howe were in a printing office together in New York in November 1776; Schlesinger notes that Hicks and Mills worked with the Robertsons on the New York *Royal American Gazette* (*Prelude*, 291); see also Thomas, *History of Printing*, 170–4.

22 Cullen, 'Talking to a Whirlwind,' 290.

23 Ibid., 291–3.

24 Grant, 'Howe,' 30–1. John Howe began publishing the *Newport Gazette* in January 1777, and married Martha Minns on 7 June 1778 while he was in Rhode Island (they evacuated Newport in October 1779). Their first child, Martha, was born on 25 December 1779 in New York. They left New York for Halifax in 1780. See J. Murray Beck, 'Howe, John,' *Dictionary of Canadian Biography*, vol. 6 (Toronto: University of Toronto Press, 1987), 332–5.

25 John Ryan married Amelia Mott, daughter of printer John Mott of Long Island, New York, on 25 June 1786. See Clarence Ward, 'Ward's Scrapbook of Early Printers and Newspapers of New Brunswick and Their Times,' Saint John Free Public Library, MC1810, F125 Inventory, Part C, microfilm reel 125, 9, Provincial Archives of New Brunswick, Fredericton, New Brunswick. See also Patrick O'Flaherty, 'Ryan, John,' *Dictionary of Canadian Biography*, vol. 7, 763–6.

26 Humphrey, 'This Popular Engine,' 21, 35; and Claude Galarneau and Gilles Gallichan, in 'Working in the Trades,' History of the Book in Canada, vol. 1 (see note 1), 86.

27 Bidwell, 'Printers' Supplies and Capitalization,' 183.

28 Humphrey, 'This Popular Engine,' 27. For a discussion of the costs of colonial printers, see Bidwell, 'Printers' Supplies and Capitalization,' 163–83.

29 Humphrey, 'This Popular Engine,' 27–9.

30 Bidwell, 'Printers' Supplies and Capitalization,' 163–4; Lawrence C. Wroth, The Colonial Printer (New York: Dover Publications, 1994; orig. 1938), 69–86; and Humphrey, 'This Popular Engine,' 28–9. To get a sense of the cost of a press in America in the aftermath of the war, see Kate Van Winkle Keller, 'Nathaniel Coverly and Son, Printers, 1767–1825,' Proceedings of the American Antiquarian Society 117 (2007): note 92.

31 Bidwell, 'Printers' Supplies and Capitalization,'164.

32 Ibid.

33 Ibid., 170–2.

34 Cullen, 'Talking to a Whirlwind,' 301–2.

35 Grant, 'Howe,' 32; Marie Tremaine surmises that Howe purchased equipment from Draper; see A Bibliography of Canadian Imprints, 1751–1800 (Toronto: University of Toronto Press, 1952), 662. If true, this could have been the source of the Franklin press.

36 Fresca, Franklin's Printing Network, 78, 255.

37 Cullen, 'Talking to a Whirlwind,' 513. See also L.F.S. Upton, 'Watson, Sir Brook,' Dictionary of Canadian Biography, vol. 5.

38 Prospectus, The Royal Gazette and The New Brunswick Advertiser, Saint John, New Brunswick, 11 October 1785.

39 Willi Paul Adams, 'The Colonial German-language Press and the American Revolution' in Press and The American Revolution (see note 6), 172–3, 216; Stephen L. Longenecker, The Christopher Sauers: Courageous Printers Who Defended Religious Freedom in Early America (Elgin, IL: Brethren Press, 1981), 136–41; Schlesinger, Prelude, 286, 292, 295; Harper, 'Sower,' 68; J. Russell Harper, 'Christopher Sower, 1754–1799: Notes Collected from various sources,' S 146–6, 1953, New Brunswick Museum, Saint John, New Brunswick, 33–4; idem, 'Sower, Christopher,' Dictionary of Canadian Biography, vol. 4, 721–2; and Bidwell, 'Printers' Supplies and Capitalization,' 166.

40 Harper, 'Sower,' 106–7; and idem, 'Sower: notes,' 76–7. On the inventory of a deceased printer's being valued lower than that for competitive sale or a partnership agreement, see Bidwell, 'Printers' Supplies and Capitalization,' 165.

41 Esther Clark Wright, *The Loyalists of New Brunswick* (Moncton, NB: Moncton Publishing, 1972; orig. 1955), 247. See also C.M. Wallace, 'Lewis, William,' *Dictionary of Canadian Biography,* vol. 4, 482–4.

42 'John Ryan Prays to bring effects from N. York,' Records of Thomas Carleton, Lieutenant Governor, Petitions: RS 330, J/1784/1, Provincial Archives of New Brunswick. Ryan had to apply for permission to bring his press from New York because of post-war restrictions on trade. See Ward Chipman to John Moore, 2 July 1785, in *The Price of Loyalty: Tory Writings from the Revolutionary Era,* ed. Catherine S. Crary (New York: McGraw Hill, 1973), 421–3; and W.S. MacNutt, *New Brunswick: A History: 1784–1867* (Toronto: Macmillan of Canada, 1963), 65.

43 Schlesinger, *Prelude,* 259–60.

44 Humphrey, *'This Popular Engine,'* 32.

45 Ibid., 30–1.

46 Wroth, *Colonial Printer,* 141.

47 Leavitt/Lovett Family Papers, S 122A-8, Item 5–38(3), New Brunswick Museum.

48 *Saint John Gazette and Weekly Advertiser,* 31 March 1789, 3, col. 2.

49 Harper, 'Sower,' 104.

50 *Saint John Gazette and General Advertiser,* 4 July 1800, 19 September 1800, 5 December 1800.

51 'Pride would stoop to Economy,' *Saint John Gazette and General Advertiser,* 15 August 1800. Thomas McCulloch's satirical Mephibosheth Stepsure sketches on morals and manners were published in the Halifax *Acadian Recorder* from 22 December 1821 to 29 March 1823. Thomas Chandler Haliburton's satirical 'Recollections of Nova Scotia' (the Clockmaker Series) were published in the Halifax *Novascotian* from 23 September 1835 to 10 February 1836.

52 Gwendolyn Davies, 'The Diary of Sarah Frost, 1783: The Sounds and Silences of a Woman's Exile,' *Papers of the Bibliographical Society of Canada* 42 (2004): 67.

53 Ward, 'Scrapbook,' 8. For the rough conditions of the first Loyalists in Saint John, also see Moses H. Perley, 'On the Early History of New Brunswick,' ts., Lecture: Mechanics' Institute, Saint John, 1841, Reel P11088, 12–14, Provincial Archives of New Brunswick.

54 J. Clarence Webster, 'The City of Saint John,' in *Saint John: Its Beginnings and Glimpses of the Early Days: A Bicentennial* Edition, no. 22, *Collections of the New Brunswick Historical Society,* 25; Ward, 'Scrapbook,' 29; and David Russell Jack, 'Early Journalism in New Brunswick,' *Acadiensis* 8 (1908): 252–5.

55 D.G. Bell, *Early Loyalist Saint John: The Origin of New Brunswick Politics: 1783–1786* (Fredericton: New Ireland Press, 1983), 62.

56 Ibid., 64–5.

57 'A Spectator,' *Royal St John's Gazette and Nova-Scotia Intelligencer,* 29 January 1784.

58 Ibid.

59 The Lewis and Ryan notice is quoted in Tremaine, *Bibliography of Canadian Imprints,* 598.

60 Bell, *Early Loyalist Saint John,* 100. Bell notes that the relevant issues of the *Royal St John's Gazette* do not survive. The 'Proposals for Printing . . . an Accurate History of the Settlement of his Majesty's Exiled Loyalists' was published on 9 September 1784 and described its proposed content.

61 This was not the first time that Sower had been a competitor of Lewis and Ryan. Sower had co-published the *New York Morning Post* in 1782–83, while Lewis and Ryan were publishing the *New York Mercury or General Advertiser.* See Cullen, 'Talking to a Whirlwind,' 640–713; Bell, *Early Loyalist Saint John,* 102; and Longenecker, *Christopher Sauers,* 144.

62 Jeffrey L. McNairn, *The Capacity to Judge: Public Opinion and Deliberative Democracy in Upper Canada: 1791–1854* (Toronto: University of Toronto Press, 2000), 135.

63 Tremaine, *Bibliography of Canadian Imprints,* 595–6.

64 Patricia Lockhart Fleming & Sandra Alston, *A Supplement to Marie Tremaine's 'A Bibliography of Canadian Imprints: 1751–1800'* (Toronto: University of Toronto Press, 1999), 621.

65 For almanac advertisements, see *Royal Gazette and the New Brunswick Advertiser,* 3 January 1786, 9 March 1799; for legal forms, 8 November 1785; for criminal confessions, 9 March 1790; for other examples, see Harper, 'Sower,' 85–6.

66 *Royal Gazette and the New Brunswick Advertiser,* 11 October 1785, quoted in Tremaine, *Bibliography of Canadian Imprints,* 595.

67 *Royal Gazette and the New Brunswick Advertiser,* 15 November 1785. See Bell, *Early Loyalist Saint John,* 105.

68 Bell, *Early Loyalist Saint John,* 104–17.

69 Ibid., 111–12.

70 Cullen, 'Talking to a Whirlwind,' 643, 654.

71 Bell, *Early Loyalist Saint John,* 112–13.

72 Ibid., 113.

73 Tremaine, *Bibliography of Canadian Imprints,* 598.

74 The supposition has always been that Lewis returned to the United States after the dissolution of his partnership with Ryan (Tremaine, *Bibliography of*

Canadian Imprints, 598, 665). However, Maudie Whelan cites the American Antiquarian Society and the *New York Journal*, 4 January 1787, as sources that Lewis died in Saint John, 27 November 1786, at age thirty-three ('Journalism in Newfoundland,' 30). I am grateful to Professor David Bell, University of New Brunswick, for providing me with the 4 January 1787 *New York Journal, or the Weekly Register* citation for Lewis's death. 'At St. John, New-Brunswick, on Wednesday evening the 27th Nov. after a lingering sickness, which he supported with fortitude and resignation, Mr. WILLIAM LEWIS, printer, in the 33rd year of his age.' No evidence of his death has thus far been found in surviving New Brunswick records.

75 See Harper, 'Sower,' 87, 96–107; see also Ward, 'Scrapbook,' chap. 14, 17–18, 25, 28.

76 Ward, 'Scrapbook,' 28; see also E.B. O'Callaghan, *A List of the Editions of the Holy Scriptures and Parts Thereof Printed in America Previous to 1860* (Albany, NY: Munsell & Rowland, 1861), 110, #5.

77 Tremaine, *Bibliography of Canadian Imprints*, 596.

78 Whelan, 'Journalism in Newfoundland,' 38. See also Don Morris, 'The Father of the Press in British North America,' *Atlantic Advocate*, September 1976, 30–1; and E.J. Devereux, 'Early Printing in Newfoundland,' *Dalhousie Review* 43 (1963): 57–66.

79 Whelan, 'Journalism in Newfoundland,' 39.

80 Gabriel Furman Mott, the eldest son of Jacob and Ann Mott, assisted his mother running the *Royal Gazette and the New Brunswick Advertiser* after Jacob's death in 1814, but, after a year, moved to St John's to work with his uncle, John Ryan. By 1819, he was editor of the *Sun* in Blakely, Alabama Territory. He then moved to New York, where he co-published the *Weekly Museum*. He married Anna Burt on 23 August 1819 in Lansburg, New York, and died in Southport, Connecticut, 1 April 1875. See Ward, 'Scrapbook,' 49–50; and David R. Jack, 'Family History, Scrapbook,' 92, Micro. F. 109, Provincial Archives of New Brunswick.

81 W.N. Glascock, *Naval Sketch-book or the Service Afloat and Ashore; Characteristic Reminiscences, Fragments and Opinions on Professional, Colonial and Political Subjects; Interspersed with Copious Notes, Biographical, Historical, Critical and Illustrative* (London, 1826), 150–7, quoted in Whelan, 'Journalism in Newfoundland,' 4–5. Whelan finds 'little doubt' that Glascock describes the Ryan family, the *Royal Gazette*, and their son-in-law Fade Goff, who married Mary Somaindyke Ryan, 6 April 1809. See also M. Brook Taylor, 'Goff, Fade,' *Dictionary of Canadian Biography*, vol. 7, 351–2, who notes that Goff immigrated to Newfoundland in spring 1809 to join his father-in-law, John Ryan.

82 Whelan, 'Journalism in Newfoundland,' 4–5. After the death of her husband Jacob, Ann Mott tried to continue publishing New Brunswick's *Royal Gazette*, at one point having 'Ann Mott & Son' on the masthead. Allegedly denied the position of king's printer because of her sex, she ceased publishing in 1815. See Jo-Ann Carr Fellows, 'Mott, Jacob S.,' *Dictionary of Canadian Biography*, vol. 5; Hudak, *Women Printers and Publishers*, appendix 9; McMurtrie, 'The Royalist Printers at Shelburne, Nova Scotia,' 13; and Wroth, *Colonial Printer*, 154–6.

83 'John Ryan, Printer, to His Excellency Sir Richard Goodwin Keats,' 26 October 1813, Provincial Archives of Newfoundland, GN 2/1/A/25/45–47. See also Whelan, 'Journalism in Newfoundland,' 66–7.

84 Robert H. Schomburgk, *The History of Barbados* (London: Longman, Brown, Green and Longmans, 1842), 405–6.

85 Trevor Burnard, 'The British Atlantic,' in *Atlantic History: A Critical Appraisal*, ed. Jack P. Greene and Philip D. Morgan (Oxford: Oxford University Press, 2009), 111.

86 Joseph Wilson Lawrence, *The Judges of New Brunswick and Their Times*, ed. Alfred A. Stockton (Saint John, NB: Collections of the New Brunswick Historical Society, 1955), 139.

87 Devereux, 'Early Printing in Newfoundland,' 58.

88 Ibid.

89 Jerry Bannister, *The Rule of the Admirals: Law, Custom, and Naval Government in Newfoundland, 1699–1832* (Toronto: University of Toronto Press, 2003), 258.

90 Ibid. See also Maudie Whelan, 'The Newspaper Press in Nineteenth-Century Newfoundland: Politics, Religion, and Personal Journalism' (PhD diss., Memorial University of Newfoundland, 2002), although Whelan does not discuss Ryan specifically.

91 Jerry Bannister, 'The Campaign for Representative Government in Newfoundland,' *Journal of the Canadian Historical Association* 5 (1994): 29, n59.

92 O'Flaherty, 'Ryan,' 766.

93 Rosalind Remer, *Printers and Men of Capital: Philadelphia Book Publishers in the New Republic* (Philadelphia: University of Pennsylvania Press, 1996), 20–1. She quotes Stephen Botein, ' "Meer Mechanics" and an Open Press: The Business and Political Strategies of Colonial American Printers,' *Perspectives in American History* 9 (1975): 127–225.

94 *Celia*, 'Messrs. Lewis and Ryan. Gentlemen,' *Royal St John's Gazette and Nova-Scotia Intelligencer*, 26 February 1784, 4, cols. 1–2.

95 Remer notes that almanacs were a mainstay of the printer's business (*Printers and Men of Capital*, 17). Lewis and Ryan published their first almanac in 1784, and Sower published one in 1786. The first almanac composed by a

New Brunswick resident was that by Loyalist schoolmaster, William Green, issued in 1791 by John Howe in Halifax. Ryan and Sower collaborated in publishing Green's 1792 almanac. See Harper, 'Sower,' 83–5; and Gwendolyn Davies, 'Green, William,' *Dictionary of Canadian Biography*, vol. 6, 300–2.

96 See, for example, 'Proposals for Printing . . . an Accurate History of the Settlement of his Majesty's Exiled Loyalists,' *Royal St John's Gazette*, 9 September 1784; 'Candid Disquisition of the Principles and Practices . . . Of the most Ancient and Honorable Society of Free and Accepted Masons,' *Royal St John's Gazette*, 8 July 1784; 'Almanacks,' *Royal St John's Gazette*, 8 July 1784; 'A Few Copies of the Laws of this Province,' *Saint John Gazette*, 19 September 1788; 'E. Sands . . . Merchandize,' *Saint John Gazette*, 30 September 1791; 'William Whitlock . . . Merchandize,' *St John Gazette*, 27 July 1798; 'William Campbell Will Sell the Following Goods,' *St John Gazette*, 2 February 1798; 'The New Gentle Shepherd,' *St John Gazette*, 10 August 1798.

97 David Hancock, *Citizens of the World: London Merchants and the Integration of the British Atlantic Community, 1735–1785* (Cambridge: Cambridge University Press, 1995), 8, 30.

98 'Hall, Lewis, Odber & Co.,' *Saint John Gazette and the Weekly Advertiser*, 11 October 1787, 1, cols. 1–3, and 19 October 1787, 7, col. 2.

99 *Saint John Gazette and the Weekly Advertiser*, 12 September 1788, 3, col. 3.

100 'Books' in 'William Campbell,' *Saint John Gazette and the Weekly Advertiser*, 2 February 1798, 1, col. 3; 19 February 1796, 1, col. 4.

101 Harper, 'Sower,' 81–2.

102 'The Father, Or American Shandyism,' *Nova-Scotia Magazine and Comprehensive Review of Literature* 2 (February 1790), 96n.

103 For a careful assessment of the growth of theatre in the early United States, see Heather S. Nathans, *Early American Theatre from the Revolution to Thomas Jefferson: Into the Hands of the People* (Cambridge: Cambridge University Press, 2003); for an evocative recreation of the theatre experience, see Liam Riordan, '"O Dear, What Can the Matter Be?" The Urban Early Republic and the Politics of Popular Song in Benjamin Carr's *Federal Overture*,' *Journal of the Early Republic* 31 (Summer 2011): 179–227.

104 For example, see advertisements in the *Saint John Gazette*, 31 March 1789 (*The Busy Body*), 17 April 1789 (*The Gamester*), 27 February 1795 (*The Citizen*), 15 February 1799 (*Douglass: Or The Noble Scotch Shepherd*).

105 'Prologue On Opening A Little Theatre In This City, On Monday the 5th January Inst.,' *Royal Gazette and the New Brunswick Advertiser*, 20 January 1795, 4, col. 4. See also Gwendolyn Davies, *Studies in Maritime Literary History* (Fredericton, NB: Acadiensis Press, 1991), 30–47.

106 David S. Shields, *Oracles of Empire: Poetry, Politics, and Commerce in British America, 1690–1750* (Chicago: University of Chicago Press, 1990), 3–27, 224–7.

107 Quoted in Harper, 'Sower,' 83.

108 Remer, *Printers and Men of Capital*, 39–68.

109 *Royal Gazette* (Newfoundland), 5 October 1847, 3, col. 2. An obituary also appeared in the Saint John *New Brunswick Courier*, 23 October 1847. See E.J. Devereux, 'Early Printing in Newfoundland,' note 6.

110 Bidwell, 'Printers' Supplies and Capitalization,' 165–6.

111 Ward, 'Scrapbook,' 52–6, 62, 76–7.

112 O'Flaherty, 'Ryan,' 766.

113 Jacob Mott's father, John, a printer and stationer, had landed in Parr Town (Saint John) in 1783 as a Loyalist when Jacob was eleven years old. The entire family returned to New York when Mrs Mott declared that she 'would never live in such a god-forsaken place as Parrtown' (Tremaine, *Bibliography of Canadian Imprints*, 666). In 1798, John Mott, Jacob, and Jacob's family returned to Saint John, where Jacob opened a stationery shop and purchased Ryan's *St John Gazette and General Advertiser* in 1799. William Durant, who arrived in Saint John as a Loyalist, apprenticed with John Ryan and later co-owned the *Times Or True Briton* (changed to the *City Gazette and General Advertiser* in 1811) with him until Ryan returned to Saint John in 1814 to close out his affairs (their partnership was dissolved 31 January 1815). Three of Durant's four sons became printers in New Brunswick. George Lugrin, who was to become king's printer in 1815, was the son of a Saint John Loyalist. James Sears of Saint John, the son of Loyalist Fletcher Sears, did his apprenticeship in the office of Loyalist printer William Minns of Halifax (brother-in-law of Loyalist printer John Howe) and was a fellow apprentice of Joseph Howe. He returned to Saint John to work at the *Morning Courier* under Henry Chubb, son of a Philadelphia Loyalist and former apprentice on the *St John Gazette* owned first by Ryan and then by Mott. Chubb's two sons also became publishers, and continued their father's newspaper after his death. These examples are a small sample of intergenerational Loyalist printing connections. Also see Ward, 'Scrapbook,' 34–110; and J. Russell Harper, *Historical Directory of New Brunswick Newspapers and Periodicals* (Fredericton: University of New Brunswick, 1961), xv.

114 Ward, 'Scrapbook,' 52–6; and Harper, *Historical Directory*, xv. See also *Loyalists' Centennial Souvenir* (Saint John, NB: J. & A. McMillan, 1887), 71.

115 George L. Parker, 'Chubb, Henry,' *Dictionary of Canadian Biography*, vol. 8; and C.M. Wallace, 'Lugrin, George Kilman,' *Dictionary of Canadian Biography*, vol. 6.

PART III

Loyalist Slavery and the Caribbean

6

Revolutionary Repercussions: Loyalist Slaves in St Augustine and Beyond

JENNIFER K. SNYDER

Mary Port Macklin, a Loyalist refugee from Savannah, arrived in St Augustine, Florida, in 1777, in flight from the revolutionary violence that engulfed the South. For the next six years, she kept a diary describing her family's struggle to survive in a port town increasingly crowded with displaced Loyalists like herself. One night, she arrived home late after caring for a sick neighbour and awoke a slave couple, Nancy and Robert, whom her husband, a part-time privateer, had stolen on the open ocean. Mary Macklin ordered Nancy to make a cup of coffee, but when it arrived, she complained that it was too cold and weak to drink, and refused it. Whether Nancy intentionally did her job poorly out of protest is, of course, impossible to know, but she may have derived some satisfaction from Macklin's annoyance. In such seemingly mundane episodes, black and white refugees displaced by war negotiated their newly entwined lives under duress. Macklin's obscure and haphazardly spelled diary helps bring greater attention to African American refugees, both willing and unwilling, during the American Revolution.[1]

The Revolutionary War uprooted thousands of people of African descent, like Nancy and Robert, and further complicated delineations between freedom and enslavement. The chaos resulting from the war offered blacks diverse opportunities: avoid conflict by staying on the plantation, fight for the Americans, flee to the British, or join any number of extra-legal groups such as the banditti. Attracted by the 1775 proclamation by the royal governor of Virginia, John Murray, the 4th Earl of Dunmore, some slaves deserted their rebel masters and sought freedom by taking up arms on behalf of the king, as is well known, or fulfilling menial roles as personal servants and labourers. But the

majority of slaves chose their families and communities over an un-
certain and risk-filled chance of freedom. An even larger and more
sustained disruption occurred in the lower South between 1776 and
1779 when 'a significant portion of the slave-labor force was removed
or dispersed' from the plantations occupying the Florida/Georgia borderlands.[2] Slaves living on these plantations made difficult decisions
to best survive the revolutionary chaos. Yet the current historical literature on the revolutionary Atlantic mostly ignores the plight of those
who remained enslaved to Loyalists.[3]

The most recent Loyalist studies have broadened their geographic
scope to include British imperial holdings in the Pacific and Indian
Oceans. Historians have begun to expand what was once an exclusively North American story, primarily through an Atlantic history
perspective. Atlantic historians believe that this new framework shows
'how areas have been brought into focus, connected one to another, and
bound up into larger networks of circulation.'[4]

Recent work primarily focusing on the *Book of Negroes*, a list of Africans and African Americans shipped from New York to relative safety
and freedom in Nova Scotia, has touched off a renewed interest in racial aspects of the American Revolution. Simon Schama has reworked
existing literature into a narrative history, *Rough Crossings: Britain, the
Slaves and the American Revolution*, and a subsequent BBC television series. Schama chronicles how Africans exerted their newly won freedom,
only to face the hardships of building new communities in Nova Scotia
and Sierra Leone. Yet, just as Loyalist studies have adopted these new
approaches, historians such as Cassandra Pybus and Maya Jasanoff
have moved beyond an Atlantic focus.

Building on Carole Watterson Troxler's black southern Loyalist
studies on migration to Nova Scotia and the Bahamas, historians have
recently begun to focus on the racial and slave aspects of the larger
migration.[5] Combining both geographical breadth and a post-colonial
emphasis on race, Cassandra Pybus's *Epic Journeys of Freedom: Runaway
Slaves of the American Revolution and Their Global Quest for Liberty* follows
the arduous route of thirty-two enslaved African Americans on their
journey to freedom, beginning with their emigration with the British to
Nova Scotia and the British Isles.[6] From there, these blacks sought liberty within two very different colonial contexts: Sierra Leone and Botany Bay in the new colony of Australia. By travelling from one corner of
the British Empire to another, these migrants forged an extensive black
British diaspora.[7] Maya Jasanoff's *Liberty's Exiles* also takes a broader

approach by using the theoretical concept of refugees to place 'loyalism in an Atlantic, imperial, and global context,' grappling with how these refugees helped build the post-war British Empire.[8]

While these works grapple with the imperial repercussions of the Loyalist diaspora, they tend to follow the lives and stories of northern blacks. The British emancipation of three thousand Africans through New York City is a fascinating journey. Scholars have devoted far less attention, however, to the fate of enslaved African Americans denied liberty by Loyalists. The majority of slaves in the thirteen colonies and the new United States, of course, lived in southern communities. Thus, the most significant wartime and post-war movement of blacks happened in the southern states. Moreover, as Andrew O'Shaughnessy has reminded us, there were twenty-six British colonies in the western hemisphere, and East Florida played a major role as one of two major Loyalist strongholds at the end of the Revolutionary War.[9] This chapter addresses this gap by highlighting historically marginalized sites, such as the lower mainland British colonies.[10] Attention to Loyalists' slaves and their Atlantic context showcases individual decisions and negotiations within their enmeshed imperial networks.

Mobility is the unifying conceptual factor in the lives of Atlantic Africans in varying states of enslavement across the British Empire. The movements analysed here belie any straightforward description of a black exodus. In the short term, a few Africans gained freedom by running away or hiding. Although historians unfortunately know little about the motivations and experiences of most blacks, we do know that the majority of them remained enslaved. The stories to follow illustrate varied situations in which mobility cannot be equated automatically with movement towards freedom. Many slaves sought safety in contested coastal towns and lost their freedom if caught. Loyalist slaves faced danger both on and off the plantation. The plight of Nancy, who was first stolen from a ship, forced into slavery in St Augustine, and subsequently faced separation from her husband in the chaotic evacuation, is just one example of the perilous course of enslaved, black refugees in the lower South.

Tracing the complex migration streams in Georgia, South Carolina, and East Florida from 1776 through 1778 reveals how enslaved and free blacks navigated the tumultuous waters of the American Revolution. Dunmore's proclamation created an unforeseen opportunity for rebel-owned slaves; it did not provide the same prospects for slaves owned by Loyalists. Shunned by British military officials, slaves in the lower

South with Loyalist masters had few options beyond joining renegade groups, staying on the plantation, or escaping to coastal towns like St Augustine. Some tried to take advantage of the turmoil to elude belligerents on both sides, yet none of these choices afforded a safe or dependable alternative.

Since the early seventeenth century, Spanish Florida had been a haven for runaway slaves from the British colonies. Blacks used Florida as a shelter for generations before white Loyalists began to flee to this last British holdout in the lower South. The departure of the royal governors of South Carolina and Georgia in 1775 and 1776 was followed by the collapse of British authority in the South, placing those colonies in the hands of Patriots. The change in government brought wholesale adjustments for Loyalists. Patriots began to target Loyalists – for example, tarring and feathering John Hopkins and Thomas Brown, the latter of whom famously carried out his revenge as the head of the Loyalist East Florida Rangers.[11] Social pressure, coupled with the fear of violence, forced many Loyalists to move to St Augustine, and many brought slaves with them. Until the British recaptured Savannah in late 1778, East and West Florida were the chief destinations for Loyalist refugees in the region. Between 1776 and 1778, a 'considerable Emigration from the rebel Provinces' fled across the swamps and lowlands of South Carolina and Georgia to the urban refuge guarded by the Castillo de San Marcos in St Augustine.[12] As a result, by 1783, the capital of British East Florida had swollen with approximately seventeen thousand refugees, both black and white.[13]

As the population boomed, so did the demand for land. Emigrants, who fled with their property, found St Augustine overcrowded and undersupplied. Larger planters relocated their entire slave population and sought to re-establish their former lifestyle. In order to continue their agricultural way of life, these planters immediately applied to the governor for major land grants. Land was such a valuable commodity that a few Loyalists attempted to bypass the local government to purchase tracts directly from local Native Americans, only to be thwarted by their own meagre offers.

Planters able to obtain land through grants, purchase, or squatting created their own agricultural niche, though not without some adaptation. Available land was not suitable for the intensive agriculture practised elsewhere in the coastal South. Instead, planters looked to alternative outlets for slave labour, especially in the timber and naval stores trade with the West Indies. As East Florida governor Patrick

Tonyn observed as early as the fall of 1776, the colony quickly became a major trader with the British West Indies, where the shortage of wood and other naval products such as tar, pitch, and turpentine created significant demand.[14] Florida, with its abundant natural resources, provided opportunities for Loyalist refugees who migrated with their slaves. Slave labour built a burgeoning naval export business that supported the sugar industry in the British Caribbean. Not surprisingly, some slaves would themselves be sold and shipped to sugar-producing islands. The export business became so profitable that once-homeless farmers began 'purchasing new Negroes,' who bolstered the number and diversity of newly founded slave communities.[15]

Loyalists from 'Georgia and others from the Back Country of Carolina' left their homes, property, and communities behind and created new frontier settlements.[16] For the most part, they saw St Augustine as a temporary haven and hoped to return home in the future. Governor Tonyn believed that 'many more would have fled, had it not been for the inconveniences & danger of losing their property.'[17] When Loyalists fled without slaves and property, they risked their livelihoods to save their lives. This 'great number' of destitute refugees arrived in St Augustine with little hope of procuring an income and shortly became dependent upon the royal colony's charity. Even as some wealthy landowners expanded their foothold, thousands of Loyalists arrived as paupers, inundating East Florida.

Lord Dunmore, the last royal governor of Virginia, added to the overcrowding in St Augustine by sending a number of distressed loyal subjects, prisoners of war, and 'some Negroes' to the town in 1776.[18] The deluge of Loyalists triggered concern, however, as Tonyn wondered how 'numbers of Indians and Emigrants Black & White [would] be fed.' His small colony could not possibly afford to clothe, feed, and house such a large group, as 'all of them [were] destitute' and they would 'incur a heavy Expence for Provisions.'[19] In exchange for support, Tonyn drafted the rapidly increasing dependant population into service, establishing and arming companies of provincial troops, which provided work for the needy population and security for the colony.

The increasing number of blacks was particularly troubling to British authorities, who expected that the 'militia . . . will be at all times useful in keeping in awe the Negroes who multiply amazingly.'[20] Governor Tonyn decided to put the black population to work as labourers, reinforcing the Castillo in case of attack or invasion. As more blacks streamed into St Augustine, forced to emigrate by masters lured by hopes of British freedom or just seeking safety from raids, Tonyn contemplated arming 'a considerable number . . . who may be trusted with arms, & rendered on such emergency very useful to His Majesty's Service.'[21] Tonyn believed they would be much better soldiers than the 'two hundred Roman Catholichs fit to bear arms at the Smyrna Settlement,' whom he forced to stay on the plantations.[22]

Tonyn commissioned other militias as well. He instructed Thomas Brown, as lieutenant colonel of the East Florida Rangers, to recruit men from among the refugees. The governor initially planned to use this force to gather cattle in Georgia to alleviate East Florida's food shortage. Brown later employed the unit to take revenge on the rebels.[23] In response to the Rangers' raids, Georgia's Patriot Council of Safety appointed Jonathan Bryan and Nathan Brownson to plan an 'irruption into the Province of East Florida' with the reduction of St Augustine a 'very considerable object.'[24] Bryan and Brownson believed that, once the rebel armies ravaged the 'cattle on the east side of Saint John's' and forced the inhabitants to 'evacuate their plantations and fly into the Castle [Castillo] the scarcity of provisions and the want of fresh supplies of many articles from the country will of itself oblige the Garrison to submit to our arms.' The rebels wished to reduce St Augustine both for military gain and to prevent slaves from running south. By driving out the British, the rebels essentially would prevent 'the loss of negroes, either by desertion or otherwise by land.' So many blacks had deserted the rebels that the Georgia Council of Safety thought attacking East Florida was the only way to safeguard their property. Finally, Bryan and Brownson argued that an attack on St Augustine would hinder privateer raids on Georgia, at least until 'we are better prepared for them.' In order to pay for this direct assault, the council members thought, 'plunder which will fall into the hands of the soldiers will well compensate them for the difficulty and toil attending their march.'[25] Plunder was surely intended to include many black families. Tonyn reported that the theft of slaves was a discernible goal of the invading Patriot army, as 'they took upwards of thirty Negroes' from the first plantations they reached.[26] In order to protect his own property, Tonyn sent several of his slaves to St Augustine to help rebuild the Castillo.

Others took similar steps to protect their valuable property, even if it meant forcibly disrupting kinship networks, communication lines, and established ways of life. Blacks who stayed on plantations, by choice or force, were victims of Patriot and Spanish raids, including invasions of East Florida in 1776, 1777, and 1778. The first attempt failed, but the two later invasions succeeded in breaching the initial lines of British border defences both on land and by coastal waterways. While no attackers reached St Augustine itself, they managed to harass the countryside between Savannah and St Augustine, burning plantations, stealing cattle, and grabbing any blacks within their reach.[27]

William Taylor, a settler on the St Mary's River in Florida, was one of those forced to flee from the invaders. He made his way to his employer William Chapman's estate on Amelia Island and from there composed a letter to Chapman describing the ensuing chaos. Taylor had an 'hourly expectation of sharing the same fate and in danger of losing our Negroes I resolved to quit the place which we did that night with all our Negroes and what effects we could carry in our boats.' Yet on Amelia Island the abundance of shellfish and crowded conditions led to widespread illness. The rest of the slaves were 'sick as are likewise one half of the people in general.'[28] A large rebel party also carried off 'Mr. Jolie, Mr. Bethune, Mr. Kennedy, & other planters and a party advanced to Nassau River and took off Negroes & Horses.'[29]

Two or three days after Taylor arrived on Amelia Island, he engaged an unnamed man to return to his employer's plantation and tend to the crops, and sent 'four of the worst of our Negroes' to assist him. Three of these black men or women were eventually carried off by the rebels, the last unable to travel when rendered lame in an ambush. Not surprisingly, Taylor felt it was unsafe to return to the plundered and burned plantation on the St Mary's River. Instead, he combined his slave population with Martin Jollie's slaves to begin shipping naval supplies. This transient black community lived on Amelia Island for two months. Taylor describes how the rebels plundered essentially every plantation between the St Mary's River and the St John's River and how rebel-scouting parties had carried off fifteen prisoners since the first raid. Rebel raiders also drove the agent Stephen Egan and more than a hundred slaves from their plantation on the St John's.[30]

On 1 July 1776 armed Georgians attacked John Wilkinson's Tobacco Bluff plantation, located west of the St John's River. The rebels 'kept concealed in the Woods, and were no[t] observed' as they surrounded the slaves labouring in the indigo fields. Patriots 'took upwards of 30 Negroes & a Family from an Adjoining plantation.'[31] These men, women, and children were abducted and marched directly to Georgia, and the plantation house and provisions were plundered or destroyed. Forced to replace his stolen slaves, Wilkinson purchased additional labourers and resumed operations two years later. These newly arrived blacks would experience the same chaos that victimized the previous labourers.

Incessant raids scared many plantation owners in the borderlands between Georgia and Florida. Charles Wright, the younger son of Georgia royal governor James Wright, took his and his father's slaves' safety into his own hands after the 1776 raids. Wright built a fort atop an old stockade on the Georgia side of the St Mary's River that had been originally built for protection against Indian raids. 'Mr. Germain & Chas Wright' retired 'from their Estate in this Province & armed their Negroes' at this makeshift fort, which was 'opposite to the Post occupied by His Majesty's Troops.' Induced by rumours of freedom, safety, or simply food and shelter, slaves from across the area joined Germain's and Wright's black outpost. When a Patriot raiding party attacked the British fort on the Florida side of the river, the fort served as a safe house, and 'a soldier of the 60th regiment in the hospital with the surgeon, and the sailors made their escape to Mr Wright Stockade.' This raid cost Wright '20 of his Negroes.'[32] On 31 July 1776, a Mr Hazard went to the council in Savannah to claim a 'negro wench and two children lately taken near Wright's Fort.' The Board ruled that she and 'her children could not be sold, but that the other negroes taken with her should be sold at vendue by Mr. Jacobs.'[33]

Numerous smaller, unauthorized raids took place over the next few years, a symptom of the growing scramble for moveable wealth in this borderland.[34] Tonyn commented on the 'numbers of fugitives from the neighboring Provinces' who flooded into St Augustine seeking safety from rebel persecution and backcountry violence. As a profitable and, more important, mobile form of wealth, blacks were prime targets for raiders. But slaves were not helpless. Many fled to East Florida on their own to seek safety. Tonyn noted a 'number of Run-away Negroes from Georgia,' who fled to St Augustine and the surrounding areas 'for protection.'[35]

Blacks in large numbers began travelling to Cockspur Island, just north of Tybee Island, on the Georgia coast during the summer of 1776. So many arrived that Edward Telfair applied to the Council of Safety in Savannah to stop his 'negro pilots from ferrying' blacks there. By confining black pilots 'in some secure place,' Telfair hoped to prevent his and other rebel property from fleeing. One month later, a Mrs Murray made an application 'to send some person to Cockspur for her runaway negroes.'[36]

In July 1776, a rebel committee composed of Jonathan Bryan, John Houstoun, and Colonel McIntosh reported that, to the 'east, the inhabitants suffer the ravages of British cruisers. Their negroes are daily inveigled and carried away from their plantations. British fleets may be supplied with beef from several large islands, well stocked with cattle, which line their coasts, and round which ships may sail.' The committee was very concerned about the 'vast number of negroes,' reporting that 'blacks exceed the whites' and that they used the backcountry to 'secure retreat which Saint Augustine affords.' The committee feared that East Florida might even use these blacks to help with the 'conquest of Georgia,' as it 'would be considered a great acquisition by Great Britain.'[37]

The growing number of defecting Africans and Loyalists – among whom was Robert Hope, a wealthy refugee from Georgia, who resettled his slaves on a five-thousand-acre tract of land close to Chief Justice James Hume's Cypress Grove plantation – clearly frustrated and alarmed Georgia Patriots like John Houstoun, who demanded an invasion of East Florida. For John Grimke, a major in the South Carolina Continentals, an invasion was needed to prevent deserters, such as the six hundred he reported fleeing to East Florida, from uniting with Loyalist refugees.[38]

News of the impending invasion reached East Florida before a force of twelve hundred Continentals began to march south in early 1777. General Augustine Prevost recommended a scorched-earth policy to keep the outlying plantations from provisioning the invading Patriot army. 'Governor Tonyn readily ordered the complete destruction of his own plantation, including two large frame houses, every outlying building and mill, and all 20,000 acres of produce and timber.'[39] He evacuated '19 male slaves, all prime 3 of them coopers and the rest Sawyers, 19 women all prime 2 of them House Wenches, and 16 children from 12 years to 6 months.'[40] These slaves were forcibly moved to the Black Creek estate to rebuild his plantation. In this process, of course, they also recreated their own communities.[41]

Samuel and Mary Tims's enterprising overseer, Richard Sill, was able to save their slaves from the rebels. Samuel Tims had bought Talbot Island in 1774 and, leaving the plantation under Sill's supervision, returned home to England to retrieve his wife. Mary Tims was pregnant when they set sail for Florida in 1777. After a disastrous stopover in

Montserrat, where the ship's captain stranded all of his passengers, Mary and Samuel finally arrived in East Florida to find that the rebel raids had destroyed their estate, plundered their provisions, and carried off most of their valuable effects a year earlier. The overseer, however, had moved their slaves to another property south of the St John's River, where he attempted to reassemble their plantation.[42]

As the Patriot forces made their way closer to St Augustine, Spencer Mann, James Penman, and Lieutenant-Colonel Robert Bissett begged Tonyn to capitulate. They even proposed to compensate rebels if 'certain properties' went unmolested. These men surely worried not only about the loss of their crops, but especially about their valuable slaves. Mann brought eleven black men and nine black women from Connecticut to St Augustine for Edward Fenwick, while Penman brought four black men and offered personally to meet the oncoming army with a flag of truce if it would help protect his property. These men set aside political ideology to preserve wealth and protect their social standing. Luckily for them, the second invasion never came close to St Augustine.[43]

At the end of April 1778, Governor Tonyn received reports of a planned third invasion. Tonyn believed the considerable force, nearly two thousand rebel troops, was 'enticed by the prospect of plunder.'[44] Rebels gathered on the St Mary's River and began raiding plantations only recently repaired after earlier attacks.[45] Among these was Jacob Wilkerson's ten-thousand-acre Padamaran Estate, which, after repeated raids in 1776 and 1778, eventually was destroyed. If any slaves remained on this plantation, they surely were ripped from loved ones and sent to live under yet another master in Georgia or South Carolina or even further afield.

Simon Munro, a Georgia Loyalist, lost part of his slave holdings and sold the rest in Antigua after his banishment in 1777. Prevented from travelling directly to East Florida, he took a circuitous route through the Bahamas, then to Jamaica, West Florida, and finally St Augustine. Appointed 'Lt. Colonel of militia' and a 'civil Majestrate,' Munro attempted to return home and visit his family after the British evacuation of Savannah, but was captured and held prisoner by the rebels. He claimed to have lost twenty-two slaves taken by 'a rebel privateer,' beyond the twenty-five he recovered, carried to Antigua, and sold. Others like 'Jack, Lear & Child, Patty, Wally, Warrick, [and] Jobas' were never found, while three slaves, 'Elsey, Fanny and Fanny's sister,' were taken by a rebel party from Munro's wife while he was away in Savannah.[46]

Thus, not only did Loyalists protecting their property forcibly move blacks, but raiders on both sides also stole them from plantations and vessels. This violent migration disrupted kinship networks and spread blacks across the revolutionary Atlantic. At the same time, blacks seeking to capitalize on the turmoil escaped by the thousands to the British to claim their liberty. Sometimes, their bold action was rewarded with freedom; more often, it was not. The British simultaneously freed and enslaved individuals, depending upon specific local circumstances.

The British retaliated against rebel raids. In a May 1779 attack on All Saints Waccamaw, situated between Myrtle Beach and Cat Island, Samuel Hasford and several other residents were 'robbed of a number of their Negroes, by a party of the British.'[47] The rebel-owned slaves were placed aboard British ships, presumably bound for a safe port such as St Augustine or New York, but the ships never made it. Captured by two rebel ships from Massachusetts, they and their human cargos were sailed to Boston. Hasford and other residents of All Saints Waccamaw, in the meantime, outfitted a seaworthy vessel to reclaim their slaves. After pursuing the captured ships all the way to Boston, Hasford sought the return of his property – Anthony, Old James, Peggy, Quash, Robert, Affa Hall, Prince Hall, Joack Philips, Jack Puddy, George Rolly, and John Rolly – or restitution. Massachusetts law, however, entitled all blacks to freedom, so Hasford petitioned Massachusetts governor John Hancock to reclaim them.[48]

Some blacks did find freedom in the northern US states and in British North America. For example, in 1779, fifteen-year-old slave William Winter left William Sams, a Loyalist turned rebel who had acted as a magistrate under the British 'to avoid bearing arms against his countrymen.' (Sams claimed that the British treated him poorly and confiscated 'upwards of forty slaves.')[49] Four years later, on 22 September 1783, Winter boarded the *Aurora* bound for Ostend, Belgium. The same day, another of William Sams's slaves, Toby Sams, a 25-year-old 'pockmarked, stout fellow,' boarded the *Charming Nancy* bound for Port Roseway, Nova Scotia.[50] Two other slaves of Sams's also managed to make their way to New York City, and were recorded in the *Book of Negroes* before reaching freedom in Nova Scotia.

Rebel Americans were not the only maritime raiders on the eastern seaboard. Since the British acquisition of Florida in 1763, Spaniards had been a constant threat to plantations along that coast, and their example led both enterprising Britons and Americans to cruise the Florida-Georgia coast in search of plunder.[51] In 1779, the rebel allies

Spain and France began to attack the southern coastline of Florida. In one instance, a Spanish privateer 'landed and carried off Eighteen Negroes from Smyrna,' and rumours of the raid travelled up the coast.[52] After another devastating raid by Spanish privateers, who destroyed his plantation, Loyalist Alexander Bissett submitted a claim for compensation of £660 and shortly thereafter moved his remaining slaves to a five-hundred-acre plantation north of St Augustine. When East Florida was returned to Spain under the terms of the Treaty of Paris in 1783, Bissett sent eighty-two of his remaining slaves to Jamaica, where they sold for £2,282.[53]

The migration of planters and their slaves and other moveable property to the apparent safety of St Augustine became so massive that the town, despite its relative prosperity after 1776, had difficulty adjusting to the influx. Governor Tonyn sent a 'detachment of the King's Troops to co-operate with the Marine for the protection of that district, and to prevent the Planters removing, some having taken the alarm and to the very great loss of their constitution have fixed nearer to this place and upon Saint John's River.'[54] Tonyn also desperately sought aid to deal with the 'increase of Negroes within these few years,' which he estimated had more than 'quadroupled.' Tonyn believed that they needed to be 'under more restraints than the Laws of England have laid upon Servants' due to the 'great deal of licentiousness that prevails amoungst them.' Further, as word spread about the flight of blacks to East Florida, the governor became concerned about the legal system's ability to handle the 'prospect of numberless claims to Negroes.'[55]

The overcrowding of so many people on a strip of land between the Florida swamps and the ocean led many to turn to privateering. When Mary Port Macklin and her husband John Macklin arrived in St Augustine, the once prosperous and resourceful restaurant owners – they had converted an old, unseaworthy vessel into a gentlemen's dining club at the Savannah docks – had little property. John Macklin then took command of the privateer *Polley* to make a new living through plunder. On his first expedition, he intercepted a vessel bound for St Eustatius and profitably netted three young black men, Primes, Jems, and Pollichor, as prizes. Leaving these slaves in the capable hands of his wife, Macklin returned to sea in search of more valuable commodities. On his second voyage, he stole two middle-aged slaves, the couple Robert and Nancy. Again, he left them with his wife, and then took two of the previously seized young men aboard the privateer for a third voyage, but this expedition ended with little property.[56] All the while, Mary Macklin kept an informative diary, but it contains many silences about the lives of the enslaved refugees in her care. Did Mary sell the young men at auction in St Augustine, and if so, for how much and to whom? John Macklin resurfaces in a later Loyalist claim, stating that he lost '2 Negroe Pilots delivered on Board the Roebuck.' These might have been the same men that he had captured on the high seas and then took privateering. He also claimed three slaves taken by rebels in 1777 or 1778. These slaves might have been stolen, or perhaps abandoned when the Macklins and the other Loyalists were forced to leave St Augustine.[57] While the names of blacks who achieved their freedom often can be recovered in the historical record, the overwhelming majority remained enslaved and undocumented.

By the war's end, the southern port towns that remained in British hands – St Augustine, Savannah, and Charleston – overflowed with black refugees. Some had fled from rebel masters to join the British; others journeyed with their Loyalist masters, had been stolen in raids by Loyalist partisans, or simply got swept up in the maelstrom. Some received freedom from the British, many more remained enslaved, and still others lived in a kind of legal limbo. When the British evacuated these towns between 1782 and 1785, most people of African descent never gained their freedom, but were destined for harsh new lives as plantation labourers throughout the British West Indies, especially Jamaica. Governor Tonyn shipped his own slaves to Dominica. Once there he arranged for their sale and coordinated additional slave sales for Jacob Wilkerson and the Earl of Egmont with a Spanish merchant from Havana. The process took so long and conditions were so poor that fifteen of the seventy-nine offered for sale – including Sam, Primus, Peggy, Amey, Sampson, Israel, Frank, Billey, Jack, Pero, Celia, Kate, Nancy, and Linda – died before they could be sold. One black man named Newport was sent to St Kitts and sold for £60.[58] The only known remaining records about them simply list their names.

Scipio Handley was a free black whose remarkable story demonstrates the varied Atlantic connections formed by people of African descent out of the uncertainty created by the Revolutionary War. Rebels caught and jailed Handley, 'a free black Charleston fisherman . . . [who] was caught carrying messages to the British, and he was condemned to death as a spy.'[59] In 1775, he hacked his way out of the rotting Charleston jail and jumped ship to Barbados. Thus, while most other Africans fled from whites, Handley chose to go to the epicentre of enslavement, the sugar-producing islands of the Caribbean. As a free man and a sojourner, however, he later was able to depart for the American mainland during the siege of Savannah, where he suffered a permanent debilitating injury when shot through the leg by a musket ball. Handley later made it to London, where he appeared before the Loyalist Claims Commission requesting compensation for his losses, one of only a handful of claims made by blacks.[60] By returning with the Loyalists as a free man, Handley seized opportunities not afforded to the majority of blacks who remained enslaved. Yet, even as a free man and the successful recipient of Claims Commission support of £20, the disabled Handley could not escape life as a member of London's vagrant, black poor after the war.

Hagar, the nurse of famed memoirist Elizabeth Lichtenstein Johnston, was one slave swept up in the tide of refugees who relocated from Georgia to St Augustine and visited many points around the British Empire. Johnston, in the last months of her pregnancy, evacuated first to Charleston, where, on 23 August 1782, she bore a daughter, named Catherine. Shortly thereafter, with her 'two little ones,' she 'embarked with a nurse on board a small schooner for St. Augustine.'[61] Like most refugees, the Johnston family attempted to set up a life in their new home until news spread that the Crown had given the Florida colonies to Spain. With no other options, William Johnston sold his slaves for 'four hundred & fifty pounds' to Colonel Brown. Elizabeth Johnston kept 'Hagar as a nurse' in preparation for another child, Lewis, who would be born in St Augustine on 10 March 1784.[62] Hagar probably travelled with the family from Georgia to Charleston and then to St Augustine. It is also very likely that Hagar went with the family on its next voyage, to Greenock, Scotland. In her memoir, Elizabeth recalls that 'Rachel, a younger sister of Mr. Johnston, and my nurse and three children, were put into the attic story' of a local inn in the Scottish port town to await the arrival of her husband.[63] Over two year later, the Johnstons and their nurse crossed the Atlantic again, this time to Jamaica, where they bought more slaves, the care of whom overwhelmed Elizabeth.[64] There is, however, little mention of Hagar in Elizabeth Johnston's memoir. Historians are left to imagine how Hagar felt about being ripped away from her community and forcibly moved south to St Augustine, east to Scotland, and finally resettled in the repressive sugar colony of Jamaica. Hagar's story is indicative of the experiences of innumerable blacks swept up by revolutionary convulsions and carried around the Empire to live out the rest of their days.

By the signing of the Treaty of Paris in 1783, the loss of slaves had become so important to Patriot negotiators that they insisted on including a treaty article stating that the British could not 'carry away any Negroes or other property of the American inhabitants.' But language failed to resolve this contentious problem. Through the remainder of the eighteenth century and the first decades of the nineteenth, the United States and Britain would negotiate over compensation for property that the Americans claimed had been stolen but that the British believed belonged to them. Thomas Jefferson and John Jay sought, but failed, to find a compromise. The British maintained that slaves who had crossed their lines, whether by choice or by accident, had become British property, while the Americans argued that the act of running to the British, whether in New York City or St Augustine, failed to change enslaved status and American ownership. The dispute simmered until 1826, when negotiations finally led Britain to agree to pay for lost slaves.[65]

The fates of Nancy and Robert, the slaves of Mary Port Macklin in St Augustine whom we met at the beginning of this chapter, illustrate the varying degrees of freedom blacks experienced in this era and locale. Caught in the tides of war, Nancy and Robert lived, loved, and lost in their attempt to create a life during and after the Revolutionary War. Mary Macklin fell ill with a debilitating disease during the last few years of the war. Losing control of her body, she became dependant on Nancy and her neighbours for care. Her husband, captured by the rebels, never returned to St Augustine and never saw his wife again. Destitute and ill, Mary was moved to the Bahamas, where she spent her final years. She was accompanied by Nancy, but Robert is not mentioned in later diary entries and seems not to have joined them. In many unwritten and lost stories, black tragedies mirror white ones. Historians can only guess what happened to Robert: perhaps he was sold to pay for Nancy's journey, or he might have run away in the chaos of the Revolution. We can assume, however, that the separation Mary and her husband endured hurt Nancy and her own husband just as profoundly. Their intertwined story is merely one example plucked from the whirlwind of wartime uncertainty, flight, and evacuation that pushed ever farther to the south as the Revolutionary War upturned thousands of lives, permanently separating black families, communities, and traditions.

To make sense of the southern theatre of the Revolutionary War, historians need to recover and retell the lives of individual people of African descent. This chapter has followed the forced movement of blacks in plantations between Savannah and St Augustine. While these stories are not triumphant depictions of Patriots, Loyalists, or the British Empire, they illustrate the varied experiences of Africans in this period. The mobility of blacks across colonies, continents, and political boundaries now makes it difficult to recover their journeys, but we need to give voice to these actors by mining the sources that explain the events that disrupted their lives in the revolutionary lower South and beyond.

NOTES

1 Mary Port Macklin, 'The Memoir of Mary (Port) Macklin,' edited and annotated by Daniel L. Schafer, *El Escribano: The St Augustine Journal of History* 41 (2004): 106–17. Following the fascinating journey of enslaved blacks from the lower South into the British Caribbean has been challenging. Sources documenting this largely illiterate black population are difficult to find. The scarcity of such sources in archival repositories is due in part to the oral tradition prevalent in the colonial period, but creative research techniques can counter this limitation. By examining traditional sources, I have been able to uncover previously ignored correspondence and other documents that describe the mobile black population.

2 Martha Condray Searcy, *The Georgia-Florida Contest in the American Revolution, 1776–1778* (Tuscaloosa: University of Alabama Press, 1985), 181.

3 Most of the scholarly literature deals with the movement of blacks north and their subsequent struggle for freedom in Nova Scotia and later Sierra Leone. See Mary Louise Clifford, *From Slavery to Freetown: Black Loyalists after the American Revolution* (Jefferson, NC: McFarland, 1999); Sidney Kaplan, *The Black Presence in the Era of the American Revolution 1770–1800* (Washington, DC: New York Graphic Society, 1973); James W. St Walker, *The Black Loyalists: The Search for a Promised Land in Nova Scotia and Sierra Leone, 1783–1870* (New York: Africana Publishing Company, 1976); Ellen Gibson Wilson, *The Loyal Blacks* (New York: Capricorn Books, 1976); and Carole Watterson Troxler, 'The Migration of Carolina and Georgia Loyalists to Nova Scotia and New Brunswick,' (PhD diss., University of North Carolina-Chapel Hill, 1974).

4 Arjun Appadurai, *Modernity at Large: Cultural Dimensions of Globalization* (Minneapolis: University of Minnesota Press, 1996), 18. Atlantic history integrates national narratives into a cohesive perspective by transcending landed political divisions. Paul Gilroy frames historical discourse in a new geographical and theoretical setting that emphasizes interconnecting

relationships of individuals, groups, and societies around the Atlantic. His work, *The Black Atlantic* (Cambridge, MA: Harvard University Press, 1993) argues that the Atlantic framework has 'created a new topography of loyalty and identity' beyond the nation state. By looking at the black diaspora within the context of the Atlantic world, we can begin to comprehend the global dispersion and settlement of Africans, who settled abroad both voluntarily and involuntarily, maintaining a consciousness of their identity and homeland while adapting to new societies.

5 Carole Watterson Troxler, 'Hidden from History: Black Loyalists at Country Harbour, Nova Scotia,' in *Moving on: Black Loyalists in the Afro-Atlantic World*, ed. John W. Pulis (New York: Garland, 1999).

6 By not including St Augustine and other southern ports, Pybus excludes the majority of blacks who left the continent with the British as enslaved people.

7 During the 1940s, British imperial historians began to explore the neglected field of black experience in the Empire. Beginning in 1948 with K.L. Little's work, *Negroes in Britain*, scholars began to illuminate the plight of British blacks. Little briefly mentions the plight of Loyalist slaves who travelled to England and 'became conspicuous among London beggars, and were known as St. Giles' Blackbirds'; Kenneth Lindsay Little, *Negroes in Britain: A Study of Racial Relations in English Society* (London: Trubner, 1948), 183. For attempts to place the abolition of slavery in the context of black history in Britain and the British West Indies, see James Walvin, *England, Slaves, and Freedom, 1776–1838* (Jackson: University Press of Mississippi, 1986); and Folarin Shyllon, *Black People in Britain 1555–1833* (London: Oxford University Press, 1977). The *Oxford History of the British Empire* fails to mention post-colonial staples such as race – leaving out the thousands of free and enslaved Africans who migrated into the Empire. This criticism resulted in a companion volume, Philip D. Morgan and Sean Hawkins, ed., *Black Experience and the Empire* (Oxford: Oxford University Press, 2004), which also overlooks the plight of the many free or enslaved Africans who plunged into Nova Scotia, Britain, and the British West Indies after the American Revolution.

8 Maya Jasanoff, ' "Notes on the Historiography of Loyalism" Revisited' (introductory lecture, 'Loyalism and the Revolutionary Atlantic World' conference, University of Maine, Orono, 4 June 2009). See also her stimulating essay, 'The Other Side of Revolution: Loyalists in the British Empire,' *William and Mary Quarterly*, 3rd series, 65 (2008): 205–32, which suggests the contours of her new book, *Liberty's Exiles: American Loyalists in the Revolutionary World* (New York: Alfred A. Knopf, 2011).

9 Andrew Jackson O'Shaughnessy, *An Empire Divided: The American Revolution and the British Caribbean* (Philadelphia: University of Pennsylvania Press, 2000).

10 Also see Carole Watterson Troxler, in this volume, on the movement of blacks into the Bahamas. For an excellent treatment of the East Florida evacuation, see her 'Loyalist Refugees and the British Evacuation of East Florida, 1783–1786,' *Florida Historical Quarterly* 60 (1981): 1–28, and 'Refuge, Resistance, and Reward: The Southern Loyalists' Claim on East Florida,' *Journal of Southern History* 55 (1989): 563–95.

11 While Brown may have sought vengeance against the Patriots, his activities were legitimate military operations. See Edward J. Cashin, *The King's Ranger: Thomas Brown and the American Revolution on the Southern Frontier* (Athens: University of Georgia Press, 1989).

12 Patrick Tonyn, St Augustine, 30 October 1776, Colonial Office Papers (hereafter cited as CO), National Archives of the United Kingdom, 5/566, no. 27.

13 Troxler, 'Refuge, Resistance, and Reward,' 580–3.

14 Patrick Tonyn, St Augustine, 1 November 1776, CO 5/566, no. 29.

15 Patrick Tonyn, St Augustine, 30 October 1776, CO 5/566, no. 27.

16 Edgar Legare Pennington, 'East Florida in the American Revolution, 1775–1778,' *Florida Historical Quarterly* 9 (1930): 31–2.

17 Patrick Tonyn, St Augustine, 30 October 1776, CO 5/566, no. 27.

18 Pennington. 'East Florida in the American Revolution, 1775–1778,' 31–2.

19 Patrick Tonyn, St Augustine, 30 October 1776, CO 5/566, no. 27.

20 Ibid.

21 Patrick Tonyn, St Augustine, 22 March 1776, CO 5/568, no. 7.

22 Ibid.

23 Cashin, *King's Ranger,* 49–62.

24 Reprinted in Allen Daniel Candler, ed., *The Revolutionary Records of Georgia 1769–1782,* vol. 1 (Atlanta: Franklin-Turner, 1908), 12.

25 Ibid., 181.

26 Pennington, 'East Florida in the American Revolution,' 25.

27 Wilbur H. Seibert, 'Slavery in East Florida, 1776–1785,' *Florida Historical Quarterly* 10 (1932): 139. 'Even a Spanish privateer was now and then successful in plundering plantations on the east coast. At the end of August 1778, a privateer entered Mosquito (now Ponce de Leon) Inlet and carried off thirty negroes.'

28 William Chapman folio, Treasury Papers, National Archives of the United Kingdom, 77/3.

29 Patrick Tonyn, St Augustine, 6 April 1777, CO 5/566, no. 35.

30 Chapman folio, Treasury Papers, 77/3.

31 Patrick Tonyn, St Augustine, 18 July 1776, CO 5/566, no. 18.

32 John Wilkinson, Treasury Papers, 77/17/16-; Treasury Papers, 77/25/frag-ments; Alexander Gray, Treasury Papers, 77/8/7.

33 Allen D. Candler, ed., *The Colonial Records of the State of Georgia*, vol. 1 (Athens: University of Georgia Press, 1976–89), 169.

34 Roger Smith, 'The Façade of Unity: British East Florida's War for Dependence' (unpublished Master's thesis, University of Florida, 2008), 65.

35 Patrick Tonyn, St Augustine, 18 October 1776, CO 5/569, no. 26.

36 Candler, ed., *Colonial Records of the State of Georgia*, vol. 1, 200.

37 Ibid.

38 John Faucherau Grimke, 'Journal of a Campaign to the Southward. May 9th to July 14th, 1778,' *South Carolina Historical and General Magazine* 12 (1911): 63–4. Grimke heard rumours that the British under Major General Prevost intended to attack Sunbury as a diversion, while other British troops would march into Georgia to be joined by one thousand to twelve hundred disaffected insurgents from North and South Carolina.

39 Smith, 'Façade of Unity,' 55.

40 Searcy, *Georgia-Florida Contest*, 88–90.

41 Smith, 'Façade of Unity,' 53.

42 Mary Tims Memorial, Treasury Papers, 77/17/8.

43 Patrick Tonyn to Lord Germain, St Augustine, 8 May 1777, CO 5/557, no. 42; Charles Loch Mowat, *East Florida as a British Province, 1763–1784* (Berkeley: University of California Press, 1943), 87; and Searcy, *Georgia-Florida Contest*, 107.

44 Patrick Tonyn, St Augustine, 15 May 1778, CO 5/569, no. 62.

45 Calvin W. Smith, 'Mermaids Riding Alligators: Divided Command on the Southern Frontier, 1776–1778,' *Florida Historical Quarterly* 54 (1976): 439.

46 Audit Office Papers, National Archives of the United Kingdom, 13:26, folios 785–6.

47 To the Honorable Hugh Rutledge, esquire, Speaker, and the rest of the Members of the Honorable House of Representatives, Records of the General Assembly, Columbia, South Carolina, Records of the General Assembly, Reel 1, 535–54.

48 Ibid.

49 To the Honorable President and Honorable Members of the Senate of the State of South Carolina, South Carolina Department of Archives and History, Columbia, South Carolina, Records of the General Assembly, Reel 2, 440–2.

50 Book of Negroes, Black Loyalist Institute, http://www.blackloyalist.com/canadiandigitalcollection/documents/ official/black_loyalist_directory_book_two.htm (accessed 12 December 2009).

51 Wright, 'Blacks in British East Florida,' 432; see also Siebert, 'Slavery in East Florida,' 139. In one instance, the British war sloop *Otter* and armed schooner *George* sailed from St Augustine in pursuit of a rebel privateer that had 'carried off 30 Negroes from the Smyrnea Settlement.' The ships were lost off Cape Canaveral in a violent storm, but the crew survived to tell the story. Patrick Tonyn, St Augustine, 20 August 1778, CO 5/569, no. 62.

52 Patrick Tonyn, St Augustine, 16 July 1780, CO 5/569, no. 90.

53 Daniel L. Schafer, 'William Elliott, Stobbs Farm at Mosquito Lagoon, and the Elliott Sugar Plantation at Indian River,' unpublished summary for Canaveral National Seashore Historic Resource Study, May 2008.

54 Patrick Tonyn, St Augustine, 16 July 1780, CO 5/569, no. 90.

55 Patrick Tonyn, St Augustine, 1 July 1779, CO 5/569 no. 79.

56 Macklin, *Memoir*, 120.

57 Ibid., 112, 125.

58 The Memorial of Patrick Tonyn, Papers of the East Florida Claims Commission, Treasury Papers, 77/10/77.

59 Walter J. Fraser, *Charleston! Charleston! The History of a Southern City* (Columbia: University of South Carolina Press, 1989), 152. See also Memorial of Scipio Handley, Audit Office Papers, 13/119/431, 12/47/117, and 12/109/160.

60 Cassandra Pybus, *Epic Journeys of Freedom: Runaway Slaves of the American Revolution and Their Global Quest for Liberty* (Boston: Beacon Press, 2006), 211–12.

61 Elizabeth Lichtenstein Johnston, *Recollections of a Georgia Loyalist*, ed. Arthur Wentworth Eaton (New York: M.F. Mansfield, 1901; reprint, Spartanburg, SC: Reprint Co., 1972), 73.

62 Ibid., 222.

63 Ibid., 76.

64 Ibid., 85.

65 For an early assessment of post-war relations between the United States and Britain regarding the return of slaves, see Arnett G. Lindsay, 'Diplomatic Relations between the United States and Great Britain bearing on the Return of Negro Slaves, 1788–1828,' *Journal of Negro History* 4 (1920): 391–419.

7

Uses of the Bahamas by Southern Loyalist Exiles

CAROLE WATTERSON TROXLER

Dislocation and rebuilding lives: these twin challenges facing refugees in any age are basic for understanding the revolutionary era in general and post-war Loyalist activities in particular. The refugee experience typically began prior to British evacuations from coastal ports, which served as funnels for persons leaving the former colonies. The largest single departure was in 1783 from New York City, the last large British military installation. For the southern colonies, there were several evacuations, ranging in area from Wilmington in North Carolina to Pensacola in West Florida and in time from 1781 to 1786.

The Bahama Islands drew newcomers directly from the New York and southern evacuations. By the end of the Loyalist settlement period, former residents of Georgia and the Carolinas made up about 70 per cent of Loyalists who received land in the Bahamas.[1] The islands also became crossing points and connectors for subsequent movement in the late 1780s and 1790s. For many Loyalists, the military evacuation was only one leg in a series of Atlantic journeys. Some who went to the Bahamas settled there. Others took a quick look and left; still others would return: to settle, to visit, to trade. As places for economic and social connections following the war, the islands were lively scenes of dislocation and efforts to rebuild lives. This chapter explores some of the ways exiles from the southern colonies used the Bahama Islands, whether they lived there or not.

The most conspicuous single use white Loyalists made of the islands was to take enslaved workers there as salvageable property following the loss of their investments on the continent. Plantation agriculture facilitated a significant re-peopling of many of the islands and brought profound changes to their economic, cultural, and natural environments. In the 1770s the only island with a non-white majority was New Providence, likely the result of Governor Montforte Browne's efforts, so far unsuccessful, to encourage cotton planting there. Overall, the pre-revolutionary decades reported a 'relatively small ratio of blacks to whites,' which, as Whittington B. Johnson observes, 'suggests that economic activities were not of the labor intensive kind.' Seafaring and shipbuilding were important, and the islands' chief trading partner was South Carolina. The 1783 population was estimated at four thousand, of whom eight hundred were enslaved and seventy-five were free blacks. More than half the inhabitants lived on New Providence. Of the other larger islands, only Long Island, Harbour Island, Exuma, Eleuthera, Cat Island, Abaco, and Turks islands were also inhabited, the last three sparsely. Loyalists settled on inhabited and uninhabited islands, most numerously on Long Island, Abaco, Cat Island, Great and Little Exuma, Watlings Island, and New Providence. They increased the population at least threefold, making the black-white ratio three to one.[2]

The Bahamian plantation period has attracted scholars for decades and deserves their continued analysis.[3] In particular, investigation of African Bahamian activity during and after the Loyalist influx is flourishing.[4] The Bahamas as a place for slavery and plantations is not the subject of this chapter, however – only its inescapable context. Rather, I sketch the migration pattern, share some research insights, and, as Anne of Green Gables would say, give 'scope to the imagination' for fellow researchers.

Many Loyalists in the southern colonies, in fact, chose not to leave but arranged with neighbours to return home from whatever pro-British activities they had pursued – typically service in Loyalist militia or provincial corps. Others, however, were motivated to leave by having become identified with the British forces, and they also knew that the British would give them transportation aboard their departing vessels.

From the Wilmington, North Carolina, evacuation, most refugees went to New York or Charleston, South Carolina. Some continued with Cornwallis into Virginia, and after Yorktown were exchanged as prisoners in New York in time for the evacuation of that city. The Savannah departure also sent people to Charleston and New York, as well as to St Augustine in East Florida and a few to Britain and the British West Indies. Charleston was the largest southern wartime evacuation. Many who had gone to Charleston from the evacuations of Wilmington and Savannah remained in the coastal South Carolina enclave until the British pulled out in late 1782. From Charleston, army transport ships went to a variety of destinations: nearby to St Augustine, the Bahamas, a few West Indies ports, but also to Nova Scotia, Britain, and New York.

Who went where from Savannah and Charleston? In very broad terms, men in the possession of large numbers of African Americans took them to Jamaica or East Florida. From Charleston to Jamaica, some twelve hundred free people (about six hundred men, three hundred women, and three hundred and fifty children) went, with about two thousand six hundred enslaved people. The Charleston evacuation list for East Florida shows about two thousand free people, nearly all of them white (about eleven hundred men, five hundred women, and four hundred children), with about two thousand five hundred blacks in their households. Savannah also sent about a thousand free people, with two thousand blacks in their households, to East Florida. Most people who went to Nova Scotia did not take slaves, although some free and enslaved blacks went there from Charleston. East Florida drew the largest number of evacuees from both Savannah and Charleston. Those who took enslaved workers to East Florida mainly took small numbers, and most took none. In the Savannah evacuation only four men took groups of fifty or more slaves to East Florida, while eight men took such groups from Charleston.[5]

At the time of the Savannah and Charleston evacuations, both Floridas were securely in British possession. Hundreds of southern Loyalists had used East Florida as a base of operation against the revolutionaries, and a lesser number had used West Florida in the same way. Some remained there at the end of the war. The governor of East Florida reported hundreds of Loyalists arriving overland from the southern backcountry in the six months after Yorktown, still prior to the evacuation of Charleston. Jennifer K. Snyder, in this volume, describes St Augustine as the focal point for forced movement of enslaved people from Savannah-area plantations.[6] The overland flow continued after the Charleston dispersion.

After Britain ceded the Floridas to Spain in January 1783, the Bahamas became significant as a site for southern Loyalists. Already, there were refugees from New York in the Bahamas, many of them former British soldiers. In East Florida, Loyalists learned of the cession in early spring and responded with anger and frustration. Some would remain under Spanish rule or venture to return to their homes. Half the enlisted men in the three southern provincial corps in East

Florida took their discharges there rather than go with their officers to receive land grants in the Bahamas or Nova Scotia. The Bahamas gained a higher profile for southern refugees when a ragged fleet of South Carolina and Georgia Loyalists attacked the Spanish at their administrative centre, Nassau, on New Providence Island, and seized it for the British in April 1783. They had not heard that Spain already had agreed to leave the Bahamas to Britain after nearly a year's possession. This flash of derring-do was rewarded, however, by land grants in the islands. Moreover, Colonel Thomas Brown's decision to follow the St Augustine garrison commander to the Bahamas influenced many of his men. For most of the war, Brown had commanded the largely Georgia corps eventually known as the King's Carolina Rangers. At least forty of that corps and several members of the South Carolina Royalists went with Brown to the Bahamas. Their comrades who did not discharge in East Florida went to Nova Scotia with most of the Royal North Carolina Regiment who did not take discharges in East Florida. Several hundred civilians left East Florida for Nova Scotia as well; like their Charleston precursors, they included whites, free blacks, and enslaved blacks.[7]

For civilians leaving East Florida, the army transports provided shipping to Britain, Nova Scotia, the Bahamas, and some West Indies locations. New York no longer was an option. More blacks were taken back to the United States (2,561) by white returnees than to any other place, according to East Florida governor Patrick Tonyn.[8]

The London government's hope that Loyalist-owned slaves would remain in British areas is reflected in Home Secretary Frederick Lord North's instructions to Tonyn in December 1783. North wrote, 'The climate of Nova Scotia not being calculated for . . . the employment of the Slaves, which will of Course be removed from East Florida, It has been a matter of much perplexity and embarrassment to the King's Servants to provide an Asylum for [southern Loyalists].' Steps were under way, North explained, to 'purchase the propriety' of the Bahama Islands, 'where Tracks of Land will be given to them (gratis) proportioned to their former situations, and ability to cultivate them. The ungranted and uncultivated Lands in the several West India Islands will also be appropriated to their use; but at present no state of those Lands can be procured of sufficient accuracy, to regulate their Movements thither.' North wished to assure Loyalists that they would have free transportation 'to any of His Majestys Possessions, either in Europe, America, or the West Indies; For those who prefer the Bahama Islands, a considerable Quantity of Provisions, has already been provided and dispatched."[9]

Destination decisions were similar to those in Charleston, with the Bahamas, Jamaica, and Dominica attracting large slaveholders still living in East Florida. Officials reported from one thousand to fifteen hundred whites and about two thousand two hundred blacks going to the Bahamas in the departures they supervised.[10]

This broad picture was neither static nor universal. Backcountry farmers went to the Bahamas along with large slaveholders, who were mainly from the lowcountry, and over the objection of the acting governor, who felt there were already too many poor refugees from the southern backcountry in the Bahamas. His preferred solution was to send any who arrived straight on, in the same vessels, to the British enclave on the Honduras coast. Witheringly assuming, but rightly, that the backcountry arrivals would be Ulster Scots, he wrote to Tonyn:

> I understand a large number of back Country Loyalists may be expected by the next Transports that arrive here, these Islands are by no means calculated for these people, who mostly subsisted on the Continent by Hunting, and like Arabs removing their habitations, and Stock from one place or province to another, and therefore could Your Excellency order them to Nova Scotia or some other Province on the Continent, or should Your Excellency be inclined to send them this way, you may think it more of His Majesty's Service to empower me to forward them in the same bottoms to the Moskito shore.[11]

His request was ignored. Crackers as well as grandees moved to the Bahama Islands and received land as Loyalists in the 1780s. The largest area of the southern backcountry for which Loyalist militia records have come to light is South Carolina's Ninety-Six and Camden districts. Bahamian land records for the late 1780s and 1790s show that the names of about 20 per cent of the men who received grants as Loyalists in the Bahamas appear on extant rolls of loyal militia for those two districts.[12] Moreover, some of the backcountry militia officers brought a few enslaved persons to East Florida, their post-war slaveholding perhaps reflecting their pre-war economic status or their prowess during 1782, when the British at Charleston encouraged them to continue raiding rebel property, or both. As was the case with slaveholders from the lowcountry, title to enslaved property sometimes was challenged in East Florida: by fellow Loyalists who said the contested workers belonged to them, by US citizens and states who appealed to the peace agreements for return of wartime property, and by blacks who claimed personal liberty for active service with British forces. Only successful litigation could legally separate slaves from the person in actual possession of them, and this rarely occurred in East Florida. In a wrangle with the newly installed Spanish governor of East Florida, Chief Justice James Hume, a Georgia Loyalist who would take land in the Bahamas, pointed out to Tonyn in July 1784, 'Your Excellency well knows, that five out of six of the Slaves in this Country, are held without any title deeds . . . parole Sales, and possession is all they [owners] can shew, which was a sufficient Title by the Laws of this Province.'[13]

Sporadic evidence suggests that some whites who arrived in East Florida with only a few slaves either sold them there or moved on and sold them in the Bahamas. Some transports taking refugees from East Florida to Nova Scotia stopped in the Bahamas, providing an opportunity for sale, and private shippers routinely stopped in the islands. In 1791, a re-enslaved black Loyalist testified that the white Loyalist with whom she had left East Florida for Nova Scotia in 1785 had forced her to travel in the vessel's hold and that they had stopped over in the Bahamas. Loyalist militia colonel David Fanning took ten black people with him to East Florida in the Charleston evacuation. After sixteen months in East Florida, six were dead. He and his party then moved on, endured a shipwreck, and stopped in the Bahamas just long enough to draw provisions before setting sail for New Brunswick. There is no indication, however, that Fanning had slaves in New Brunswick.[14]

Unaccountably, passenger lists of two transport ships arriving in the Bahamas early in the eighteen-month-long East Florida evacuation were filed among land records in Nassau in June 1784. The *Elizabeth* carried mainly slaves, 86 per cent of whom belonged to three owners, who were not on the vessel. Five free blacks, four white men, and three white women (one of them the wife of an overseer) brought the passenger total to 141. The transport *Charlotte* carried mainly white Loyalists. One had been the overseer of former East Florida governor James Grant's rice plantation. Workers on the plantation were moved to the Bahamas, but later were sold back into South Carolina. Eighteen white heads of households were listed aboard the *Charlotte*, among whom two were women with children and seven were men with wives and children. A trading company, one woman, and six men were listed singly. Eight of the men have been identified as belonging to southern provincial or militia units, and another five left indications in Georgia or South Carolina that they were active Loyalists or were perceived as such. The shipmaster, Thomas Pearson, had commanded a regiment of loyal militia in backcountry South Carolina. He would settle in Nova Scotia, but there are no indications that the named heads of households on his passenger list did so. That Bahamian land grants to Loyalists include the names of only three of the fourteen men on the *Charlotte* could reflect further movement, or perhaps a loose relationship between Loyalists' landing in the Bahamas and their seeking or obtaining a land grant.[15]

Initially, even the owners of substantial work forces were not enthusiastic about the Bahamas. Visiting the islands in 1783 with a view to relocating there, Georgia planter Lewis Johnston was dismayed by the thin soil, which he judged would be exhausted after two or three years' cultivation. 'My expectations by no means sanguine,' he wrote, are 'cruelly disappointed[.] I intend to embark for St. Augustine in 7 or 8 days as much at a loss as ever where to direct my steps . . . The West Indies would on many accounts be the country I would prefer, but the great expense of living there and the uncertainty of . . . employ[ing] my few Negroes to any advantage deters me from it, so that after all if better prospects do not open to me on my return to St. Augustine it is probable I will be obliged to return to this poor Country on the evacuation of Florida.'[16]

The wealthiest New York settlers in the Bahamas provided newcomers with mercantile and financial alliances for a slave-based economy. With the influx of some wealth and much labour, the islands went through a brief but transforming cotton boom. Already, in the 1770s, the governor had encouraged cultivation of the long-staple, or 'sea-island,' cotton that suited the climate, but with little effect. After the Loyalist-era cotton boom, a top-producing Loyalist planter from Georgia, Roger Kelsall on Little Exuma, complained that post-war newcomers had been 'unable to procure from *the few cotton planters whom they found in the country*, any information that could be relied on.' Similarly, former Georgian Thomas Brown on Caicos Island complained to the Agricultural Society that, 'in other countries the planters have profited by the experience of others, in this, we never found a person of skill or experience, to direct our agricultural pursuits.'[17] Slash-and-burn farming already was altering some of the islands before the Loyalists came; in the late 1780s and 1790s, deforestation, cultivation, and resulting erosion quickly removed the topsoil and left the land unable to support such

crops as cotton. Hurricanes and chenille bugs were secondary discour-
agements. The best year for cotton was 1790, after which productivity
declined sharply, even while more land was brought under cultivation
in the following years. During the cotton success, planters and merchants improved Nassau's public facilities and brought new cultural
amenities. These included plays, a lending library, and a newspaper
that had moved from Charleston to St Augustine. The new planters
and merchants disdained the native white Bahamians' way of life, de-
riding them as 'Conchs.' Eventually, however, most newcomers who
remained – or their children – adapted to fishing, wrecking, and small
farming, although there were significant regional variations in this adaptation.[18]

In political life, the new planter-merchant group clashed with Governor John Maxwell, who was not eager to share power. The group
organized a Board of American Loyalists with the stated intention of
maintaining Loyalists' rights against Maxwell and the old inhabitants.
Not all Loyalists in the Bahamas identified with the group, however.
The governor courted backcountry southerners, former British soldiers,
and those New York Loyalists who were outside the merchant-investor
circles. In the 1960s, Thelma Peters, the pioneering analyst of the Loyalist presence in the Bahamas, described the tension as between former
East Floridians and West Floridians, depicting East Florida Loyalists as
planters and merchants and those from West Florida as largely backcountry farmers, a dichotomy that has been retained in subsequent
scholarship.[19] The political division, however, does not seem to have
been between these two groups. Newcomers who had spent time in either of the Floridas included both lowcountry and backcountry southerners. In West Florida, 'Loyalists' had included office holders and
merchants at Pensacola, and in the Bahamas such men were part of the
planter interest. Some Loyalists in West Florida, as in East Florida, were
backcountry people who had moved overland during the war to join
the British forces and/or to get away from the internecine and Indian
warfare of the Carolina-Georgia frontiers. J. Barton Starr estimates that
at least two thousand people fled to West Florida during the Revolution, and he notes that approximately 40 per cent of the thirteen to sixteen hundred petitioners for land there were from South Carolina and
Georgia. Their sparse military records indicate service with the Indian
Department and show that some West Floridians who moved to the
Bahamas came by way of New York following the Spanish seizure of
Pensacola in May 1781.[20]

Bahamian planter Richard Pearis conspicuously illustrates the complexity of 'West Florida' Loyalists in the islands. Formerly a South
Carolina trader with the Cherokees, he was active in West Florida as
a commander of Loyalists from his home area of western South Carolina. Another who does not fit any West Florida-*cum*-governor vs East
Florida-*cum*-planter political alignment is Adam Chrystie. He had been
a planter in West Florida and commanded a West Florida provincial
corps, the remnant of which transferred to New York after the fall of
Pensacola. At least two of the unit went from New York to the Bahamas
in 1783, while several others, including a deserter and prisoners of the
Spanish at Pensacola, later showed up in the Bahamas; these men were
from South Carolina and Georgia. Chrystie returned to Scotland after
the war, then returned to the Bahamas as an official in 1790.[21] Still another example is provided by the Scottish-based Indian traders, Panton,
Leslie and Company. They had established themselves in both Floridas
before the war and continued to operate there with Spanish permission
afterwards, but Nassau was their post-war nerve centre, with connections throughout the Bahamian planter-merchant interests. Governor
Maxwell, however, favoured a rival company headed by John Miller,
another former Pensacola merchant.[22]

The basic pro- and anti-Maxwell division was between people with
resources to pursue cotton planting or its allied activities and those
who were not invested in planting and its support system. The easi-
est distinction between the two groups was whether or not they possessed unfree labour. Maxwell's challengers appropriated the term
'Loyalist' as a socially and politically partisan term for themselves,
tacitly excluding other white and all black Loyalists in the islands.
By narrowing their Loyalist identity in this way, they demonstrated
the kaleidoscopic potential of post-war constructs of 'loyalism' in a
manner fitting Keith Mason's discussion in this volume. Moreover, the
notion of imperial loyalty helped to institutionalize the slaveholder-
merchant dominance in the Bahamas. By their wartime initiatives,
they had sacrificed for British interests, it could be said, in a manner
that indigenous whites had not. The notion of loyalty to the Empire
by the founders of the post-war Bahamas positioned the dominant
families and their interests for tense dealings with imperial authorities
for decades.

The governor's challengers, indeed, were too much for him. The
president of the Board of American Loyalists, James Hepburn, a lawyer from Wilmington and now a planter on Cat Island, had proved

himself an adept politician and attorney in New York, Charleston, and St Augustine. The struggle came to a head with the election of an assembly in late 1784. There were disputes over election returns, several Loyalists walked out, and Maxwell prorogued the assembly. Hepburn and his board enjoyed the assistance of Patrick Tonyn, the retiring East Florida governor, whose administration they praised in a statement to the home secretary. Tonyn forwarded their petitions to London while repeatedly delaying his final withdrawal from East Florida, perhaps (as the Spanish governor suspected) in hopes of the Bahamian governorship.[23] These troubles resulted in Maxwell's recall. Controversies continued between the pro-Maxwell forces and the Board of American Loyalists while the administration was temporarily in the hands of a former coastal Georgian; he was elderly and not politically ambitious but solidly in the planter group. This was the official who in 1785 tried to prevent backcountry Loyalists from entering the Bahamas.

For Hepburn and his allies, the perfect outcome would have been Maxwell's replacement with one of their own kind. They asked London for a governor who had been a southern Loyalist, and a willing North Carolinian was ready at hand. John Hamilton had commanded North Carolina provincials during the war and had promoted the Nova Scotia settlement of men from the three southern provincial corps. In 1784, nearly one thousand people had moved from East Florida to Country Harbour, a remote estuary in eastern Nova Scotia. Hamilton himself had gone to Britain to pursue his career and compensation for his losses. In 1788 and 1789 he took grants in the Bahamas. Already, eighty-one southern Loyalists in London, mainly North Carolina Scots, had petitioned the home secretary to appoint Hamilton governor of the Bahamas. Instead of Hamilton, however, the Bahamians in 1787 got John Murray, earl of Dunmore, the last royal governor of Virginia and, like Hamilton, a Scot. The planters, however, abhorred Murray because of his 1776 offer of freedom to enslaved people who would serve with the British forces.[24]

Slave control was a vital issue for the planter-merchant network. By 1785, grand juries reflected fears that maroon communities, at first short lived or transient, would become permanent features in remote island interiors. At least 60 per cent of the Bahamas population of about thirteen thousand was black by that time. About 15 per cent of the total was free non-white, three-quarters of them living in Nassau,[25] where, south of the town centre, they had created a distinct community that assisted and protected escapees. Nassau was a market for hired services and goods, and thereby presented economic opportunities for non-whites, whether recognized as free or not. These realities had figured in Maxwell's troubles, and complaints regarding them faced Dunmore when he arrived in the autumn of 1787.

The new governor's immediate objective was order. Dunmore was appalled by the cruelty with which escapees were pursued and by the re-enslavement of black Loyalists by white Loyalists. Maxwell had accused some white Loyalists of promising freedom to slaves on reaching the Bahamas as a way to entice blacks to accompany them to the islands: 'some of the venders came to the possession of [slaves] in no other way than that of plunder and false promises,' he remarked.[26] Dunmore instituted a series of 'freedom courts' where amnestied maroons and other runaways could present evidence of free status and where the burden of proof was on the person who claimed ownership. These courts seem to have upheld slavery as often as they freed claimants, but the procedure was perceived as a threat to the merchant-planter network, coming in tandem as it did with abolitionist activity in Britain and with parliamentary efforts to 'ameliorate' slavery in the colonies. Dunmore's governorship was 'the peak period' for gaining freedom by government order, with more than forty successful cases. Eleven persons were manumitted by proclamation during the period from 1783 to 1787, forty-one from 1788 to 1796, and only seven after 1796. Elsewhere, however, the burden of proof was on the black person who claimed to be free. A woman named Betty acted on this and had her manumission record (made by Thomas Skottowe in Charleston at the time of the British evacuation) recorded in East Florida in February 1784 and again in Nassau in November 1785.[27]

It took the planter group ten years to force Dunmore out of the Bahamas. Many Loyalist planters gave up their Bahamian cotton dream around the turn of the century, returning to the United States and leaving the islands to the Conchs, the backcountry Loyalists, and the people of African and Euro-African ancestry, whose numbers they had increased. Significantly, departing planters took some enslaved people with them to their former homes in lowcountry South Carolina and Georgia. When it was understood that returnees would bring slaves with them, legislatures pardoned men they had exiled earlier. Already, there was talk of closing the United States to imports of enslaved people directly from Africa, reflected in a spate of successful petitions to the South Carolina legislature around 1800. Clearly, for individuals with people to sell, falling demand for unfree workers in the Bahamas and rising demand for them in the United States converged at the turn of the century. Former lowcountry residents of South Carolina and Georgia stressed that, if given permission to move to South Carolina, they would bring their 'families' of 'negroes' to market.[28]

Planter movement from the Bahamas to the southern United States helped promote commercial cotton there. The shift in personnel figured in the invention and manufacture of a cotton gin that could be used for the short-stapled fibre that would transform the southern interior. About 1800 Joseph Eve, a Loyalist from Philadelphia via New York, moved his cotton gin manufactory from the Bahamas to the Georgia-South Carolina lowcountry, where he had relatives. Eve's gin was an improved roller gin for the long-staple 'sea island' cotton grown near the coast. Eli Whitney examined one of Eve's gins on land that Georgia had granted to General Nathanael Greene and then tackled the problem of ginning the short-staple plant that would thrive in the Piedmont.[29]

For exiles from the southern states who settled in Nova Scotia or its 1784 offshoot, New Brunswick, the Bahamas could facilitate trade and family ties with their former homes. Several southern Loyalists moved from Nova Scotia and New Brunswick to the Bahamas, and others visited and traded. One of the most conspicuous and enduring was William Wylly, who arrived from New Brunswick in 1787 and joined the critics of Governor Dunmore. The Georgia native had spent two years in Saint John as an attorney and member of the governor's council, vainly seeking a judicial appointment among a surfeit of New England lawyers. He had been educated in England and admitted to the Georgia bar in 1780 and the English bar in 1784 after having led a company of the King's Carolina Rangers in Georgia, South Carolina, and East Florida. Landing a judgeship on his arrival at Nassau, Wylly for years would be a spokesman for the planter interest. He exclaimed to a New Brunswick friend in 1789, 'I can not fail as a planter – for men who have Negroes here do monstrous things with them – they count with certainty upon clearing every year between 25 and £40 a hand with them – which is from 50 to 100 per cent for a nabs misery.'[30] Already acknowledging the 'misery' of slavery, Wylly's perspective as an owner and his impact on his new home would grow more complex during his next decades in the Bahamas.

From the 1790s onward, tension over the issue of slave amelioration dominated Bahamian politics. Governors arrived in Nassau with

instructions to obtain local legislation to improve the physical conditions and enlarge the judicial rights of the enslaved and to enforce
imperial limits on the slave trade. Typically, a governor became worn
down by planter-merchant resistance in the Assembly and then was
replaced by a fresh man with similar instructions. An early result was a
1797 revision of the slave code, the first since 1780. In addition to modest physical and judicial innovations, it codified restrictions on slaves
that protected owners' security.[31]

Wylly's role in the tension over amelioration was twofold: as a judicial official and as a prominent slave owner on three plantations. He
became solicitor general in 1787, the year of his arrival, and he served
briefly as chief justice in 1797. In 1799 Wylly was appointed attorney
general, and he served as king's advocate and procurator general from
1800 to 1821, when he became chief justice on the island of St Vincent.
As a jurist supporting the metropolitan-mandated reforms, he enforced
the 1797 slave code and the strictures on international trade that were
embodied in the British Abolition of the Slave Trade Act of 1807. The
merchant-planter elite widely regarded Wylly as a traitor. They endured
more subtle pressures from his private policies as a slaveholder. His
slaves were reputed to have better living conditions and looser on-site
restrictions, which he published, than most owners provided; perhaps
exaggerated at the time, the reputation has scholarly confirmation. The
health and social stability of his workforce benefited Wylly. Moreover,
his conversion to Methodism was significant in Wylly's orientation as a
slave owner and judicial official. Presenting himself as a reformer and
denying the charge of abolitionism, Wylly is regarded as a 'conservative humanitarian.'[32] Even so, the 1983 assessment of Wylly by Sandra Riley suggests an internal struggle that was not unique to him but
may have been rendered more conspicuous by his vanity and legalism.
Wylly, she concludes, 'recognized . . . that kind treatment did not justify the basic and undeniable evil of owning other human beings.'[33] He
was well matched to serve during the 1812–27 tenure of Henry Lord
Bathurst as secretary of state for war and the colonies. Abolitionist
evangelicals relentlessly pushed Bathurst towards intervention in West
Indies governance in order to protect blacks. Bathurst combined policies of amelioration with a desire to restrict the latitude long enjoyed by
West Indies and Bahamian legislatures.

In the context of mounting British pressures, Wylly's orientation, his tactlessness, and his public and private policies alarmed
the planter-merchant network even more than Dunmore had done

decades earlier. Tension flurried to hysteria in 1817. The immediate issue was a clash between the Assembly and Governor Charles Cameron over a parliamentary requirement of slave registration in British colonies to limit slave smuggling. A committee of the Assembly conducted a survey of large slaveholders and officials with the intention of convincing Parliament that registration of enslaved Bahamians was unnecessary. Wylly's caustic responses to the survey questions went beyond their content and somehow his responses, or at least a summary paraphrase, ended up in publications linked with a London abolitionist group with whom he corresponded. Ever the legal expert, Wylly referred to the Assembly's fifty-year suspension in 1802 of an act of George II pertaining to judicial rights of free people of colour; the Assembly took offence and ordered his arrest for contempt. At his plantation near Nassau, Wylly armed some of his slaves. They denied the arresting officer entrance when he refused to state his business. Three days later, in Nassau, Wylly was arrested for arming his slaves against an Assembly officer. Following a writ of *habeas corpus* and more arrest warrants, the governor stepped in and dissolved the Assembly. The controversy raged for years in and out of court. A horse-whipping in a Nassau street by a member of the Assembly increased Wylly's anxiety, and he moved to St Vincent in 1821, the year in which the Bahamas Assembly passed a slave registration act that met parliamentary requirements.[34]

Also conspicuous, but lacking the drama surrounding Wylly, were North Carolina Scots who used the Bahamas for social and trade connections. They found the islands appealing at the time of John Hamilton's interest in the governorship. This was particularly true of officers he had commanded in the Royal North Carolina Regiment, and they obtained grants in the islands in the late 1780s, some of them having briefly tried Nova Scotia. For Scots who remained in Nova Scotia, it was easier to travel to the Bahamas than to the Carolinas – direct sailing, or at least trade in certain items, was prohibited from Nova Scotia and New Brunswick to the 'American states' during some periods. The *Bahama Gazette* noted frequent shipping arrivals from Nova Scotia and New Brunswick: a three-week period at the end of 1789 saw three vessels arriving from New Brunswick and Shelburne, the new Loyalist town in southwestern Nova Scotia, and during two weeks in February 1791, there were three sailings from Nassau to Halifax. The newspaper listed the names of about a dozen individuals and families arriving from New Brunswick and Nova Scotia.[35]

Highland Scots in North Carolina and the Bahamas maintained connections. For example, visits, trade, and marriages linked Long Island with North Carolina's Upper Cape Fear region through the Taylor and McNeil families. Archibald Taylor had been a major in the Bladen County, North Carolina, militia, and was among the Highlanders who joined Colonel David Fanning in seizing the North Carolina governor in 1781 and turning him over to British forces, one of the most remarkable militia feats of the war. Taylor also commanded marines in the 1783 Loyalist seizure of Nassau. Settling afterward on Long Island, he went back to North Carolina to marry Eliza McNeil in the autumn of 1789. Less than two years later, members of Taylor's wife's family went to Long Island for the wedding of her sister Margaret McNeil and Archibald's brother Duncan.[36] A 1789 marriage that linked North Carolina, the Bahamas, and Nova Scotia was that of Christiana McDonald and Miles McInnis. McInnis, who was engaged in trade connecting the three places, had lived in Anson County, North Carolina, where he had been an officer in the loyal militia. He obtained land adjacent to James Hepburn in the Bahamas on Cat Island when other former Carolina residents arrived from Nova Scotia, but the couple married in Nova Scotia and remained there.[37]

For white Loyalists who moved from Nova Scotia to the Bahamas in the late 1780s, the high demand for enslaved labour in the islands raised the temptation to kidnap black Loyalists in Nova Scotia and sell them in the Bahamas. A few officers of the Royal North Carolina Regiment seized two other members of that corps and their wives after the two couples had left their remote settlement at Country Harbour and moved to Halifax. The black men had served in the regiment in the Carolinas and in East Florida. They had belonged to John Hamilton, the regiment's commander, until he sold them to a rebel early in the war, but they escaped and joined the British. Their wives also struck for freedom and worked for British forces during the war. The couples' white Loyalist captors acted in tandem with one of Nova Scotia's highest officials and were not punished: the Halifax merchant who was their middleman was Michael Wallace, a member of the governor's council who soon would be acting governor. A Scot, Wallace had been a merchant in Charleston before the war. He had a purchaser in the Bahamas, and a ship's captain ready to take the captives there. Apparently, Wallace acted on behalf of Hamilton's cousin, with whom the two couples had lived at Country Harbour for about two years as unpaid servants. This episode is known only because of the escape and the successful litigation by the four captives, raising the question of how many other people were illegally seized by white Loyalists as they left Nova Scotia to move to or trade with the Bahamas, the West Indies, and the United States.[38]

At least two hundred free black civilians had gone directly to Nova Scotia in the evacuations of Charleston and East Florida, in addition to those who went from those ports with military units and the thousands who went to Nova Scotia from New York. Yet, free black Loyalists around the busy port of Shelburne lived in fear of sale to the West Indies or the Bahamas during the post-war decade. Using the local court to challenge claims of ownership, they alleged illegal sales and shipment, and documented their widespread fears. Sometimes their litigation was successful.[39] The known seizures in Nova Scotia reflect the attraction the Bahamas held in the 1780s and 1790s for people who had human chattel to sell, legally or illegally. 'The scramble for moveable property,' to use Jennifer Snyder's phrase in this volume, continued well after the war and operated by sea as it had in the southern borderlands during the war. More calmly, later in the nineteenth century, the slave trade between Nova Scotia and the Bahamas switched directions. The 1807 Abolition of the Slave Trade Act forbade export of enslaved residents of British-ruled areas only to non-British areas, and for decades after the cotton era, the Bahamas was a source of enslaved people brought to Cape Breton Island.[40]

The Bahamas as a site of black Loyalist re-enslavement was established as early as their first arrival from New York City in August 1783, even before the onset of the cotton boom. Within two months, about four hundred 'Negroes' had arrived at Abaco from New York; passenger lists indicate that some were freeborn, while others got certificates of freedom during the war. All the blacks were accompanied by white persons 'in whose possession they are now.' Similar ambiguous language was used in Nova Scotia as blacks entered Loyalist settlements.[41] Three years later, in June 1786, a Bahamian observer noted: 'It is with great Pain of Mind that I every day see the Negroes, who came here from America, with the British Generals' Free Passes, treated with unheard cruelty by Men who call themselves Loyalists. These unhappy People, after being drawn from their Masters by Promises of Freedom and the King's Protection, are every day stolen away.'[42]

During the cotton boom, slaves produced salt in the 'down' cycle of cotton production on some of the plantation islands. Large, shallow salinas, or salt pans, were dug in which to evaporate sea water. The resulting salt crust was broken and raked ashore into piles, packed for shipping, and moved to a port. Beginning in 1789, there was some supervision of salt production from Nassau, largely for price and quality control. There was looser oversight at the southern extreme of the island chain, where the Turks, Inagua, and Caicos Islands (the latter after its own brief cotton period) were the giants of salt production and export. Both during and after the cotton excitement, the labour-intensive salt pans of these islands offered a constant and unsupervised market for able-bodied workers. In 1807, the Turks Islands, with only forty white inhabitants – no more than in 1773 – reportedly had thirteen hundred enslaved workers. The salt pans were deadly, requiring a constant influx of new labourers. The salt operation on and near the Turks Islands may have served as a safe market in which to sell persons who had been plucked forcibly from a free life, as well as a dumping ground for known troublemakers. With salt a high-demand trade item, it is not surprising that sailing records of links among the southern United States, the Bahamas, and Nova Scotia carry frequent references to the Turks Islands,[43] an ominous fact that offers scope to the researcher's imagination and invites further enquiry, particularly into sailing records.

This exploration of the ways Loyalists from the southern colonies used the Bahamas in the 1780s and 1790s underscores the islands' function as points of connection for the Atlantic world. Their post-war linkages were seized by exiles who experienced, as Keith Mason notes in this volume, 'a series of social deaths and rebirths, a repeating circuit of dislocation and dismemberment, marked nevertheless by an unceasing desire to reconstitute the self through family, friends, and community.'[44] The disruptions and dislocations grounded in the American Revolution called for restoring connections and forging new ones, whether familial, social, financial, entrepreneurial, legal, or resource based. For white and black, resident and non-resident alike, the Bahamas provided crossing points and linkages with other colonies, states, Britain, and the world beyond. As such, the islands were central to the dynamic with which the Atlantic world entered the nineteenth century. Laws that soon would limit the international slave trade notwithstanding, the Atlantic world began the century with slavery more entrenched than ever. In the last two decades of the eighteenth century, the Bahamian function in Atlantic linkages served the international 'peculiar institution' well.

NOTES

1 Bahamas Registrar General Department (microfilm copies in P.K. Yonge Library, University of Florida, hereafter cited as Bahamas Registrar General microfilm), Index to Crown Grants and Conveyances; Bahamas Registrar General, Crown Grants and Conveyances Books A/1, B/1, C/1, D/1, E/1,F/1, G/1, A/2, D/2, C/4, M.

2 Ibid.; Whittington B. Johnson, *Race Relations in the Bahamas, 1784–1834: The Nonviolent Transformation from a Slave to a Free Society* (Fayetteville: University of Arkansas Press, 2000), xvi (quotation)–xxi; Michael Craton and D. Gail Saunders, *Islanders in the Stream: A History of the Bahamian People*, vol. 1, *From Aboriginal Times to the End of Slavery* (Athens: University of Georgia Press, 1999), 179; and Thelma Peters, 'Loyalists and the Plantation Period in the Bahamas' (PhD diss., University of Florida, 1960), 34.

3 Pioneering research on southern Loyalists in the Bahamas was done by Lydia Austin Parrish and Thelma Peters: Parrish, 'Records of some Southern loyalists: being a collection of manuscripts about some 80 families, most of whom immigrated to the Bahamas during and after the American Revolution' (typescript, 1940–53) Houghton Library, MS Am 1547, Harvard University; and Peters, 'Loyalists and the Plantation Period.' Sandra Riley, *Homeward Bound: A History of the Bahama Islands to 1850* (Miami: Island Research, 1983), incorporates Peters's work and is strong for Abaco.

4 This study was facilitated by Whittington B. Johnson, *Race Relations*, and Craton and Saunders, *Islanders in the Stream*, as well as Peters's older work; other recent helpful and inclusive works include D. Gail Saunders, *Slavery in the Bahamas, 1648–1838* (Nassau: Nassau *Guardian*, 1985); Howard Johnson, *The Bahamas from Slavery to Servitude, 1783–1933* (Gainesville: University Press of Florida, 1996); Laurie A. Wilkie and Paul Farnsworth, *Sampling Many Pots: An Archaeology of Memory and Tradition at a Bahamian Plantation.* (Gainesville: University Press of Florida, 2005); and John D. Burton, 'American Loyalists, Slaves and the Creation of an Afro-Bahamian World: Sandy Point Plantation and the Prince Storr Murder Case,' *Journal of the Bahamas Historical Society* 26 (2004): 13–22.

5 Colonial Office Papers (hereafter cited as CO) 5/560, 403–11, National Archives of the United Kingdom (hereafter cited as UKNA); *Year Book of the City of Charleston, 1883* (Charleston, SC: n.d.), 416.

6 Patrick Tonyn to Lord George Germain, 1 May 1782, CO 5/560, 211–12; see Jennifer K. Snyder, in this volume.

7 The Georgia Loyalists and the Florida Rangers were incorporated as King's Carolina Rangers in 1782. Treasury Papers, UKNA, 64–23, Reduced Officers,

Florida Rangers; Audit Office Papers, UKNA, 13:79, 383, Alexander Mc-
Donald claim; Audit Office Papers 13:25, 378, James Moore claim; Audit
Office Papers 13:37, 215, William Wylly certificate in John Mullryne
Tattnall claim; Alexander Prevost to Sir Henry Clinton, 30 July 1779, CO
5/98, 217–8; 'Return of Persons who Emigrated from East Florida,' 2 May
1786, enclosed in Patrick Tonyn to Evan Nepean, 2 May 1786, CO 5/561,
817–20; Carole Watterson Troxler, 'Loyalist Refugees and the British Evacuation of East Florida, 1783–1785,' *Florida Historical Quarterly* 60 (1981): 1–28.

8 'Return of Persons who Emigrated from East Florida,' 2 May 1786, reprinted in Troxler, 'Loyalist Refugees,' 21.

9 Frederick Lord North to Patrick Tonyn, CO 5/560, 724–7 (quotation); Troxler, 'Loyalist Refugees,' 21.

10 Ibid.; Tonyn to Nepean, 2 May 1786; Archibald MacArthur to Sir Guy
Carleton, 30 May 1783, Guy Carleton, 1st Baron Dorchester Papers, PRO
30/55, UKNA; statement by 'Capt. Touyn [Tonyn] Governor General,
Nassau,' quoted in A. Talbot Bethell, *The Early Settlers of the Bahamas and
Colonists of North America*, 3rd ed. (Norfolk, UK, 1937; reprinted Baltimore:
Genealogical Publishing, 2007), 100.

11 James Edward Powell to Patrick Tonyn, 9 June 1785, enclosed in Tonyn to
Thomas Townsend, Lord Sydney, 29 August 1785, CO 5/561, 721–3. Some
conflicts of class and culture in the southern backcountry are described in
Robert S. Davis, 'Loyalism and Patriotism at Askance: Community, Conspiracy, and Conflict on the Southern Frontier,' in *Tory Insurgents: The Loyalist Perception and Other Essays*, ed. Robert M. Calhoon et al. (1989; rev. and
expanded ed., Columbia: University of South Carolina Press, 2010), 229–83;
and Harry M. Ward, *Between the Lines: Banditti of the American Revolution*
(Westport, CT: Praeger, 2002), 187–91, 200–40.

12 Bahamas Registrar General microfilm; Treasury Papers 50, vols. 1–6 (microfilm copies in North Carolina Collection, Wilson Research Library,
University of North Carolina). Camden District Militia lists are vol. 1, unnumbered pay abstracts for John Phillips's Regiment; vol. 2, pay abstracts
8, 127 (two lists), 159, 171, 172, and unnumbered pay abstracts for John
Phillips's Regiment; vol. 3, pay abstracts 46, 136, 152–4; vol. 6, pay abstracts 2, 7, 9–16, 31, 35, 77, 99, 118, 126, and 129. Ninety-Six District Militia
lists are vol. 1, pay abstract 38 and unnumbered pay abstracts of Patrick
Cunningham's Regiment, Richard King's Regiment, John Cotton's Regiment, Daniel Clary's Regiment, and Zachariah Gibbs's Regiment; vol. 2,
pay abstracts 1–5, 9–10, 12–13, 20, 22, 28–30, 32, 37, 42–3, 49, 54, 58, 61,
66–9, 80, 90, 92, 94, 103, 111, 117, 124, 134, 155, 162, 170, and unnumbered
pay abstracts of Robert Anderson's Regiment, Richard King's Regiment,
John Cotton's Regiment, Daniel Clary's Regiment, Zachariah Gibbs's

Regiment, Patrick Cunningham's Regiment, Daniel Plummer's Regiment, Thomas Pearson's Regiment, John Hamilton's Regiment, and William Cunningham's Troop; vol. 3, pay abstracts 62–4, 71, 74, 76, 104, 113, 123, 137–9, 116, 162, 169–70; vol. 6, pay abstracts 34, 43, 60, 65, 70, 93, 97, 100, 109, 115, 128, and 130.

13 James Hume to Tonyn, 26 July 1784, enclosed in Tonyn to Sydney, CO 5/561, 50 (quotation), 83.

14 Carole Watterson Troxler, 'Re-enslavement of Black Loyalists: Mary Postell in South Carolina, East Florida and Nova Scotia,' *Acadiensis* 37 (2008): 70–85; idem, ' "To Git Out of a Troublesome Neighborhood": David Fanning in New Brunswick, 1784–1800,' *North Carolina Historical Review* 56 (1979): 343–65; and Jonas Howe transcript of David Fanning Journal, Jonas Howe Papers, New Brunswick Museum, Saint John.

15 Bahamas Registrar General microfilm, L: 29, 31, 'Return of the Cargo of the *Elizabeth* Thomas Church from East Florida 30 June 1784,' and 'Return of Blacks and Whites landed out of the Transport *Charlotte*, Thomas Pearson Master 23 June 1784 from East Florida'; Daniel L. Schafer, *Governor James Grant's Villa: A British East Florida Indigo Plantation* (St Augustine, FL: St Augustine Historical Society, 2000); Florida Historical Markers Program, St Johns County, 'Governor Grant's Plantations'; Carole Watterson Troxler, 'Community and Cohesion in the Rawdon Loyalist Settlement,' *Nova Scotia Historical Review* 12 (1992): 41–66.

16 Troxler, 'Loyalist Refugees,' 22.

17 Emphasis added; quoted in Whittington B. Johnson, *Race Relations,* 20 (Kelsall), 27 (Brown).

18 *Bahama Gazette* 11 January 1786; *Bahama Gazette* 11 April 1789; Peters, 'Loyalists and the Plantation Period,' 52, 172–9; D. Gail Saunders, *Bahamian Loyalists and Their Slaves* (Oxford: Macmillan Caribbean, 1983), 9–14; and Whittington B. Johnson, *Race Relations,* xxi, 304.

19 Thelma Peters, 'The American Loyalists in the Bahama Islands: Who They Were,' *Florida Historical Quarterly* 40 (1962): 226–40; Peters, 'Loyalists and the Plantation Period,' 85–6; Saunders, *Bahamian Loyalists and Their Slaves,* 14; and Whittington B. Johnson, *Race Relations,* 2.

20 J. Barton Starr, *Tories, Dons, and Rebels: The American Revolution in British West Florida* (Gainesville: University Press of Florida, 1976), 230–1; Muster Rolls of West Florida Royal Foresters, Lawrence Collection, Ward Chipman Fonds, vol. 27, Library and Archives Canada.

21 Indian Commissioners to Lords of the Treasury, 14 July 1779, Intercepted Letters – British, 2:28, and William McIntosh, Returns of Royal Refugees, 30 April 1779 and 30 June 1779, 2:40, 28, both in Papers of the Continental

Congress, National Archives of the United States; Jim Piecuch, *Three Peoples, One King: Loyalists, Indians, and Slaves in the Revolutionary South, 1775–1782* (Columbia: University of South Carolina Press, 2008), 54–6, 204.

22 William S. Coker and Thomas D. Watson, *Indian Traders of the Southeastern Spanish Borderlands: Panton, Leslie & Company and John Forbes & Company, 1783–1847* (Pensacola: University Press of Florida, 1986); Wilbur Henry Siebert, *The Legacy of the American Revolution to the British West Indies and Bahamas* (Columbus: Ohio State University, 1913), 12–33.

23 William L. Saunders, ed., *Colonial Records of North Carolina* (Raleigh, NC: State Printer, 1886–90), 10: 72–3, 141, 173, 175, 586, 846; Bahamas Registrar General microfilm, A/1: 20, 177 and B/1: 26; Tonyn to Sydney, 14 December 1784, CO 5/561, 345–52; 'Resolution of the Board of American Loyalists,' 1 September 1784, enclosure in Tonyn to Sydney, 21 October 1784, CO 5/561; Vicente Manuel de Zéspedes to Bernardo de Galvez, 24 December 1785, East Florida Papers, bundle 43, Library of Congress (microfilm copy); Whittington B. Johnson, *Race Relations*, 2–4.

24 *Bahama Gazette*, 7 January 1791; Foreign Office Papers 4:1, UKNA, copies in English Records, North Carolina State Archives; Edmund Rush Wegg account, 4 August 1788, CO 23/28, English Records, North Carolina State Archives; Bahamas Registrar General microfilm B/1:26.

25 Michael Craton, 'Bay Street, Black Power and the Conchy Joes: Race and Class in the Colony and Commonwealth of the Bahamas, 1850–2000,' in Howard Johnson and Karl Watson, eds., *The White Minority in the Caribbean* (Kingston, Jamaica: Ian Randle, 1998), 73; Paul Shirley, 'Tek Force Wid Force,' *History Today* 54 (2004): 30–5; Saunders, *Slavery in the Bahamas*; Whittington B. Johnson, *Race Relations*, xvii, xxi; and Howard Johnson, *Bahamas from Slavery to Servitude*.

26 Quoted in Whittington B. Johnson, *Race Relations*, 2.

27 Ibid., 42–3; Bahamas Registrar General microfilm, M: 243.

28 Petitions of Richard Pearis, Martha and Eliza Wilkins, Moses Glover, William Blacklock, Thomas Hunt, Andrew Deveaux, Buderade Mathews, Mary Eliza Kelsall, David English, William and Elizabeth Telfair to the General Assembly, 1776–1883, South Carolina Archives.

29 *Bahama Gazette*, 7 January 1791; Peters, 'American Loyalists in the Bahama Islands,' 238.

30 William Wylly to Ward Chipman, 12 September 1789, Ward Chipman Papers 4:1450, New Brunswick Museum (quotation); Audit Office Papers 13:3, William Wylly claim; New Brunswick Land Grants and Petitions, Saint John County, Petition of William Wylly, 1785, Record Group 108, Provincial Archives of New Brunswick; Muster rolls of King's Carolina

Rangers, Record Group 8 (British Military Records), Library and Archives Canada.

31 Whittington B. Johnson, *Race Relations*, 6.

32 Cecilia A. Green, ' "A Civil Inconvenience"? The Vexed Question of Slave Marriage in the British West Indies,' *Law and History Review* 21 (2007): 27, note 2 (quotation); William Wylly, *Regulations for the Government of Slaves at Clifton and Tusculum in New Providence* (Nassau: *Royal Gazette and Bahamas Advertiser*, 1815); D. Gail Saunders, 'William Wylly and his Slaves at the Clifton Plantation,' *Journal of the Bahamas Historical Society* 20 (1998): 27–31; Craton and Saunders, *Islanders in the Stream*, 221–4, 297–303; and Whittington B. Johnson, *Race Relations*, 95–9.

33 Riley, *Homeward Bound*, 203–4.

34 Ibid., 203–6; D. Gail Saunders 'William Wylly and the "Wylly Affair,"' 8 March 2006 posting, Environmental Issues in the Islands of the Bahamas, http://www.reearth.org.

35 Arrivals who were named included Robert Ross, Norman Macleod, Benjamin Douglas, Robert Thompson, Mr McLeod, Mr Patton and family, Mr Ferguson and family, Mr Prior and family, Mr French, Mr Darlington, and Mr McCulloch – see *Bahama Gazette*, 17 January 1789, 14 March 1789, 25 April 1789, 11 July 1789, 8 February 1791, 15 February 1791, 22 February 1791.

36 *Bahama Gazette*, 24 October 1789, 4 March 1791; Audit Officer Papers 12:109, 13:124, Archibald Taylor claim.

37 On entering the port for the Wilmington area, McInnis's vessel carried fruit, nails, sugar, paint, wine, fish, oil, and unnamed 'merchandise.' When he cleared for Nova Scotia, he carried lumber, tar, flour, hogs, rice, and tobacco. Treasurers' and Comptroller's Papers, Ports, boxes 9, 10 North Carolina State Archives; Petition of Christiana McInnis, 4 June 1819, Treasury Papers 79:121; Audit Office Papers 13:102, part 1, 44; Audit Office Papers 13:121 and 12:100, 54, Miles McInnis claim; Bahamas Registrar General microfilm C/1:198.

38 Carole Watterson Troxler, 'Hidden from History: Black Loyalists at Country Harbour, Nova Scotia,' in *Moving On: Black Loyalists after the American Revolution*, ed. John Pulis (New York; London: Garland, 1999), 39–57.

39 Troxler, 'Re-enslavement of Black Loyalists'; Shelburne Miscellaneous, Record Group 34–321, Library and Archives Canada; Shelburne Records, Record Group 60, Nova Scotia Archives and Records Management.

40 Ken Donovan, *Slaves in Cape Breton, 1713–1815* (University of Toronto Press and University of Nebraska Press, forthcoming); Georgii III, Session 1, cap. XXXVI.

41 Michael Craton, 'Loyalists Mainly to Themselves: The "Black Loyalist" Diaspora to the Bahamas, 1783–c. 1820,' in *Working Slavery, Pricing Freedom: Perspectives from the Caribbean, Africa and the African Diaspora*, ed. Verene A. Shepherd (New York: Palgrave 2001), 47–8 (quotation); William Shaw to Edmund Winslow, 15 June 1784, Lawrence Collection, Ward Chipman Fonds, 24: 251, Library and Archives Canada.

42 Quoted in Craton and Saunders, *Islanders in the Stream*, 87.

43 *Year Book of the City of Charleston, 1883*, 416; D.C. Harvey, ed., *The Diary of Simeon Perkins, 1780–1789* (Toronto: Champlain Society, 1958), 365, 420; idem, *The Diary of Simeon Perkins, 1790–1796* (Toronto: Champlain Society, 1958), 394; Treasurers' and Comptroller's Papers, Ports, boxes 9–12, North Carolina State Archives; and Craton, 'Bay Street, Black Power and the Conchy Joes,' 90.

44 See above, 41.

PART IV

Loyalist Religious Politics after the American Revolution

8

Loyal Orangemen and Republican Nativists: Anti-Catholicism and Historical Memory in Canada and the United States, 1837–67

ALLISON O'MAHEN MALCOM[1]

Within one generation of the War for American Independence, Loyalists in Upper Canada had established their adopted colony as a place that existed in contrast to its republican neighbour. Given a second chance to rebel during the War of 1812, Canadians remained loyal to the British Empire. While the initial republican values of the United States evolved in a democratic fashion, the Rebellion of 1837 failed in Upper Canada. An insurgency in Quebec met a similar end, while calls for reform in the heavily Loyalist Maritimes never reached the point of armed revolt. Scholars thus often interpret Canadian history as the story of ongoing Loyalist triumph, and many argue that Canada matured as a colonial entity, and later as a nation, as a rebuke to the revolutionary United States.[2] Upper Canadian colonial ideology was, therefore, conservative and reactionary. It was based on a shared allegiance to the Crown, the English language, the Protestant religion, and anti-Americanism.

Yet loyalism, like republicanism, was an evolving identity based on politics, religion, social needs, and historical memory, and scholars have challenged the common assumption that Upper Canadian society was necessarily reactionary, backwards, or static. Instead, as Jeffrey McNairn, Carol Wilton, and others have argued, subjects in Upper Canada did move towards popular democracy in the nineteenth century, even if this developed within the framework of constitutional monarchy. Petitioning, public protest, voluntary associations, and a popular press – all normally associated with the democratizing process in the United States – characterized early nineteenth-century Canadian society as well. These manifestations of the public sphere often operated despite both official and unofficial governmental opposition, but some of those in power also tended to tolerate and even encourage such actions.[3]

A central theme of this volume is that the Loyalist experience was anything but uniform during the initial revolutionary era, and this chapter advocates that view for the following generations as well. Neither the Loyalist experience of nation-building nor the Loyalist understanding of that experience was consistent. Limited democratization, such as the type that developed in the Upper Canadian case, demonstrates the relationship between questions of ideology and the framework upon which actors developed these ideologies. The ideology of loyalism was contested, as was the extent to which a Loyalist could also be a democrat; the only consistency was that the Upper Canadian world in which the Loyalists lived was unequivocally British.

As the decades passed, however, interpretations of the Loyalist experience began to change. In the nineteenth century, the processes of memory creation funnelled the actual diverse histories of the Loyalists into a series of archetypes in the developing public sphere, one of which I examine in this chapter. Norman Knowles has identified five markers of what is normally regarded as the Loyalist tradition as it later developed: 'unfailing devotion to the British Crown and Empire, a strong and pervasive anti-Americanism, suffering and sacrifice endured for the sake of principle, elite social origins, and a conservative social vision.'[4] According to Knowles, these principles came together into a single functioning form of English-Canadian nationalism only after the turn of the twentieth century.[5] Nevertheless, these standards for English-Canadian identity took root in the early nineteenth century in Upper Canada as colonial subjects sought to define themselves politically and culturally. One additional useful category of self-definition for early English-speaking Canadians was religion. Ultra-Protestantism, loyalism, anti-Americanism, and conservatism came together in this period to create a totalizing model for Loyal Canadian identity: Orangeism. While not the only version of Canadian loyalism to survive into the twentieth century, it was nonetheless one of the most clearly articulated, and one of the most popular.

The development of the Upper Canadian public sphere was at once monarchical and democratic, and the Loyal Orange Association of British North America reflected this inherent contradiction. Fraternal organizations such as the Orange Association are normally considered major forces in the democratization of society in both the United States and Upper Canada. Yet Orangeism itself represented the most monarchical and reactionary of developing Upper Canadian nationalisms. Beginning in the late eighteenth century, within a few years of the organization's founding in Ireland, large numbers of men in British North America joined Orange lodges, which would become pervasive strongholds of Loyalist nationalism. Many of the more conservative elements of the Upper Canadian Protestant population especially embraced the reactionary anti-Catholicism that helped to define Orange identity. Their ideology closely resembled American nativism. Like nativist fraternities in the United States, the Orange Order was a nationalistic organization with an unyielding vision of the proper position of politics and religion within its host society.[6] Of course, the Order did not claim to represent democracy. Yet its organizational apparatus was a vehicle through which many subjects of the Crown in Upper Canada entered the public sphere. They made their voices known through the Orange Press, Orange parades, and occasional Orange mobs.[7] In ideology, Orangemen and nativists had much in common. Both groups understood history as a story of the triumph of Protestantism and free government over Catholicism and despotism.[8] Their collective memories regarding historical enemies and threats were steadfast but not particularly parochial. Rather, their views fit within the framework of the purpose of history as comprehended by many mainstream Anglo-American intellectuals of the day. Theirs was a history different in degree, but not in basic understanding.

Like many mid-nineteenth century western liberal thinkers, Protestant nationalists in North America understood history to be a forward progression towards greater civility and polity in human society. In this story, Europe rose up out of the Middle Ages and modern nations were born out of the ashes of a defunct feudal system. Out of the Renaissance came art and beauty. Out of the Protestant Reformation came an understanding of religion superior to medieval Christianity. Out of the Enlightenment came new thoughts about government and humanity. To proud American citizens, the settling of the New World, and eventually the American Revolution, were the next great events in history, and the logical culmination of this improvement. As the children of Loyalists, their neighbours in British North America also generally held this view of history – up to 1776. To the Upper Canadian, the American Revolution was an evolutionary mistake. On the timeline of history, it marked the beginning of an unnaturally radical course that stood outside of this tempered advancement over time.[9]

Yet many North Americans on both sides of the border concurred on the value of an earlier revolution, one that gave the Loyal Orange Association its name. Though interpretations varied, Protestants in both the United States and Canada tended to agree that the Glorious Revolution of 1688 marked the death knell of medieval Catholic tyranny in Great Britain, and was thus a celebrated moment in the history of English-speaking people. When they looked back over a century and a half, they concluded that the conspiracy to overthrow James II, which they termed a righteous parliamentary 'invitation' to William of Orange to take the throne, represented two causes, as later celebrated in an Orange song: 'true British freedom and Protestant laws.'[10] The Glorious Revolution was for many Patriots a necessary precursor to the American Revolution, which threw off the chains of monarchy entirely. Loyal British subjects, of course, would see no justification for 1776 in the events of 1688. The Glorious Revolution cemented Britons' belief that their constitution was Protestant, and that it was from this Protestantism that they enjoyed both civil and religious freedoms.[11] The Revolution of 1688 was seen as the just and measured overthrow of an unreasonable monarch and a foreign religion, not an attack on the monarchy itself. By the nineteenth century, Protestant Loyalists generally cherished the Glorious Revolution as a major point of progress in both political and religious freedoms.[12]

Upper Canadians who chose to be Orangemen raised the ante of this particular understanding of history, and in doing so added a key element to their brand of Loyalism: ultra-Protestantism. They venerated William III and annually marked the dates of his victories in both England and Ireland. The greatest of these – 12 July 1690, the date of the Battle of the Boyne – stemmed from the Orange Order's Irish roots and its part in sectarian animosity there; aspects of these hostilities are described by Allan Blackstock in this volume. The Order crossed the Atlantic in the last years of the eighteenth century, first through British army units, later through Irish immigrants, and soon spread beyond the Irish community to become one of the most popular fraternities in British North America.[13] Despite continued Protestant Irish immigration that fuelled its growth over the course of the nineteenth century, the Orange Order became an outlet for many Upper Canadian men who valued both loyalism and Protestantism in the Empire.[14] In Upper Canada, the Order remained an organization that stressed loyalty to the British monarch above all. However, this Irish institution added a religious, reactionary dimension to what had been a simpler test of Canadian Loyalist identity; merely choosing to accept British rule was not loyal enough for the Orangemen. Orangeism changed in reaction to the Canadian situation as well. In North America, revolutionaries who had successfully broken from the king proved to be as much of a concern to Upper Canadians as the possibility of an Irish-Catholic rebellion – especially after a number of nationally minded Irish Catholics moved to British North America. Despite not having originated among United Empire Loyalists, and while maintaining its unique Irish identity in its songs and regalia, the Orange Order also adopted a Canadian version of loyalism that directly contrasted with the republicanism of the United States.[15]

Yet even as the Orange Order's role in Upper Canada evolved, it continued its remembrance of the Glorious Revolution. Orange Loyalist ideology thus combined anti-American sentiment with persistent adherence to the commemoration of William of Orange's victory in Ireland. In Orange memory, the Patriots of the Revolution and Catholic James II became a common historical enemy. Both stood in opposition to British order, religion, and the rightful monarch. In contrast, the same history as told in the United States illustrated a different understanding of the same events. In the memory of many American Protestant nationalists, by establishing its primacy over the monarch, the Convention Parliament of 1689 was the antecedent to a government of the people, by the people, and for the people. And only by saving British liberty from the control of the pope could the colonies be free from the yoke of Rome and thus open for the development of both political and religious freedom.

The common ideological factor here was anti-Catholicism. Ironically, the Patriots in the United States who most often articulated these views – the nativists – had much in common with the Orangemen who stood in opposition to them.[16] Both were Protestant, understood Protestant countries as being superior to Catholic counties, and did not hesitate to espouse their anti-Catholicism. Their mutual belief was that Catholicism was medieval, rightfully dying out in the world, and antithetical to true freedom – of both religion and the state. As Linda Colley and others have argued, the development of modern British nationalism connected closely to this type of militant Protestantism in the eighteenth and nineteenth centuries.[17] Accompanying this was both popular and intellectual anti-Catholicism, which played a central role in the political and popular culture of nineteenth-century Britain.[18] Similarly, as John Higham has stated, many Americans, like most English-speaking Canadians, inherited Protestantism as a central part of their national myth, paving the road for anti-Catholic nativism to flourish.[19] The spread of evangelical Protestantism in the early nineteenth century, as facilitated by disestablishment in the United States and Upper Canada, additionally influenced the close connection between Protestantism and nationalism.[20] The international revival in the Roman Catholic Church, as well as an increase in Irish Catholic immigration to both the United States and British North America, amplified the perceived threat to those Protestant national myths, regardless of whether they were a threat to the nations themselves.[21]

Loyalism and American independence thus became two contrasting but logical consequences of the Glorious Revolution in historical memory, according to two similarly structured groups of ultra-Protestant nationalists in North America. By the mid-nineteenth century, both the United States and English-speaking Upper Canada had developed conflicting anti-Catholic ideologies coloured by their respective views of the American Revolution. In turn, men and women in both places used their anti-Catholicism to justify the national status of their own home territory as a rational and correct outcome of history. In Upper Canada, this process was well under way by the 1830s and 1840s, when rebellions and changing governments prompted colonists to reconsider their place in the Empire. The Orange Order, a popular organization uniquely tolerated by powerful politicians, became an institution that served a key role in the development of Canadian Loyalist identity.

English speakers settled Upper Canada relatively late. In the wake of the American Revolution, approximately seven thousand United Empire Loyalists relocated to what was then western Quebec. They were soon vastly outnumbered, first by settlers from the United States, and later by migrants from Britain and Ireland. In 1791 Parliament split the sparsely populated western region from the French-speaking east. The British government sought to increase the population of this new colony, promising low taxes and cheap land to Americans willing to take an oath of allegiance to the Empire. Such inducements, combined with the fluid borders of the Great Lakes region, meant that many American nationals settled alongside British and Irish migrants. Initially, Parliament attempted to recreate a British constitutional model in the colony, granting limited representative government within an oligarchic framework, in order to guarantee a measured liberty to the colony's inhabitants. The end of the War of 1812 brought relative stability to the region, paving the way for increased immigration. In the wake of the war, however, the British government stepped back from encouraging American settlers and instead turned to Ireland and Scotland. Like the United Empire Loyalists, the settlers from the British Isles tended to reflect a conservative, group-oriented, anti-democratic, Protestant mind-set.[22] Thus, a third major element in the story of Canadian loyalism was introduced to the colony. Throughout the nineteenth century, Irish Protestants in Upper Canada outnumbered Irish Catholics two to one.[23] In contrast to the United States and eastern colonies such as Newfoundland, Irish did not become synonymous with 'Catholic.' Nor was the population largely urban. While Toronto and other cities received their share of migrants, the Irish in Ontario spread throughout the townships and rural areas.[24]

This sheer Irishness of Upper Canada meant that Orangeism made a successful leap from Ireland to Upper Canada. The Orange lodges in the new province grew and multiplied due to large numbers of Irish immigrants. However, the organization attracted other groups as well, and before long English and Scottish Canadians outnumbered their Irish counterparts. Almost from the beginning, the Orange Order became the premier fraternity in Upper Canada. Often the first social institution in a community, the Orange lodge provided fraternal aid and hosted social activities. Unlike, for example, a church, the organization was interdenominational and did not require a pastor. In addition, it was an honourable place for men to congregate in a society where women often made up the bulk of churchgoers.[25] Like the United States, Upper Canada had a large number of voluntary associations from a very early period. McNairn notes that, in 1834, York, a city of fewer than ten thousand people, had at least twenty-two associations, including religious, temperance, charity, literary, and civic societies.[26] Yet even in the midst of so many groups, the Orange lodge stood out.

In 1830, a newly arrived Irishman in Brockville, Ogle R. Gowan, unified the existing Orange lodges in Upper and Lower Canada under a Grand Orange lodge of British North America. The twenty-six-year-old Gowan had made his living as an anti-Catholic writer in Ireland, and upon landing in Upper Canada he became nothing less than 'a full-time organizer and agitator.'[27] Gowan went on to become a Conservative leader in a political career occasionally noted for its ruthless and extralegal campaigning. As Donald Akenson has noted, 'Gowan, like his followers, became at least semi-respectable.'[28] With this respectability came popularity. In the meantime, the spread of democratic and patriotic tendencies among American settlers in the face of a particularly unresponsive regime eventually led to the Rebellion of 1837. After the Rebellion failed, the British government sent Lord Durham to assess the situation, and his 1839 *Report* was instrumental to the Union of the Canadas. 'Responsible government,' as advocated by Durham and many others, was established a decade later. Vindicated once again with a (now more) representative government still tempered by conservative, monarchical elements, Loyalists celebrated the defeat of American extremism and the responsiveness of the British government to their colonial situation.[29] One estimate suggests that, a generation later, one-third of the Canadian male Protestant population was or had been a member of what was now called the Loyal Orange Association of British North America.[30] By 1870, all but twenty-five of Ontario's four hundred settled townships were home to Orange lodges, with as many as two hundred thousand Orangemen in British North America out of a population of under four million.[31] All male Protestants were eligible for membership and the Order often traversed class and denominational lines.[32] The massive growth of the Order over this forty-year period suggests that the Loyal Orange Association's specific interpretation of the history and purpose of loyalism must have had widespread appeal among Upper Canadian Protestants.

Orangemen, like nativists in the United States, were concerned about Rome upsetting the delicate balance of Loyalist society.[33] Their anti-Catholicism reinforced and was reinforced by their concern for what we might call 'the Great American Loyalist Experiment.'[34] It remained relatively consistent in the forty-year period after Gowan first united the Loyal Orange Association. Orangemen continually worried that Canadians had forgotten the threat of Catholicism: 'the present generation had grown up so ignorant of the machinations of Popery and the true causes of the Penal Enactments,' stated one Orangeman in 1851, referring to Catholic Emancipation in the United Kingdom and the colonies that had had penal laws, 'that many rejoiced in their total repeal.' The author described this mindset as a mistake: 'From all this we have been suddenly awakened, and we find (as the better-informed well know) that the principles of Popery are ever the same. It tolerates no other religion and suffers no other opinions than its own.' Roman despotism had brought down the revolutions of 1848 and threatened the United States. It had a stranglehold on Canada East and, if loyal subjects were not careful, Canada West would be next. Orangemen called on Canadians to emulate the followers of King William to overcome the papal threat.[35]

Orangemen saw themselves as having none of the prejudiced fanaticism of which they accused their Catholic adversaries. They 'disclaim[ed] an intolerant spirit,' and claimed to allow membership only to those 'believed to be incapable of persecuting or injuring another one on account of his religious opinions; the duty of every Orangeman being to aid and defend all *loyal subjects*, of every religious persuasion, in the enjoyment of their constitutional rights.'[36] Whether an individual Catholic *could* be a loyal subject was another question entirely, however, and one that Orangemen could not always answer. Certainly, Catholics as a group, and the Roman Catholic hierarchy specifically, were always suspect.

Similar to the debate over nativism in the United States, Canadian historians have disagreed over the nature of the Orangemen's ideology, their politics, their meetings, and their marches. Were Canadian Orangemen paranoid extremists given to violent outbursts and a faith-based mobocracy? Alternatively, were they the nationally minded members of a healthy social club dedicated to the protection of loyalist interests? While historians in the United States have been inclined to marginalize nativists to downplay the wide appeal of their ideology and the popularity of their political message, Canadian historians have tended in the opposite direction.[37] Since Orangeism was such a popular manifestation of nineteenth-century Loyalist spirit, according to this interpretation, Orangemen could not have been fanatics. This difference reflects a larger English-Canadian historiography that tends to emphasize the relative stability of Canadian society as compared to that of the United States – a view shared by many nineteenth-century Canadian observers.[38]

Orangemen, like nativists, were nationalists above all. The newspaper press in Canada West reported on myriad peaceful events in which the Orange Order celebrated their Canadian, British, and Irish identities. For the queen's birthday in 1854, Orangemen marched in Toronto along with local firemen and other assemblages, such as the St George's, St Andrew's, and St Patrick's societies.[39] At the Orange Order's annual rally in Kent in 1859, over three thousand people attended outdoor religious services that included several speakers and a choir.[40] There is little in such reports to separate Orangeism from any number of benevolent societies and voluntary associations given to outbursts of patriotic memory, the type of which have been well noted by scholars of the early American republic. Yet, a second common characteristic to both American nativists and Orangemen was the role of semi-secret voluntary associations. Nativists routinely organized themselves as members of such associations in the 1820s to 1850s; these groups had such innocuous names as the Order of United Americans and the Junior

Order of United American Mechanics. The Upper Canada Orangemen inherited their organizational structure from the Irish group. Nonetheless, the make-up of the hierarchical, ceremony-laden, oath-bound society looked very similar to these American nativist fraternities.[41]

Orangeism, like nativism, had both affirmative and negative aspects *inherent* to its ideology: to accept Orangeism was to accept its anti-Catholicism as an incontrovertible fact. In both the United States and Upper Canada, anti-Catholic fervour could lead to discrimination and the occasional violent outburst.[42] While there was no single overarching nativist institution in the United States – instead there were competing local and regional societies – the two ultranationalisms closely resembled each other. Both came from the same British colonial tradition. Even the Orange Order itself, a very specifically 'British' institution, did not disappear in the young republic but blended with other anti-Catholic organizations. The nationalism inherent in each may have evolved towards different ends but the fear of Rome remained.

The Upper Canadian and later united Canadian governments generally tolerated the Orange Order, even when its actions tended towards violence and intimidation, in a way that the disparate nativist groups in the United States would have envied. The Order's conservative nature meant that any mob activity more often than not purported to support the existing governmental structure. Just as the Orange Order itself channelled ultra-Protestant Loyalist ideology into a working model of Canadian colonial nationalism for one major facet of the public sphere, the institutional structure of the colony channelled anti-reform and anti-Catholic mob violence.[43] It should be noted, however, that the colonial government's support did not extended to corporate status for the organization: the fight for Orange incorporation began in 1856, but it was not granted for nearly thirty-five years.[44]

The Orange Order actively spread an anti-Catholic policy while defending the offensive as reasonable. 'We deny *in toto* that all sorts of religion should be *respected*. It is a question even whether they should be *tolerated*,' chastened one Orange newspaper critic. After all, 'we have laws against the existence of Jesuit institutions in the country, and against papal processions in our streets, and against the usurpation of territorial titles by the nominees of a foreign lordly ecclesiastic. These, and many other laws, prove that restraints are necessarily put on certain developments of false religions, but for which anarchy and confusion would prevail.'[45] In its defence of Orange activities, the Canadian press sometimes ignored obvious evidence that the Loyal Orange Association was an active anti-Catholic organization. For example, in the *Chatham Planet*, a medium-sized regional paper, a glowing account of the 1860 Boyne anniversary in Kent covered its front page. The paper reprinted the addresses given that day, including an anti-papal invective worthy of the most ardent of American nativists. Yet it went on to say, 'not a single angry word, insulting word, or expression that could by any possibility offend the most fastidious opponent of the Orange Order was uttered by any Orangeman in our hearing.'[46] The point is not so much that these Orangemen were anti-Catholic, which of course they were, as it is clear that mainstream Protestant society in Upper Canada was susceptible to the same anti-popery as the Protestant United States.

Such susceptibility meant that many of the Protestant critics of the organization did not question Orangemen's hyper-Protestantism, which was a manifestation of a rather mainstream type of British nationalism, but rather their techniques to combat popery. Members of the Order, one minister wrote, 'call themselves Protestants, but they have no religion, and consequently no true Protestantism, for real Protestantism consists in leading a life so pure and holy, as to prove that you are quite earnest in protesting against sin.' The Reverend Hilton was so confident in his own faith that it should be a small thing to win over 'Romanists,' whose religion was so 'sinful,' 'by love, and by prayer, and by the word of God.'[47] That Catholicism was a faulty religion that tended towards the spiritual and political despotism of the individual remained an incontrovertible fact for the minister. But he could not abide the Orange Order, and questioned Protestant Canadians' need to ban together in an organization so given to upsetting the public peace.

The Loyal Orange Association's emphasis on the impossibility of Catholicism's place in a free society translated into sectarian animosity hidden under the guise of loyalism.[48] Scott See argues that New Brunswick in the 1840s was the site of legal and economic discrimination against Irish Catholics, enabled by the Orange stranglehold on the local government. There, the Loyal Orange lodges had 'an inherent paramilitary nature' and carried out violent retributions on the Irish Catholic community.[49] Although there is no equivalent study for Upper Canada, contemporary sources point to the real danger of sectarian violence. In his report, Lord Durham viewed the Loyal Orange Association as good for little more than sectional animosity: 'The Irish Catholics complain very loudly and justly of the existence of Orangeism in this colony,' he wrote. He argued that, 'the organization of this body enables its leaders to exert a powerful influence over the populace' and that mobs were generally the end result. He did not even acknowledge that the loyalism attributed to the organization had any validity. Disagreeing with the notion that the Loyal Orange Association had any particular religious or national purpose, he instead accused its leaders of political expediency, claiming that they 'probably hope to make use of this kind of permanent conspiracy and illegal organization to gain power for themselves.'[50] In Lord Durham's account, the members of the society were a rather ignorant lot, drawn in by false claims of patriotism and without any comprehension of the wicked nature of the organization or the cynical pragmatism of its leaders.[51]

As Durham's report indicates, Orangemen took an active part in politics before the 1837 Rebellion, and while they were the primary anti-Catholic organization in the colony, they also served as a vehicle for conservative Canadian politics in general. Denied the vote, many members of Orange lodges nonetheless found political voice, acting as a group to promote conservative goals. Through the 1830s, mob action often marked public meetings and elections; such violence was meant to intimidate and to make clear the views of its members, a situation tolerated and even encouraged by conservative political leaders, some of whom, such as Gowan, were themselves affiliated with the organization. Thus the colony's conservative ruling elite engaged with the Order within the limits of a closed political structure, and used it against those who favoured reform. Such actions paradoxically created a role for individuals in the public sphere at the same time as it undermined the legitimacy of the colonial state. There would be both rebellion *and* reform, partially in response to such actions, and Orangemen, who had supported the old regime, would have to re-imagine their place within a new governmental structure.[52]

Evidence suggests that the Orange lodges continued their engagement in mob action to further both conservative and Protestant ends, and that this activity actually increased in the period after the Union of the Canadas. The first elections of the new United Canada saw major election-day clashes that involved many Orangemen.[53] At the same time, the Orange Order attained greater legitimacy, re-imagining its role on a larger scale in the public sphere.[54] In the 1840s and 1850s, Orangemen began more elaborate parades and uniforms and to take part regularly in public celebrations. Such public expressions of Orangeism occurred despite a Reform-led government's having banned Orange parades in 1843, though the law was repealed in 1851.[55]

Orangeism's anti-Catholic side also continued. When, on Saint Patrick's Day in 1858, Irish nationalist and future Canadian statesman Thomas D'Arcy McGee was scheduled to lecture after an Irish-Catholic parade in Toronto, Orangemen broke up the gathering 'unimpeded by the police or the military.' In Brantford in 1860, Orangemen gathered threateningly outside a hall where McGee was scheduled to speak and caused the address to be postponed.[56] In 1864, in response to the announcement that a procession and outdoor Mass to celebrate Corpus Christi would take place on the grounds of a Catholic church, armed Orangemen thronged to the site, endangering the children who had been in the procession.[57] Between 1870 and 1879, there were eighteen major Orange riots in Toronto alone, two-thirds of them prompted by parading on relevant holidays: the Twelfth of July, Saint Patrick's Day, and Guy Fawkes Day.[58] Generally, Orange parades would wind their way through Irish-Catholic neighbourhoods while marchers sang songs and displayed banners designed to taunt and humiliate the inhabitants. The combination of crowds, alcohol, and ethnic, religious, and class tensions often resulted in marchers and observers coming to blows. While few people died in these skirmishes, property damage was often considerable.[59] And although Upper Canadian cities with a large Orange presence usually had smaller, opposing organizations such as the Fenian Brotherhood or similar Irish nationalist groups,[60] the Loyal Orange Association was far more powerful. The institutional structure of Orangeism gave access to officials and credit unavailable to the Catholic community.[61] The organization was also a major player among Conservatives in the mid-nineteenth century. On a local level, it resembled a Tammany-type organization that handed out patronage jobs.[62] By 1844, for example, six of Toronto's ten aldermen were Orangemen in a city where Irish Catholics could claim their largest presence in the colony, a situation that would endure for the next several decades.

   The Orange Order's reputation for having an institutional stranglehold on the community spread beyond Canada. Cautioning the public about Orangemen in the United States, the *New York Times* stated in 1870 that there were 'townships [in Western Canada] in which no Roman Catholic is allowed to dwell in peace, and cities in which the jury box is invaded by secret oaths, and obligations at variance with the administration of justice.'[63] The Loyal Orange Association also had its own newspapers. One, the *Orange Lily and Protestant Vindicator*, published in Bytown (later Ottawa) in the 1850s, mixed a conservative political philosophy with patriotic songs and articles such as 'The Spirit of Popery Unchanged' and 'Popery a Hindrance to National Prosperity.'[64] In addition, the Loyal Orange Association in Canada continued to be a parallel organization to the Orange Order in Ireland and Britain. Such measures as Catholic Emancipation in 1829, the funding of a Catholic seminary at Maynooth, Ireland, and the Irish Church Disestablishment Act of 1869, drew Orange-led dissent. In enormous public demonstrations, they burned effigies of Daniel O'Connell alongside Guy Fawkes, events followed by reporters in the United States and Canada.[65] Indeed, an Irish-Catholic immigrant might not have been able to distinguish Canadian Orangemen from their Irish brethren, especially since Orange immigrants were welcomed immediately into the lodges of the colony.[66] Both Britain and the United States saw an increase in anti-Catholicism in this period; it seems incongruent that Canada would have escaped the same pattern.[67]

Despite its connections to Canadian conservatism, Orangeism was at its most powerful as a fraternal association, not as an explicitly political organization, since the structure of Canadian politics limited its efficacy within the body politic. In fact, on the political issues of the day, the Orange Order seemed at times to contradict itself. The separate school issue is a good example of this internal contradiction. The organization's conservative stance on the connection between church and state meant that it most often opposed the expansion of a single colony-wide nondenominational school system, instead favouring schools more closely connected to individual churches: Orangemen were among the few supporters of the Anglican Church's desire to run its own schools with public funds. To further this end, Orangemen found themselves in the odd position of supporting Catholic separate schools in the colony. In Orange thinking, it was entirely consistent that Catholics should have separate schools; the alternative was the watering down of traditional Protestant religion within the 'authentic' common schools of Canada West.[68] The irony of the Orange Order's role in the debates over separate schools thus illustrates the larger role it played in Upper Canadian society, consistently reinforcing the interconnectedness of Protestantism, Canadian national identity, and loyalty to the Empire. While its political conservatism sometimes resulted in oddly paradoxical support for Catholic causes, socially it was very much the bastion of traditional Protestant culture. Thus, it was in the Order's actions outside the existing political structure – its use of intimidation and mob violence, its networks of power and money, and its ideological harnessing of a large portion of the population – that Orangeism saw most of its influence and success.

Whatever the Order was in practice, the Irish overtones to Canadian Orangeism necessarily complicated the tenor and terms of its avowed Loyalist ideology. In its justifications for its own existence, there always existed a tension between different loyalisms: simple colonial fidelity to the Empire (unlike Americans); a loyalism infused with historical meaning as understood by many early and mid-century Protestant evangelicals (that the nineteenth-century Empire was the end result of the Glorious Revolution, unencumbered by the bastardization of the American Revolution); and finally loyalism as it existed in Ireland (that of a fearful minority in the face of constant rebellion, which magnified the meaning behind every historical event and symbol). In songs and speeches, the Orange Order paid relatively little attention to the original Loyalists who had fled the American Revolution.

Like those first United Empire Loyalists, Orangemen were undoubtedly a diverse lot. The collective ideology of Orangemen, however, was something different. Orangemen – through their parading, their publications, their speeches, their regalia, their songs, and their meetings – created a uniform usable memory from past events, the ultimate expression of which lay in the commemoration of the Glorious Revolution. Thus, the present and the past became one in Orange language. Colley states that, even in the nineteenth century, 'intolerance . . . was rooted in something . . . intangible, in fear most of all, and in the way that Britons chose to remember and interpret their own past.' If this historical interpretation was indeed, as Colley puts it, 'a soap opera written by God,' then the Orangemen's version was especially dramatic.[69]

When an Orange officer announced in mid-century that, 'All the hosts of Rome shall never be able to vanquish the small band of William's followers,' he was referring to what he saw as contemporary intrusions of the Roman Catholic Church into Canadian society. But his language of loyalty was tied to the monarchy of the past (King William), not the present (Queen Victoria).[70] Like nativists in the United States, many Protestants in Canada argued against the removal of the King James Bible from public schools and other public forums in deference to Catholic wishes. In Orange (and nativist) history, then, the Bible represented a single symbolic expression of Protestant freedom. An Orange song on this contemporary issue is telling: 'Our Bible we carry, and practice its truth,/We seen it respected in days of our youth,/By all who have passed to our forefathers' our graves,/Their watchword was

"Freedom, no Protestant slaves!" '[71] The forefathers in this case dated back to the Glorious Revolution, and before that to the Reformation. The past, recreated and resurrected to support the present, became a powerful rhetorical weapon in the Orange arsenal.

The glorious past could, indeed, be far superior to the present. Without the appreciation of the sacrifice of ancestors, it was difficult to maintain optimism about the future. James Campbell, who was killed in a skirmish between Catholics and Orangemen following an 1851 Twelfth of July celebration, became the subject of a popular song. Frustrated by what they concluded was a fixed trial, the Orangemen sang this final verse: 'Will we support to power and place/Those Protestants who grieve us,/By courting Rome in every case;/We know those that deceive us/Such barter all our rights with Rome –/Rights of the reformation – /Once settled by King William's throne,/Now's lost in legislation.'[72] Although Parliament had 'invited' King William to take the throne, Orangemen no longer held the same faith for officials in the government. Due to this distrust of the present, Orangemen, like nativists in the United States, wavered between fear for and dire warnings of the future, on the one hand, and satisfaction that their God-given place in history was preordained, on the other. In another song, they warned of a difficult prospect: 'On our old English Bible, boys, were framed the British law,/And from it's light, the nation yet her freedom's standard draws;/But if that day will ever come to cast that Bible down,/With it will fall the nation's pride,/it's honor and it's crown [sic].'[73] Yet, at the same time, the Orangemen were confident that Rome would fall, thus assuring the future of the Empire. They sang, 'When trees are showing forth their buds,/We know that Spring is near;/So watch the signs in prophecy,/Which now to us appear,/The fall of ancient Rome has come,/She shall not rule our Land;/Since kings no more shall worship her,/Nor bow at her command.'[74] In their notion of history, Rome was a thing of the past, and any nineteenth-century revival of Catholicism was both puzzling and troubling. And since Catholicism could not naturally succeed, any success that the Roman Church had must have been the result of dubious action on the part of the Church, its clergy, or its flock. A strong Protestant government, however, could stand up to Pius IX and arrest any momentum in his mid-century Catholicism.

Similarly, democratic rebellion remained a threat to the British monarchy. In a reply to a letter from the Grand Orange Lodge in County Antrim written not long after the events of 1837, the Loyal Orange Association of North America connected Canadian rebellion and Rome:

'May our loyal Institution prosper daily more and more, until all staunch good and the true, present a barrier, which neither Popery at home, nor Rebellion here, can penetrate.'[75] A later Orange song poking fun at American policies on slavery and trade was mockingly set to the tune of 'Yankee Doodle.'[76] Orangemen were suspicious of the democratic character of the United States, and also saw it as particularly susceptible to papist influence. The 1861 autobiography of the late Vincent Philip Mayerhoffer, purported to have been the Grand Chaplain of the Orangemen in Canada, illustrated a career arc that moved gradually from Catholic Continental Europe to free Protestant Canada. Mayerhoffer detailed his early career as a Catholic priest, his arrival in Pennsylvania, and his eventual escape from the priesthood and the Jesuits who controlled his diocese there. He married and became an Anglican minister in Upper Canada. But his newfound contentment was threatened by local church politics and the Rebellion of 1837. The rebels showed their animosity to both Canadian loyalty and righteous religion by locking Mayerhoffer out of his church. He noted fondly the actions of the Loyalist 'Orange boys,' his only allies in those days.[77]

Though Orangemen like Mayerhoffer were quick to point to their own part in suppressing rebellion, the United Empire Loyalists themselves remained outside the Orange tradition. One might at least expect Ogle Gowan's own 1859 history of the Orange Order, *Orangeism: Its Origin and History*, eventually to make its way to Canada, as he himself had done, but it does not. His history begins with the Roman Empire and later the usurping of true Christianity by the Roman Church in the first millennium after Christ. The first institution he sees as Orange in spirit is a secret Christian organization, founded in 55 AD, that protected the faith against the excesses of Nero.[78] He highlights the reclaiming of Christianity by Protestants during the Reformation, details the defeat of every Catholic plot against Elizabeth I, and dissects Irish history in the same way. After many pages, he finally reaches the early life of William himself. The actual founding of an Orange organization in Ireland would not occur for another hundred years, and Gowan finally does address it several hundred pages later. But the modern organization remains practically irrelevant compared to the tradition upon which it was founded. As for the Loyalists and Canadian loyalism, they are lost in this Orange history.[79]

The struggle between an imagined historic loyalism as created by Orangemen and the realities of contemporary loyalism culminated in the third generation during the visit of the Prince of Wales to North

America in the late summer and fall of 1860.[80] The tour was an enormous success and Canadians turned out in droves to visit the prince, illustrating the continued close connection between nascent Canadian nationalism and the British imperial claim.[81] After a visit to Quebec, the royal retinue moved on to Ontario, where Orangemen were keen to claim the same rights of ceremony that they felt the Roman Catholic hierarchy had been accorded in their sister colony. The prince first visited Ottawa, where a parade in his honour included both the local Orange lodges and members of the Catholic clergy.[82] In Kingston, however, Orangemen decided to chair the prince's welcome committee and parade. They erected two arches in the business district, inscribed with phrases such as 'Our God, our Country, and our Queen,' '1690,' and 'Garibaldi, 1860' – again suggestive of the connections between historical and contemporary fights against Catholicism.[83] As secretary of state for the colonies, Henry Clinton, the Duke of Newcastle, was in charge of the prince's visit. Wanting neither 'religious feuds' nor 'breaches of the peace,' he announced his intention not to allow the prince to land if the Orange Order continued its display.[84] In the duke's England, Orange marches had been illegal for a decade, and he had little patience for Orange sentiment. Because the prince had greeted leaders of Catholic organizations in Quebec, however, the Orangemen in turn refused to call off their parade.[85] The prince's entourage left Kingston without landing, and Orangemen rented a steamer to follow its boat on Lake Ontario.[86]

Orangemen considered the prince's refusal to land an enormous insult. They were determined to parade at the next scheduled stop, Belleville, so again the duke moved his young charge on. Only in Cobourg, where there was no Orange demonstration, did the entourage land.[87] Meanwhile, Orangemen in Toronto resolutely announced their intention to march. They burnt effigies of the duke and decorated the city. The prince did land in Toronto, but the duke made every effort to avoid Orangemen.[88] Within a few days of the incidents, more than one hundred thousand signatures were collected protesting the duke's actions.[89]

English Canadians felt the insult because in this case they equated Orangeism with both Protestantism and loyalism. 'The Protestant community of Lower Canada has without question been slighted in a most marked manner,' editorialized the *Chatham Planet*, remarking that, as the majority of the population in Canada West, Protestants should have been recognized in turn.[90] At the same time, this sentiment exposed a paranoia about Catholics and the attention paid to them by the royal party: 'The Roman Catholic body on the other hand, has been the recipient of unusual attentions and favors,' the paper continued, 'the Protestants should assert their privileges against all opposition.'[91] One Canadian correspondent for an American paper contended that aggressive Catholics, and specifically the Irish-nationalist-turned-Canadian-politician McGee, were as responsible as the duke for the slight.[92] *Harper's Weekly* agreed that Catholics were to blame, justifying Orangeism even as it condemned its 'destructive . . . tendencies.' The magazine stated, 'Canada is ruled by a priest . . . He rules the Archbishop; the Archbishop rules the Catholic members of Parliament . . . [T]hese members . . . control the Canadian Legislature.'[93] Therefore, Orangemen had every right to remind the prince of Protestantism's own beleaguered status in the Empire. Despite these assertions of Catholic power, however, the few Catholics in the area were silent about the events at Kingston.

Some journalists emphasized a distinctive Canadian 'nationalism' in order to defend the Orange Order. In this reasoning, the duke had ignored the 'liberty' of Upper Canada, as the Orange Order was both legal and popular there, even within the Canadian government.[94] Others, who wanted to show that the prince did not object to Orangeism, insisted that the boy was virtually a prisoner. Trapped on his boat, the teenager actually 'burst into tears' at the thought of disappointing his subjects. This account also stressed liberty as the issue at hand, in this case the liberty of Kingston to govern itself.[95] If Ontario wanted to be Orange, it had a right to be so under British law. By the eve of Confederation, then, it was clear that anti-Catholicism actually tempered the loyalism of the Orange Order. While Orangemen venerated King William, their Loyalist ideology was so entwined with Protestantism as to make even decisions made by the Prince of Wales suspect. A later Orange song about the incident was far more confident about Orangemen than about the future monarch: 'God save the youthful Prince of Wales/From Puseyites, and learn/How he may all their mimicry/From Protestant discern./Long live the Kingston Orangemen,/With all that's good in store;/Likewise their Belleville brethren–/They have my bosom's core.'[96] Loyalism to a Protestant monarch, then, extended only so far.

Both Canadian Orangeism and American nativism had two sides: an affirmative nationalism as well as traditional anti-Catholicism. While Upper Canadian Loyalists celebrated their status as subjects,

American nativists, descendants of those who had rebelled against the king, more often associated subjecthood with popery and therefore slavery. Samuel F.B. Morse, who would become one of the country's leading nativists in the 1830s, echoed a common American sentiment of the time. American men, unlike Europeans, could claim status as citizens, a departure from what he and others regarded as the degraded European model of ranked subjecthood. Subjects, always beholden to others, could not achieve full manhood. Rather, as Morse states, they were pathetic creatures, 'enslaved,' 'priest-ridden,' and 'tax burdened.'[97] In Morse's mind, the twin follies of faulty government and faulty religion made up 'these antiquated remnants of feudal barbarism' and *together* created the man not fully realized – the subject.[98] If a citizen was fully a man because he bowed before no other human being, it was still necessary for him to bow before God – directly before God – without the intervention of an institutional church. Nativists regarded citizenship in terms of their understanding of Protestant Christianity as inherently linked with the history and success of the republic. A citizen was a man who had the privilege of both free government and free religion. A Canadian subject of the British monarch fell short of this ideal.

The Glorious Revolution was also a major event in the American colonies, and the proceedings of the 1770s would mirror the earlier New England resistance to the rule of James II. The Orange overthrow led to the end of the despised Dominion of New England and a return to significant colonial autonomy. It also marked the end of the royal charter for Calvert family rule in colonial Maryland, a historical occurrence dear to the hearts of mid-nineteenth-century Maryland Protestants.[99] Like Orangemen, nativists also found and reprinted stories of seventeenth-century events in Britain and Ireland to support their cause against popery and to warn of the dangers of political Romanism.[100] Their understanding of history reflected mainstream interpretations. For example, to conclude the first volume of his history of the United States, published in 1859, George Bancroft assures the reader that, 'Priestcraft did not emigrate [to the colonies] . . . Nothing came from Europe but a free people.' He adds, 'Our fathers were not only Christians; they were, even in Maryland by a vast majority, elsewhere almost unanimously Protestants. Now the Protestant reformation, *considered in its largest influence of politics*, was the awakening of the common people to freedom of mind.'[101] Bancroft, educator and democratic statesman, was certainly not a nativist. But he, and any number of authors of similar texts, wrote history as a patriotic citizen attempting to explain the origin of his national system.[102]

According to such a mindset, Christianity continued to be a necessary influence on the United States. The American Protestant Association, for instance, was an anti-Catholic organization and in later years would have close ties to Canadian Orangemen, but that was not how it presented itself. In a publication written for the association in 1844, Andrew Lipscomb argued that, 'The farther man progresses in civilization, and the greater his improvement in civil polity, the more need is there of the presence and purity of Christianity; for every advance is removing society from physical means of government, and resting it on moral influence.'[103] His view, again, was not unusual in nineteenth-century America. Protestant Christianity was seen to be a necessary forerunner to progress, and enlightened progress continued to recreate the United States. Nativism, like Orangeism, was different in degree, but not necessarily in kind, from a more general Protestant viewpoint.

Morse understood that this close connection between government and religion was not coincidental. He cited Frederick Schlegel, a Catholic in the Austrian cabinet, as admitting, even boasting, '*Protestantism* favors *Republicanism*, while Popery as naturally supports *Monarchical Power*.'[104] In a different volume, he reinforced this point: 'Every religious sect has certain principles of government growing out of its particular religious belief, and which will be found to agree or disagree with the principles of any given form of civil government.'[105] He went on to assert that, while Austrians and Americans agreed that authority to govern was God-derived, the two peoples disagreed as to the delegation of this authority. Just as Catholics believed that God spoke through the pope, so too Austrians believed that civil authority was delegated to the emperor. As Protestants believed that God spoke through the individual, so Americans believed that civil authority was delegated to the people.[106] Likewise, nativists understood that republican governments failed without Protestantism to support them. Lipscomb of the American Protestant Association argued, for example, that a lack of a Christian citizenry had doomed the French Revolution.[107] As long as the United States remained Protestant, however, the republican experiment would succeed.

If, as Morse stated, 'the civil polity of Popery is in direct opposition to all which he deems sacred in government,' the Roman Catholic clergy would actively keep Catholics from becoming good citizens able to engage in their public duty.[108] Given that many European immigrants had been raised under such despotic conditions, it was only a short step of logic to conclude, as nativist Joseph Tinker Buckingham did in 1844, that naturalized Catholics would 'attempt to control our legislators, nominate our magistrates, and to browbeat our voters at the ballot-box,' and that the most ignorant ones would simply 'sell their votes to the more enlightened and crafty demagogue, and perjure their souls [at] the command of profligate leaders.'[109] Echoing many other nativists of the period, Morse concluded that European Catholic immigrants 'form[ed] a body of men whose habits of *action*, (for I cannot say *thought*,) are opposed to the principles of our free institutions, for they are not accessible to the reasoning of the press, they cannot and do not think for themselves.'[110] Simply put, Catholics could not be good citizens.

Mainstream Protestant nationalist opinion against nativists in the United States and criticisms of Orangemen in Canada were very similar. Like the Reverend Hilton, many American Protestants who were not active in nativist groups agreed that Catholics were a problem but thought that prayer was the best way to overcome it. Unlike nativists, they would not seek any sort of political solution to favour Protestantism over its rival. The most optimistic writers saw the Catholic Church as imploding from within, without the need for political activity on the part of Americans.[111]

To American nativists, Protestant immigrants, while subjects, were less suspect than their Catholic equivalent. Thanks to the Glorious Revolution, British subjects, for instance, were only a step short of citizenship: they were perceived as well educated in both representative government and Protestant Christianity. In American eyes, however, Canadians still suffered from their colonial identity. One American newspaper scoffed at Canadian ethnic infighting just months before the passage of the British North America Act: 'All these antagonistic elements go to form what is falsely known as the Canadian people. There is no such people, nor will there ever be, so long as Canada remains a colony.'[112] An American nation might overcome its diversity, but Canada, made up of mere colonial subjects, could not.

If Canadians were less than impressed with American nativists, Americans were less impressed than Canadian Orangemen with King Billy's actions in Ireland. While perfectly willing to claim the Glorious Revolution's impact on English, or even British, representative government, the Irish overtones of Orangeism were not so appealing. Accounts suggest that the Irish-Catholic migrant in North America especially saw Orangeism in terms of its activities in the British Isles. In both Canada and the United States, the press reported on Orange activity in the United Kingdom. The regular mention, and condemnation, of current Orange activity there reinforced the immigrants' historical fear of Orangeism as an aggressor against Irish Catholics.[113] The *Brooklyn Daily Eagle* labelled one report of a riot in Ireland, 'Always a Disgrace to Protestantism.'[114] In 1864, the *New York Times* reported on a forty-thousand-man demonstration and convent burning that occurred in Belfast after the unveiling of a statue dedicated to Daniel O'Connell in Dublin. In that case, it called Orangeism a 'national madness.' The report noted that, in Ulster, 'to be willing to eat a Papist is a sufficient evidence of a practical piety to fit a man for church membership.'[115] Reporting on the incident, *Harper's Weekly* noted that the Orangemen behaved in an 'outrageous manner against the Catholics.'[116] Of course, newspapers not aimed at Irish Americans usually paired these attacks on Orangeism with equal sarcasm about Irish Catholics. In regard to the origin of one riot in Ireland, the *Times* editorialized: '[W]e are probably safe in assuming that either some rabid Orangeman gave utterance to sinister anticipations as to the prospects of Pius IX in the next world, or that some fervid Roman Catholic expressed himself disrespectfully with regard to King William III or his glorious, pious, and immortal memory.'[117] Orange organization in the United States thus remained confined mostly to working-class Irish-Protestant immigrants in urban areas.[118] Though Orange parades sparked many disturbances throughout the century, including major riots in New York City in 1870 and 1871, the organization there was generally not well known.[119] It remained strictly an immigrant institution.[120]

Though they did not found an official organization until 1867, Orangemen had arrived in the United States by 1800.[121] Between the 1830s and the 1860s, the organization faded from view, blending in with more explicitly American nativist groups such as the American Protestant Association, though the relationship between the two societies was often strained.[122] When it became an official centralized association, the Orange Order in the United States looked much like its sister societies in Canada, Scotland, and Australia. Members, who had to have been born Protestants and who could not marry Catholics, still swore to defend the memory of William, adding only the following line to their oath: 'will to the utmost of my power support the laws of these United States as long as they maintain civil and religious freedom.'[123] This addendum did not endear Americans, even many nativists, to the

Orange cause. The *Brooklyn Daily Eagle*, after the first of the two major July 12 riots in New York, wrote, 'The English Government, for shame's sake, has forbidden by law Orange processions in Ireland on the 12th of July.' Orange processions would always cause riots, as they brought to mind only 'the memory of vengeance, humiliation, and defeat.'[124] The *New York Daily Tribune* agreed: 'If the great Orange anniversary were nothing but a commemoration of the triumph of Protestantism, or the celebration of a national victory, no one could object to Protestants keeping it. Everybody knows, however, that the cause it exalts was not national, but sectional, and that the festival, whatever it be in name, is in reality not so much the celebration of a victory as a taunt for the vanquished.'[125] Though the newspapers mostly defended the Orangemen's right to march through American streets, Orangeism was seen as a particularly Irish phenomenon, and thus unworthy of the American republic. Despite this, or perhaps due to it, critics of American anti-Catholicism well into the twentieth century used 'Orangeman' as shorthand for any Protestant who admitted sectional rivalry with the Catholics.[126]

Interestingly enough, the *Irish American*, in reaction to the riots, used the same comparison of subject to slave as had the nativistic Morse, editorializing that, 'an "Orangeman," everywhere, is a self-constituted slave in the service of England; and whether he comes in a red uniform or out of it, he is the enemy of liberty and Ireland; and as such only can we recognize him.'[127] Irish Catholics in Canada, most of whom distinguished between the British colonial situation in North America and British rule in Ireland, might have dismissed this attitude as lacking in subtlety.[128] The same article also took a shot at American nativists. Orangemen were Tories in the Revolution, it claimed, and these were the same men that later formed and joined the American Protestant Association.[129] American nativists, exceedingly proud of their revolutionary ancestry, would have been extremely offended by such a suggestion.

In fact, the small American organization that was the American Orange Institution saw no need for loyalism in its Loyalist ideology at all. Rather, its by-laws reflected a nativist attitude towards history, drawing a direct line from the Reformation to both the Pilgrim Fathers and William of Orange and then on to Washington: 'We cherish the memories of noble men of every age and country, who have contributed to establish civil and religious freedom for the people. Among those worthy of special honor we place Wycliffe, Knox, Luther, Melanthon, Coligny, the "Pilgrim fathers," William of Orange, President of the Dutch Republic, Washington and his compeers, and all other heroes in the same cause.'[130] Their loyalism – limited in this case to Protestant Christianity and *all* free government – seemed to them to be completely consistent.

By the mid-nineteenth century, Orange loyalism and nativist republicanism represented two sides of the same coin. Orangeism was not a harmless outlet for what might have become nativist hostility; rather, they were one and the same. The ultra-Loyalist, the ultra-Tory, the Orangeman – these were manifestations of usable loyalism, recreated in the generations succeeding the American Revolution for purposes of political, cultural, and social power. As current and former subjects, respectively, of the British Crown, Orangemen and nativists understood history, and the role of Protestantism in history, in similar ways. Yet faced with different political realities, they adjusted their understanding of history to justify their own present. The Glorious Revolution was the common historical event, and the American Revolution served as the point of departure. The long-standing and continually reinforced fear of popery in English-speaking North America supplied the common thread. These American citizens and British subjects might have despised each other's politics; the Orange Order served as an occasionally extralegal organization that propped up some of the most antidemocratic voices in the Upper Canadian government, while nativists claimed to be republicans first, and saw their own organizations as representative of the best parts of American democracy. Yet, both often looked in equal horror at what seemed to be an autocratic and superstitious medieval institution resurrected.

Of course, this was a problematic attitude in the end. Developing nationalisms in both countries had to account for significant Catholic populations. Canada included Quebec as well as large Catholic minorities elsewhere, but Orangemen's version of nationalism included only one religion and one people.[131] The Canadian Orange Order's loyalism as it developed through the course of the nineteenth century was of a specific kind. Somewhere in their telling of the Loyalist story, Orangemen usurped the original Canadian Loyalist tradition. The memory of the actual United Empire Loyalists, forced from their homes to Upper Canada after the American Revolution, became lost. In its place, Orangemen created a new tradition of Upper Canadian loyalism, one based on Protestantism and the memory of a king whose thoughts likely never strayed to what was then a large swath of little-explored territory in French North America.

NOTES

1 This chapter began as a paper in Professor Michael Perman's graduate seminar at the University of Illinois at Chicago. Some of the research for the chapter was completed while the author was a Legacy Fellow at the American Antiquarian Society.

2 Most standard works in Canadian history have dealt with this topic. See, for instance, Arthur R.M. Lower, *Colony to Nation: A History of Canada* (Toronto: Longmans, Green and Company, 1946); J.M.S. Careless, *Canada: A Story of Challenge*, rev. and expanded ed. (Toronto: Macmillan, 1953), esp. 116–21, 131–6, 164; S.F. Wise and R.C. Brown, *Canada Views the United States: Nineteenth Century Political Attitudes* (Toronto: Macmillan, 1967); Jane Errington, *The Lion, the Eagle, and Upper Canada: A Developing Colonial Ideology* (Montreal; Kingston, ON: McGill-Queen's University Press, 1987); David Mills, *The Idea of Loyalty in Upper Canada, 1784–1850* (Montreal; Kingston, ON: McGill-Queen's University Press, 1988); and, for the later period, Carl Berger, *The Sense of Power: Studies in the Ideas of Canadian Imperialism, 1867–1914* (Toronto: University of Toronto Press, 1970). Errington tempers this generalization, arguing that Upper Canadian settlers, who had closer ties to New York than to England, were generally 'ambivalent' towards the United States (*The Lion and the Eagle*, 36). At least one contemporary source, though, affirms the continuity in Canadian Loyalist anti-Americanism into the second and third generations:

> The aversion, with which [Loyalists] regarded the revolutionists never decayed, and was, of course, communicated to their descendants, who now form a considerable part of the population of Upper Canada. – The Americans returned their hostility with vehemence; and the two nations became so completely estranged from each other, that the long peace which followed the rebellion had little effect in restoring harmony between them. However, the invasion of Canada in 1812 removed all chance at reconciliation, and made both parties more personal, and more inveterate, in their dislike. And, as the social and moral condition of the two countries is growing more dissimilar every day, the aversion, with which their inhabitants regard each other, is not likely to diminish.

See John Howison, *Sketches of Upper Canada, Domestic, Local, and Characteristic: To Which Are Added, Practical Details For the Information of Emigrants of Every Class; And Some Recollections of The United States of America* (Edinburgh: Oliver & Boyd, 1821; reprint n.p.; S.R. Publishers, 1965), 277–8.

3 Jeffrey L. McNairn, *The Capacity to Judge: Public Opinion and Deliberative Democracy in Upper Canada, 1791–1854* (Toronto: University of Toronto Press, 2000); and Carol Wilton, *Popular Politics and Political Culture in Upper Canada* (Montreal; Kingston, ON: McGill-Queen's University Press, 2000), 12–13. For the American view of associations as a tool for democratizing, see Johann Neem, *Creating a Nation of Joiners: Democracy and Civil Society in Early National Massachusetts* (Cambridge, MA: Harvard University Press, 2008).

4 Norman Knowles examines the evolving nature of Canadian Loyalist ideology and the use of historical memory and commemorations to create and recreate this Loyalist identity; see *Inventing the Loyalists: The Ontario Loyalist Tradition and the Creation of Usable Pasts* (Toronto: University of Toronto Press, 1997), 3, 5–7.

5 Ibid.

6 Scott W. See connects the success of both Orangemen and nativists to 'burgeoning nationalism,' despite the lack of an independent nation in Canada's case, citing 'British colonial nationalism'; see *Riots in New Brunswick: Orange Nativism and Social Violence in the 1840s* (Toronto: University of Toronto Press, 1993), 11. I tend to use to word 'nation' when referring to colonial Canada here mostly for expediency's sake, but certainly 'British colonial nationalism' in practice was not completely unlike other types of nationalism that developed in the nineteenth century, as described by, for example, Benedict Anderson; see *Imagined Communities: Reflections on the Origin and Spread of Nationalism*, rev. ed. (London: Verso, 1991). Of course, Canadian historians have addressed the gradual development of a true Canadian 'nationalism' in the late nineteenth and early twentieth centuries. See, for example, Berger, *The Sense of Power*. In the United States, the term nationalism came into use in the 1830s, though what we might call 'nationalism' predated the use of the word. See Daniel Walker Howe, *What Hath God Wrought: The Transformation of America, 1815–1848* (New York: Oxford University Press), 116.

7 McNairn, *Capacity to Judge*, 102–3.

8 The connection between American nativists and the Loyal Orange Association of British North America has been made most recently by See, but also initially by the Orangemen themselves – see, for instance, 'Orangeism,' *Toronto Patriot*, 4 January 1860. Contemporaneous critics of both Orangemen and nativists agreed that there was a connection: 'It is an indisputable fact that the Orange organization was the original germ and nucleus of Know Nothingism,' stated one American newspaper, 'and the tests and obligations of the Know Nothing Councils were but modifications of the oaths administered in the Orange lodges' ('Premonitory Symptoms,' *Brooklyn Daily Eagle*, 15 September 1860, 2). In the secondary literature, Cecil J. Houston and

William J. Smyth describe how Irish-Protestant immigrants in the United States tended to join specifically American organizations such as the American Protestant Association rather than the Orange Order; see 'Transferred Loyalties: Orangeism in the United States and Ontario,' *American Review of Canadian Studies* 14 (1984): 193–211.

9 My use of the word 'liberal' in this paragraph refers entirely to the view of history as progress, a common idea in both the Scottish and French Enlightenments and among many, if not most, classical liberal thinkers of the eighteenth and nineteenth centuries. While the proposed path to progress was often a point of contention between opposing groups of people, the belief in progress transcended national borders, religious affiliations, and political parties. Howe argues that, in the United States, the millennialism of evangelical Protestantism combined with Enlightenment thought, leading to a surge in national confidence; see *What Hath God Wrought*, 3, 285–327. Linda Colley discusses this mindset in regards to Britons of the eighteenth and early nineteenth centuries, for whom *their* Empire stood as the ultimate example of human society at its best; see *Britons: Forging the Nation, 1707–1837* (New Haven, CT: Yale University Press, 1992), 368–9. As the nineteenth century continued, ideas about racial hierarchy entered this version of history: white, Anglo-Saxon men had progressed the farthest. Such an attitude became a justification for imperialism in Britain and the United States, and also in Canada specifically; see Berger, *The Sense of Power*, 147–52. On the interconnected nature of the English Civil War, the Glorious Revolution, and the American Revolution, see Eliga H. Gould, 'Revolution and Counter-Revolution,' in *The British Atlantic World, 1500–1700*, ed. David Armitage and Michael J. Braddick (London: Palgrave Macmillan, 2002), 196–213.

10 'Come to Our Standard; Or, Union Is Strength to Our Protestant Cause,' in Robert McBride, *The Canadian Orange Minstrel for 1860* (London: Free Press Steam Printing Office, 1860), 3.

11 D.G. Paz, *Popular Anti-Catholicism in Mid-Victorian England* (Stanford, CA: Stanford University Press, 1992), 3; and Owen Stanwood, 'The Protestant Moment: Antipopery, the Revolution of 1688–1689, and the Making of an Anglo-American Empire,' *Journal of British Studies* 46 (2007): 481–508.

12 McNairn calls the belief in the Glorious Revolution as the last important moment in the history of the British Constitution a 'fairly standard Whig strategy' (*Capacity to Judge*, 38). This understanding of the Glorious Revolution as a major moment in Protestant history also developed by the early nineteenth century due to an increasingly vocal new generation of evangelical and ecumenical Protestants. As the number of Christian-themed

publications and their markets increased, so too did the number of volumes that made generalizations about the history of Protestantism in world history; see, for instance, Howe, *What Hath God Wrought*, 194.

13 Donald Harmon Akenson, *The Irish in Ontario: A Study in Rural History*, rev. ed. (Montreal; Kingston, ON: McGill-Queen's University Press, 1999), 170.

14 As might be expected, the Orange tradition tended to be politically conservative, so it is probable that many Reformers did not feel welcome in the local lodges. There was also a Tory overtone to mid-century Loyalist ideology in general; see Knowles, *Inventing the Loyalist Past*, 3.

15 William J. Houston and Cecil J. Smyth, 'The Orange Order in Nineteenth-Century Ontario: A Study in Institutional Cultural Transfer' (Discussion paper, University of Toronto, Department of Geography, 1977), 4.

16 See has called for historians to recognize such similarities across the US-Canadian border, despite respective historiographies that stress different national myths, one peaceful and one violent. See 'Nineteenth-Century Collective Violence: Toward a North American Context,' *Labour* 39 (1997): 13–38.

17 Colley, *Britons*. See also J.C.D. Clark, *The Language of Liberty, 1660–1832: Political Discourse and Social Dynamics in the Anglo-American World* (Cambridge: Cambridge University Press, 1994).

18 See E.R. Norman, *Anti-Catholicism in Victorian England* (London: George Allan and Unwin, 1968); Walter Arnstein, *Protestant versus Catholic in Mid-Victorian England: Mr. Newdegate and the Nuns* (Columbia: University of Missouri Press, 1982); Robert J. Klaus, *The Pope, the Protestants, and the Irish: Papal Aggression and Anti-Catholicism in Mid-Nineteenth Century England* (New York: Garland, 1987); John Wolffe, *The Protestant Crusade in Great Britain, 1829–1860* (Oxford: Clarendon Press, 1991); and David Hempton, *Religion and Political Culture in Britain and Ireland* (Cambridge: Cambridge University Press, 1996).

19 John Higham, *Strangers in the Land: Patterns of American Nativism, 1860–1925*, 2nd ed. (New York: Atheneum, 1968), 3–11. Higham identifies anti-Catholicism as one of three major expressions of nativism in the United States.

20 Whether Upper Canada ever had an 'established religion' depends on how one defines the term. The Constitution Act of 1791 established 'the Protestant religion' in the area outside of Quebec – that is, Upper Canada – whereby the Church of England and later the Church of Scotland would receive 'lands, privileges and the right to marry'; see H.V. Nelles, *A Little History of Canada* (Don Mills, ON: Oxford University Press, 2004), 82. The Act of Union did not clarify this point. From 1823 on, no tithes were

permitted by law and there were none before that in actuality. After the
Act of Union, the Church of England repeatedly conceded privileges; see
William Westfall, *Two Worlds: The Protestant Culture of Nineteenth-Century
Ontario* (Montreal; Kingston, ON: McGill-Queen's University Press, 1989),
93–4, 107.

21 Howe, *What Hath God Wrought*, 165–6, 320–3. Various strands of evangelical Christianity travelled to Canada both before and after the American
Revolution, and Canada was heavily influenced by both British and American Methodists and other evangelical groups; see, for example, Mark A.
Noll, David W. Bebbington, and George A. Rawlyk, eds., *Evangelism: Comparative Studies of Popular Protestantism in North America, the British Isles,
and Beyond, 1700–1990* (Oxford: Oxford University Press, 1994); and Todd
Webb, 'How the Canadian Methodists Became British: Unity, Schism, and
Transatlantic Identity, 1827–54,' in *Transatlantic Subjects: Ideas, Institutions,
and Social Experience in Post-Revolution British North America*, ed. Nancy
Christie (Montreal; Kingston, ON: McGill-Queen's University Press, 2008),
159–98.

22 Elizabeth Jane Errington, 'British Migration and British America, 1783–
1867,' in *Canada and the British Empire*, ed. Phillip Buckner (Oxford: Oxford
University Press, 2008), 146–7.

23 Akenson, *Irish in Ontario*, 8–20, 26, 34; and Brian Clarke, *Piety and Nationalism: Lay Voluntary Associations and the Creation of an Irish Catholic Community
in Toronto, 1850–1895* (Montreal; Kingston, ON: McGill-Queen's University
Press, 1993), 12.

24 Akenson, *Irish in Ontario*, 41–2.

25 Tony Gray, *The Orange Order* (London: The Bodley Head, 1972), 265; William J. Houston and Cecil J. Smyth, *The Sash Canada Wore: A Historical Geography of the Orange Order in Canada* (Toronto: University of Toronto Press,
1980), 6, 35; and J.M. Bumstead, 'Consolidation of British North America,
1783–1860,' in *Canada and the British Empire* (see note 22), 48–9, 52. For the
ongoing impact of Orangeism as an outlet for Canadian masculinity, see
David Wilson's introduction to *The Orange Order in Canada*, ed. David Wilson (Dublin: Four Courts Press, 2007), 19.

26 McNairn, *Capacity to Judge*, 67.

27 Akenson, *Irish in Ontario*, 169–71, 172–92, 193.

28 One (Green) Irish paper at least questioned the 'respectability' of any
Orangeman's holding office: 'It has been rumoured that Mr. Gowan, ex-
Orange Grand Master, has been offered a seat in the Cabinet,' the *By-Town
Packet* remarked after a murder-stabbing brought on by Orange Activity
in 1847. 'Sincerely we hope the country may be spared such an infliction,

such a disgrace'; see 'Fruits of Orangeism,' *By-Town Packet* [later the *Ottawa Citizen*], 17 April 1847.

29 Alan Taylor, 'The Late Loyalists: Northern Reflections of the Early American Republic,' *Journal of the Early Republic* 27 (2007): 1–34; [John George Lambton, 1st Earl of Durham], *Lord Durham's Report on the Affairs in British North America*, 3 vols., ed. Sir Charles Lucas (Oxford: Clarendon Press, 1912; reprint, New York: Augustus M. Kelley, 1970). Taylor and others note that Canadian revisionist historians overemphasize the republican nature of these 'Late Loyalist' settlers from the United States (32–3).

30 Kevin Haddick-Flynn, *Orangeism: The Making of a Tradition* (Dublin: Wolfhound Press, 1999), 393–4.

31 Gray gives the former number, Houston and Smyth the latter. Both figures could be wildly exaggerated because they appear to be taken from statistics reported by the Loyal Orange Association itself. See Houston and Smyth, *Sash Canada Wore*, 37, 84; Houston and Smyth, 'Transferred Loyalties,' 194; and Gray, *Orange Order*, 263.

32 Houston and Smyth, *Sash Canada Wore*, 3, 18–19; in Canada, a greater portion of the Loyal Orange Association's members was Anglican or Methodist than Presbyterian (95).

33 Loyal Orange Association of British North America, *Laws, Rules and Regulations for the Government of the Orange Association of British North America; Revised, Amended, and Enlarged, at a Meeting of the Grand Lodge, Held in the City of Hamilton, on Tuesday, 18th Day of June, 1850. The Right Worshipful The Grand Master in the Chair* (Belleville, ON: Intelligencer Office, 1850), 46.

34 In no way do I mean to present Roman Catholics, the Catholic Church in Canada, or the Catholic Church in Rome as innocent or passive victims of Protestant bigotry. It could be quite logical in nineteenth-century terms to suspect the Catholic Church's influence in the governments of North America, especially in the face of international events. In Upper Canada, which shared a government with Catholic Quebec from the 1840 Act of Union until the creation of the Dominion in 1867, religion was a real and complicating force in politics. This is best illustrated in the separate school debates, when the Orange Order, which as a conservative organization that preferred denominational schools to new, publicly funded nondenominational institutions, at times actually supported Catholics in their successful bid for separate schools in Upper Canada. The complicated nature of politics in cases like this has led some historians to argue that Orangeism was not primarily concerned with religion in Canada. On this point, see Mills, *Loyalty in Upper Canada*, 79–82, 85–9, 106; and Houston and Smyth, *Sash Canada Wore*, 146–7. On the schools issue, see Franklin Walker, *Catholic*

Education and Politics in Upper Canada, vol. 1, *A Study of the Documentation Relative to the Origin of Catholic Elementary Schools in the Ontario School System* (Toronto: English Catholic Educational Association of Ontario, 1955).

35 *Supplement to 'The Church.' A Charge Delivered to the Clergy of the Dioceses of Toronto at the Visitation in May, by John, Lord Bishop of Toronto, with Appendix* (Toronto: Diocesan Press, 1851), in 'Pamphlets, 1840–1869,' Gowan-Ferguson Family Fonds (vol. 3, folder 7), Library and Archives Canada, 6.

36 Loyal Orange Association of British North America, *Laws, Rules, and Regulations, for the Government of the Orange Association of British North America. Adopted by the first meeting of the Grand Lodge of B.N.A., held in the Court House of Brockville, C.W., on the 1st day of Jan'y, 1830; and further revised, enlarged, and confirmed, at a meeting of the Grand Lodge held in the City of Toronto, on the 9th of June, 1840; and now also still further revised, and amended, and enlarged, at a meeting of the Grand Lodge, held in Belleville, C.W., on Tuesday, the 9th day of June, 1846, and by adjournment on Wednesday, the 10th. The Right Worshipful Grand Master in the Chair, Adopted by the Grand Lodge of New Brunswick and Nova Scotia, and Re-Printed by their Order* (St John, NB: Chronicle Office, 1848), 4.

37 In the United States, contemporary Catholics and early Catholic historians, who tended to be parochial in their outlook, understood that anti-Catholicism was next to universal. By understandably defining this very real cultural leaning as a prejudice, they denied the reality of Catholic aggression, and even Catholic agency. Thus, Catholics became helpless victims, and anti-Catholics intolerant aggressors. The historian who took the subject of anti-Catholicism mainstream in US history brought with him some of these early assumptions. In Ray Allen Billington's work, the 'Protestant Crusaders,' as he terms the anti-Catholics, were central actors in nineteenth-century US history. As a secular social historian, however, Billington, like the parochial Catholic historians before him, has little patience for the other aspects of his subjects' worldview, making no distinction between extremists and mainstream Protestant thinkers – a lack of subtlety that makes it easier to dismiss all of them. Critics like Richard Hofstadter take Billington's stance even farther, and through one unfortunately named book relegate anti-Catholicism in the United States to the paranoid fringe of history. See Ray Allen Billington, *The Protestant Crusade, 1800–1860: A Study in the Origins of American Nativism*, 2nd ed. (New York: Rinehart and Company, 1952); and Richard Hofstadter, *The Paranoid Style in American Politics and Other Essays* (New York: Vintage Books, 1965). More recent scholarship has corrected this view to some extent, but the sentiment remains.

38 Berger, *Sense of Power*, 155–65. Houston and Smyth, *Sash Canada Wore*, 6; Hereward Senior, *Orangeism: The Canadian Phase* (Toronto: Frontenac Library, 1972), 82; Gregory S. Kealey, 'The Orange Order in Toronto: Religious Riot and the Working Class,' in *Essays in Canadian Working Class History*, ed. Gregory Kealey and Peter Warrian (Toronto: McClelland and Stewart, 1976), 13–34; and Donald Akenson, *Small Differences: Irish Catholics and Irish Protestants, 1815–1922: An International Perspective* (Montreal; Kingston, ON: McGill-Queen's University Press, 1988), 88.

39 'Canadian Affairs,' *New York Times*, 5 June 1854.

40 *Chatham Planet*, 14 July 1859.

41 William J. Novak, 'The American Law of Association: The Legal-Political Construction of Civil Society,' *Studies in American Political Development* 15 (2001): 163–88. This article demonstrates how a legal environment favourable to corporations encouraged the development of, among other organizations, voluntary and patriotic societies, many of them arranged much like the Loyal Orange Association. While Albrecht Koschnik places a number of organizations that might specifically be labelled nativist in the larger tradition of collective action in the United States, Dale T. Knobel explores several of these in a single city, and Steven C. Bullock addresses the Masons and how they integrated themselves into the power structure of the early republic. See Albrecht Kosch, *'Let a Common Interest Bind Us Together': Associations, Partisanship, and Culture in Philadelphia, 1775–1840* (Charlottesville: University of Virginia Press, 2007); Dale T. Knobel, *'America for the Americans': The Nativist Movement in the United States* (New York: Twayne, 1996); and Steven C. Bullock, *Revolutionary Brotherhood: Freemasonry and the Transformation of the American Social Order, 1730–1840* (Chapel Hill: University of North Carolina Press, 1996). For a description of the general Upper Canadian equivalent, especially the important role of Freemasonry, see McNairn, *Capacity to Judge*, 63–115.

43 While actual discrimination against Irish Catholics in the United States certainly existed, scholars such as Richard Jensen have pointed to how such bias has been exaggerated in American history; see ' "No Irish Need Apply": A Myth of Victimization,' *Journal of Social History* 36 (2002): 405–29. Jensen argues that the phrase 'no Irish need apply,' for example, was far more popular in England than it was in the United States and that the song of the same name originated there.

43 Donald M. MacRaild argues, 'Orangeism may be one of the persistent and continuous instances of fraternity in the British world,' and as such, should be studied further in a transnational context; see 'The Associationalism of the Orange Diaspora,' in *Orange Order in Canada* (see note 25), 25.

MacRaild cites the same points about Orange fraternalism as do scholars of such American organizations: 'Orangeism was a training ground. It provided numerous opportunities for ordinary men and women to pick up the habits of writing minutes, chairing communities and accounting for income and expenditure' (40). Paul Gilje may provide us with an older model as a lens through which to view this early Orange rioting. In the eighteenth-century model, rioting was part of a corporate structure of society: 'As long as consensus was the goal, a community might join together and riot to purge itself of deviants or to protect itself from outside intrusions.' Upper Canada before 1840 existed under such a corporate model; thus, Orange mobs might be viewed in this reactionary way. See Paul Gilje, *The Road to Mobocracy: Popular Disorder in New York City, 1763–1834* (Chapel Hill: University of North Carolina Press, 1987), vii, 3–36. Daniel A. Cohen makes a similar argument about corporate government and mobbing in 'Passing the Torch: Boston Firemen, 'Tea Party' Patriots, and the Burning of the Charlestown Convent,' *Journal of the Early Republic* 24 (2004): 536.

44 Ian Radforth, 'Orangemen and the Crown,' in *Orange Order in Canada* (see note 25), 78–9. The organization could have incorporated under the general law of incorporation, as other fraternal orders had done, but wanted special parliamentary recognition, seeing themselves as a special Loyalist organization crucial in the development of the Canadian state.

45 'The Expulsion of the Bible from English Schools,' *Protestant Review: A Literary and Religious Magazine for Christian Families* 3 (February 1870): 353–6. While this magazine was published in New Brunswick, a March 1871 issue lists an agent for the magazine in Ontario.

46 *Chatham Planet*, 17 July 1860, 2.

47 John Hilton, *An Address to the Orangemen of Canada, July 12, 1858* (Port Hope, ON: Guide JGB Office, 1859), 2–3, 9.

48 Akenson admits that Orange events did often contain an anti-Catholic overtone, but he finds little evidence to support the idea that anti-popery had any literal meaning in Upper Canadian life: 'Locally, the Orangemen went through their anti-Roman rituals with all the solemnity of a politician deprecating governmental waste, while day by day they got along peacefully with the Catholics who lived on the next farm' (*Irish in Ontario*, 280).

49 See *Riots in New Brunswick*, 12, 61, 72, 195; see also Robert McLaughlin, 'Irish Canadians and the Struggle for Irish Independence, 1920–1925: A Study of Ethnic Identity and Cultural Heritage' (PhD diss., University of Maine, 2004).

50 *Lord Durham's Report*, vol. 2, 180.

51 Lord Durham's liberal politics would have made him rather predisposed to dislike Orangeism, which was so closely aligned with ultra-Toryism at home; see Janet Ajzenstat, *The Political Thought of Lord Durham* (Montreal; Kingston, ON: McGill-Queen's University Press, 1988).

52 Erringon, 'British Migration and British America,' 157; Wilton, *Popular Politics*, 13–20, 130–6, 148–54, 182, 185, 187, 211. Orangemen were not the only Upper Canadians to make use of violence to further political ends, with or without the government's consent (106–7).

53 Careless, *Union of the Canadas*, 45.

54 As Wilton points out, the presence of political parties depends on each side's seeing the other as legitimate. In the period before 1840, each side – conservative and reform – claimed to be the only reasonable voice in the colonies. Hence, if the Orangemen were to achieve respectability, they would have to do so within the context of a genuine party system, something that did not exist until the 1840s. See Wilton, *Popular Politics*, 142–3. Ironically, given their politics, Orangemen at times supported a move towards American-style republicanism as an alternative to the developing parliamentary system in the 1850s. However, as McNairn points out, the 'republicanism' of these conservatives was 'almost exclusively institutional,' not a re-imagining of ideology; he explains, 'Although not ultimately successful, "Tory republicans" proved to be conservatives first and monarchists second; Canadians first and Britons second; and more thoughtful and discerning than they have been given credit for' (*Capacity to Judge*, 288, 292).

55 Wilson, introduction to *Orange Order in Canada* (see note 25), 15. In reaction to the passage of the law, an Orange mob burnt effigies of reform leaders. Eliza Baldwin wrote her father, Robert Baldwin, 'Mr. Hinks blazed nicely – but they could not get you to burn at all'; see Careless, *Union of the Canadas*, 82.

56 Peter Toner, 'The Fanatic Heart of the North,' in *Irish Nationalism in Canada*, ed. David A. Wilson (Montreal; Kingston, ON: McGill-Queen's University Press, 2009), 34; and *New York Times*, 23 January 1860, 1. Orangemen had two reasons to dislike McGee, the first of which was his ardent Irish nationalism. But even after McGee abandoned the Irish revolutionary cause, his work still favoured the rights of Roman Catholics in the colony, including the right to separate schools. McGee and Orangemen may have come to a permanent rapport under the umbrella of the new Liberal-Conservative Party after 1867 as they had earlier on the separate schools issue, but McGee was killed in 1868, to this day the only Canadian politician at the national level to be assassinated. While a militant Fenian was

hanged for the crime, some Irish-Catholic Canadians continued to blame a Protestant conspiracy for his death. See David A. Wilson, ' "Orange Influences of the Right Kind": Thomas D'Arcy McGee, the Orange Order, and the New Nationality,' in *Orange Order in Canada* (see note 25), 89–108.

57 Clarke, *Piety and Nationalism*, 185–6.

58 Brian Clarke gives a larger number in a more recent essay, pointing responsibility for these riots in the 1870s to a group of youthful Orangemen, the Young Britons; see 'Religious Riot as Pastime: Orange Young Britons, Parades and Public Life in Victorian Toronto,' in *Orange Order in Canada* (see note 25), 109–27.

59 Clarke, *Piety and Nationalism*, 208.

60 Wilson, introduction to *Irish Nationalism in Canada* (see note 56), 7; and Errington, 'British Migration and British America,' 156–7.

61 Akenson, *Small Differences*, 98.

62 Kealey, 'Orange Order in Toronto,' 24; and Haddick-Flynn, *Orangeism*, 394.

63 'Are Ireland's animosities to be naturalized in America?' *New York Times*, 15 July 1870, 4.

64 *Orange Lily and Protestant Vindicator*, 15 July 1850, 18; 1 August 1849, 24.

65 There are numerous examples: in 1867, an account of repeated attacks on church services during a mission week in Portadown that injured constables, smashed windows, and stoned a priest; the next month, a report on an Orange rally to support the Church of Ireland; in January 1868, an article denouncing the judicial system that allowed Orangemen to be above the law in Ulster; in May, a reprimand of an Orange threat of repeal if disestablishment should pass; in August, three columns on Orange riots in Dublin; in 1869, the story of Orange jury-packing to prevent the prosecution of Orangemen in riots in County Monaghan; that August, the killing of a Presbyterian minister who had sheltered earlier Orange victims; and most summers, news of Orange riots in Manchester, Bainbridge, Blackburn, Portadown, Londonderry, Hiltore, and always Belfast. On one occasion, Orangemen were reported to have burnt down seventeen homes. See *Irish Citizen*, 26 October 1867, 6; 8 November 1867, 2; 16 November 1867, 2; 4 January 1868, 3; 9 May 1868, 2; 8 May 1869, 234; 8 August 1868, 2; 21 August 1869, 354; 27 June 1868, 3; 24 July 1869, 327; 7 August 1869, 338; 19 September 1869, 2–3; 24 July 1869, 322; 4 July 1868, 2; 22 May 1869, 252; 26 June 1869, 291; 14 August 1869, 346. Representative reports in the *Irish American* can be found in 'Our Irish Letters,' *Irish American*, 15 August 1868, 1.

66 Robert McLaughlin argues that Irish-Canadians 'most definitely' maintained an interest in their homeland well into the period of the Irish Civil

War; see 'Irish Nationalism and Orange Unionism in Canada: A Reappraisal,' *Eire-Ireland* 41 (2006): 80–109, esp. 84–5.

67 Paz, *Popular Anti-Catholicism*; Norman, *Anti-Catholicism in Victorian England*; Arnstein, *Protestant versus Catholic*; Klaus, *Pope, the Protestants, and the Irish*; Wolffe, *Protestant Crusade*; Higham, *Strangers in the Land*; and Billington, *Protestant Crusade*.

68 This contradiction led to a temporary political split within the Orange lodges on the schools issue; see Careless, *Union of the Canadas*, 188.

69 Clark, *Language of Liberty*, 239; and Colley, *Britons*, 19.

70 Nassau C. Gowan, 'Orangism' (pamphlet, probably read aloud, written after June 1858 and before 1867), in 'Speeches and Addresses: n.d.,' Gowan-Ferguson Family Fonds (vol. 2, folder 1), Library and Archives Canada, 1. Here he stressed the minority status of Orangemen, referring to the Roman Church as 'Goliah' [*sic*] and the Orange Order as 'the little David.' Some sources repeated decades-old accusations that the Orangemen were especially disloyal towards Victoria, implicating them in a plot that had been meant to keep the royal line of succession away from the young princess; see 'Orange disloyalty: Attempt to assassinate a Viceroy and to discrown the Queen,' *Irish Canadian*, 12 August 1848, 3. After Victoria, the heir to the throne was Ernest Augustus, duke of Cumberland and later king of Hanover, who was Grand Master of the Orange lodges in Ireland and had actively opposed Catholic emancipation. At the time of Victoria's accession, rumours about such a plot plagued the duke and Orangemen of the kingdom.

71 'Come to Our Standard,' in McBride, *Canadian Orange Minstrel for 1860*, 4.

72 'On the Murder of James Campbell by the Oneida Papists, July 12, 1851,' in McBride, *Canadian Orange Minstrel for 1860*, 18. The version of the song from the following decade has the murder (and the song title) occurring in 1850.

73 'On Our Old English Bible being Suppressed in Schools,' in Robert McBride, *The Canadian Orange Minstrel for 1870* (Toronto: n.p., 1870), 16–18.

74 Garibaldi, 'On the Downfall of Rome,' in McBride, *Canadian Orange Minstrel for 1870*, 13. As the last stanza begins, 'Watch her well Canadians, then, Partake not of her sins,' I imagine that this 'Garibaldi' was a Canadian.

75 Loyal Orange Association of British North America, *Proceedings of the Grand Lodge of British North America* (Toronto: Rogers and Thompson, 1840), 13.

76 'Imprisonment for Debt Illustrated,' in McBride, *Canadian Orange Minstrel for 1860*, 4–5.

77 V[incent] P[hilip] Mayerhoffer, *Twelve Years a Roman Catholic Priest, Or, The Autobiography of the Rev. V.P. Mayerhoffer, M.A. Late Military Chaplain to the Austrian Army, and Grand Chaplain of the Orders of Freemasons and Orangemen, In Canada, B.N.A. Containing an Account of His Career as Military Chaplain, Monk of the Order of St. Francis, and Clergyman of the Church of England in Vaughan, Markham and Whitby, C.W.* (Toronto: Rowsell & Ellis, 1861), esp. 96.

78 Ogle Robert Gowan, *Orangeism: Its Origin and History* (Toronto: Lovell and Gibson, 1859), 5–7.

79 Ibid., 10–35, *passim.*

80 The details of this two-month-long trip can be found in Ian Radforth, *Royal Spectacle: The 1860 Visit of the Prince of Wales to Canada and the United States* (Toronto: University of Toronto Press, 2004).

81 Phillip Buckner, 'The Creation of the Dominion of Canada, 1860–1901,' in *Canada and the British Empire* (see note 22), 67.

82 'The Prince's progress,' *Chatham Planet*, 4 September 1860, 2.

83 'The Prince of Wales,' *Chatham Planet*, 5 September 1860, 4.

84 'Foreign News,' *Harper's Weekly*, 15 September 1860, 583.

85 Senior, *Orangeism*, 57.

86 'The excitement in Canada,' *New York Times*, 6 September 1860, 8.

87 'The royal party refuse to land at Belleville, and proceed to Coburg,' *New York Times*, 7 September 1860, 1.

88 'The Canadian Excitement,' *New York Times*, 8 September 1860, 1.

89 Senior, *Orangeism*, 59.

90 *Chatham Planet*, 6 September 1860, 2.

91 Ibid.

92 'The Duke and the Orangemen,' *New York Times* 7 September 1860, 1.

93 'The Prince's Troubles in Upper Canada,' *Harper's Weekly*, 15 September 1860, 578.

94 'The Duke and the Orangemen,' *New York Times*, 7 September 1860, 1; 'Where are the Prince's advisers?' *Chatham Planet*, 13 September 1860, 2.

95 'The Prince's progress,' *Chatham Planet*, 8 September 1860, 2.

96 'The Prince of Wales Travels under the Duke of Newcastle's Puseyite Cloud,' in McBride, *Canadian Orange Minstrel for 1870*, 11–13.

97 Brutus [Samuel F.B. Morse], *Foreign Conspiracy Against the Liberties of the United States* (New York: Leavitt, Lord, 1835; reprint, New York: Arno Press, 1977), 19.

98 Samuel F.B. Morse, *Samuel F.B. Morse: His Letters and Journals*, vol. 1, ed. Edward Lind Morse (New York: Da Capo Press, 1973), 428.

99 Many published histories from mid-century argued over the reasons for and the outcome of Protestant rule in Maryland and the origin of 'religious

toleration' in that colony. See, for example, George Lynn-Lachlan Davis, *The Day-Star of American Freedom: or, The Birth and Early Growth of Toleration in the Province of Maryland* (New York: Scribner, 1855); Richard H[enry] Clarke, *Mr. Gladstone and Maryland Toleration* (New York: Catholic Publication Society, 1875); J[ohn] P[endleton] Kennedy, *Reply of J.P. Kennedy to the Review of his Discourse on the Life and Character of Calvert: Published in the United States Catholic Magazine, April, 1846* (Baltimore: J. Murphy, 1846); John McCaffrey, *Church and State: A Lecture Delivered before the Catholic Institute of Baltimore* (Baltimore: Hedian & O'Brien, 1854); E[dward] D[uffield] N[eill], *Maryland Not a Roman Catholic Colony: Stated in Three Letters* (Minneapolis: Johnson & Smith, 1875); and Josiah F. Polk, *The Claim of the Church of Rome to the Exercise of Religious Toleration During the Proprietary Government of Maryland, Examined* (Washington, DC: J.N. Davis, 1846).

100 For an example, see Matthew Meek [attributed to Richard Ramsey], *The Tale of the Butter Horn*, 2nd American ed. (Rochester, NY: Printed for the Purchaser, 1836).

101 George Bancroft, *History of the United States of America, From the Discovery of the Continent*, the Author's Last Revision, vol. 1 (New York: D. Appleton, 1859, 1924), 604; italics added.

102 For other, more nativistic examples of this type of progressive thought regarding history, see James Rowland, *The Glorious Mission of the American People: A Thanksgiving Discourse by James Rowland, Pastor of the First Presbyterian Church, Circleville, Ohio. Nov., 28, 1850* (Circleville, OH: Published by Request, 1850); Frederick Saunders, *A Voice to America; or, the Model Republic, its Glory, or its Fall: With a Review of the Republics of South America, Mexico, and of the Old World; Applied to the Present Crisis in the United States*, 2nd ed. (New York: Edward Walker, 1855); and *The Dawn of Modern Civilization: or, Sketches of the Social Condition of Europe, From the Twelfth to the Sixteenth Century*, revised by D[aniel] P[arish] Kidder (New York: Lane & Tippett, 1847).

103 A[ndrew] A[dgate] Lipscomb, *Our Country: Its Danger and Duty* (New York: American Protestant Society, 1844), 37. There were at least two separate American Protestant Associations founded in the 1840s alone, and their histories are difficult to untangle.

104 An American [Samuel F.B. Morse], *Imminent Dangers to the Free Institutions of the United States Through Foreign Immigration, and the Present State of the Naturalization Laws. A Series of Letters Originally Published in the New-York Journal of Commerce* (New York: E.B. Clayton, 1835; reprint, New York: Arno Press, 1869), 8.

105 Morse, *Foreign Conspiracy*, 33–5.

106 Ibid.
107 Lipscomb, *Our Country*, 39.
108 Morse, *Foreign Conspiracy*, 129.
109 J[oseph] T[inker] Buckingham, *Golden Sentiments: Being An Address to the Native Americans of The Old Bay State and Especially The Citizens of Boston. Together With Their Declaration of Sentiments* (Boston: H.B. Skinner, 1844), 4.
110 Morse, *Foreign Conspiracy*, 58.
111 For examples, see W.P. Strickland, *The History of the American Bible Society From Its Organization to the Present Time* (New York: Harper and Brothers, 1849), xxix; George W. Burnap, 'The Errors and Superstitions of the Church of Rome [Being the Dudleian Lecture Delivered in the Chapel of Harvard College, on Wednesday May 11, 1853],' *Christian Examiner and Religious Miscellany* 55 (July 1853): 62; and 'Popery and the Signs of the Times,' *Presbyterian Magazine* 3 (June 1853): 297.
112 *Brooklyn Daily Eagle*, 26 March 1867, 2.
113 See Clarke, *Piety and Nationalism*, 208.
114 'The Belfast riots,' *Brooklyn Daily Eagle*, 23 August 1872, 4.
115 'Our London correspondence,' *New York Times*, 24 August 1864, 1.
116 'Foreign News,' *Harper's Weekly*, 17 September 1864, 595.
117 'The religious riot in Londonderry,' *New York Times*, 30 April 1869, 4.
118 Houston and Smyth, 'Transferred Loyalties,' 204.
119 For more on these riots, see Michael A. Gordon, *The Orange Riots: Irish Political Violence in New York City, 1870 and 1871* (Ithaca, NY: Cornell University Press, 1993).
120 Houston and Smyth, 'Transferred Loyalties,' 194.
121 Haddick-Flynn, *Orangeism*, 396.
122 Gordon, *Orange Riots*, 22; and Dale B. Light, *Rome and the New Republic: Conflict and Community in Philadelphia Catholicism between the Revolution and the Civil War* (Notre Dame, IN: University of Notre Dame, 1996), 298.
123 'What Orangeism means,' *New York Times*, 11 July 1871, 1.
124 'The riot in New York yesterday,' *Brooklyn Daily Eagle*, 14 July 1870, 4.
125 'The riot,' *New York Daily Tribune*, 14 July 1870, 4. Many newspapers pointed to the celebration of Saint Patrick's Day as a similar type of unnecessary sectional statement, and argued that the celebration of both July 12 and March 17 should be abandoned at taking citizenship. See, for example, *New York Daily Tribune*, 15 July 1870, 4; 'Are Ireland's animosities to be naturalized in America?' *New York Times*, 15 July 1870, 4; and 'The law and public processions,' *Brooklyn Daily Eagle*, 6 August 1870, 2.
126 For instance, see the use of the word in Sister M. Evangeline Thomas, 'Nativism in the Old Northwest, 1850–1860' (PhD diss., Catholic

University, 1936), 45. Robert Francis Hueston says that the Catholic press constantly saw 'Orangemen' at work, for example during the nativist Philadelphia riots of 1844; see *The Catholic Press and Nativism, 1840–1860* (New York: Arno Press 1976), 85.

127 'The Twelfth of July: What it means in America,' *Irish American*, 23 July 1870, 4.

128 Senior, *Orangeism*, 67–8; Senior argues this is one reason Fenianism remained unpopular in Canada.

129 'The Twelfth of July,' *Irish American*, 23 July 1870, 4.

130 *By-Laws of Worcester L.O.I., No. 255, Approved by the Supreme Grand Officers, July 19, 1894* (Worcester, MA: Cummings and McKenzie, 1896), 4–5. Orangemen were marching in the United States by the 1820s – though extant early official by-laws are less common. In the United States, '[t]he Orangemen set aside their monarchist baggage, transformed their King Billy from his parochial identity as savior of Protestant and British Ireland to his larger role of deliverer of the Protestant faith' (Houston and Smyth, 'Transferred Loyalties,' 207). In addition, their major political issue – the defence of American public schools – mirrored that of other American nativist organizations; see *By-Laws of Worcester L.O.I., No. 255,* 4.

131 Berger, *Sense of Power*, 134–47.

9

'Papineau-O'Connell instruments': Irish Loyalism and the Transnational Dimensions of the 1837 Rebellions in Upper and Lower Canada

In January 1838, the *Sligo Journal* described locally discovered pike heads linked to the Ribbonmen, a Catholic secret society, as 'Papineau-O'Connell instruments.'[1] This deliberate conflation of the leader of Irish nationalism with the French-Canadian *patriote*, Louis-Joseph Papineau, directed attention to the rebellions in Canada, which, though thousands of miles away, resonated across the Atlantic. Most studies dealing with transatlantic comparisons focus on the east-to-west connection, but in this chapter I take the opposite orientation: a transnational approach that analyses the flow of information from the New World back to the Old. Recent work has examined the Irish end of this west-to-east flow with respect to parallels between French Canadians and Irish Catholics, but the same has not been attempted with the primary focus on loyalism.[2]

Accordingly, I address this historiographical gap by dealing with the transmission, manipulation, and reception of news from Canada in specific examples from the provincial Irish loyalist newspaper press in Ulster and Connacht. I argue that, while the reception of this information was facilitated by links fostered by westward emigration and the transmission of Orangeism, its editorial manipulation was conditioned by Irish circumstances. The press drew parallels between the Canadian revolts and Daniel O'Connell's campaign to repeal the 1801 Act of Union, which closed the Dublin parliament and concentrated Irish representation at Westminster. Additionally, while these comparisons were made at a macro level in both in Ulster and Connacht, Canadian news was further finessed to suit specific local situations loyalists faced in both provinces. There were marked differences, however, between the positions of Protestants in the western province and those in Ulster.

In Ulster there was heavy Protestant settlement, but their political outlook was divided between conservatism, on the one hand, and liberalism or radicalism, on the other. There were also denominational divisions, mainly between Anglican and Presbyterian. Connacht's Protestants were predominantly Anglican, but thin on the ground and massively outnumbered by Catholics.

Before I analyse the loyalist newspaper press, however, it is necessary to outline the Canadian and Irish contexts and to situate this study in the historiographies of both countries.

– I –

The origins of the Canadian problems went back to the British conquest of New France during the Seven Years' War, but the immediate backdrop to the rebellions was escalating political tension in the 1820s and 1830s.[3] Pitt's Constitution Act of 1791, influenced by concerns over the French Revolution, created the provinces of Lower Canada and Upper Canada, the latter as a refuge for United Empire Loyalists who fled the American Revolution and wanted separation from Quebec.[4] The bulk of Lower Canada's populace was francophone, Catholic, and relatively poor; most *habitants* were, like the Irish peasantry, near-subsistence farmers. There were also a few *seigneurs*, like Papineau himself: landowners with rights based on the old French tenurial system, a variant of feudalism. Another minority was an English-speaking mercantile group, whose small numbers belied their political dominance, and who were instinctively loyal to Britain and commercial in their outlook.

These profound political and cultural differences were given institutional structure by Lower Canada's governmental system of elected assemblies but with executive and legislative councils appointed by the governor. The anglophone minority and a few token *seigneurs* comprised the 'Château Clique,' which dominated the councils but was opposed by the *patriotes* in the Assembly. The Clique defended *canadien* customs and agitated over grievances such as the use of parliamentary privilege, control over taxation, and the partial exercise of patronage.[5] Though Lower Canada's population was four-fifths French Canadian by the 1830s, anglophones held most public offices.[6] The *patriotes* wanted to replace the non-elected parts of the system with an American-style senate that controlled revenue and thus curtailed the governor's power. These demands, like Catholic emancipation in Ireland, had little practical relevance for the *habitants*, who had their own grievances as their precarious economic position was worsened by successive bad harvests. In 1837 Lord John Russell's Whig government rejected *patriote* demands and removed Papineau's threat to withhold revenue by authorising the governor to dispose of funds without legislative approval.[7]

Upper Canada's first governor, John Graves Simcoe, predicted that the province would reflect its Loyalist origins and become a bastion of British imperial power. Each June George III's birthday was celebrated as enthusiastically as in Ireland or elsewhere in the Empire. Yet, despite Simcoe's vision of a governmental system mirroring the liberty of the British constitution, the province, like Lower Canada, was tightly controlled by an elected Assembly and an appointed Legislative Council.[8] The Assembly's decisions could be overruled by the Council, the lieutenant-governor and, ultimately, the British government.[9] The original Upper Canadian leadership was drawn from Loyalist refugees. Although there were not parties in the Assembly so much as loose affiliations of like-minded people, adjustment to colonial realities saw an opposition emerge to challenge the governing elite. Between 1805 and 1807, William Weekes and Robert Thorpe championed 'the people' against governmental 'tyranny.'[10] As well, geographical contiguity with the New England states and New York meant official nervousness about the new republic.[11]

Fears of American encroachment were given tangible form in 1812 when war broke out between Britain and the United States. An American invasion of Upper Canada was repulsed by British regulars and Canadian militia, though Tories claimed the victory had been due primarily to its Loyalist inhabitants.[12] The conflict reflected the complexities of British North America, as many Canadian Loyalists felt they were fighting against the tyranny of France and her republican allies who exercised despotism over Federalists in the United States.[13] The war helped stimulate a distinctive 'colonial consciousness,' but also brought forward a new generation of leaders who had proved their loyalty in the conflict. They were not necessarily of elite or of Loyalist ancestry; indeed, the father of the archetypal authoritarian Tory, the Reverend John Strachan, had been an overseer in a Scottish granite quarry.[14] However, the key characteristic of this group, which by the 1820s formed the core of the 'Family Compact,' was its support for the colonial administration.[15]

American immigrants were a growing element as the population rose from twenty thousand in the 1790s to around one hundred thousand in 1820.[16] Unlike its American counterpart, however, the Upper Canadian economy languished, leading to criticism of the status quo over economic and political issues that later formed the basis of the demand for responsible government. Economic stagnation allowed the Reformer Robert Gourlay to argue that such immigrants were an asset and could be naturalized. Though many American immigrants had fought for Canada in the War of 1812, Tories still doubted their loyalty, and Strachan favoured British settlement.[17] In this fractured polity, the highly divisive 'alien' question coalesced with other reform grievances in the 1820s.[18] These included religion. Since many immigrants were Dissenters, issues such as education and the 'clergy reserves' (land reserved for the Anglican Church) were controversial, and Strachan, wanting to protect the church's privileged position, pushed for an Anglican university.[19] Like the *patriotes* in Lower Canada, the Reformers dominated Upper Canada's Assembly. Their leader, the Scottish-born journalist William Lyon Mackenzie, headed extensive petitioning campaigns complaining to London that the colonial government was ignoring public opinion about the Council's veto over the Assembly. The Tory reaction saw Mackenzie expelled from the Assembly and then re-elected, a process repeated several times, and a parallel and sometimes threatening mobilization of Loyalist public opinion in 1832.[20]

In response, the Reformers established political unions on the British model to convert popular support into electoral organization. Though they achieved an Assembly majority in 1834, events turned against them. A key Reformer, the Methodist Egerton Ryerson, defected to the Tories, and Mackenzie himself inadvisably published a letter from his ally, the British radical Joseph Hume, suggesting that Canadians seek independence and end Britain's 'baleful domination.' The replacement at the Colonial Office of the sympathetic Lord Goderich by Edward Stanley removed a gateway to influence with the British government. Sir Francis Bond Head's appointment as lieutenant-governor in late 1835 briefly raised Reformers' hopes because he had pledged non-interference in local affairs. In fact, he demolished their cause in the 1836 'loyalty' election, helped by electoral intimation and the brokering of an unlikely anti-Reform coalition of Orangemen, Catholics, and Ryerson's Methodists. Moderate Reformers attempted to revive political unions, but Mackenzie issued a 'Declaration' echoing the American Declaration of Independence and sought a delegate convention from both Canadas before he decided to revolt.[21]

These crises resonated across the Atlantic and interacted with political developments in Britain and Ireland that, in turn, influenced Canadian policy. The initial response of the Whig government of Lord Grey to Irish agrarian violence and riots between Catholic Ribbonmen and Orangemen was coercion, but the cabinet was divided and Grey resigned in July 1834, to be replaced by Melbourne. In November a Conservative administration under Sir Robert Peel came to power. In March 1835 the Whigs, now in opposition, entered the 'Lichfield House Compact' with O'Connell and the Radicals, who agreed to topple Peel and support a minority Whig government in return for favours. For O'Connell this meant dropping agitation for repeal of the Irish Act of Union in return for a conciliatory policy to reform abuses by the Protestant Ascendancy. British politics now entered a confusing phase. Peel, while in power, had adopted a policy of 'liberal Toryism'; in opposition, however, he frequently voted with the government. His motives were to keep the Whigs from falling under the influence of radicals and also to strike against ultra-Tories in his own party. These were extremists who, with Irish Orange support, had resisted Catholic emancipation to the last and now utterly opposed any change in the church-state relationship or any dilution of the 'Protestant Ascendancy.' The 1837 general election saw the Whigs remain in power, but heavily reliant on O'Connellite MPs.[22]

Irish Protestants saw O'Connell's repeal plans as a smokescreen for Catholic Ascendancy. Orangemen, claiming ideological ancestry from the eighteenth-century 'True Whigs,' were disgusted with 'modern Whigs . . . determined to conciliate the Molock of Popery.' Whig measures, such as the 1835 parliamentary enquiry that resulted in the Orange Order's temporary dissolution, were seen as arbitrary infringements of the libertarian principles of the Glorious Revolution of 1688. The Whigs' Irish viceroy, Mulgrave, whom O'Connell called 'the best Englishman ever to come to Ireland,' was dubbed 'O'Mulgrave,' an O'Connellite sycophant wilfully blind to Ribbon violence.[23] With such a shaky majority, Canadian agitation was the last thing the Whigs needed. Melbourne's return to power was followed in June 1835 by the appointment of an Irish peer, Lord Gosford, as lieutenant-governor of Lower Canada, whose brief was to extend Britain's Irish policy and conciliate where possible. Though Gosford had fought on the Loyalist side in 1798, he was a 'liberal Protestant' who had lambasted Orange rioters in Ulster and voted for Catholic emancipation.[24] O'Connell welcomed Gosford's appointment, and sent him an analysis of the Canadian situation, but events were moving beyond politics.

The Lower Canadian *patriotes* dropped constitutional agitation, held protest meetings, and established the paramilitary 'Sons of Liberty.' Arrest warrants were issued for Papineau and his followers. Despite his revolutionary rhetoric, however, Papineau held back from personal involvement in armed insurrection, hoping to exploit the crisis to force the government to concede virtual independence. The social radical Wolfred Nelson – who, unlike Papineau, sought abolition of seigneurial rights – led several thousand badly armed insurgents. After an initial victory at St-Denis, they were routed in November and December 1837 at St-Charles and St-Eustache, with the loss of around two hundred and fifty lives.[25] Nelson and many insurgents were arrested, while others escaped to the United States and planned a second rebellion, which, failing to attract substantive American support, was crushed in late 1838.[26]

The Upper Canadian rising was also badly organized. With the government's concentration on Lower Canada, Mackenzie planned to march on Toronto to effect a *coup d'état*, but the affair ended in confusion. An initial advance saw the rebels panic on meeting a Loyalist picket, and many simply went home. Outnumbered and against the advice of his militarily experienced supporter, Anthony Van Egmond, Mackenzie then attacked government communication links. This effort was also defeated, but false rumours of Mackenzie's success in Toronto triggered rebel mobilizations in the western region under Charles Duncome; these were also dispersed by Loyalists.[27] Mackenzie fled to Buffalo, where he found American sympathy but little armed commitment, and a series of border raids during the following year were also repulsed. The casualties were minimal compared with those in Lower Canada, but, in a province with strong memories of 1812, there were many arrests, fifty-six treason trials, and two executions.[28]

– II –

Canadian historians have tended to treat these two rebellions and their precipitating crises separately. For anglophone historians, the Upper Canadian revolt interrupted moderate Reformers' legitimate ambitions for responsible government, whereas their francophone counterparts saw 1837–38 as part of the struggle for French-Canadian cultural and national identity. After the 1970s, these Whiggish narratives were superseded by socio-economic studies of the rebellions, shifting the spotlight from the leaders to the actual participants.[29] Micro-histories have explored military and diplomatic aspects, while the fashionable social history of the 1980s concentrated on ordinary participants.[30] This work has broken down impressions of homogeneity. Fernand Ouellet distinguishes between conservative nationalists like Papineau and middle-class (and often anglophone) social radicals like Wolfred Nelson, and attributes the revolt's failure to a self-interested francophone middle class gulling the *habitants*, who lacked initiative due to their lack of class consciousness.[31] However, the mutually exclusive nature of studies of English and French Canada has been criticized. Magda Fahrni argues that microhistories actually perpetuate the 'lack of communication between the two historiographies.'[32] Allan Greer complains about the 'comparative isolation of Canadian historiography from larger international currents' and a 'yawning chasm' between studies of both Canadas, which, he argues, were gripped by a single 'revolutionary crisis.'[33] Above all, he contends that a full conceptual understanding requires a broad comparative framework that recognizes parallels elsewhere in the Atlantic world.

Several historians now have adopted broader approaches that include transnational studies of migration, imperial analyses, and investigations of memory and commemoration.[34] Building on the Atlantic history of J.G.A. Pocock and others, Michel Ducharme argues for an intellectual history based on the North Atlantic world. This allows him to see the 1837–38 rebellions as the 'last chapter in the Atlantic Revolutions,' with similarities between Canadian debates of the 1830s and those of the original American Patriots. For Ducharme, the oppositions were not liberalism versus conservatism but between court and country as in eighteenth-century England.[35] Philip Girard characterizes the pre-Rebellion political debates as driven by different concepts of liberty. Mackenzie and Papineau adopted a classical republican understanding of liberty, which some argue had its roots in Irish, rather than English Whig, thought, at least in Upper Canada. The government and its supporters, on the other hand, espoused a modern notion of liberty based on a mixed and balanced constitution.[36] Such transatlantic comparisons clearly have relevance, as a brief glance at the long history of interconnections between Ireland and Canada suggests.

The 1774 Quebec Act, designed to reconcile the *habitants* to British rule, included an oath of allegiance replicated in the Irish Catholic Relief Act of that year.[37] The American Patriots had strong kin links with

Ulster Presbyterians, many of whose ancestors had emigrated.[38] Indeed, mirroring the complexities of Canadian loyalty, the Irish Volunteers of 1779–82 were amateur soldiers loyal to king and country in opposing invasion from the Patriots' Catholic allies; but they themselves were 'patriots' in supporting the colonists against central autocracy, seeing parallels with Ireland, where parliamentary legislation was subject to Westminster's veto.[39] The more radical Volunteers who helped form the United Irishmen saw the American and French Revolutions as precedents. In 1812 many United Irish exiles supported the invasion of Canada, including Richard Caldwell, a rebel 'general' in 1798 who organized a large force from Orange County, New York.[40] Irish influence also came through associational transfer. Canadian Orange lodges began in 1800 and reached eighteen thousand members by the 1830s, many of them recent immigrants, including the prominent Tory Ogle Gowan, a Wexford Loyalist whose father had experienced the 1798 uprising.[41]

Loyalism was part of this interchange, and intellectual history allows historians to untangle the complex warp and weft of contemporary ideologies. This naturally leads to more sophisticated analyses of loyalism. Jerry Bannister recognizes the wider context and also emphasizes the particularly Canadian nature concerning the key issues of liberalism and loyalism in the struggle between Reformer and Conservative. He argues that Canadian loyalism has 'received considerably less scholarly attention' than liberalism, and draws a category distinction between 'Loyalists' and the ideology of 'loyalism,' which was not necessarily coeval with reaction and should be distinguished from the 'Loyalist tradition' of American refugees.[42] Ducharme contends that historical preoccupation with Loyalist migrations looks rather threadbare from the Atlantic angle.[43] As Allison O'Mahen Malcom notes, in this volume, Canadian loyalism and American republicanism had common roots in the libertarian tradition of the Glorious Revolution of 1688. The difference lay not in necessarily blind obedience to Britain, but in the limits of resistance. British historians used to see loyalism as a crude, simplistic elite-driven reaction to 1790s radicalism, but interpretations have moved significantly, and loyalism is now viewed as an empowering and integrative phenomenon with deep historical roots and ideologically broad enough to comprehend ultra-conservatism and reformism.[44] Reassessments of Irish loyalism have also moved beyond simplistic interpretations, which depicted it simply as the Orange and reactionary foil against which

Irish nationalism emerged, to emphasize that it also contained liberal and Catholics variants.[45] While several historians recognize Irish Orange links to Canada, and the British North Atlantic world context for Orangeism has been recently explored, the dynamic relationship between Canadian and Irish loyalism *in Ireland* remains to be investigated.[46]

This relationship can be explored fruitfully by examining the transmission and reception of information, particularly in newspapers. Print media, voluntary associations, and political conflict were forums for public discussion and dissemination of information to an increasingly wide audience. Though this concept of the 'public sphere' was developed originally in a European context, several Canadian historians have applied it. Jeffrey McNairn recognizes the breadth of the public sphere and the remarkable growth of newspapers in Upper Canada, and argues that the colony 'participated fully in this international process.'[47] There was certainly acute awareness of the importance of public opinion on both sides of the Atlantic. Carol Wilton argues that Mackenzie's marshalling of Upper Canadian public opinion in petitioning was heavily influenced by British petitioning for parliamentary reform. This stimulated counter-petitioning by government supporters, and before the Rebellion both sides worked within the framework of British constitutional politics.[48] Upper Canadian papers also reflected their readers' interest in American news, and indeed European news often reached Canada quicker via New York and Boston.[49]

Jason King recently has examined the Irish dimension of this public sphere in the nationalist *Nation* newspaper and the Protestant *Dublin University Magazine*, arguing that, up to the late 1840s, both periodicals 'projected their cultural and political aspirations for Ireland' onto Canada. The *Nation* identified the plight of Irish Catholics with French Canadians, whose exertions provided the model for action. The *Dublin University Magazine* opposed conciliation or erosion of Anglican privilege in Canada as the beginning of a slippery slope leading to disestablishment in Ireland. Emancipation, repeal, and the Canadian revolts were seen not as local issues but as a malign transatlantic combination, a threat exacerbated by conciliation and requiring cultural and religious proselytism in Ireland and Canada to counteract it.[50] King's refreshing approach emphasizes the symbiotic nature of Irish and Canadian events as mediated through reportage. The *Dublin University Magazine*, however, was not representative of Loyalist opinion: it had an educated readership and, as its fixation with disestablishment shows, it was Anglican in ethos. Moreover, it was metropolitan in orientation and could not provide the regional reaction to Canadian events, particularly in Ulster, where Protestants were divided politically and denominationally. The extent and scope of Canadian information in the Irish Loyalist press supports the notion of an expanding public sphere, a veritable loyal Atlantic.

– III –

Belfast had long had its eyes on North America. During the 1812 American invasion of Canada, the former United Irishman John Templeton told Belfast's Historical Society, 'If the Americans are now worsted, Liberty . . . must again retire to the wilderness.' In 1816, toasts by his fellow radicals at a Saint Patrick's Day dinner in the town's Academical Institution included, 'May the Exiles of Erin find more happiness under the Republican eagle, than they found under the Monarchical Lion.'[51] Such provocation did not go long unanswered, and those who drank the toast were forced to resign their positions. Both the toast and the Loyalist response reveal the politics of a town where the United Irishmen had originated among the Presbyterian merchant community. Belfast-published newspapers reflected these divisions and intra-Conservative tensions.

The *Ulster Times* and the *Belfast News-Letter* were both broadly Conservative and loyal, but beyond this, their politics diverged sharply. The *Ulster Times* had been started in 1836 by then-Orangeman and later Home Ruler Isaac Butt, in reaction to the *News-Letter*'s perceived failure to represent adequately the ultra-Tory view. It championed zealots like Lord Roden, who opposed 'democracy' whether in the 1832 Reform Act or in Whig administrations. The *Ulster Times* focused on law and order, accusing the Whigs of bureaucratically destroying the old system, where power resided with local Orange magistrates, and advocated armed defence of Protestantism, recalling the Loyalist yeomanry corps of 1798.[52] Though violent separatism was a thing of the past, a strong Liberal, even Radical, presence remained. Like their British counterparts, Belfast Radicals demanded democratic reform but opposed repeal, though it had sufficient support for O'Connell to visit Belfast in 1841. Liberalism was largely Presbyterian but increasingly included Catholics as the town expanded. Other Presbyterians, however, led by Henry Cooke, were Conservative and allied politically with the

Anglicans.[53] It is against this kaleidoscopic backdrop, where local and national politics intersected, that the Canadian reportage needs to be understood.

The ultra-Tory *Ulster Times* used a battery of information from British and Canadian papers primed and aimed by its editorial commentary.[54] Papineau was represented as a villain, and his links to O'Connell were frequently highlighted. In addition to negative comparisons with Ireland, however, the paper emphasized that loyalism existed in Lower Canada. In September 1837, news of a Loyalist meeting in Quebec was given an Irish gloss as it threw into stark relief 'the bare-faced disloyalty of Papineau, not less audacious . . . than that of O'Connell and his myrmidons on this side of the water.' The Loyalist meeting's law-abiding resolutions were negatively contrasted with Ireland under Whig government: 'Happy Canadians! Who have no Mulgrave to exercise a dispensing power.' An Irish immigrant's speech confirmed the 'good feeling' of Lower Canada's Irish settlers in contradistinction to the *patriotes*, who, like the French revolutionaries of 1789, wanted unbridled liberty leading to 'Lynch Law or Mob Rule.' The editor did not baulk at tokenism. A loyal French Canadian's testimony was seized on to prove that the *patriotes* were only a 'faction,' which was the designation Loyalists gave O'Connell's organizations. They imitated their Irish prototypes to 'delude the British nation by styling themselves '*the Canadian People*,' echoing O'Connell's assertion that 'Popish rebels are the Irish People and the Protestants or loyal population, Sassenachs or interlopers.'[55] In selecting evidence that contrasted respectable loyal meetings with anarchic mob rule, the *Ulster Times* presented a crude dichotomy between civility and barbarism with clear Irish resonance. Perhaps the most prominent feature of its Canadian coverage, though, was the use of the Rebellions to flay the Whigs through Lord Gosford.

On the eve of rebellion, the paper contrasted Lower Canada's ominous state, where Gosford was governor, with Upper Canada's loyalty, where Sir Frederick Bond Head claimed that Loyalist volunteers could defend the colony despite its being 'stripped of every soldier.'[56] This line of attack was mediated through editorial commentary and a deliberately selective choice of material from British, Canadian, and American newspapers. Commentary in the (London) *Times* was recycled for Ulster readers, creating the impression that the Whigs had misinterpreted the Canadian situation. Due to the ministry's 'dread of the ultra-radical faction' that voted with them, instead of rigorously enforcing the laws, they sent Gosford on a foolish conciliatory mission.

The anti-bureaucratic animus came out in the derogatory dismissal of 'Lord Gosford and his red tape men,' whose blundering concessions were stimulating war, while Bond Head maintained British supremacy. Gosford's un-British policy would prove King William IV's 'prophetic admonition' that 'Canada would be lost or given away' and England would lose its last American possession.[57] 'Instead of nipping rebellion in the bud,' the Whigs had 'bought the favour of the English radicals by affecting to conciliate Papineau, as they purchased the support of Irish agitators by . . . succumbing to O'Connell.' Papineau was 'a restless political adventurer and ci-devant lawyer,' a 'grievance monger,' and 'precisely like O'Connell.' The Canadian 'mine' was 'sprung first,' but the delight of the 'Irish conspirators' at the Rebellions was revealing. Gosford was equated with Mulgrave as Whig Irish policy spread its baneful influence across the Atlantic: 'The Canadians see this and say what is good in Dublin is good in Quebec: Lord Gosford feasts Papineau and Lord Mulgrave feasts O'Connell.'[58]

The 30 December edition contained an adroit editorial selection of Canadian material from other British sources carefully painting the picture for its readers. First came the Tory *Morning Post*'s Canadian intelligence, emphasizing the moderation of British rule from the Quebec Act of 1774 to Pitt's Canada Act of 1791. Papineau's followers simply 'hated the English' and, like Robespierre and O'Connell, he was a 'crafty and cowardly conspirator' who would 'goad his followers to . . . destruction.' Next, the editor printed appropriately filtered material supplied to the Whig *Morning Chronicle* from its Philadelphian correspondent, including a disclaimer that neither Britain nor America anticipated the unrest due to Papineau's secrecy. The revolt was 'not a war for liberty' but national hatred of the British aggravated by sectarian bigotry; it did not have American support because the *patriote* cause was not 'just and holy as the cause of the founders of this great republic.' Finally, the *Ulster Times*'s editor completed his three-card trick by disingenuously asking why readers would need any further information, 'as the case is so well stated by the correspondent of the *Morning Chronicle* that we need do no more than refer to that writer's narrative.' This, he recapitulated, showed that 'the *Canadian People* as the rebels, in imitation of a disaffected party nearer home love to style themselves' had no real grievances, and 'their disaffection is . . . national hatred inflamed by sectarian bigotry.'[59]

Subsequent issues continued to highlight accusations of sectarian motivations in ministerial prints (doubtless intended in those papers to deflect criticism of government culpability) as evidence that there existed 'unanimity' that the Lower Canadian Rebellion was 'a purely wanton outbreak of national hostility pampered into insolence by mistaken indulgence.'[60] With the new parliamentary session looming, this apparent consensus supported the ultra-Tory argument that Peel should seek a vote of censure on the government. Though news of Mackenzie's revolt had reached Ireland, the *Ulster Times* confined itself to factual information about Upper Canada. Rather than focusing on the insurrection, it highlighted Upper Canadian loyalism. A letter from Toronto stressed how many volunteers were willing to go and fight in Lower Canada and noted that six thousand stand of arms were entrusted to the city's mayor and commonalty.[61] If the Conservative party continued to support this Whig 'rope-dancing cabinet,' then it would forfeit all claims to support.[62] Papineau's revolt fitted the ultras' high political agenda on Peel's pragmatic dallying with the Whigs, while the paper's coverage of Upper Canadian loyalism chimed with the ultras' Irish policy of stimulating armed loyalism to defend the Protestant Ascendancy.

By contrast, the *Belfast News-Letter*'s Canadian reportage appeared balanced. Its readers were presented with information gleaned from Canadian, American, and British papers, but cautioned that 'the statements contained in the Canadian papers are not to be implicitly trusted, because they are all on the one side [Loyalist] and on the other hand, considerable deductions must be made from the representations of the American journalists who are, with very few exceptions, equally ardent in favour of the insurrectionists.' Editorial comment appeared tactfully judicious about the government's handling of the crisis. As the Reformers' demands would lead to *de facto* independence, the British government's refusal to give in was understandable; yet intransigence made conflict inevitable. The moderate tone continued with the statement that, 'Questions of this kind are generally of a mixed character – errors are to be found on both sides.' Limited concession might have reconciled Canadian Reformers to 'theoretic anomalies in the constitution,' yet a 'spirit of sufficient concession has scarcely been shown to them by the British Government.'[63] Culpability, however, was mainly pinned on an American government that had 'long cast an anxious eye upon Canada.' Though the Americans could not formally intervene, they would render 'secret assistance' to 'protract the civil war.' Though written in the knowledge of the *patriote* victory at St-Denis, the report in the *News-Letter* claimed that the 'insurgent faction' would be formidable in the long term only 'through the surreptitious aid of the Republicans of the United States.' Although the Rebellion's roots were ethnic, 'the descendants of the Old French Colonists having never submitted to British rule,' republicanism – that old enemy for Belfast loyalists of the 1790s – lay at its heart and had even influenced some Canadians of British origin, as reports of Upper Canada's tranquillity and loyalty had to be treated with scepticism.[64]

The apparently supportive line on the Whigs disguised the *News-Letter*'s real target of radicalism in its British and, particularly, Belfast manifestations. Its Belfast rival was the *Northern Whig*, which, notwithstanding its masthead title, was a Radical paper. The Canadian emergency had forced the government to abandon conciliation and resort to coercion. Given their conciliatory and reformist instincts, this made the Whigs vulnerable to criticism and raised tensions with their erstwhile Radical allies, which Conservatives were quick to exploit. Struggling to extricate the government from political embarrassment, the English Whig *Morning Chronicle* had played the ethnic card. Belfast's *Northern Whig* responded bitterly to the *Chronicle*'s claim that no true Briton would allow ignorant French peasants to prevail, asking, 'What was this but the old cry against ignorant Irish papists?' How could the Whigs support Irish Catholics against the Protestant Ascendancy and simultaneously endorse 'Orange domination' of *canadien* Catholics? With regard to Mackenzie, the *Northern Whig* claimed that his demand for democracy was just and his supporters were, like the American Patriots of 1776, 'goaded' into rebellion by those denying 'the liberties of the people.'[65]

The *News-Letter*'s emphasis on American aggression, therefore, needs to be seen in the context of these Whig-Radical tensions and the fact that Belfast radicalism had antecedents in United Irish republicanism. Having recast the Canadian situation as republican aggression, it widened the blame to encompass statements in the House of Commons by English Radicals who exulted in the 'prospective disgrace of British arms.'[66] In January 1838, this attack developed an economic aspect guaranteed to appeal in industrializing Belfast. The *News-Letter* published material suggesting that Papineau's economic grievances were unjustified because Lower Canadians were better off than inhabitants of the mother country, who paid heavy taxes for 'relatively worthless' Canadian timber.[67] The negative parallels with the Patriot precept of 'No taxation without representation' were thrown in the faces of Belfast's Radicals.

After the insurgents' defeat, the *News-Letter*'s treatment of Gosford continued to be balanced. His proclamation to the beaten rebels evinced a 'temperate, conciliatory, and prudential tone . . . highly honourable to his character as a statesman' and would appeal to all but the most unregenerate insurgents, proving that the government wanted to avoid unnecessary bloodshed. This shunning of the opportunity to criticize the Whigs was not, however, objective journalism. Gosford's proclamation became ammunition in ongoing inter-Conservative divisions; the editorial noted how '[m]ost of the ultra party papers, both in Canada and this country assail the document . . . as a pusillanimous effusion,' which would actually encourage the rebels. While elevating conflict over conciliation 'may be congenial to the dispositions of some ultra zealous individuals,' it had nothing of morality or humanity.[68] This also wrong-footed the *Northern Whig*, which was subsequently compelled to admit that Gosford's 'amnesty' had 'redeemed his character,' especially as it was opposed by vindictive Canadian Loyalists.[69]

Though the Conservative and Loyalist *Belfast News-Letter* took a different tack on Gosford than either the *Ulster Times* or, indeed, Canadian Loyalists, it used the revolts to grind its axe against the ultra-Tories and Belfast's Radicals. The paper ostentatiously shunned a sectarian or ethnic interpretation of the revolts in favour of a political explanation that connected radicalism, republicanism, and revolution in Ireland, Britain, and North America. This was the main contemporary Loyalist critique of Belfast's Presbyterian radicals – that they were little altered from their 1798 predecessors. Having radicalism as its main target, the *News-Letter* ignored the Papineau-O'Connell connection but repeatedly emphasized links between the *patriote* leader and British Radicals, as the seizure of Papineau's papers implicated both Hume and Roebuck in the 'Papineau and Mackenzie rebellion.'[70]

When we move from Ulster to Connacht, however, a very different inflexion of the Canadian Rebellions is evident. Connacht's leading Loyalist newspaper, the *Sligo Journal*, began in 1796 in the teeth of United Irish opposition. It circulated in the counties of Leitrim, Roscommon, and Mayo, and in parts of Donegal, as well as in Sligo itself. Though Protestants were in a minority in Sligo and the wider area, an Orange tradition went back to the 1790s. County Sligo witnessed action in 1798 at the Battle of Collooney and generated extensive anti-Catholic emancipation petitioning in 1828.[71] Yet Protestants were under pressure. In 1829, the year of emancipation, following intimidation of witnesses at the Sligo Assizes, it was noted that the anti-Catholic Brunswick Clubs were more necessary 'to protect the scattered loyalist of every creed in this rebellious, ill-regulated, ingrate land' than in England, where these clubs originated.[72] The omnipresent nightmare was the Ribbonmen, a Catholic secret society, which the *Journal* called 'midnight legislators' dedicated to 'Protestant extermination.'[73] Orangeism struggled in these conditions. On 12 July 1833, only one lodge, LOL 465, 'the Old Tirerill,' made much of a show, and the *Journal* 'regretted that the spirited example . . . is not more generally imitated in . . . Sligo.'[74] In July 1836, as associations formed in Ulster and northern England to create a 'bond of union' among all Protestant denominations, the Collooney Protestant Brotherhood was established. Its resolutions pledged members 'to collect and place before the Empire, through the instrumentality of the Conservative members of parliament, all important information concerning the outrages committed against the lives and properties of Protestants.'[75] The following month, however, 'O'Connell's puppet,' Mulgrave, visited Sligo and was welcomed by green arches emblazoned with the United Irish motto, 'Erin Go Bragh,' Liberal Clubs, trades unionists, and, worst of all, 'wavering half-Protestants and papists.' Despite this, the uptake for the new Protestant association remained poor. The *Journal* noted how this 'cement of loyal brotherhood will, in the worst emergency, prove the best safeguard against treacherous aliens or domestic foes.' 'What,' it asked, 'were the Protestants of Sligo thinking of?' They could no longer 'slumber . . . in the hope of conciliating the Catholic Association who no concession short of Ascendancy can satisfy.'[76]

The newspaper carried reports from Irish, British, and Canadian newspapers selectively reprinted with editorial gloss. Several articles comprised material from the main national Ascendancy paper, the *Dublin Evening Mail*. The *Sligo Journal* followed its line, emphasizing links between O'Connell and Papineau. When news of the Rebellions reached Ireland, it reproduced O'Connell's parliamentary speech on Russell's Resolutions, in which he had claimed that 'the issue between Canadians and the government was the same which had distracted Ireland for centuries.' It noted that the analogy was perfect except that he had an 'O' at the beginning of his name and the *patriote* leader had one (eau) at the end. The Canadian 'British party' was like 'the Orange party' in Ireland and aimed at monopoly. The same edition quoted the *Evening Packet*'s claim that a Canadian insurgent, Thomas Storrow Browne, had once edited the O'Connellite *Dublin Comet*, and that the Radicals, Hume and Roebuck, had struck a bargain with the Whigs: 'as

Ireland was surrendered to that incendiary (O'Connell), to propitiate the Popish priests, so also was Canada sacrificed to appease the Papineau Papists.'[77]

A 'Letter from Montreal' claimed a priest had administered the sacrament to rebels to make them 'stand or die.' The editor glossed this, noting, 'of course he [the priest] did, it followed a longstanding Irish pattern of Catholic rebellions and massacres of Protestants, for 'in 1641 the Pope issued a bull of indulgence for the rebels, in 1798 priests blessed the arms and banners of the insurgent forces and at the elections of Waterford and Clare the crucifix was held up in the Altar and the poll booth.' The tactical manipulation of transatlantic news for local consumption can be seen from a reprinted article from the British Tory *Morning Post* describing the difficulties of Loyalists during the Canadian revolts. The *Sligo Journal*'s editor assured readers that their fellow-Loyalists in Canada would eventually triumph, but he equated the position of isolated and outnumbered Protestants on both sides of the Atlantic and warned that 'it must end in the discomfiture of the rebels but in the meantime the troops and loyalists with the British settlers in remote disaffected districts, may suffer severely.'[78] This again evoked memories of 1798, when the United Irishmen were initially successful in Connacht.

Canadian intelligence was deliberately amalgamated with reportage of local issues, including the danger that wavering Protestants would defect. Following O'Connell's loyal overtures to Queen Victoria, who favoured the Whigs, Sligo Radicals met in December 1837 to address the new monarch.[79] The *Journal* dubbed it '[a] hole and corner meeting . . . composed of the Popish agitators and a few Protestant Radicals that have deserted their colours.' This made it 'necessary for the upright, truly loyal, determined and independent Protestants of the county to present an address to Her Majesty.' Militancy and danger, always the best cement for Protestant unity whether in 1798 or in 1837, were provided by the Canadian parallel: 'should the standard of rebellion be again unfurled, should a Papineau or an O'Connell . . . draw the sword and endeavour to dissolve the union with England and attempt to establish a Popish dominion on the ruins of our Protestant establishment, there will be found in the county of Sligo no small body of Protestant loyalty and true sterling courage to protect our institutions from the rebels.'

The *Sligo Journal* repeatedly highlighted the supposed Catholic nature of the Lower Canadian Rebellion: 'The priests in Canada have openly given the sacrament to the rebels . . . would the Romish clergy in this country be backward?' Whereas the O'Connellite *Sligo Champion* supported Mulgrave's assertion that Ireland was quiet by claiming that 'not a single outrage was recorded in the last *Sligo Journal,*' the latter print eagerly seized upon any evidence of Ribbon outrages. This was the context for branding a recently discovered 'specimen of one of those Ribbon Pikes' a 'Papineau-O'Connell instrument.' This description linked the national and international reportage of the Canadian revolts with specific local affairs and pointed readers in a familiar direction, back to 1798, when the pike was the rebels' trademark weapon.[80]

In early 1838, as news came through of insurgent defeats, subsequent issues of the *Sligo Journal* continued to translate North American affairs into a local context. Comparisons were drawn between Ireland and Canada to highlight the detrimental effects of concession and conciliation. The *Journal* amplified comments from another Orange periodical, the *Warder*, asserting that the Rebellions proved that the 1774 Quebec Act was misconceived, yet the Whigs continued mistakenly to assume that 'a Popish people can be reconciled and allegiant [*sic*] to Protestant rule.' The 'Hiberno-Canadian agitation' was like O'Connell's 'Justice for Ireland' demands of the Whigs.

These anti-Catholic hits found their mark: a reader's letter advocated repeal of the Catholic Emancipation Act, withdrawal of the grant to Maynooth College, and the banishment of Jesuits. This would make Ireland peaceful and prosperous, free of 'superstition, priestcraft, idolatry and crime.' The anti-Catholic interpretation of the Canadian situation also served electioneering purposes. A letter supporting the Conservative John Martin, defeated in the 1837 general election for Sligo Borough by a liberal, J.P. Somers, used Radical support for the Canadian insurgents to make a case to unseat Somers.[81] Sligo Conservatives had established an electoral society that was attracting support from Protestant artisans, so it seems that this kind of political manipulation was to insulate them from the '*so-called* Protestants who have joined . . . the Sligo destructives.'[82]

Thus, the Canadian Rebellions were ideal ammunition for the defence of Protestants from the perceived external Catholic threat and from internal defections. The *Sligo Journal*'s Canadian reportage played on present fears and fearful memories in the psyche of its Protestant readership. These current fears included being outnumbered. With their demographically weak position in an Ireland where numbers now mattered politically, the emigration of Protestants to Canada was another source of fear. As a key Ascendancy figure noted following emancipation, 'emigration of Protestants is of all things the most to be dreaded.'[83]

In early February 1838, the *Journal* published a letter of an emigrant, currently in New York but previously resident in Canada, to his father in Sligo town. It described the genesis of the Rebellions, highlighting the French and Catholic nature of Lower Canada, where agitators misled *habitants* in the same way Irish demagogues exploited Catholics. Most members of the Assembly could not even write their names, and Canada's deleterious state should 'deter emigrants . . . until matters are in a more settled and prosperous condition.' The letter appeared in the editorial section with prefatory remarks cautioning that 'persons intending to emigrate will act wisely by adhering to the advice which the writer so forcibly inculcates'; the point was re-emphasized in a subsequent editorial. The *Journal's* partisan and disingenuous manipulation of information showed clearly, however, in its equal willingness to capitalize on Irish immigrants. A letter to a Sligo doctor from a 'relative residing in Toronto' described the Upper Canadian Rebellion and boasted of his role in its suppression as a Loyalist volunteer. It highlighted how Toronto Loyalists were not only able to arm and defend themselves but, when Mackenzie's insurgents were at Niagara, to muster a thousand men ready to march at a moment's notice.[84]

Several points emerge from this analysis. Aside from the general Ascendancy critique of Whig government, the *Sligo Journal's* main themes – anti-Catholicism, electioneering, opposition to Protestant emigration, and law and order – had clear local contexts. The critique of the French-Canadian Catholic clergy was blunt but blinkered. The reality of priestly opposition to rebellion was ignored: 'In this conflict it is complained that the priests are in favour of the British constitution. It may be so, but it will be found it is from interested motives, as . . . should the Canadians succeed in throwing off the British yoke, they will be put upon the voluntary system.' Unashamedly playing the card of popular memory, however, the paper noted, 'their tacit conduct prior to the breaking out of the rebellion of 1798 has taught us a lesson not to place too much confidence in them, or construe their silence and inactivity with loyalty.'[85] The uncomfortable fact that Upper Canadian Orangemen had cooperated with the Roman Catholic hierarchy against the Reformers in the 1836 loyalty election was also ignored.

Thus, for Connacht Protestants, the meanings of the Canadian Rebellions were filtered through a selective and present-centred historical memory.

– IV –

In summary, there are revealing differences in the ways these provincial Loyalist papers presented information about Canada that are relevant to the debate over the public sphere and the loyal Atlantic. The *Belfast News-Letter*'s eagerness to use the American and republican aspect of the revolts as a stick to beat local Radicals underscores the strong transatlantic dimension of Canadian history. The growth in the public sphere meant extended geographical distances and a time-lag for news to travel, which could result in distortion. But the very elasticity of this loyal public sphere facilitated the reconstituting of Canadian material as propaganda for local consumption.

Popular memory played a vital role in this manipulation on both sides of the Atlantic. Alison O'Mahen Malcom (in this volume) notes how Canadian Orangemen's selectively reinterpreted memories of the Glorious Revolution focused on William III's military victory at the Boyne in 1690. Jessica Harland-Jacobs cites a ballad, 'Our sires may boast of '*Ninety-eight*; We boast of *Thirty-seven*,' to illustrate the danger from American republicans in 1837 that helped Canadian Orangemen elide memories of both rebellions to form an origin legend.[86] On the Irish side, the potency of popular memories of 1798 was a common factor to these papers, even though the interpretation the editors sought to validate by their Canadian examples was creatively tailored to local circumstances. The evocation of historical memory by current circumstance triggered an emotive reaction that made sequential time disappear – the past inhabited the present – and drew distant geographical entities together by repeated reiteration of political or religious similarities.

In Sligo, the transnational nature of loyalism allowed the memory of far-off events like 1641 and 1798 to be dynamically integrated with the Rebellions in Canada to conjure up the ghosts of massacred Protestants in the Sligo of 1837. In Ulster, the apparent re-enactment of 1798 across the Atlantic could be used to resurrect armed volunteer loyalism or to counteract Protestant divisions. The fraught political climate in Britain, Ireland, and Canada meant that the hyphens linking neologies like the *Ulster Times*'s 'Papineau-Roebuck party,' the *Belfast News-Letter*'s

'Papineau and Mackenzie rebellion,' and the *Sligo Journal*'s 'Papineau-O'Connell instruments,' were small enough to signify subtle local differences, yet wide enough to bridge the Atlantic.

NOTES

1 *Sligo Journal*, 5 January 1838.
2 Jason King, ' "Their Colonial Condition": Connections between French-Canadians and Irish Catholics in the *Nation* and the *Dublin University Magazine*,' *Eire-Ireland*, 41–2 (Spring/Summer 2007): 108–31.
3 Jerry Bannister, 'Canada as Counter-Revolution: The Loyalist Order Framework in Canadian History, 1750–1840,' in *Liberalism and Hegemony: Debating the Canadian Revolution*, ed. Jean-François Constant and Michel Ducharme (Toronto: University of Toronto Press, 2009), 100.
4 For loyalism, see Bannister, 'Canada as Counter-Revolution'; Norman Knowles, *Inventing the Loyalists: The Ontario Loyalist Tradition and the Invention of Useable Pasts* (Toronto: University of Toronto Press, 1997), chap. 1; Jane Errington, *The Lion, the Eagle, and Upper Canada* (Montreal; Kingston, ON, McGill-Queen's University Press, 1987); and David Mills, *The Idea of Loyalty in Upper Canada* (Montreal; Kingston, ON: McGill-Queen's University Press, 1988).
5 F. Murray Greenwood and Barry Wright, 'Introduction: Rebellion, Invasion, and the Crisis of the Colonial State in the Canadas, 1837–9,' in *Canadian State Trials*, vol. 2, *Rebellion and Invasion in the Canadas, 1837–39*, ed. F. Murray Greenwood and Barry Wright (Toronto: University of Toronto Press and the Osgoode Society for Canadian Legal History, 2002), 10–11.
6 Joseph Schull, *Rebellion: The Rising in French Canada, 1837* (Toronto: Macmillan, 1971), 14; Arthur M. Lower, *Colony to Nation* (Toronto: McClelland and Stewart, 1977), 221.
7 Greenwood and Wright, 'Introduction,' 12–13.
8 Errington, *Lion, the Eagle, and Upper Canada*, 13, 23.
9 Carol Wilton, *Popular Politics and Political Culture in Upper Canada, 1800–1850* (Montreal; Kingston, ON: McGill-Queen's University Press, 2000), 163.
10 Errington, *Lion, the Eagle, and Upper Canada*, 49–51.
11 Greenwood and Wright, 'Introduction,' 18.
12 Jon Latimer, *1812: War with America* (Cambridge, MA: Harvard University Press, 2007), 2–3; Knowles, *Inventing the Loyalists*, 19.
13 Errington, *Lion, the Eagle, and Upper Canada*, 83–5.

14 Alexander Neil Bethune, *Memoir of RT Reverend John Strachan, First Bishop of Toronto* (Toronto: H. Rowsell, 1870), 1.

15 Errington, *Lion, the Eagle, and Upper Canada*, 85, 92–4; Knowles, *Inventing the Loyalists*, 19.

16 Wilton, *Popular Politics and Political Culture in Upper Canada*, 9.

17 Errington, *Lion, the Eagle, and Upper Canada*, 158, 163, 167–8.

18 Greenwood and Wright, 'Introduction,' 18.

19 Wilton, *Popular Politics and Political Culture in Upper Canada*, 44–5.

20 Ibid., 56–70, 130–1, 148.

21 Ibid., 154–5, 168, 183–7; Greenwood and Wright, 'Introduction,' 19.

22 Boyd Hilton, *A Mad, Bad and Dangerous People: England, 1783–1846* (Oxford: University Press, 2006), 494–500; and Oliver MacDonagh, *O'Connell: The Life of Daniel O'Connell, 1775–1847* (London: Weidenfeld and Nicolson, 1991), 403–4.

23 Allan Blackstock, 'Orange Songs in Green Books,' in *Politics and Political Culture in Britain and Ireland, 1750–1850*, ed. Allan Blackstock and Eoin Magennis (Belfast: Ulster Historical Foundation, 2007), 72, 75.

24 T.B. Browning, 'Acheson, Archibald, second earl of Gosford (1776–1849),' rev. Phillip Buckner, in *Oxford Dictionary of National Biography*, ed. H.C.G. Matthew and Brian Harrison (Oxford: Oxford University Press, 2004), online ed., Lawerence Goldman, January 2008, http://www.oxforddnb.com/view/article/58 (accessed 10 August 2009); O'Connell to Gosford, 21 July 1835, Public Record Office of Northern Ireland, Gosford Papers, D2995/8/7.

25 Greenwood and Wright, 'Introduction,' 13–4; Allan Greer, *The Patriots and the People: The Rebellion of 1837 in Rural Lower Canada* (Toronto: University of Toronto Press, 1993), 3.

26 Greenwood and Wright, *Canadian State Trials*, 15

27 Ibid., 20–1; Colin Read, *The Rebellion of 1837 in Upper Canada* (Ottawa: Canadian Historical Association, 1988), 11–15.

28 Greenwood and Wright, 'Introduction,' 22; Read, *Rebellion of 1837*, 20–2.

29 Greenwood and Wright, 'Introduction,' 8–9, 12; Allan Greer, '1837–38: Rebellion Reconsidered,' *Canadian Historical Review* 76 (1995): 4–5.

30 Greer, 'Rebellion Reconsidered,' 2–4.

31 Fernand Ouellet, *Lower Canada, 1791–1840: Social Change and Nationalism* (Toronto: McClelland and Stewart), 326–7, 338.

32 Magda Fahrni, 'Reflections on the Place of Quebec in Historical Writing on Canada,' in *Contesting Clio's Craft: New Directions and Debates in Canadian History*, ed. Christopher Dummitt and Michael Dawson (London: Institute for the Study of the Americas Press and the Brookings Institution, 2009), 1–5.

33 Greer, *Patriots and the People*, x, xi, 5–7; 11, 16; idem, 'Rebellion Reconsidered,' 6–9.

34 Greenwood and Wright, 'Introduction,' 19. See also Nancy Christie, 'Introduction: Theorizing a Colonial Past: Canada as a Society of British Settlement,' in *Transatlantic Subjects: Ideas, Institutions, and Social Experiences in Post-Revolutionary British North America*, ed. Nancy Christie (Montreal; Kingston, ON: McGill-Queen's University Press, 2008), 11–15.

35 M. Ducharme, 'Canada in the Age of Revolutions: Rethinking Canadian Intellectual History in an Atlantic Perspective,' in *Contesting Clio's Craft* (see note 32), 162–9, 173–4, 181.

36 Philip Girard, 'Liberty, Order and Pluralism,' in *Exclusionary Empire: English Liberty Overseas, 1600–1900*, ed. Jack Greene (Cambridge: Cambridge University Press, 2010), 178, 180.

37 Thomas Bartlett, *The Fall and Rise of the Irish Nation: The Catholic Question, 1690–1830* (Dublin: Gill and Macmillan, 1992), 81–3.

38 Ian McBride, *Eighteenth-Century Ireland: The Isle of Slaves* (Dublin: Gill and Macmillan, 2009), 375.

39 Allan Blackstock, 'Loyal Clubs and Societies in Ulster, 1770–1800,' in *Clubs and Societies in Eighteenth-Century Ireland*, ed. James Kelly and Martyn Powell (Dublin: Four Courts Press, forthcoming).

40 David Wilson, *United Irishmen, United States: Immigrant Radicals in the Early Republic* (Ithaca, NY: Cornell University Press, 1998), 84.

41 Wilton, *Popular Politics and Political Culture in Upper Canada*, 75–6; Hereward Senior, *Orangeism in Britain and Ireland, 1795–1836* (Toronto: Ryerson Press, 1966), 97.

42 Bannister, 'Canada as Counter-Revolution,' 112, 126–7.

43 Ducharme, 'Canada in the Age of Revolutions,' 172–3.

44 Frank O'Gorman, 'English Loyalism Revisited,' in *Politics and Political Culture in Britain and Ireland* (see note 23), 224–5.

45 Allan Blackstock, *Loyalism in Ireland, 1789–1829* (Woodbridge, UK: Boydell & Brewer, 2007), 276–8.

46 Donald Harmon Akenson, *The Irish in Ontario: A Study in Rural History* (Montreal; Kingston, ON: McGill-Queen's University Press, 1999); Hereward Senior, *Orangeism: The Canadian Phase* (Toronto: McGraw-Hill, 1972). For recent research on Orangeism, see Jessica Harland Jacobs ' "Maintaining the Connexion": Orangeism in the British North Atlantic World, 1795–1844,' *Atlantic Studies* 5 (April 2008): 27–49.

47 Jeffrey L. McNairn, *The Capacity to Judge: Public Opinion and Deliberative Democracy in Upper Canada, 1791–1854* (Toronto: University of Toronto Press, 2000), 9–19.

48 Wilton, *Popular Politics and Political Culture in Upper Canada*, 14–16.

49 Errington, *Lion, the Eagle, and Upper Canada*, 36–7.

50 Jason King, 'Their Colonial Condition,' 108–31.

51 John Templeton's Journals, 19 January 1813, 9 May 1816, Ulster Museum.

52 John Bew, *The Glory of Being Britons: Civic Unionism in Nineteenth-Century Belfast* (Dublin: Irish Academic Press, 2009), 16, 148–52.

53 Finlay Holmes, *Henry Cooke* (Belfast: Christian Journals, 1981), 115, 148; idem, *The Presbyterianism Church in Ireland* (Dublin: Columba Press, 2000), 90–6.

54 *Ulster Times*, 7 December 1837.

55 *Ulster Times*, 12 September 1837.

56 *Ulster Times*, 30 November 1837.

57 *Ulster Times*, 26, 28 December 1837.

58 *Ulster Times*, 23, 26, 28 December 1837, 11 January 1838.

59 *Ulster Times*, 30 December 1837.

60 *Ulster Times*, 4, 6 January 1838.

61 *Ulster Times*, 19, 23 December 1837.

62 *Ulster Times*, 30 December 1837.

63 *Belfast News-Letter*, 26 December 1837.

64 Ibid.

65 *Northern Whig*, 14 October, 9, 26, 30 December 1837, 4 January 1838.

66 *Belfast News-Letter*, 29 December 1837.

67 *Belfast News-Letter*, 2 January 1838.

68 Ibid.

69 *Northern Whig*, 6 January 1838.

70 *Belfast News-Letter*, 16, 23 January 1838.

71 Grand Orange Lodge of Ireland (G.O.L.I.) Grand Lodge of Ireland Minute Book, 1798–1818, fol. 32; *The Formation of the Orange Order, 1795–1798: The Edited Papers of Colonel William Blacker and Colonel Robert H. Wallace*, ed. G.O.L.I. Education Committee (Belfast: Grand Orange Lodge of Ireland, 1994), 96–7; Blackstock, *Loyalism in Ireland*, 208, 231.

72 *Sligo Journal*, 15 May 1829.

73 *Sligo Journal*, 23 October 1829.

74 *Sligo Journal*, 18 July 1833.

75 Notice: Collooney Protestant Meeting, 29 July 1836, Public Record Office of Northern Ireland, Coopershill Papers, D4031/F/12/10.

76 *Sligo Journal*, 26 August, 22 September 1836.

77 *Sligo Journal*, 29 December 1837.

78 *Sligo Journal*, 5 January 1838. The Waterford (1826) and Clare (1828) elections saw Catholic Association candidates victorious, including O'Connell

himself in Clare, a crucial turning point in forcing the government to give
way on emancipation.

79 James H. Murphy, *Abject Loyalty: Nationalism and Monarchy in Ireland during the Reign of Queen Victoria* (Cork: Cork University Press, 2001), 26.

80 *Sligo Journal*, 5 January 1838.

81 *Sligo Journal*, 29 December 1829, 12, 19, 26 January 1838; Brian M. Walker, *Parliamentary Election Results in Ireland, 1801–1922* (Dublin: Royal Irish Academy, 1978), 66.

82 *Sligo Journal*, 5 January 1838; K. Theodore Hoppen, *Elections, Politics and Society in Ireland, 1832–1885* (Oxford: Clarendon Press, 1984), 282.

83 Barre Beresford to Sir George Hill, 17 August 1829, Public Record Office of Northern Ireland, Hill of Brook Hall Papers, D642/221B.

84 *Sligo Journal*, 2, 9 February 1838.

85 *Sligo Journal*, 5 January 1838.

86 Harland-Jacobs, 'Maintaining the Connexion,' 38–9.

Afterword: Loyalist Cosmopolitanism

ROBERT M. CALHOON

Loyalist history is a history of complementarity. Though foes of independence and champions of the imperial connection, the Loyalists as well as their Patriot counterparts were also kinsmen, fellow subjects, and common inhabitants of North American provinces; although some Loyalists prized organic conservatism, more were Whiggish Lockeans; whereas there would be Loyalist losers and Patriot winners in the American Revolution, no one knew with any certainty in 1776 who would end up with which fate; and while Loyalist refugees would populate Canada and other imperial territories, the revolutionary experience of the Loyalists preordained neither British constitutionalism nor Tory survivalism as the ideological foundation of Loyalist diaspora nation-building.

As I told the 'Loyalism and the Revolutionary Atlantic World' conference in my keynote address, historians of loyalism have, sometimes serendipitously, sometimes intentionally, paired off with scholarly predecessors or contemporaries to explore the Janus-faced empirical, interpretive, and conceptual divides of the Revolution to complicate our understanding of Patriot achievements and Loyalist intentions. While incorporating these intrepid tales into the folklore of the sub-field of Loyalist studies risks romanticizing the historiographical process, done with a light touch these antecedents and remembrances are part of the literary art embossing the harder analytical work of historical interpretation.

The earliest of four identifiable surges in Loyalist scholarship reacted forcefully to counter the oblivion into which the memory of the Loyalists in the United States seemed to be slipping by the early twentieth century. Lorenzo Sabine began ransacking Revolutionary War records for lists of Loyalists' names: muster rolls; legal arcana such as confiscation, amercement, and attainder; banishment proceedings in revolutionary courts; friendly addresses that made the departure of Crown officials from colonial America into media events. Utilizing this master list of some three thousand four hundred names, Sabine put a human face on the Loyalist tragedy.[1] His book-length introductory essay enabled Woodrow Wilson to incorporate Loyalist exiles into his popular *History of the American People*, and a century later the Sabine model made credible Clifford K. Shipton's discovery that some 15 per cent of Harvard graduates who lived through the Revolution were either Loyalists, neutralists, or very conservative Whigs who suffered for their doubts about the imperial breach.[2] The early twentieth-century professionalization of history and the training of historians in graduate schools assured that Loyalists (along with other parties and interests) would, at least, be acknowledged, categorized, and assigned significance. This social scientific approach locked in Sabine's and Shipton's prosopographical efforts to preserve the memory of loyalism in the United States.

The post-war era, from 1945 through the mid-1960s, provided early American history in general, and topics like revolutionary allegiance in particular, with a new impetus away from narrow empiricism or anecdotal trivialization. In Edmund S. Morgan's far-reaching project for historical revitalization, made famous by his essay, 'Revisions in Need of Revising,' and also in Jack P. Greene's equally influential essay announcing the 'Neo-Whig' interpretation of revolutionary history, an engaged diagnostic historiography became a defining preoccupation of early American historians.[3] Sharply challenging the Imperial and Progressive schools of interpreting the American Revolution, Neo-Whig scholarship – fashioned in large part by Morgan, Greene, Bernard Bailyn, and their graduate students – made the coming of the Revolution into a transatlantic event in which personal volition, Enlightenment ideas, and political cosmopolitanism among both rising colonial elites and ordinary folk transformed the public sphere of British American society.

Two of the most stunning moments in this new assessment of the coming of the Revolution involved Loyalist-Patriot interaction at the highest levels. In the Morgans' *The Stamp Act Crisis: Prologue to Revolution*, Massachusetts lieutenant-governor Thomas Hutchinson discerned from his own historical research that the Puritan founders had raised their own capital and their descendants had taxed and governed themselves and paid more than their share of the cost of wars against the French. Hutchinson's private letter to Massachusetts agent Richard Jackson in London enabled the pro-American Member of Parliament, Isaac Barré, to skewer Charles Townshend with the humiliating retort: 'Planted by your care? No! your oppressions planted 'em; nourished by your indulgence? They grew by your neglect of 'em! protected by your arms? They have nobly taken up arms in your defense!' Edmund Morgan then rendered this timeless verdict: 'It was his prudence, his moderation, his fundamental conservatism that made Hutchinson seem an enemy of the people in 1765,' recalling from his Cambridge Latin School education Thucydides's teaching that prudence and moderation were classical Greek synonyms for courage and coolness in battle, and the first targets for bombast and demagoguery in war.[4]

Likewise, Bernard Bailyn's groundbreaking analysis of the pamphlets of the American Revolution peeled layer after layer from more than a decade of imperial and constitutional debate until he reached the core of their meaning. He found this meaning *not* in a pamphlet by Adams or Jefferson or Paine, but in a challenge to Whig ideology penned by the high Tory theorist and polemicist Thomas Bradbury Chandler, who demanded to know 'whether some degree of respect be not always due from inferiors to superiors . . . and whether the refusal on this or any other occasion be not a violation of the general laws of society?' 'How else could it end?' Bailyn wanted to know. 'What reasonable social and political order could conceivably be built and maintained where authority was questioned before it was obeyed, where social differences were considered incidental rather than essential to community order, and where superiority, suspect in principle, was not allowed to concentrate in the hands of a few but was scattered throughout the populace? No one could clearly say.'[5] Chandler's fundamental question about obedience and subordination was not one that most Patriots had first asked themselves. To the contrary, the deepest level of revolutionary consciousness reverberated in the most reactionary, polemically shrill American Tories, men unafraid in the white hot heat of rebellion to speak of 'general laws of society,' the most advanced of Condorcet's Enlightenment categories.[6]

The Bicentennial of the Revolution opened a third window of opportunity in Loyalist history. In 1975 Mary Beth Norton and Linda K. Kerber quietly planned a unique bicentennial and gender-based project. Each would complete what coincidentally both scholars had already begun: new histories of women in the Revolution. But they would cease communicating their findings until their books were published in 1980. The result was two historians with comparable skills and ambitions producing independent assessments of the same complex historical phenomenon. Those two books – Norton's *Liberty's Daughters: The Revolutionary Experience of American Women* and Kerber's *Women of the Republic: Intellect and Ideology in Revolutionary America* – complemented each other effectively (Norton writing a social history, Kerber an intellectual and textual study) and were simultaneously breathtakingly counterintuitive. *Liberty's Daughters* included widows of Loyalists who filed their own claims for compensation from the British Treasury and documented the entrepreneurial responsibilities of colonial wives when their husbands were away from home in military service, or speculating in land, or drumming up new business. It fell to sons in *Women of the Republic* to sue in American courts to reclaim property once belonging to their mothers, and to insist that the wives of Loyalist husbands were politically and ideologically inert, and thus could not rightly have their property seized by Patriot state authorities.[7]

For early American historians in Canada, especially those exploring Canada's political identity, the stakes in Loyalist historiography are even higher than they had been for Shipton, Morgan, Bailyn, Norton, or Kerber. Were prominent exiles in Nova Scotia and New Brunswick founding fathers and mothers of British North America? Were aboriginal people pushed northward? Were African American Loyalists victims of ethnocentric racism common to the Empire and the new republic alike? Were the Whiggish Canadian provincials who educated Lord Durham in the spirit of the British constitution in the 1830s revisiting issues that John and Abigail Adams and their son, John Quincy, had successfully negotiated years before?

No Canadian historians have worked *outside* the boxes of heritage, hegemony, and politics as freely and creatively as the Canadian-born George A. Rawlyk, trained at the University of Rochester, or the American-born Elizabeth Mancke, trained in part at the University of British Columbia, who, more than any other constitutional scholar, has conceptualized Canadian constitutionalism as a unique product of North American and imperial history. Rawlyk's earliest scholarship dealt with New England-Maritime British North American relations, and then pivoted into North American evangelical history with *A People Highly Favoured of God: The Nova Scotia Yankees and the American Revolution* (co-authored with his first doctoral student, Gordon Stewart). Rawlyk's agenda encompassed nothing less than a fundamental reassessment of the value systems of Massachusetts and Nova Scotia. The Reverend Henry Alline emerged in Rawlyk's four successive books on Canadian evangelicalism as a Maritime Jonathan Edwards, a Canadian founding father of immense emotional, psychic, and spiritual dimensions as a man of peace. A Loyalist country, Rawlyk realized, deserved and needed a national narrative entirely different from that fashioned since the 1960s by early American historians in the United States.[8]

Given the groundwork laid by Rawlyk, it was fitting that Elizabeth Mancke would migrate from her early graduate training in British Columbia to Jack Greene's seminar at The Johns Hopkins University to test her hypothesis that Canadian constitutionalism had deep roots in Atlantic political culture. These big questions, she realized, arose from specific social origins. In *Fault Lines of Empire: Political Differentiation in Massachusetts and Nova Scotia, ca. 1760–1830,* Mancke subjected two towns, Machias, Massachusetts (now Maine), and Liverpool, Nova Scotia – a Patriot town and a Loyalist town – to microscopic examination. No less than the famous Demos, Greven, Lockridge, and Zuckerman town studies of 1970, Mancke's Machias/Liverpool project produced an array of new analytical insights and social patterns.[9] In just one of her many post-doctoral essays, 'Early Modern Imperial Governance and the Origins of Canadian Political Culture,' Mancke transformed the historiographical landscape: 'However much John A. Macdonald and the other fathers of Confederation wanted to build a strong centralized government, Ottawa did not replace London, and the Privy Council legitimated the distinctive powers that provinces brought with them into Confederation. The challenge that Canadians inherited from the empire was not how to build a single organic state, but how to domesticate a composite state system.'[10] A *domesticated, composite state system* is an entirely new ideological and institutional formulation. It harkens back not only to Hume's and Madison's 'extended republic' but more deeply to the origins of Machiavellian political science in Renaissance diplomacy when Florence, Milan, and Venice organized one set of city-state alliances after another – some grounded in Athenian political economy, others in Spartan moral solidarity, and still others in opportunism.

Joseph Galloway and William Smith, Jr, were only the most prominent Loyalists to perceive that the conflict over allegiance within the Empire demanded constitutional reform. Whereas Galloway believed that personal ambition would drive such reform, Smith was convinced that constitutional readjustments were implicit in the very constitutional flaws that fomented political unrest. For that reason, Jack Greene included the 'reintegration of the Loyalists and the disaffected' as one of fifteen substantial short-term political achievements the Revolution achieved decades before the staying power of republicanism, the security of the rule of law, or the efficacy of nationalism as a cohesive force came into their own.[11]

In the course of demonstrating that the Patriots began reincorporating Loyalists into the life of the revolutionary polity as early as 1774 and that the process was largely complete by 1785, I borrowed Ronald Walters's distinction between 'causal' and 'contextual' history. In causal history, the historian determines who participated in a past event and what they did, whereas the contextual historian asked what that event and those actions meant to affected individuals and to the people and culture surrounding them. 'Contextual history,' Walters explains, 'is a history of commonality and structure rather than distinctiveness and movement.'[12] Interpreting Loyalist reintegration as contextual history explicated the social logic of the Revolution as unplanned and shaped first by ideas and visions and secondarily by social needs. At the same time, I called for a causal history of Loyalist reintegration to be written. I acknowledged that localist republicans, no less than cosmopolitan Lockeans, saw the merit of rehabilitating Tories, and I cited Norton's study of the wives of Loyalist exiles and Peter Marshall's account of Indian allies of the Crown becoming victims of American racism as well as being clients of British imperial statecraft. I capped these concessions with an appreciation of J. Leitch Wright's unfinished project on the Gulf Coast and Mississippi Valley as an international zone of competition, which, but for the Napoleonic Wars, would have frustrated Manifest Destiny for decades. Fortunately, I hedged my bets by calling on historians to integrate causal as well as contextual perspectives into their accounts of Loyalist trauma and persistence.[13]

The Neo-Whig historiography on the coming of the Revolution that I had employed in writing my dissertation on pre-revolutionary loyalism, and in revising and expanding it into *The Loyalists in Revolutionary America, 1760–1781*, sensitized me to Loyalist anguish in the 1770s and 1780s, and following my lead both Rick Ashton and Carole Watterson Troxler wrote books about 'Loyalist Experience.'[14] But when Jeffrey M. Nelson excoriated me for settling for *experience* as the sum and substance of loyalism, he directed his readers, myself included, back to English Toryism in the reign of Queen Anne as a badly neglected ideological reservoir for the American Tory.[15] His timely, if opinionated, review essay thereby kept William Nelson's *The American Tory* exactly where it deserved to be: at the centre of what John Ferling calls 'The Loyalist Mind.'[16] *The Loyalist Perception and Other Essays* (1989), as well as its revised and expanded 2010 edition, chart my step-by-step reconsideration of the merits of my own formulation of Loyalist historiography. Responding to challenges in reviews of my first book, and then to wide-ranging work by Leslie Upton, Carol Berkin, Mary Beth Norton, Ann Zimmer, Janice Potter, and William Pencak in a brilliant series of studies,[17] my scholarship has been a bridge between Loyalist historiography and the intellectual history of American constitutionalism created by Bernard Bailyn, Gordon S. Wood, J.G.A. Pocock, and Quentin Skinner.[18]

Little did I anticipate the robust Atlanticism that was about to make its presence known so dramatically at the 'Loyalism and the Revolutionary Atlantic World' conference in June 2009, but the essays from the Maine conference, published in this volume, put my metaphorical bridge to good use by trafficking back-and-forth in ideas and actions, in values, and in a transformed political and social environment. Conference participant Jerry Bannister had already produced a powerful reimagining of the place of a Loyal Order in his essay, 'Canada as Counter-Revolution,' an argument that unfolds still further in the opening chapter of this volume, co-written with Liam Riordan.[19] The shift we see here to a more fully comparative assessment of the past, built upon a deep reading of colonial and imperial history, is bearing fruit in work that helps us to revisit the revolutionary era in wholly new ways. Keith Mason's searching examination of Loyalist identity fuses causality and contextualism by emphasizing how mercurial and troubled that identity – indeed, the very concept of identity itself – became as the processes of revolution unfolded. 'The evils of civil war,' he quotes one Loyalist, prevented Loyalists from being 'true to ourselves.' Revolutionary violence was an overlay of hatred and alienation, on top of a fraternal process of conversation and reasoned conciliation. The allegiance of the king's supporters in the Maritimes, John G. Reid discovers, was cemented by an aboriginal concept of political and constitutional 'friendship' in which the manifest integrity of colonial administration bespoke a bond between allies.

The changing conception of print culture in the late eighteenth century becomes itself a bond of empire in Philip Gould's treatment of the struggle over Thomas Paine's *Common Sense* and a communal bond

for exiles in Gwendolyn Davies's study of Loyalist printers in the diasporic communities of Atlantic Canada. Gould probes legal, cultural,
and commercial debates about authorship and the role of the press,
and Davies reveals exiled Loyalist printers as '[d]isseminators of public
debate, prisms of insight into societal patterns, and representatives of
Loyalist views.' Both Gould's and Davies's Loyalist cohorts lived fuller,
richer, and more risk-filled, productive lives on their side of the revolutionary divide, and their scholarly craftsmanship dissolves the parti-
tion between causality and contextualism that constricted my analysis
of Loyalist historiography in the 1980s.

Nowhere in the emergent historiography of loyalism does the concept of the *Loyal Atlantic* function so dramatically as in Jennifer K.
Snyder's and Carole Watterson Troxler's treatments of the whirlwind
ripping through the enslaved and British North American slaveholding
diaspora of the 1770s and 1780s. Some individual Africans struck out
on their own when Georgia, the Carolinas, and soon enough the Floridas slipped out of British control, but for the great majority of enslaved
people of colour, especially those in family units, staying together
meant continued bondage even in exile. No aspect of Loyalist history
lends itself more readily to a causal analysis than the persistence of
slaveholding by Patriots and Loyalists alike.

As gifted essayists, Snyder and Troxler plumb those deterministic
depths to sketch poignant stories of human tragedy implied in the
often fragmentary historical evidence. Snyder locates Nancy and Robert, married bondspeople of a South Carolina Loyalist woman, fending
for themselves amid chaotic flight from Savannah to St Augustine and
thence to resettlement in the West Indies. Troxler reveals that, during
the revolutionary endgame, Loyalist and Patriot slaveholders alike stole
each other's human property and then, in retaliation, plundered more
victims to profit from this chaotic situation. She concludes her moving
portrayal by overhearing, as it were, the voice of a long-time Bahamian
settler, who observes 'with great Pain of Mind that I everyday see the
Negroes, who came here from America with the British Generals' free
passes, treated with unheard cruelty . . . after being drawn from their
Masters by Promises of Freedom and the King's protection, [and] are
every day stolen away' – truly a nuanced, almost slow-motion, render-
ing of human cruelty and confusion.

If the new historiography of the Loyal Atlantic has unfolded intelli-
gibly thus far, along lines that I might have anticipated, the final pair of
essays here by Allison O'Mahen Malcom and Allan Blackstock explore

an Atlantic political culture violently troubled by anti-Catholicism in the nineteenth century that surprises me with its vehemence. Suffice it to say, the Loyalists who settled the Maritime provinces in the 1780s could not have seen this storm coming, and it reminds us to be wary of static assumptions of the meaning of something as polyvalent as loyalism. The values and worldview that were transmuted to the grandchildren of the Loyalist refugees by the complexity of their diasporic experience and the changes that accompanied continued social development meant that the Loyalist tradition instructed nineteenth-century Canadians and Britons to confront political trouble with a conservatism deeper and more intractable than the conservative Whiggery or, in some instances, the Tory organic conservatism, of their Loyalist ancestors.

NOTES

1 Lorenzo Sabine, *Biographical Sketches of Loyalists in the American Revolution with an Historical Essay* (Boston: Little, Brown, 1864), 138–52.

2 Arthur S. Link et al., eds., *The Papers of Woodrow Wilson*, vol. 14 (Princeton, NJ: Princeton University Press, 1973), 312; Wilson included Sabine's monograph on fisheries in the New England and Maritime economies, but not his *Sketches of the Loyalists* – see *The Papers of Woodrow Wilson*, vol. 6 (Princeton, NJ: Princeton University Press, 1969), 579, 604. Robert M. Calhoon, *The Loyalists in Revolutionary America, 1760–1781* (New York: Harcourt, Brace, Jovanovich, 1973), 273–4, 561.

3 Edmund S. Morgan, 'The American Revolution: Revisions in Need of Revising,' *William and Mary Quarterly* 14 (1957): 3–15; Jack P. Greene, 'The Flight from Determinism: A Review of Recent Literature on the Coming of the American Revolution'; and idem, 'Beyond the Neo-Whig Paradigm: Trends in the Historiography of the American Revolution,' in *Interpreting Early America: Historiographical Essays* (Charlottesville: University Press of Virginia, 1996), 311–33, 441–59.

4 Edmund S. Morgan and Helen M. Morgan, *The Stamp Act Crisis: Prologue to Revolution* (Chapel Hill: University of North Carolina Press, 1953, 1995), 221–9; on Morgan's prescient use of the term 'moderation,' see Robert M. Calhoon, *Political Moderation in America's First Two Centuries* (New York: Cambridge University Press, 2009), 1–3.

5 Bernard Bailyn, *The Ideological Origins of the American Revolution* (Cambridge, MA: Harvard University Press, 1968, 1992), 319.

6 David Williams, *Condorcet and Modernity* (Cambridge: Cambridge University Press, 2004), 69–71, 172–5.

7 Mary Beth Norton, *Liberty's Daughters: The Revolutionary Experience of American Women, 1750–1800* (Boston: Little Brown, 1980); and Linda K. Kerber, *Women of the Republic: Intellect and Ideology in Revolutionary America* (Chapel Hill: University of North Carolina Press, 1980). They explore these Loyalist cases even more directly in Mary Beth Norton, 'Eighteenth-Century American Women in Peace and War: The Case of the Loyalists,' *William and Mary Quarterly* 33 (1976): 386–409; and Linda K. Kerber, 'The Paradox of Women's Citizenship in the Early Republic,' *American Historical Review* 97 (1992): 349–78.

8 Gordon Stewart and George A. Rawlyk, *A People Highly Favoured of God: The Nova Scotia Yankees and the American Revolution* (Hamden, CT: Archon Books, 1972); and George A. Rawlyk, *The Canadian Fire: Radical Evangelicalism in British North America, 1775–1812* (Montreal; Kingston, ON: McGill-Queen's University Press, 1994).

9 John Demos, *A Little Commonwealth: Family Life in Plymouth* (New York: Oxford University Press, 1970); Philip Greven, *Four Generations: Population, Land, and Family in Colonial Andover* (Ithaca, NY: Cornell University Press, 1970); Kenneth A. Lockridge, *A New England Town: The First Hundred Years, Dedham, Massachusetts* (New York: W.W. Norton, 1970); Michael Zuckerman, *Peaceable Kingdoms: New England Towns in the Eighteenth Century* (New York: Alfred A. Knopf, 1970); and Jack P. Greene, 'Autonomy and Stability: New England and the British Colonial Experience in Colonial America,' in *Interpreting Early America* (see note 3), 126–51.

10 Elizabeth Mancke, *The Fault Lines of Empire: Political Differentiation in Massachusetts and Nova Scotia, ca. 1760–1830* (New York: Routledge, 2005); idem, 'Early Modern Imperial Governance and the Origins of Canadian Political Culture,' *Canadian Journal of Political Culture* 32 (2006): 20.

11 Jack P. Greene, 'Introduction: The Limits of the American Revolution,' 1–4, 12, and Robert M. Calhoon, 'The Reintegration of the Loyalists and the Disaffected,' 67–9, both in *The American Revolution: Its Character and Limits*, ed. Jack P. Greene (New York: New York University Press, 1987).

12 Ronald G. Walters, *The Anti-Slavery Appeal: American Abolitionism after 1830* (Baltimore: Johns Hopkins University Press, 1976), 147.

13 Calhoon, 'Reintegration' (see note 11), 68–9, 73–4, and notes 48–51.

14 Carole Watterson Troxler, *The Loyalist Experience in North Carolina* (Raleigh, NC: Department of Cultural Resources, 1976); and Rick J. Ashton, 'The Loyalist Experience, New York' (PhD diss., Northwestern University, 1973).

15 Jeffrey M. Nelson, 'Ideology in Search of a Context: Eighteenth-Century British Political Thought and the Loyalists of the American Revolution,' *Historical Journal* 20 (1977): 741–9. My book was also ably assessed by William H. Nelson in *Canadian Historical Review* 56 (1975): 491–3.

16 William H. Nelson, *The American Tory* (Oxford: Clarendon, 1961); and John E. Ferling, *The Loyalist Mind: Joseph Galloway and the American Revolution* (University Park: Pennsylvania State University Press, 1977).

17 L.F.S. Upton, *The Loyal Whig: William Smith of New York and Quebec* (Toronto: University of Toronto Press, 1961); Carol Berkin, *Jonathan Sewall: Odyssey of an American Loyalist* (New York: Columbia University Press, 1974); Mary Beth Norton, *The British Americans: The Loyalist Exiles in England, 1774–1789* (Boston: Little, Brown, 1972); Anne Y. Zimmer, *Jonathan Boucher: Loyalist in Exile* (Detroit: Wayne State University Press, 1978); Janice Potter, *The Liberty We Seek: Loyalist Ideology in New York and Massachusetts* (Cambridge, MA: Harvard University Press, 1983); William Pencak, *War, Politics, & Revolution in Provincial Massachusetts* (Boston: Northeastern University Press, 1981); and idem, *America's Burke: The Mind of Thomas Hutchinson* (Washington, DC: University Press of America, 1982).

18 Calhoon, 'Ideology as a Way of Thinking about the American Revolution,' in *Dominion and Liberty: Ideology in the Anglo-American World, 1660–1801* (Arlington Heights, IL: Harlan Davidson, 1994), 1–17.

19 Jerry Bannister, 'Canada as Counter-Revolution: The Loyalist Order Framework in Canadian History, 1750–1840,' in *Liberalism and Hegemony: Debating the Canadian Liberal Revolution*, ed. Jean-François Constant and Michel Ducharme (Toronto: University of Toronto Press, 2009), 98–146.

Contributors

Jerry Bannister is Associate Professor of History at Dalhousie University and author of *The Rule of the Admirals: Law, Custom, and Naval Government in Newfoundland, 1699–1832* (2003).

Allan Blackstock is Reader in History at the University of Ulster and author of *Loyalism in Ireland, 1789–1829* (2007). He is currently working on a monograph, *Science, Politics and Society in Early Nineteenth-century Ireland: The Reverend William Richardson*, and will be co-editing with Professor Frank O'Gorman a collection of essays on *Loyalism and the Formation of the British World, c. 1775–1880*.

Robert M. Calhoon taught at the University of North Carolina at Greensboro from 1964 to 2009. His most recent books are *Political Moderation in America's First Two Centuries* (2009) and *Tory Insurgents: The Loyalist Perception and Other Essays, Revised and Expanded Edition* (2010).

Gwendolyn Davies, FRSC, is Professor and Dean Emerita in English and the School of Graduate Studies at the University of New Brunswick. The author and editor of various publications on the history of the book in Canada and on the literature of the Maritime provinces, she is currently working on a book on the literary voice of Loyalist women in late eighteenth-century Atlantic Canada.

Philip Gould is Professor of English at Brown University. He is currently working on a monograph entitled, *Writing the Rebellion: Loyalists and the Literature of Politics in British America*.

Allison O'Mahen Malcom earned her PhD in history in 2011 from the University of Illinois at Chicago. Her dissertation project, which she is revising for publication, is entitled 'Anti-Catholicism and the Rise of Protestant Nationhood in North America, 1830–1871.'

Keith Mason is Lecturer in North American, Caribbean, and Atlantic History at the University of Liverpool. He is the author of 'The American Loyalist Diaspora and the Reconfiguration of the British Atlantic World,' in *Empire and Nation: The American Revolution in the Atlantic World*, ed. Peter Onuf and Eliga Gould (2005). His current research centres around two book-length studies: *Revolution and Civil War in the British Atlantic, 1760–1815* (Blackwell) and *Slaveries and Emancipations in the Atlantic World: Haiti, the British Caribbean, and North America* (Manchester University Press).

John G. Reid is Professor of History at Saint Mary's University. His books include *Viola Florence Barnes, 1885–1979: A Historian's Biography* (2005) and *Essays on Northeastern North America, Seventeenth and Eighteenth Centuries* (2008). His current research focuses on native-imperial relations in eastern British North America during the Loyalist era.

Liam Riordan is Associate Professor of History at the University of Maine. He is completing a comparative biography about five Loyalists from diverse walks of life who travelled all around the Atlantic world as a result of their opposition to the American Revolution. He also wrote the annotated bibliography, 'Loyalism,' in *Oxford Bibliographies Online: Atlantic History*, ed. Trevor Burnard (http://www.oxfordbiblio graphiesonline.com/).

Jennifer K. Snyder is completing her doctoral dissertation, entitled 'Black Flight: Tracing the Loyalist Slave Diaspora throughout the Revolutionary Atlantic World,' at the University of Florida.

Carole Watterson Troxler is Professor Emeritus at Elon University. Her many loyalist publications focus on the southern backcountry and on black and white migration from the southern colonies to areas of British control and beyond. Her books featuring Loyalist content are *The Loyalist Experience in North Carolina* (1976); *Pyle's*

Defeat: Deception at the Race Path (2003); and *Farming Dissenters: The Regulator Movement in Piedmont North Carolina* (2011). With her husband George W. Troxler, she is the 2010 recipient of the Christopher Crittenden Award from the North Carolina Literary and Historical Association.

Index

Abolition of the Slave Trade Act (1807), 197, 200
aboriginals/natives: aboriginal and Native American Loyalists, 7, 17, 41, 43, 49, 94–5; aboriginal populations of Nova Scotia, 77, 79–81, 83–6, 87–94; of Acadie, 78; Brant's bargaining on behalf of the Haudenosaunee, 43; and the British Army, 91–3, 94; British-Houdenasaunee relations as 'chain of friendship,' 78, 94; British-Mi'kmaw treaty of 1752, 81; Cape Breton Mi'kmaq, 89; changing balances of imperial, colonial, and aboriginal power in the British empire, 11; Cherokees, 193; Cherokees and Creeks abandoned to encroachments of the US by 1783 peace treaty, 43; French-aboriginal relations, 78, 80; French-Houdenasaunee peace agreement of 1701, 78; 'friendship' as imperial term used in negotiations with, 77–8, 79–82, 90, 93–5, 283; and gift-giving, 43, 80, 81, 82–3, 84, 86, 88–9, 90, 91, 92, 93, 94; Houdenasaunee, 43, 76, 78; imperial-aboriginal friendship in Mi'kma'ki/Wulstukwik, 9, 43, 75–95; Indian warfare of the Carolina-Georgia frontiers, 192; 'Indians' distinguished from 'His Majesties Subjects,' 81; intermarriage between colonists and, 79, 80; loyalty as issue of diplomatic negotiation for, 7–8, 43, 77, 84; Maliseet and Passamaquoddy treaty of 1760, 81; Mi'kmaq and Wulstukwiuk attack on Fort Cumberland, 85; Mi'kmaw treaties of 1760–61, 81; Mohawk Loyalists, 7; Monk's exchanges with Mi'kmaq concerning gifts, 88–9; native experiences during the American Revolution, 76; neutrality of, 76–7, 85, 91, 92–3; of New England, 83; Royal Proclamation of 1763 as aboriginal people's Magna Carta, 9; Scottish-based Indian traders, Panton, Leslie and Company, 193; terms Mi'kma'ki and Wulstukwik, 96n. 7; treaty negotiations in Boston, 81, 82

Duncome, Charles, 257
Dundas, Henry, 91
Dunlap, William: *The Father; or,*
 American Shandyism, 149
Dunlap's Pennsylvania Packet, 119
Dunmore, Lord. *See* John Murray
 (earl of Dunmore)
Dunmore's Proclamation (1775), 167,
 194
Durant, William, 151, 161n. 113
Durham, Lord, 10, 245n. 51, 280;
 Durham's 1839 report on British
 North America, 22, 218, 222

Egan, Stephen, 171
English Civil War, 10; invoked to
 oppose *Common Sense*, 49; and the
 Patriot movement, 8–9
evangelicalism: Abolitionist evangelicals, 197; black Loyalists and, 43;
 and the close connection between
 Protestantism and nationalism,
 216, 225, 238n. 9; and the development of Protestant history, 239n.
 12; Evangelical Atlantic, 4; evangelical Christianity in Canada,
 240n. 21; North American evangelical history, 280–1
Eve, Joseph, 196
Evening Packet, 267–8

Fanning, David, 190, 199
Fahrni, Magda, 258
Fawkes, Guy, 223, 224
Fenwick, Edward, 174
Ferling, John, 283
Florida: Britain's cession of the
 Floridas to Spain, 187–8, 194;
 Charleston evacuation list for
 East Florida, 187; East Florida as

Loyalist stronghold, 167, 187; East
 Florida Rangers, 168, 170; Florida
 as haven for runaway slaves, 168,
 172, 173; number of refugees in
 West Florida, 192; Patriot raids in
 Georgia and, 170–2, 173–4, 174;
 Scottish-based Indian traders in
 193; southern evacuations from
 Pensacola, 185; Spanish seizure
 of Pensacola, 192, 193; tension between former East Floridians and
 West Floridians in the Bahamas,
 192; trade between East Florida
 and British West Indies, 168–9;
 trajectories of civilians leaving
 East Florida, 188; 'West Florida'
 Loyalists in the Bahamas, 193. *See
 also* St Augustine
Foucault, Michel, 124n. 10; on the
 'author function,' 108–9, 123n. 8
France: French-aboriginal relations,
 78, 80; French financial and military support of Patriots, 18, 175–6;
 French-Houdenasaunee peace
 agreement of 1701, 78; French
 North America, 236; French Revolution, 19, 77, 232, 253, 259, 262,
 263. *See also* French Canada
Francklin, Michael, 84–5, 86, 87–8, 91
Franklin, Benjamin, 131, 133, 134,
 151
Fredericton Telegraph, 143
freedom of the press, 106, 118–21
French Canada, 236; anglophone
 and francophone historians' treatments of the 1837–38 Rebellions,
 257–8; anglophones in Lower
 Canada, 253; Catholic populations
 in Quebec/Lower Canada, 235,
 241–2n. 34; 'Chateau Clique,' 253;